Red Lodge

and the mythic west

Red Lodge

and the mythic west

COAL MINERS TO COWBOYS

Bonnie Christensen

UNIVERSITY PRESS OF KANSAS

© 2002 by the University Press of Kansas

Published by the University Press of Kansas (Lawrence, Kansas
66049), which was organized by the Kansas Board of Regents and is
operated and funded by Emporia State University, Fort Hays State
University, Kansas State University, Pittsburg State University, the
University of Kansas, and Wichita State University

Library of Congress Cataloging-in-Publication Data

Christensen, Bonnie, 1966–
    Red Lodge and the mythic West : coal miners to cowboys / Bonnie
Christensen.
        p. cm.
Includes bibliographical references and index.
    ISBN 0-7006-1198-3 (cloth : alk. paper)
    1. Red Lodge (Mont.)—History.   2. Red Lodge (Mont.)—Social
life and customs.   3. Frontier and pioneer life—Montana—Red
Lodge.   4. Historic sites—Montana—Red Lodge.   5. Festivals—
Social aspects—Montana—Red Lodge.   6. Rodeos—Social
aspects—Montana—Red Lodge.   7. Memory—Social aspects—
Montana—Red Lodge.   8. Historic preservation—Social aspects—
Montana—Red Lodge.   9. Memory—Social aspects—West (U.S.)
10. Historic preservation—Social aspects—West (U.S.)   I. Title.
    F739.R43 C48 2002
    978.6'652—dc21   2002005433

British Library Cataloguing in Publication Data is available.

Printed in the United States of America

10 9 8 7 6 5 4 3 2 1

The paper used in this publication meets the minimum requirements
of the American National Standard for Permanence of Paper for
Printed Library Materials Z39.48-1984.

To my mother,

Judy Patton Christensen

CONTENTS

List of Illustrations, *viii*

Acknowledgments, *ix*

Introduction: Red Lodge, Montana, *xi*

1 Western at the Fringes: Red Lodge in the 1890s, *1*

2 "Nothing Up Here but Foreigners and Coal Slack":
   The Industrial West, *40*

3 The End of an Era, *73*

4 Everyone's a Cowboy: The "Wild West" in the Twentieth Century, *88*

5 "Hardy Pioneers, American and Foreign":
   Public Ethnicity in the West, *127*

6 Nature's West, *168*

7 Preserving a Past, *212*

Notes, *239*

Bibliography, *281*

Index, *297*

ILLUSTRATIONS

The county displays its "treasures" of grains and vegetables, *15*
The solid brick buildings of Red Lodge's main street, *38*
Depiction of idealized local workers from 1892 *Northwest Magazine, 46*
Depiction of workers' homes from 1892 *Northwest Magazine, 47*
The East Side Mine, *51*
Hi Bug home, *52*
Jewelry store along Broadway Avenue, *54*
Sconfienza Bakery and Grocery Store in 1908, *61*
Unionized miners pause for a picture, *64*
Alice Greenough at the Red Lodge rodeo, *98*
Sally Rand at Ben Greenough's ranch house, *111*
1953 advertisement from a promotional brochure, *124*
Downtown windows during the first Festival of Nations, *144*
Red Lodge Cafe sign and flags flying for the Festival of Nations, *148*
Finnish wedding portrait from turn-of-the-century Red Lodge, *150*
Ethnic identities merging with western identities, *156*
The Beartooth Highway as scenic backdrop, *190*
Red Lodge Zoo postcard, *198*
1974 cartoon ridiculing Cody, Wyoming, *214*
1984 advertisement in publicity brochure, *216*
Coal Miners Memorial Park, *218*
Suburban subdivisions in the shadow of Beartooth Mountains, *233*

ACKNOWLEDGMENTS

Many people helped to make this book possible. First, I'd like to thank my dissertation adviser at the University of Washington, Richard White, whose insights and invaluable commentaries guided so much of my research and writing. My reading committee of John Findlay and Susan Glenn did much to clean up many of my arguments and make me think more deeply about Red Lodge and its people. Kathy Morse and Robert Self, my graduate school colleagues, did more than they'll ever know to get me through the dark days of dissertation writing. The University of Washington Graduate School and History Department provided support during the writing process; the Charles Redd Center for Western Studies helped make possible a summer of research in Red Lodge. The people at the Carbon County Historical Society and Peaks to Plains Museum made much appreciated efforts to help me through the long process of researching Red Lodge's history. I will always be grateful to Ardyce Jenkins, Carbon County historic preservation officer, who put me up for an entire summer in the Winnebago parked in her driveway. Ardyce's generosity of spirit and love of life lent a spark to my work; she is sorely missed. Jeanne Parker at the Carbon County Historical Society archives provided much appreciated assistance and cheerful conversation as I slowly worked my way through every shelf of material in the Courthouse Annex basement. Penny Clark helped immensely with my efforts in the photo archives. David Walter and Jodie Foley of the Montana Historical Society walked me through the materials at the Helena archives, especially the extensive and invaluable oral history collections. I need to thank the wonderful people in my Makani Kai ohana for being the best neighbors possible; your aloha for me and my baby girl meant so much as I struggled to finish this project. And to my husband, Rusty, thank you for putting up with this for so many years. Now I can get back to varnishing the boat.

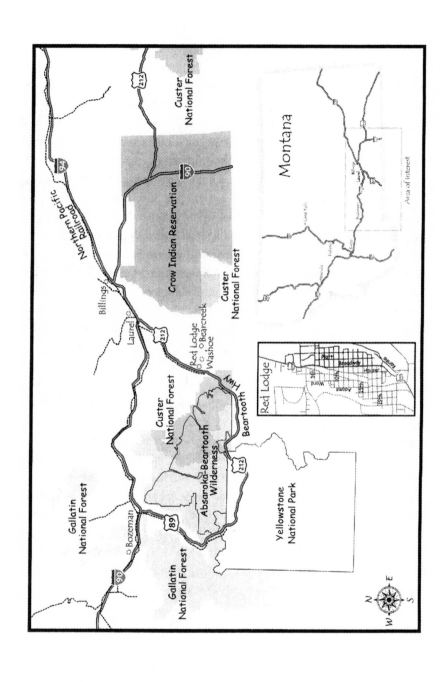

Most people see Red Lodge from behind the windshields of their cars. It's the little town with the speed limit that slows them down for a mile or so as they drive to or from Yellowstone National Park. Sometimes these drivers take an interest in the quaint-looking brick buildings of the downtown area; they may stop for a sandwich or soda at the Red Lodge Café or perhaps purchase a T-shirt from the Mountain People store. And then, they're on their way again, speeding off to see more natural wonders or maybe just heading back to Billings or Sheridan. On the way through town they may notice the straight grid pattern of streets leading away from Broadway Avenue, looking like so many other street patterns in the right-angled American West. They might pay attention to the trout stream that runs along the edge of the road on the south side of town — the end that leads toward Yellowstone. Many, however, see little beyond the mile markers telling them that it's seventy-two miles to the national park or sixty miles to Billings.

But if you have the time, pause for a moment and really *look* at Red Lodge. Look closely and critically and try to figure out this little town and its reason for being. Where did this place come from, you might ask? What is its history? Why is it here? The pretty little downtown, first of all, suggests a prosperous past; around the turn of the century this town had some money. How was that money made? The log cabin at the edge of town, the Fourth of July rodeo, and a preponderance of cowboy hats and boots indicate, perhaps, a local history of ranching. Yes, some ranching was done in the area, but cattle and cattle-men did not build this town. What else? The town abounds in references to an annual ethnic celebration, the Festival of Nations, which suggests a multi-cultural past in this overwhelmingly white community. If there were immi-grants here, what did they do? The abandoned mill works on the east bench above town mark a mining past; most people notice that. But don't be fooled by that obvious tunnel entrance. Yes, this once was a mining town, but that particular structure dates back only to the 1950s when a short-lived chrome operation tried to make a go of it here. You'll need to look a lot harder to find the boarded-up coal mine tunnel across the river and under the weeds, near the grassy hollow that used to be a settling pond and where deer now some-times feed. That coal entrance is the real history of this town, the source of its original wealth and reason for being. Other markers of the coal-driven past can be found around the community, but again, they're hard to locate. Just at the north entrance to town, for example, there's a football field where the Red Lodge High School football team, the Redskins, plays. Kneel down and look at that field, and you'll notice a bunch of shiny black flakes that feel almost greasy to the touch; you'd need to ask, though, to find out that the playing field sits on a government-reclaimed slack pile — an industrial waste site from the boom days of coal. The pile used to loom hundreds of feet above the town, covering more than the length of the football field. Like much of the mining past, though, the tower of waste has been cleaned up, removed from sight, and almost forgotten until very recently.

From the town's founding in 1889 into the 1930s, Red Lodge's public identity revolved around coal, coal miners, and industrial development. But, for many different reasons, it is much easier today to find images of cowboys, ranching, and Indians around town than it is to find references to Red Lodge's coal mines. Red Lodge, like other towns scattered around the country, seems to possess a kind of fractured public identity that does not really make sense. It's a town built by miners that presents itself as a town of cowboys. It's a community of white Americans who every year celebrate their cultural diversity. Many residents now favor environmentalist positions about wilderness, yet the town was built on the extraction of coal and has survived into the present through the construction of a highway that has brought automobiles into the heart of some of the most remote wild areas in the nation.

In its apparently fractured identities, Red Lodge is both quirky and typical. Investigating the historical creation of these overlapping, sometimes contradictory identities reveals a lot not only about Red Lodge itself but also about the ways in which thousands of communities have chosen to remember their pasts and project images of what they want their present to be. Looking into the development of Red Lodge we get a clearer understanding of the motivations behind the creation of "theme towns" like Leavenworth, Washington ("America's Bavarian Village"), and Solvang, California ("Little Denmark"), nostalgic neighborhood hubs such as Pike Place Market in Seattle, and pioneer museum complexes like that in Fort Dodge, Iowa. Analyzing the shifting role of the cowboy in Red Lodge offers insights into the role of myths and mythmaking in American communities. We can see that "myth" doesn't necessarily mean "false," that people can have differing interpretations of what is historical "reality." Investigating the construction of an ethnic celebration like the Festival of Nations helps to explain why residents and developers in other communities have created ersatz historic districts like New York's South Street Seaport and Wild West Days in Cody, Wyoming. Unique in its particular, chosen identities, Red Lodge illuminates broader processes of identity formation employed by thousands of communities across the United States.

Americans have always shaped the particular identities of their own particular places, influenced, of course, by wider regional and national pressures and trends — local places do not stand outside widespread influences like the environmental movement, cold war fears, or preservationism. Significantly, however, towns like Red Lodge and Leavenworth and Cody have responded to these larger pressures in their own ways; local people make local choices about identity and imagery even as they adapt these choices to larger considerations of American or western identity. Thus, Red Lodge did not develop exactly the same public imagery and identity as did Cody, although parts may be very similar because both towns responded to popular national ideas about what western towns should look like.

Although very different in many ways, all these towns have a lot in common. The stories of all these places are intertwined with concerns of community identity, local heritage, tourism, survival, and the efforts of especially energetic residents with specific visions for their town or neighborhood. The story of Red Lodge, in particular, opens up a window onto how and why communities have shaped and adapted their public identities in response to local, regional, and national concerns.

Identity is a slippery term; it's hard to pin down because scholars have employed it so generally and loosely. First put into popular use by social scientists in the 1950s, identity emerged as a convenient way to locate studies of national character. People started to refer to concepts such as "ethnic identity" and "national identity" as academics tried to explain the relationships between individuals and society. Although scholars initially sought to pinpoint cohesive group identities, more recently investigators in this field have shown that groups and individuals can adopt a variety of distinct identities that may be contradictory, fragmented, and incomplete. According to these new theories, individuals can align themselves with more than one identity at a time and through a natural kind of "doublethink" easily resolve contradictions between competing identities.[1] An insurance salesman from Red Lodge, for example, might simultaneously identify himself as a westerner (complete with cowboy hat), Croatian-American (son of an immigrant coal miner), and athlete (as a former college basketball star). While the pastoral imagery of the cowboy hat might seem to contradict the industrial legacy of the miner's son and the modern sportsmanship of college athletics, an individual like John Barovich could easily assume all of these identities as his rightful heritage and not think twice about the legitimacy of his various personas.

Collective identities involve similar contradictions and overlapping, but these larger identities — membership in a specific group, town, state, ethnic group, or nation — are even more complicated because of the number of people who make up the collective. "American," for example, can mean vastly different things to different people all of whom consider themselves to be American. An American Indian from Utah might hold a completely different conception of what being American is about than would a white factory worker in Ohio; at the same time, the two might share some similar perceptions of this collective identity based on shared military experiences or because they grew up watching the same movies.

Public identity — the messages about the group that are communicated both within and outside the collective — is less personal and intimate than the individual experiences and memories of each particular member. Although a group's identity rests, ultimately, in the individuals who make up the group, the articulation of public identity is often the product of a few people with the time, energy, money, or prestige to project that identity in a public manner. Newspaper editors, published writers, movie producers, and politicians, after all, have taken the lead in shaping and defining what it means to be "American." Think about how much power textbook publishers or movie distributors have in telling the nation and the world what America represents. Individuals like Abraham Lincoln or Henry Ford have shaped the public identity of the nation in enormously influential ways. Their sweeping pronouncements about what it means to be American cannot possibly encompass the disparate views, beliefs, and experiences of millions of citizens, but their ideas have helped define the ways in which Americans view themselves and how others view Americans.

Image is a facet of identity — the part that is perceived by others. Every town projects a series of images that can include things like cowboy hats, abandoned buildings, polluted waterways, picturesque gardens, or strip malls. Taken together, these images create a set of visual markers that can be fitted into something bigger — a particular identity such as a "western" town, post-industrial community, New England village, or suburbia. Residents create these images either intentionally or unintentionally; visitors and residents alike then interpret these visual markers according to established ideas about what such images represent. Not everyone, of course, sees the same identity when observing certain town images. Where one person sees a run-down, dying community, someone else can see a paradise of open land and recreational opportunities. In the creation of public identities, however, community members often work quite hard to manufacture "appropriate" imagery that will guide the viewer to see what group members want to be seen. Town leaders erect welcome signs, banners, and flags to inform visitors about local identity. Residents select certain themes to reinforce selected or preferred identities. A preponderance of cowboy and Indian images, for example, guides the observer into identifying a certain community with "the West" — even if the community itself is in the Midwest or indeed Germany (a country with a decided fascination for western mythology and imagery). Imagery, thus, is created out of identity, while at the same time imagery reinforces identity.[2]

Ultimately, much of this manufacturing of public identity and imagery comes down to the selection and construction of collective memories. A group's cultural identity changes through historical time as collective memories are selected and changed according to external and internal influences.[3] On a national scale, leaders can emphasize (or even manufacture) certain stories of the past to promote patriotism. Recent events in Yugoslavia show how effective such an appeal to selective histories can be. The collective Serb memory stretches back hundreds of years to keep alive stories of atrocities committed against Serbs by Croats, Bosnians, and Albanians yet conveniently blacks out reciprocal histories of cruelties perpetrated by the Serbs against these same ethnic peoples. On a much more intimate (and less bloody) scale, towns like Red Lodge have presented certain, selected versions of the local past in an effort by leaders to instill town pride in residents and present an attractive public image for visitors. At various points in the town's history, residents have emphasized the region's Wild West history, its immigrant past, and its industrial heritage; sometimes all are displayed at once. Just as individuals choose to tell their grandchildren stories about only selected parts of their pasts, so too communities and nations choose which memories to validate and valorize and which to ignore or simply forget about. [4]

Questions of identity and public memory have been central to many recent academic discussions, but relatively few of these discussions have looked at the evolution of local or regional identities over a considerable time frame. Scholars have written much about American and western identities, but while broad, sweeping studies of the "myth of the frontier" and the "American character" provide valuable frameworks for the investigation of local identities, they leave many gaps in our understanding of how people in specific places have adapted or rejected national or regional identities in the construction of their own public presentations of who they are. Richard Slotkin's books on the myth of the frontier, for example, have shed light on the ways in which the ideas of "the West" spread throughout the nation and gained great power. Red Lodge residents' struggles against the imagery of the West in the 1890s and their embrace of it in the 1930s certainly illustrate the validity of some of Slotkin's arguments about the pervasiveness of the mythology of the West. But such broad studies cannot explain or explore all the different nuances and variations of how and why local peoples have responded to certain aspects of national culture. As this study of Red Lodge shows, townspeople certainly found themselves wrapped up in nationally generated trends and concepts, but they also adapted such larger ideas to their own local situations.

To look closely at identities such as "western" and "American" in a particular place such as Red Lodge is to understand how complicated their constructions are and to recognize that local, regional, and national identities can be symbiotic as well as antithetical. The American West is a particularly fertile place to examine these questions. Everyone seems to know what a "westerner" and "the West" look like; Americans, and indeed people around the world, have been bombarded with these images for centuries. The West has come to mean cowboys, Indians, pioneer farmers, deserts, mountains, and vast plains. It represents masculinity, wilderness, rugged individualism, democracy. These images and meanings — distributed through dime novels, newspaper stories, magazines, and, in the twentieth century, by radio, movies, and television — have had great cultural power and appeal in the United States. [5]

These are national images, mass-produced cultural representations. But they are something more for westerners who have used these popular images of the West to create their own local identities. Westerners have imbibed these images along with everyone else and have recognized the power that such identities might offer them. Thus, even in a coal town like Red Lodge, local people learned to wear cowboy boots and hats in the mid–twentieth century because that was part of what it meant to be a westerner. Local western identities, grounded in specific places, have become inextricably intertwined with national ideas about the West and the people who inhabit it. In this study I pick apart these specific and local western identities to see how and why they developed over time and to understand the ways in which people have generated and used them explain who they are, both to themselves and to outsiders. I do so by examining one small town, looking particularly at the construction of *public* identities drawn both from interpretations of the past and the community's location in the Rocky Mountain West.

The choice of Red Lodge, first of all, deserves some explanation. A small town of about two thousand residents on the eastern edge of the Rocky Mountains, Red Lodge's history and location typify a variety of very "western" aspects. Red Lodge, like much of the West, had a history in resource extraction (in this case coal mining); it lay close to an immense swath of national forest and park lands and also within a few dozen miles of an Indian reservation; its early population was made up largely of European immigrants; and the town itself was created by a huge national corporation, the Northern Pacific Railroad. Red Lodge has also had a variety of intriguing public festivals and monuments including an annual rodeo, an annual ethnic celebration, a county museum, and an entire downtown district on the National Register of Historic Places. The town has made a point of staging its history for public consumption.

Red Lodge, in short, is a wonderful place to investigate questions of western identity and the creation of public memory. Digging into the town's past, one does not find simple definitions of who belongs and who doesn't, of what it means to be from Red Lodge. The townspeople have drawn their identities as much from American reverence for the Yellowstone area and complex ideas about Indian peoples as they have from the coal mining industry that dominated the town's economy and culture from the 1880s into the 1930s. Red Lodge's location near thousands of acres of public lands, its industrial past and tourism-driven present, and the inhabitants' studied celebration of their history through festivals and ceremonies make this town a fascinating and illuminating site for this type of study. Between their desires to create colorful and interesting tourist attractions and to erase troublesome social divisions, Red Lodge inhabitants have developed celebrations that have reinforced certain appealing identities. The celebrations and identities created through them have become part of the town's image and how residents understand themselves and their past.

On the other hand, Red Lodge has not been inflicted with the "theme town" craze that hit so many little communities from Iowa to California. Red Lodge certainly sells its public identities as a cowboy or ethnic town, but it has not gone to the extremes exemplified by communities like Leavenworth, Washington. Leavenworth, a dying timber town, invented itself as "America's Bavarian Village" in the 1960s for the express purpose of attracting tourist dollars into the area. Even though the town had little or no connection to German heritage, the surrounding scenery — mountains, forests, rivers — looked "alpine" enough to inspire several residents to push for remodeling the entire community into an Old World village complete with pitched roofs, gingerbread trim, German signs, and European-style flower boxes at every window on main street. During the summer, polka music provides an auditory backdrop for visitors who stroll by baskets of edelweiss and pause to watch costumed residents perform folk dances under "Bavarian" streetlights. Like Solvang, California (little Denmark), Fort Dodge, Iowa (Pioneer Village), and Williamsburg, Virginia (colonial village), Leavenworth secured a tourism niche by making itself over according to a theme — a script that mandated how buildings should look, how residents should perform for tourists, and the direction in which the town should develop.[6]

Red Lodge's approach to identity formation was never so structured or focused on one single public identity. Organizers in Leavenworth, after all, took on the monumental task of convincing hundreds of residents to transform a main street of false-fronted western buildings into a façade of a Bavarian village; the process included detailed plans and guidelines to direct the transformation. In Red Lodge, the application of Wild West exteriors evolved much more gradually and at the instigation of individual business owners; ethnic imagery appeared once a year at the Festival of Nations rather than year-round as in Leavenworth. Although the town's various public identities received much guidance from community leaders, the "theming" of Red Lodge was never applied with such broad brush strokes. And, significantly, all the prominent public identities drew very directly from some part of the community's history.

Red Lodge is also a very small community, which, although greatly influenced by national ideas and economic forces, never attracted the kind of mega-corporate presence that transformed such communities as Sun Valley, Aspen, and Park City in the twentieth century. The sort of corporate "colonization" discussed by historian Hal K. Rothman in his study of western tourism did not take place in Red Lodge (at least not yet). Red Lodge residents never faced the monolithic power W. Averell Harriman's Union Pacific Railroad wielded in Sun Valley, for example, or that Walter Paepcke had in Aspen.⁷ In Red Lodge, tourism — and the desire to attract tourist dollars to the community — certainly influenced the development of the town's public identity, but, at least into the early 1990s, local tourism remained very much a *local* concern. Without the influence of multimillion-dollar corporations arranging grand attractions and events (think of the Vegas strip, for example), local people had to create their own attractions that reflected *their* interpretations of what might draw tourists to this small town. Public celebrations like the annual rodeo and Festival of Nations really did become community efforts to create an attractive and appealing public identity for the town.

Red Lodge, thus, provides an ideal location to investigate the development of *public* identity in a local western place. The emphasis here is on public. This study looks at celebrations, architecture, publications, and monuments designed for public consumption, and I make the distinction between what Yi-Fu Tuan refers to as "public symbols" and "fields of care." Fields of care are areas holding personal, private meanings for individuals — their particular homes, special taverns, private places. Public symbols, on the other hand, "command attention and even awe"; they project specific images to observers. Public symbols include not only physical buildings and public events but also images of the ideal city: printed pictures and word portraits of how residents *want* the town to be perceived by outsiders.⁸ In Red Lodge, local people shaped and reshaped this public identity over the course of a century as they responded to a variety of new conditions, challenges, and changes.

Granted, this focus on the "public" shaping of identity means looking most specifically at the actions and activities of an elite set of local leaders — those with the time or money to write newspaper stories, to form rodeo committees, or to sit on the board of the county historical society. And much of this study does rely on the presentation of public identity found in the local newspapers, which constituted one of the community's main means of communicating a vision of itself to readers both in Red Lodge and outside the town's boundaries. These newspapers represented the voices of the people who made the most vigorous efforts to shape the town's public imagery. The actions of other residents are also examined, although in less direct ways. For example, through their willingness (or unwillingness) to dress up as Slovenian immigrants or Wild West cowboys, local people lent their support (or lack thereof) to the efforts of groups like the Chamber of Commerce, Woman's Club, and Italian Girls Victory Club as they tried to create specific public identities for the little town. I have also used the oral histories of longtime residents to add depth and differing perspectives to many discussions of how the town developed its various public personas. As is evidenced in Chapter 5's discussion of the Festival of Nations, local people often fit their personal memories around popular narratives of local heritage; however, their personal histories also revealed some of the town's lingering class, ethnic, and racial tensions that the studied public performances and displays had eventually smoothed over or eliminated.

Heritage is a second important factor in this study. Heritage, first of all, needs to be understood as a version of history that explains the local past in ways its residents prefer it to be understood. This distinction between heritage and history is important. According to David Lowenthal, "while it borrows from and enlivens historical study, heritage is not an inquiry into the past but a celebration of it." Where history "explores and explains pasts grown ever more opaque over time, heritage clarifies pasts so as to infuse them with present purposes."[9] Heritage, as it were, consists of the stories we *want* to tell about ourselves and how we came to be. In creating Red Lodge's public identity, residents pulled from various versions of the past — some of it not even really the local past — to create a heritage appropriate to what they wanted Red Lodge, and themselves, to represent.

Finally, I use a fairly broad interpretation of "local," which can be a tricky term, especially in the mobile West where residency persistence averaged about ten years at the turn of the century. By itself, as historian Louis S. Warren notes, "the word *local* masks varying degrees of rootedness."[10] Red Lodge "locals" came and went continuously in the almost one hundred years of this study. And these locals never shared a common view of what "Red Lodge" meant; their conceptions of the town and its identity split along class, ethnic, racial, and gender lines. Some, it seemed, had little in common beyond the fact that they lived in the same community. However, that proximity of residence *is* something. "Local" is an important term, which I use to differentiate between residents (of whatever duration) and the visitors, tourists, and potential investors whose experiences with the town were much more fleeting than those who invested years of work and hopes in the community. So, even though some Red Lodge old-timers still might reserve "local" only for those whose family roots in the town extend back at least two generations, this book accepts a much broader definition that, basically, equates local with resident.

The study proceeds both chronologically and topically through an examination of how Red Lodge residents produced their local public identity. Chapter 1, first of all, looks at the townspeople's initial attempts in the 1890s to eliminate the imagery of the popular "Wild West" from their environs as the community strove to create an identity as a safe, progressive, prosperous town. Chapters 2 and 3 study the development of Red Lodge's industrial and immigrant identities, while Chapters 4 and 5 investigate how and why residents in the mid–twentieth century chose to redesign that industrial history to create a heritage more appropriate to their contemporary needs. The results show how these local people selected particular story lines from the town's past, which they then interwove with powerful national narratives of "the West" and American pluralism. Chapter 6 examines the impact of federal lands — specifically Yellowstone National Park and the Beartooth Mountains — on the town's public identity. The western ruggedness and outdoor ability associated in the national imagination with such vast acres of wild forested lands became part of the town's defining identity. Finally, the conclusion looks at more recent attempts to construct a cleaned-up version of a mining heritage into the town's public identity. Ironically, with the last remnants of that past almost gone — slack piles and miners alike have disappeared — residents have finally started to create public markers to commemorate the industry and men that created the town.

This book, then, lays out a story of salesmanship, adaptation, and, ultimately, survival in one little town that managed to endure through the turbulent ups and downs of the West's unpredictable extractive industries economy. It is significant because it tells a little bit about who we all are — how and why we pick and choose among various versions of the past to find the meanings that fit who we want to be and who we want others to think we are. In this story of Red Lodge we see the contradictions, ironies, and humor that are part of all our lives as we continually invent and reinvent ourselves.

Over the course of a few decades, after all, Red Lodge had miners dressed up like cowboys, miners dressed up like Italian immigrants, cowboys wrestling steers from speeding cars, cowboys who were really Indians (and vice versa), and trout dumped from airplanes to make nature more "natural." More than giving a humorous glimpse into our attempts to remake ourselves, Red Lodge's story reveals the enduring power of a nationally created western mythology, which has enticed local westerners with no roots at all in ranching or farming or mountaineering to assume these mythic identities as part of their contemporary identity and culture. This study also shows the ways in which national ideas about "Americanness" have intertwined with local histories as residents interpreted their own past against a larger story of American progress and exceptionalism. We need to acknowledge and understand the power of these narratives that have become so ingrained into our modern lives and cultures.

As the story of Red Lodge's evolving and shifting identities shows, local people can put both the past and the natural world to a variety of uses. But, as this study also shows, local heritage and understandings of the environment have not stood outside of much larger, national and regional developments. From the townspeople's early attempts to obscure Wild West associations to their claims that the Festival of Nations represented a quintessentially "American multiculturalism," Red Lodge residents have drawn their very local public identities from national ideas about the West, immigration, nature, small towns, and the preservation of history. But these national trends never determined exactly how local people would develop their public identities. Yes, the Wild West exerted a powerful influence on the West, but other places, like Cody, Wyoming, embraced that imagery much more so than Red Lodge did. And lots of mining towns with large immigrant populations — like Belt and Roundup in Montana — never started up ethnic celebrations like the Festival of Nations. Members of the Red Lodge historical society *chose* to work for the town's inclusion on the National Register even though many other towns in the state never made such an effort.

In the end, what's important to this study is the hows and whys and ways in which local residents developed complicated, shifting public identities. Red Lodge created itself into an industrial coal town with a "Wild West" cowboy heritage populated by "hardy" European immigrants with special ties to the great outdoors. Separating these different images, following their development over time, and thus examining how one little town established such a complex and intriguing public heritage illustrate the fascinating ways in which people combine the local, regional, and national to create peculiar and particular public identities and presentations of heritage.

Western at the Fringes
Red Lodge in the 1890s

Destined to Greatness: Red Lodge Is a Good Place to Invest Your Money and
Suddenly Grow Into Comfortable Circumstances.
—Red Lodge *Picket*, 19 December 1891

A Runaway Kid: Johnny Southward, an eleven-year-old, took the dime novel notion
of starting out on his own hook. He borrowed a horse from his father for the occasion
and rode to Billings preparatory to taking a freight train for the west. His father
learning of his whereabouts went down to the train and captured the runaway, who
was glad enough to come back home.
—Red Lodge *Picket*, 14 May 1892

In May 1892, eleven-year-old Johnny Southward "borrowed" his father's horse
and galloped off to Billings planning to hop a freight train "for the west." After
soaking up exciting dime-novel stories of the outlaws, cowboys, and opportunity that beckoned in that fantastic region, he had made his getaway, determined to find his own adventures in the West he had read so much about.
Like so many other young runaways, he did not get very far on his romantic
journey. His father (who presumably had more than one horse) soon caught
up with Johnny and returned him to what was apparently the "un-western"
town of Red Lodge, Montana.

This seems a pretty typical story: a young boy with dreams runs away (but
not too far), looking for adventure and seeking (perhaps) to escape from an
overly strict parent or the drudgery of daily chores. What's significant here is
Southward's assumptions about where and what the West was. According to
the Red Lodge *Picket*, Southward had fled Red Lodge heading for "the west."
Both Johnny and the newspaper writer, it seems, assumed that the West was
not in Red Lodge. To find the real West, Southward needed to travel away
from Red Lodge (the town I've chosen as "typical" of "the West") and toward
something that perhaps existed only in his, and millions of other Americans',
imagination.

In 1892 Red Lodge was a raw, growing town in south-central Montana. In terms of location, Red Lodge seemed fairly "western." Montana, after all, is west of both the Missouri River and the 100th meridian, two popular markers of the West's geographical place. Red Lodge stood at the intersection of the high plains and the Rocky Mountains, which seems pretty western. There was an Indian reservation only a dozen or so miles away, cowboys and ranchers driving cattle to the new railroad depot, lots of saloons and brothels, and even the start of some false-fronted buildings along the main street. Red Lodge was also a product of the western geography that created stunning mountains and seemingly endless prairies and the western climate that brought hard winters and dry summers to the region. We recognize all of these as symbols of the West, as would any late-nineteenth-century American.

But there was a lot more to Red Lodge than these popular "western" icons. With its urban population of miners, bankers, merchants, prostitutes, boardinghouse keepers, children, and immigrants, Red Lodge also contained many of the markers of a modern West of cities, industry, and capitalism. Its residents lived with the presence of a strong federal government and alongside millions of acres of government-owned forests and parklands. Smokestacks, tipples, railroad engines, and coal dust dominated the townscape and sustained the industrial heart of the growing community. Red Lodge was western like Bisbee, Cripple Creek, Virginia City, and San Francisco were western. It was a West of steel and capital that disappointed young boys like Johnny Southward with their dime-novel visions of what the West *should* be. In Red Lodge, the mythical West of six-shooters and cowboys merged with the modern West of industry and corporations, and for Southward, at least, the mixture had too much of the latter and not enough of the former. He could not find "the West" in the coal fields and immigrant working-class neighborhoods of Red Lodge even though the town was most definitely in "the West."

Johnny Southward's aborted quest for western excitement and adventure, thus, points toward the central question of western identity: What is the West? What does it mean to be in the West, of the West, western, a westerner? Is the West a place, a region, a process, an idea? The answers to these questions are not fixed. In fact, scholars disagree quite vehemently on the subject, as do westerners themselves — all of which is not surprising since the West is such a large, diverse area with so many national mythologies about what it is and what it is supposed to be.

One way to investigate some of the complicated questions about western identity is to look closely at one particular place and what "western" came to mean there over time. This means looking not only at national perceptions of "the West" but also at how local peoples accepted, adapted, and defied such larger notions of westernness, for the West never really stood apart from national forces that shaped and tried to define the region. In Red Lodge, as in other western places, residents negotiated a public identity that both embraced and rejected popular ideas and images of "westernness."

First of all, by the late nineteenth century, "the West" had become a mythical site, a place that Americans invested with a lot of cultural baggage. Popular perceptions of the West drew from some very real people, places, and events, but in the course of their transmission to the East and their appropriation by Americans, the West became transformed into mythology. Americans created meanings and stories out of the western experience that represented not so much the West itself, but what Americans wanted to believe about themselves and their nation. Bombarded by paintings, photographs, books, newspaper stories, and live performances — like those presented by Buffalo Bill — Americans readily associated the West with a variety of images, values, and personalities: farmers, log cabins, independence, cowboys, Indians, masculinity.

These real people and real things took on the heavy weight of cultural significance in the national imagination as the popular media spread stories about the West and what it meant. Jesse James, as a specific example, lived and died as a real, complicated, not very nice person who liked to shoot people; in his *mythology,* however, he became so much more: a force of righteousness battling corporate greed, a symbol of the triumphant bandit championing the cause of the little people.[1] In a much broader way, farmers came to symbolize the triumph of the American virtues of democracy and egalitarianism as the plow conquered an entire continent, and the cowboy riding free on the plains epitomized freedom and independence. The West as a region became mythologized into more than it ever was, and for most venturers the place could never live up to the dreams and expectations built up by stories of valor, victory, excitement, opportunity, and high-blown ideals.

The West as a real, physical place existed in conjunction with the mythology that Americans built up around the region. The two could never really be separated even by those who actually lived in the West—the mythology exerted that powerful an influence on the minds of all involved. Part of being in and of the West thus involved negotiating, consciously or subconsciously, the disjunctures between what the West *was* and what it was *supposed* to be. If the West of free land guaranteed success to those willing to work hard enough to turn the prairies into wheat, then the farmer driven off the land by successive years of drought or low grain prices had to reconcile his personal failure with the myth of western opportunity. He either had to blame his own lack of hard work (when he had certainly worked plenty hard) or turn to scapegoats like railroad corporations or government policies. Mythology often proved stronger than personal experience in such cases. People, it seems, really wanted to believe in the myth of the West even when contradicted by direct experience. If towns like Red Lodge did not offer excitement and opportunities to adventurous young boys like Southward, then the "real" West must lie someplace else.

Just to complicate matters even more, there was never just one simple mythology of the West. By the late nineteenth century, however, two particular mythologies had clearly begun to take shape as the most compelling narratives explaining the nation's advance westward and identifying the important characteristics of the West as a region. In the one, the heroic pioneer farmer civilized the region with his plow and log cabin; in the other, the noble cowboy tamed the plains by shooting his six-gun at Indians. Both represented the domination of white men over the western region, but each told that story in a different way and with different heroes.[2] Each narrative became an important part of how westerners and nonwesterners alike understood the region and its promise. As much as some people valued the simple virtues of the pioneer farmer, others (like Johnny Southward) eagerly embraced the more exciting, dangerous icon of the cowboy and the Wild West. In their own local places, westerners sought to create their own preferred version of western progress while also contending with the people, beliefs, and practices that did not fit with these selected views. Public identity in western communities emerged out of this complex, often contradictory mix of images, mythologies, real people, real places, and dreams.

The first installment in the story of Red Lodge's developing public identity covers the 1890s, the decade of settlement and promotion when local town builders sought to create the "correct" western identity and imagery to boost their growing community. New entrepreneurs in a developing town, these men and women found themselves caught up not only in their own visions of what the West should be but also in the preconceptions and misconceptions that outsiders had about the region. Although they never put their struggle into such neat terms, Red Lodge town builders in effect embraced one particular mythology of the West — the "agrarian West" of the farmer — while rejecting another — the "Wild West" of the cowboy. Their preferred identity had everything to do with agriculture and farmers and the mythology of plows conquering the West; it rejected the Wild West of Indian attacks, ranchers who controlled the prairies, and aggressive cowhands. Not only did these latter figures represent a West of violence that might frighten potential settlers and investors, but they also controlled lands that town builders wanted in the hands of farmers and developers who would make them profitable for the entire region. Red Lodge boosters despised both the appearance of wildness and also the power of those "wild" westerners who seemed to threaten the growth and prosperity of the new mining camp. Western mythology and its representatives were all well and good as long as they did not damage the fragile economic system that town builders were constructing.

Interestingly, though, even as town builders sought to eliminate cowboys, Indians, and ranchers from the town's public identity, some local promoters had actually begun to incorporate a different kind of Wild West figure into the community's imagery. Even in the early 1890s, townspeople realized that certain not-so-wild representatives of the Wild West might be used to boost Red Lodge's public image. The "mountain man" — an older icon of the West — promised a safe public association between the town and the masculinity of the Wild West. This remained a minor effort, making Red Lodge "wild western" only at the fringes, but it pointed toward the path later town boosters would follow, for the period of fighting against the Wild West did not last for long. It lasted, really, only so long as the actual figures of that cultural narrative still retained some power in the real West. That power faded quickly as farmers closed off the open range, Indians settled onto ever-smaller reservations, and local government curtailed the gun-slinging fun of rowdy cowhands

But the real power of the Wild West — its grip on the national imagination — lasted far longer, and eventually enveloped the very western communities that had once despised and feared Indians, cowboys, and ranchers. Towns like Red Lodge, which in the 1890s had accepted only safe, "fringe" elements of the Wild West, would quickly learn how to manipulate these popular images to their own advantage.[3] Once cowboys and Indians seemed "safe," even they were readily adopted into local imagery.

The West as a real, physical place existed, but never fully separate from the mythology that Americans had built up around the region. Red Lodge, even if it disappointed dreamers like Southward, *was* the West. The point is that part of being of the West involved living with, fighting against, and tweaking around the popular imagery of what the West should be. In the junction between the mythologized West and the modern West, westerners like those in Red Lodge negotiated a working public identity, one that combined local needs and desires with powerful national and regional forces of capital and legend.

Red Lodge, Montana, did not have to be. The town owed its existence as much to the whims of political boundaries and the shrewd business sense of eastern capitalists as it did to the abundant resources of rich, dark, bituminous coal that lay beneath its streets. Capital, hand in hand with the federal government, created Red Lodge. Northern Pacific Railroad (NPRR) officials invented the town in 1887 because the railroad needed coal and corporate insiders wanted to make money. Territorial governor Samuel T. Hauser, owner of the largest bank in Montana, Henry Villard, president of the NPRR, and Frederick Billings, former NPRR president, played key roles in the game of developing the Red Lodge mine, railroad, and town site. All were capitalists used to gambling for big stakes, looking out for their own interests, and recognizing how each could use the other for his own gain. Hauser, who had made his initial fortune by securing eastern investment in Montana gold mines in the 1860s, wielded great influence within the territorial government, while Villard and Billings had close ties not only to the NPRR but also to other power brokers at the national level. They did not choose Red Lodge as the NPRR's newest coal source because of its proximity to the railroad's main line or because of the quality of the coal there; other fields lay closer and had better-burning coal. The Red Lodge field caught the attention of these investors because it lay within the boundaries of the Crow Indian Reservation in the early 1880s, off-limits to speculators who had already laid claim to the territory's other coal resources. If the three men had selected the Bull Mountain fields, for example, they would have had to negotiate with these earlier arrivals, who were sitting on those claims just waiting for the NPRR to come seeking coal reserves.[4] If only the federal government could be persuaded to redraw the reservation boundaries, Hauser, Villard, and Billings stood to save thousands or even millions in property purchases.

Not surprisingly, three such well-connected men had little trouble attaining their desired goal. By 1887, the Crow Indian Reservation boundaries were suitably renegotiated, and Hauser and his cronies had secured claims to the coal lands, funded construction of the new mine and railroad line, and even wrangled federal consent for a railroad right-of-way through the ever-shrinking Crow Reservation.[5] Determined to make money from every aspect of local development, the major investors controlled not only the coal mine and railroad branch line but also all sales of electricity and town lots. In 1889, the forty-four-mile-long Rocky Fork Railway connected Red Lodge to the main line of the NPRR, the mines came into operation, and the population at the new town site almost immediately swelled to over five hundred. By early 1890, Hauser and his partners had created a boomtown that promised to enhance their already considerable personal fortunes.[6] The lesson: western resources offered the greatest wealth to those who already had enough money and political power to claim and exploit the area.

Like many other towns in the West, Red Lodge developed as a creature of corporate interests. Hauser and his partners manipulated both town and residents to secure maximum profits in the new community. The mines, the railroad, the mansions of the corporate managers, and even the street names marked the very unegalitarian distribution of resources in the new boomtown. On the plats for the new town site, developers carefully penned in "Hauser" and "Billings" avenues as they paid homage to the capitalists who had funded the town's creation; the names of smaller streets and boulevards honored a variety of other prominent Northern Pacific officials.[7] Mine managers, such as Dr. J. M. Fox, who supervised the Rocky Fork Coal Company from 1887 to 1900, settled into the ostentatious mansions on Hauser Street that reflected their power and prestige as corporate representatives.

When it wanted to, capital could even stifle Red Lodge in one place and resurrect in another. In 1893, denied clear title to the land around the new mine because of the presence of an opportunistic homesteader with a somewhat spurious competing claim, Hauser and his associates in the Rocky Fork Town and Electric Company (RFT&EC) simply moved the center of town further west, away from the mine and toward the railroad tracks. Borrowing money from the NPRR, town site trustees erected the town's first brick structure, the

Spofford Hotel, and declared that it stood in the center of Red Lodge's downtown. Sitting alone in the middle of acres of mud and muck, the three-story Spofford seemed a very tall center of nothing by the end of 1894, while the town's business life continued to hum along in the motley collection of huts and tents clustered around the mine entrance half a mile away. Like a magnet, however, capital gradually pulled the entire "old town" of merchant houses, saloons, bordellos, and professionals over to where Hauser and his colleagues declared the downtown to be.[8]

Access to capital trumped possession of land in town building.[9] In 1901, Fox's daughters quite literally marked this social hierarchy on the town. While entertaining eastern friends, the girls arranged an expedition to climb the mountain at the edge of town. Upon reaching the top, the party broke open a bottle of champagne and christened the peak Mt. Maurice after Dr. Fox. Instead of a nameless peak, now Mt. Maurice (the name stuck) loomed over the little town, a reminder of who sat at the top of the local class structure at the turn of the century.[10]

But, of course, other, more lowly mortals also sought out success and fortune in such western boomtowns. Into this modern West of industrial mining, eastern capital, and mountains named after corporate managers streamed the workers who would bring life to Red Lodge and the entrepreneurs who would shape the new town's culture, civic life, and public image. Undaunted by the symbolism of Mt. Maurice, these men and women approached Red Lodge as a place alive with the possibility of wealth and success, the opportunity inherent in western mythology. For them, capitalistic investment — the corporate creation of towns like Red Lodge — offered the chances for success that had brought them West. These were men like Johnny Southward's father — men who saw Red Lodge not as a dingy, dirty, little mining camp, but as a western place ripe with possibilities that a quick-thinking, hard-working fellow could take advantage of. Capital had already replicated its structures in the West, but there was plenty of room for maneuvering up the social and economic ladder in new boomtowns.

Most of the new arrivals were workers, many of them immigrants, who came searching for jobs in and around the mines. For them, the West's opportunity was not great wealth but the chance to earn a wage and perhaps save enough money to establish a small business, take out a homestead claim, or return to the Old World in triumph. Above these wage laborers sat a smaller group of entrepreneurs who, as the new community's incipient middle class, laid a stronger claim to the town's opportunities for riches. Although they possessed far less money, influence, and power than men like Hauser and Billings or even Fox, these new residents — merchants, lawyers, and other professionals — made substantial capital investments in Red Lodge, gambling that this western place would return them handsome profits.

Red Lodge's "pioneer" moment provided plenty of possibilities for big dreams. Here the imagined West of bonanzas and great wealth might actually come true. Economic niches were up for grabs, and minimal investments by early arrivals might yield hefty returns.[11] Entrepreneurs rushed in, eager to get in on the ground floor of a booming town. Saloon keepers and brothel madams moved in first, putting up hastily built tent businesses in 1887 to reap the quick profits to be made serving the desires of railroad and mine workers.[12] They were quickly followed by people like Jim Virtue, who started a small livery barn in the town in 1888, and Charles Bowlen, whose lumber business opened a year later. These smaller operations stood side by side with branches of statewide businesses such as the J. H. Conrad Company, which in 1889 added Red Lodge to its network of merchant and banking houses.[13] By 1891, the local paper contained advertisements for a stage company, various restaurants and clothing stores, a druggist, barbers, a bank, insurance and real estate services, a meat market, a lumberyard, a bakery, saloons, and an assayer, as well as people selling ice, jewelry, groceries, and shoes and providing paper-hanging services.[14] Many of these men and women moved on quickly, disappointed by conditions in Red Lodge or drawn by the promise of better profits in other places. Others stayed on, encouraged by their success in occupying economic niches during the town's founding period and expecting to find even greater success by sticking with this one town and making it grow. These merchants, professionals, and business managers — the ones who stayed for at least a few years — created Red Lodge's initial business class.

Local growth meant everything to this business class. Quite simply, if Red Lodge got bigger, they got richer. Unlike corporate investors such as Hauser and Villard, who depended on regional or national markets, local entrepreneurs provided goods and services for consumers within a very limited area. Hauser and his partners spread their investments over the entire region; Virtue and Bowlen and other local business owners, although tied through workers' wages to the larger corporate market, had much of their lives and capital wrapped up in one town. Small capitalists in the West pinned their hopes for success on their ability to choose a promising site, invest their time and money in that place, and then sell it as aggressively as possible to newcomers. Essentially, these men and women worked within a limited vision of what the West was and should be.

In effect, these middle-class entrepreneurs believed that the West was simply a preliminary stage toward becoming the East. As Richard Slotkin has argued, town builders really wanted to replicate the "Metropolis," the eastern city, in their western landscape.[15] Optimistic entrepreneurs visualized the transformation of towns like Red Lodge from a scattered collection of rickety shacks into a "live and progressive little city composed of cozy and comfortable residences and substantial business blocks."[16] Success to the business class meant re-creating familiar economic and social structures with *themselves* in the prominent civic roles reserved for entrenched elites in older communities. Every increase in the local population — each successful "sale" of Red Lodge — meant more customers for Jim Virtue's livery barn, the rise in value of his Main Street property, and an improvement in his status as a town founder and leading businessman. Virtue's success depended on selling, or "boosting," Red Lodge: creating and marketing a local image that would convince outsiders to settle and invest in this emerging town.

But a lot stood in the way of Red Lodge and these dreams of vast fortunes. Ironically enough, Red Lodge was just too "western" in many ways. Although town builders appreciated such western assets as abundant natural resources and open spaces, they complained endlessly about other typically western attributes of the region: the landscape was too rugged, the federal government controlled too many resources, corporate industries were too powerful, and there were, quite simply, way too many Indians on way too much land. If Red Lodge were to grow, it would have to do so in spite of the intransigence of the land, government, Northern Pacific Railroad, and Indians.

The western topography, first of all, was maddeningly inconvenient to Red Lodge entrepreneurs, whose inability to reshape geography cut off growth and increased the town's dependence on the Northern Pacific Railroad. The new town's promise depended, in large part, on the convergence of coal and railroads, but their convergence at Red Lodge was also geographically unfortunate. The town's rich hinterland was inaccessible. Red Lodge stood at the edge of the Rocky Mountains, where the high lands swept down to the Great Plains.

It was a place of stunning beauty; snow-capped mountains, heavy forests, and rushing streams promised bounties of ore, wood, and water. But the towering Beartooth Range and snow-fed rivers separated the town from potential customers, making transportation difficult and cutting off the expansion of the town's merchant trade into the gold fields of Cooke City, ranches of northern Wyoming, and farmlands of the Clark's Fork Valley in Montana. Lacking the resources to reshape the western topography, local entrepreneurs had to depend on the Rocky Fork Railway Company and the NPRR for reliable, if expensive and limited, transportation and connections to a wider marketplace.[17] As the only railroad running to Red Lodge, the NPRR could, of course, set its own rates and schedules, while town leaders could only beg for extra trains and lower prices.

As if mountains and monopolies weren't enough, boosters also found themselves fighting against the most powerful presence in the West — the federal government — whose agents seemed determined to stymie the "natural" growth of the new community. Red Lodge town builders watched in horror as the government's Yellowstone Park Timberland Reserve Act of 1891 permanently prevented the private acquisition of thousands of acres of forestland near Red Lodge. The government did not exactly "lock up" this land, as some opponents claimed, but the federal presence in and control of the forests limited development. The federal role in locking up land was even more evident on the Crow Reservation, where troops and agents kept settlers out of over six million acres of reservation land in the early 1890s. To local promoters, these expansive grasslands, which stretched out toward the Pryor and Crazy Mountains far to the east and north, were the right and natural site for the homes and fields of hundreds of farmers who would make the prairie blossom — and bring business to the town. To dispossess the weakened Crow Indians from their lands only a few miles from Red Lodge, entrepreneurs had to lobby a federal government over two thousand miles away, and they were never satisfied with however many millions of acres the Crow lost as the U.S. government forced one treaty renegotiation after another on the tribe. Through successive treaties the federal government reduced the reservation from 6.5 million acres in 1882 to 4.5 million acres in 1892 and to 3.4 million acres in 1904.[18] To promoters intent on rapid development, the process of taking Crow land and turning it into farmland was painfully slow and an affront to western promises of progress and transformation.

Unable to speed up the government, move mountains, or remove Indians by themselves, town builders relied on constructing vivid images of Red Lodge to lure settlers and investors whose work and money would reshape the land and economy according to local wishes (or so boosters assumed). Boosting assumed grand dimensions in the nineteenth-century West as town builders across the region competed against each other in a serious, though often absurd, game of salesmanship. Image was everything. Promoters from every town in the West, not just Red Lodge, churned out newspaper stories and promotional brochures promising a "Grand Future" for their community and assuring potential settlers and investors that it was "destined in time to be a great city."[19] Immune to shame, boosters sold places with a ridiculous mixture of hyperbole and mythology, marketing locales with vivid descriptions of fertile lands and assurances of industrial development. The "Coal Metropolis," as boosters quickly labeled Red Lodge, had an official population of only 624 in the early 1890s, when local boosters described it as a city "of over two thousand inhabitants" or, more eloquently, as "a young giant stretching his sinewy limbs in all directions."[20] According to various booster reports, the Red Lodge area not only possessed "an unequaled and vast expanse of agricultural country" and coal enough "to supply a million people for centuries,"[21] but it also was destined to produce "a veritable bonanza" of gold mines in the near future.[22] Town builders promised, in short, that Red Lodge would live up to the promises of the West.

Boosters, of course, recognized the power of western mythology and eagerly mobilized its national images in service to their cause. One would expect no less from such flamboyant salesmen. Significantly, these boosters carefully separated out certain versions of the western story, emphasizing only those facets of the mythology that served their own, promotional interests, for in the 1890s, the "West" (the idea) was not simply one thing. It was a jumble of contradictory images and symbols and stories that merged around two broad narratives of American westward advancement. Similar in many ways, these twinned narratives explained the West as a site of conquest. One version, elegantly summarized by Frederick Jackson Turner in his 1893 essay "The Significance of the Frontier in American History," centered on the independent farmer whose plow brought civilization to the wild region as the culmination of an orderly series of population waves: "the Indian, the fur-trader and hunter, the cattle-raiser, the pioneer farmer."[23] This version of the West most clearly promoted the region as the site of democratic opportunity and egalitarian values. Significantly, Turner virtually ignored Indian and Mexican land claims to the West; his tale of conquest assumed free land for white advancement and predicted a steady progression of capitalist expansion in the region.

In contrast, a second narrative of westward expansion focused on the bloody struggle between white and nonwhite peoples in the conquest of the West. The "Wild West," as made popular by showman Buffalo Bill Cody, presented six-gun–wielding cowboys as the heroes of a violent region. More blatantly elitist and racist than Turner's West of farmers and fields, the Wild West stressed the region's freedom but suggested that natural aristocracy and talent outweighed democratic egalitarianism in this place of men and guns. These two western stories mingled and merged in the physical and imagined Wests of the 1890s, up for grabs by Red Lodge boosters who, almost of accord, favored Turner's farmer over Buffalo Bill's cowboys and Indians.

In fact, as they grasped at national images of the West to support their dreams of gain, Red Lodge entrepreneurs, in effect, separated these two strands of the American westering mythology and pitted them against each other — advancing the narrative of the agrarian hero while deriding, and seeking to control, the Wild West figures. Boosters championed the farmer and vilified the rancher, cowboy, and Indian. In later years, movie producers would re-create this mythic struggle in popular Westerns like *Shane,* in which the farmer and rancher battled for the right to determine the destiny of the region's resources. Would it be wheat or cattle? Fences or open range? Of course, in the movies there could be little doubt about the outcome: cattle and Indians inevitably yielded to the farmers and the town builders. The Wild West always lost in the end; its glamour lay in its ephemeral quality of being an era that was over almost before it began.[24] Shane himself, as a figure of the Wild West, had to disappear at the end of the movie, riding off into the night and away from a world that no longer had a place for him. With the Wild West's ranchers and cowboys under control, the story implied, farmer Joe Starrett and his friends would continue their efforts of building farms, homes, towns, and churches in the newly opened lands. This was the kind of simple, comprehensible narrative Red Lodge boosters yearned for as they mobilized local resources to champion the sturdy pioneer farmer as their western icon of choice.

In their quest to promote both the imagery and physical bodies of the pioneer farmer, Red Lodge was following a common western course in the 1890s.

As the Wild West increasingly became the purview of Wild West shows and cheap literature, western towns sold themselves to prospective settlers as the antithesis of the popular imagery. That imagery, while it could sell show tickets and paperbacks (and could later help promote tourism), did nothing to promote settlement. Instead, most entrepreneurial town builders around the West promoted "the farmer," a powerful national image that ensnared nineteenth-century middle-class Americans in a deeply rooted pastoralism.[25]

Although well aware of their deepening dependence on industrial goods and services, Americans, including Red Lodge entrepreneurs, had not yet shed an earlier Jeffersonian agrarianism. They believed deeply in the necessary role of the farmer and his plow as the agents of civilization, stability, and morality. According to Leo Marx, this belief in the pastoral ideal in the face of the "machine's" appearance in the landscape "enabled the nation to continue defining its purpose as the pursuit of rural happiness while devoting itself to productivity, wealth, and power."[26] By the late nineteenth century, the farmer embodied a mythology of American progress that denied the social and economic changes that were accompanying the nation's rapid industrialization.[27] In the West, according to this mythology, the pioneer farmer confronted a land without artificial class structures, where wealth and social position in fact meant nothing compared to courage and hard work.[28] The imagery of the frontier farmer thus allowed Americans faced with a nation divided by race and class to retain their faith in American democratic and egalitarian ideals. On their own small scale, Red Lodge boosters echoed this larger, national infatuation with the American farmer with an emphasis on this figure's ability to bolster a struggling regional economy. Entrepreneurs could not look at the industrial landscape of Red Lodge without painting in the small farms, industrious farmers, and bountiful harvests that made the picture "complete."[29]

The small, independent farmer, both as a symbol and as an actual person with a family to provide for (preferably with goods purchased in Red Lodge), became a touchstone of local boosterism in the town's early years. A consumer as well as a producer, the farmer embodied dual images: he was at once a link to older, more stable precapitalist values and also a small entrepreneur who would help the town's economic growth.[30] Farmers promised economic diversity to a town that seemed painfully dependent on a single corporate industry. While grateful, even boastful, of the economic advantages offered by the Rocky Fork Coal Company and the Rocky Fork Railroad, local entrepreneurs

Hopes for an agricultural Eden around Red Lodge died hard. Here the county displays its "treasures" of grains and vegetables in the hope of luring farmers into the area. (Carbon County Historical Society photo)

feared being held hostage to these powerful companies. The mines and railroads represented the modern technological progress that had created Red Lodge, but boosters wanted that industrial core buffered by an older, more familiar form of extractive enterprise. "The farms that are tributary to this city," the local newspaper stated in 1893, "will give Red Lodge a permanency that other industries cannot assure."[31] Independent, capitalist farmers would protect local entrepreneurs from the frightening vicissitudes of an industrial economy that seemed increasingly prone to financial panics, booms, and busts. Economic stability, at least in the minds of local businessmen, resided in small freeholders steadily tilling fields and harvesting crops.

Local entrepreneurs also tried to use the powerful national appeal of the farmer to secure their own ends. In Red Lodge, the independent farmer became both a goal and a tool to persuade influential easterners to "open up" more western lands to the very farming that local entrepreneurs wanted in the area. Wrapped up themselves in convictions about the role of agriculture in "civilizing" a region, boosters readily used agrarian imagery to play to eastern concerns about the nation's increasing industrialization and urbanization. In so doing, they laid bare the class and racial assumptions that underlay the egalitarian agrarian mythology.

Red Lodge boosters played to class- and race-based fears among middle- and upper-class easterners as they constructed their case for more farming opportunities in Carbon County. Western farming, boosters argued, could ameliorate eastern labor troubles. As industrial tensions mounted in the factory towns of the East — sensationalized by the Haymarket Riot of 1886 and the violent Homestead Strike of 1892 — Red Lodge town builders stepped up to offer the solution of western lands. The "discouraged industrial classes of the overcrowded East," the Red Lodge *Picket* suggested, could find hope and financial security on the lands around Red Lodge. The agency of earth, plow, and private property could transform discontented industrial workers into property-owning farmers who would work within the American capitalist system instead of against it. Drawing on popular ideas of the time, Red Lodge entrepreneurs marketed the arable land around their town as a "safety valve" that might save eastern city dwellers from the eruption of an increasingly violent, urban working class.[32]

First, however, the federal government would have to take the land away from the Crow Indians who claimed it.[33] Opportunity for the white farmer, which represented the salvation of American capitalism and democracy, depended on the dispossession of Indians, and Red Lodge boosters were eager to convince easterners of the need to open up more Crow land to non-Indian settlement. Of course, as numerous scholars have pointed out and as many thinking Americans recognized at the time, few really "miserable" workers from the industrial classes could afford to travel out West, buy seed and tools to plant a first crop, and wait out a year with no income before a homestead farm might begin to pay off. Only those with ready cash could afford to take advantage of the "free" land offered under the various federal Homestead Acts. Industrial workers with dreams of western success more often struggled for jobs and survival in the deep mine shafts under industrial towns like Red Lodge or Butte or Bisbee, not on agricultural lands seized from Indians. The power of the Jeffersonian image of the farmer overwhelmed these mundane statistics, however, promising to solve the heightening industrial (read class) problems of the East through the simple expedient of taking land away from

Indians. Red Lodge's emerging middle class thus mustered the democratic image of Turner's frontier farmer in service to their own (and easterners') class interests and at the expense of dispossessed Crow Indians. As Red Lodge town builders quickly discovered, for an egalitarian figure, the farmer could serve a variety of decidedly unegalitarian ends.

Though enmeshed in the agrarian imagery of the frontier farmer, Red Lodge entrepreneurs, as they demonstrated in their arguments about Crow lands, were never simply the creatures of this national mythology. Boosters eagerly manipulated the image of the farmer to their own advantage whenever they could, even when it might not seem particularly appropriate. Red Lodge entrepreneurs, for example, early on took control of the very terminology of the pioneer farmer, cloaking themselves in the culturally weighted language of "the pioneer" to lend legitimacy to their assumption of local leadership roles in the urban space of Red Lodge. Entrepreneurs understood that "pioneer" and "farmer," intimately intertwined in national thought, shared a kind of veneration in American popular culture.[34] The terms evoked images like those in Walt Whitman's "Pioneers! O Pioneers!" (1865): "We the youthful sinewy races, all the rest on us depend.... We the virgin soil upheaving, Pioneers! O Pioneers!"[35]

According to the popular mythology, restless and ambitious farmers had led much of America's westward movement, earning the designation "pioneer" through their struggles to settle and farm the nation's western boundaries.[36] Anyone calling himself a pioneer invoked this agrarian association. Academic historians like Frederick Jackson Turner recognized and reinforced the popular connection, pointing out, if town builders had cared to look, that pioneers were farmers, not townsmen. In his essay on the frontier, Turner explicitly defined pioneers as agrarian people; they cleared and tamed the wilderness, making way for the towns that would come several stages later. Although heroic in their own way, the town builders were, in frontiering myths, farther removed from the crucible of the frontier — the "pioneering" stage — and thus closer to the corruption of the Old World. The towns brought "gardens, colleges, and churches" to the West but were also prone toward "luxuries, elegances, frivolities, and fashions."[37] Pioneers, in American culture, embodied the *agrarian* strand of western mythology.

In Red Lodge, however, the local entrepreneurial class assumed the right to determine who might be called pioneer in their community.[38] The original entrepreneurs justified their possession of the title of "pioneer" — and the exclusion of workers, Indians, and later arrivals — by pointing out that in the Red Lodge area, the pioneer risk-takers had been the town builders who had stuck with the community and worked to make it prosper and succeed. In the local newspaper, use of "pioneer" was extensive but selective; schoolteachers, businessmen, and farmers might be called pioneers, but never miners, Indians, prostitutes, or immigrants.[39] When Red Lodge was only a few years old, consisting of a rickety and disorganized collection of shacks and tents surrounding the Rocky Fork Coal Company mine, a local editor argued that residents enjoyed "comfortable circumstances" at the present time only because of the efforts and sacrifices of the early town builders, "the pioneers of Red Lodge, who first discovered and opened up our immense coal fields and splendid agricultural resources and made them accessible."[40] Reversing the Turnerian process, townsmen had taken the land away from the Indians and made it safe for farmers. In a telling statement meant to reassure new settlers, the Red Lodge *Picket* made this point clearly: "The Indian has disappeared," it proudly claimed, "and the land is yours for the asking."[41] (Of course, the Indians had not quite disappeared, but exaggeration was standard operating procedure for western boosters.) Almost as soon as they could, the spokesmen of the developing middle class created themselves as pioneers, borrowing from the mystique of Jeffersonian farmers to assert their own moral authority to lead the new community.

Red Lodge boosters invented nothing new in these manipulations of frontier imagery. Such appropriations of pioneer terminology were fairly common in the American West whenever local entrepreneurs sought to secure their positions and fortunes in developing communities. As Richard Slotkin has observed, this appropriation of mythological language ensured that the "dangerous or dubious form of the bourgeois could be made to disappear into the mystique of the buckskin pioneer."[42] Entrepreneurs masked their goals through an egalitarian imagery that, in fact, excluded almost everyone else in the community. They made this point clearly in their exclusive possession of the term "pioneer." As the town matured and social classes became better established, the business classes would loosen their grip on this frontier imagery. Gradually, other local groups would appropriate the terminology of the pioneer as they, too, laid claim to the town's history and sought to advance their own social status. Eventually, even the middle-class descendants of the town's immigrant miners could proudly identify their working-class ancestors as true "pioneers" of Red Lodge.[43] In the early 1890s, however, the entre-preneurial classes kept much tighter rein over this powerful imagery, even as they manipulated it for their own gain.

But imagery could go only so far in the American West, and boosting re-mained a limited tool. Printed descriptions of fertile fields and pioneer farm-ers might convince some settlers to purchase local lands or persuade a lawmaker to vote in favor of Indian land cessions, but these promotional tools could do little to change a climate, influence an intractable (and distant) fed-eral bureaucracy, or lower rates on a corporate railroad monopoly. Continu-ally rebuffed by the land, NPRR, and federal government, Red Lodge entrepreneurs clung to the image of the independent farmer and the prom-ise of local control over local resources. But events and conditions conspired against Red Lodge boosters' plans to achieve wealth rapidly and easily. Even when the federal government threw open 1.8 million acres of the Crow Reser-vation to settlers in 1892, local promoters felt profoundly ill-used. They expected a land rush and instead got something more like a trickle. The Panic of 1893, which closely followed the reservation opening, devastated the national economy and stifled interest in western lands. And the prospective settlers who braved the poor economy to purchase land rejected much of the available acreage around Red Lodge. The provisions of the Dawes Allotment Act of 1887 had allowed individual Crow Indians to retain some of the best creek bottomlands on the ceded reservation, and what remained was too arid to be very appealing in hard times. At the very moment they expected the golden influx of hardy farmers, boosters instead faced more disappointment.

Angered at the continual frustration of the "natural" progression of west-ern land from wilderness to ranch to farm and cities, local boosters cast around for convenient scapegoats to explain the failure of their model of western progress. Interestingly, the figures these town builders chose to blame for Red Lodge's failure to prosper happened to be the key figures from the popular ver-sion of the Wild West: the Indian, the rancher, and the cowboy. Boosters, of course, never employed the neat label of "Wild West" to identify the people who seemed to stand in the way of progress, but in the early 1890s, town builders spoke out — sometimes viciously — against these representative fig-ures of the Wild West and the danger (wildness) they brought to the public imagery of the little town. Through their newspaper articles and editorials, boosters essentially created a dichotomy between the agrarian and wild Wests around Red Lodge, blaming the latter for the failure of the former to establish an agricultural paradise in the area.[44]

Ironically, much of the nation in the 1890s remained transfixed by the very mythology of the Wild West that regional boosters fought against. The very popularity of the Wild West was part of the boosters' problem. Even as western townsmen derided and attacked local Indians, ranchers, and cowboys, the nation developed an insatiable appetite for stories about these exotic characters and their adventures in a West full of danger and excitement. The Wild West offered Americans and Europeans a chance to escape the sense of over-civilization and artificiality that seemed to permeate urban society by the end of the century. Although still attached to the agrarian imagery of the egalitarian farmer, Americans grew increasingly fascinated with the Wild West's bloody and violent narrative of expansion into a rough frontier. The appeal was widespread, with dime-novel Westerns, churned out by writers paid by the page, featuring extravagant adventures set in a West full of Indians, bandits, cowboys, and masked women.

Young boys and workers snapped up sensational tales of intrepid, valiant men like Wild Bill Hickok, who could track a murderer across miles of desert and then single-handedly kill two dozen desperadoes in a good day's work. Germans in the 1890s could not get enough of Karl May's stirring stories about "Old Shatterhand" and the Indian chief "Winnetou," who battled evil villains against the wild and beautiful backdrop of the American Southwest.[45] Buffalo Bill Cody's Wild West extravaganza brought these dime novels to glorious life for middle-class viewers, with "authentic" reproductions of western scenes that turned the conquest of the West into a glamorous spectacle of racialized violence. From 1883 into the 1910s, Cody and his Wild West performers toured the world, thrilling audiences with such dramatic episodes as "A Prairie Immigrant Train Crossing the Plains," in which cowboys rescued settlers from attacks by genuine Indian actors, and "Capture of the Deadwood Mail Coach by the Indians" (the title speaks for the story line).[46] Like Deadwood Dick, Calamity Jane, Winnetou, and Wild Bill Hickok, Buffalo Bill lived in a West rippling with enough danger and intrigue to raise the blood pressure of excitable readers who, like Mark Twain's Huckleberry Finn, dreamed of "lightin' out fer the territories."

But the Wild West's messages ran much deeper than simple danger and excitement, although these facets appealed greatly to urban dwellers safe in warm homes. The Wild West also presented the West as the proving ground of Anglo-American superiority. Unlike the pioneer farmer mythology, which obscured its racist and classist foundations beneath the stalwart image of the egalitarian farmer, the Wild West assumed a clearly stated racial and class hierarchy.[47] To Cody's largely middle-class white audience, the Indians' atrocities and the skill of the cowboys and scouts who defeated them reaffirmed the racial superiority of white Americans over Indian savages and, by extension, over other "colored" races. The conquest of the West *proved* the superiority of white America.

Theodore Roosevelt refined this message for a more elite audience but essentially reiterated in print what Cody presented in the arena. Denouncing "sentimentalists" who decried the fate of conquered Indians, Roosevelt replied that "*war was inevitable. . . . It is wholly impossible to avoid conflicts with a weaker race.*"[48] Race in this case was not a simple white/black or white/red equation. Roosevelt, like many other Americans, was heavily influenced by the social Darwinism and biological racism popular in the late nineteenth century. His friend Owen Wister made this point bluntly in the classic 1901 Western, *The Virginian*. Men like Wister's Virginian succeeded in the West not through hard work alone, but because they were better than those around them, especially Indians, Mexicans, Chinese, and eastern European immigrants. Anglo-Saxon men rose to the top in the West, socially and economically, because of natural abilities borne out of racial superiority. "Equality is a great big bluff," the Virginian pointed out to the eastern greenhorn. "It's easy called."[49] The harsh, uncivilized Wild West proved his point.

For the most part, Red Lodge entrepreneurs had little trouble accepting, even embracing, the racist and class assumptions of the Wild West narrative, which after all reflected much wider national ideas of the late nineteenth century. Town builders readily advocated stripping Indians of treaty lands and asserted their own class rights to dominate local leadership roles.[50] But violence — the very heart of the Wild West — was bad for business. Affirming Anglo-Saxon superiority was all well and good, but stories of ambushes and massacres painted the region as a place without law, order, or progress. Wildness meant crime, Indian attacks, and lack of protection for property and capital investments. Middle-class families and farmers, who might enjoy seeing a Wild West show, did not move to "wild" places themselves or invest in businesses there. Besides, two of the Wild West's representative characters — the rancher and the Indian — threatened local progress by monopolizing arable lands that might support thousands of farmers and their families. The Wild West not only presented the wrong image of the West, but the real-life representatives of that narrative controlled too much land. Except for minor, fringe elements of this narrative, local boosters were determined to fight the Wild West in and around Red Lodge in their quest to make the town into a model, eastern-style city surrounded by respectable, and profitable, farmlands rather than by Indians, ranchers, and cowboys.

The most evocative and powerful symbol of the Wild West, Indians posed multiple threats to Red Lodge business interests. The Crow not only monopolized some of the region's best land, but they also frightened prospective settlers who remained culturally convinced that all Indians were terrifying savages intent on massacring and scalping white victims. Surprisingly, remnants of this attitude toward Indians persisted even into the late nineteenth century. The perception, after all, had deep roots in a nation obsessed since colonial days with Indian atrocities against white settlers. Americans had long memorialized white victimization, virtually ignoring accompanying white atrocities against Indians. Buffalo Bill's Wild West, for example, regularly featured Indian attacks on helpless white settlers but never presented tableaux of white Americans massacring or dispossessing Indians. That was not part of the popular story. The Custer Battlefield became a national monument; the site of the Marias massacre, where U.S. soldiers killed 173 Blackfeet Indians, mostly women and children, in 1870, never even warranted a marker.[51] Western mythologies effectively inverted the story of American conquest. As Richard White argues, spectacles like Buffalo Bill's presented the American conquest of the West as a site where whites were victims and Indians aggressors. Such images permeated American culture, and Americans learned well the lesson of white victimization, as Red Lodge boosters soon discovered.[52]

In the early 1890s, the Red Lodge area resounded with stories of white victims of Indian aggression.[53] Although white settlers invariably initiated any violent encounters between Indians and non-Indians, whites insisted that Indian savagery endangered their lives and property. Conditioned by the mythology of the Wild West, new migrants to the region *expected* Indian violence and saw it everywhere. In 1892 and 1893, dozens of rural residents fled their homes in anticipation of Crow uprisings, and a favorite story in Red Lodge family reminiscences tells of a farmwife just settled on former Crow land who scurried into her cellar any time an Indian approached her house, fearfully awaiting the inevitable attack that never came.[54] The presence of these new settlers on former reservation land did produce tensions, but mostly because white newcomers illegally claimed land and other resources owned by individual Crows. Rumors of Indian attacks that swept through the Red Lodge area in the early 1890s developed out of white violence toward Indian landholders, not the other way around.

In October 1892, for example, two white settlers who took claims on Indian lands drove off the Crow owner with guns when he protested the intrusion. The incident set off a series of rumors that Indians were gathering for an attack on the settlers.[55] A few months later, two men shot and killed an Indian who protested their theft of lumber from his allotted land. When about 150 Indians gathered to demonstrate against the killing, the terrified residents of the town of Wilsey (about thirty miles north of Red Lodge) fled to Laurel on the main line of the Northern Pacific.[56] Fears of an Indian uprising were unfounded, the local newspaper assured its readers; the Crow would not engage in such "foolishness," knowing as they did that any such attack would mean that "the entire tribe would be wiped out of existence in a few days."[57] But new settlers were slow to accept such reassurances. Masking their own aggressiveness, they believed that all Indians were eager to massacre white victims in the manner of the bloodthirsty Sioux in Buffalo Bill's Wild West.

Local boosters dismissed the "absurd rumors" about Indian attacks, but they quickly realized that the very presence of Indians spawned such rumors. Indians, quite simply, were bad for the region's image. Rumors of Indian uprisings, even if unfounded, produced "highly sensational reports" that eastern newspapers seized upon to generate dramatic stories about the dangers of the Wild West in Red Lodge.[58] To identify the Red Lodge area as a peaceful and settled part of the West, boosters would have to make the Indians disappear.[59] Entrepreneurs and new settlers did not care that the Crow had been military allies of the United States since 1825 or that these Indians had engaged in a vigorous and important barter economy with earlier American settlers in the Yellowstone area.[60] The complete elimination of Indians from nonreservation lands was needed to put an end to the bad publicity inevitably arising from the interaction of two seemingly incompatible groups. The local paper put it bluntly: "We all know that when Indians come in contact with the western settler the effect is about the same as planting a red flag in the face of a maddened bull. The two classes will never assimilate. The proper remedy is to remove those

Indians to the reservation."[61] Final removal of the Indians ("red" flags) from their former lands would serve the dual purposes of opening up more acreage to farmers and eliminating a vital element of the Wild West from Red Lodge's public image. Indians in the area were safe only as a distant memory or restricted within the ever-shrinking boundaries of a reservation.

In later years, tourism promoters would actively solicit Indians to appear in Red Lodge rodeos and festivals as symbols of the town's Wild West past, but in the early 1890s Indians were too much of a presence and retained too many associations with real danger and economic troubles to be welcomed in the community. Town leaders preferred to have them completely out of sight. Local boosters even tried to change the town's name to Villard in 1889, dropping its connection to Indian dwellings while currying favor with the president of the Northern Pacific Railroad. Henry Villard requested, however, that the name not be changed, and the "Indian" name of the town would eventually become one of its most effective marketing features. By the 1920s, boosters began to incorporate Indian symbols into the town logo, and promotional campaigns played up the area's "Indian past." Outside of ceremonial events, however, real Indians remained largely unwelcome in the community for much of the twentieth century.[62] Unlike the other Wild West characters of the rancher and the cowboy, the Indian's presence stayed almost entirely symbolic in Red Lodge's developing "western" identity.

If Indians represented the racialized, savage "other" on the western landscape, then the rancher embodied the Anglo-American success story of the Wild West. White, male, wealthy property holders, ranchers controlled huge acreages of land in the region, often living in grand style at luxurious ranch headquarters with imported furnishings and foods. For many eastern observers, ranchers epitomized the western dream. Theodore Roosevelt championed the rancher lifestyle; he played at being a rancher in the Dakotas for several years and idolized men such as Granville Stuart, owner of one of the largest ranches in Montana in the 1880s. Owen Wister hobnobbed with the rancher elite at the Cheyenne Club in Wyoming and admired the town's radical egalitarianism: the newly rich rubbed shoulders democratically with the sons of eastern millionaires.[63] Ranchers such as those who befriended Wister and Roosevelt did not terrify settlers, threaten public safety, or provoke wild rumors about massacres. But in the early 1890s, Red Lodge boosters despised these figures as much as, if not more than, the Crow Indians.

Local battles against ranchers centered on land, or more particularly on accusations that cattle owners monopolized arable acres that might more profitably support farmers than cows. Ranchers represented the Wild West of the open range; they controlled enormous acreages in the region, both through the manipulation of federal law and through sometimes shady alliances with the Crow Indians.[64] Cattlemen's consolidation of local lands actually began a few years before the founding of Red Lodge, when the killing winter of 1886–1887 ended the days of the open range. The harsh winter decimated herds and destroyed many of the big cattle companies.[65] Cattlemen used any method at hand, legal or illegal, to gain control over key parcels of land on which they could grow fodder to feed their herds through the winter months. Local rancher J. R. Dilworth, for example, filed on a Desert Land Act claim that he never lived on himself, but that his outfit, the Dilworth Cattle Company, "fenced and cultivated" for its own benefit. Dilworth's successor, J. N. Tolman, also took out filings under the Homestead and Desert Land Acts, and Tolman's cousin claimed a Timber Culture Act filing for the company, which was headquartered in Kansas. In a typical manipulation of these land acts' stipulations, Tolman swore to use the acreage only for his own benefit, then offered the company "full use of the Land so long as they may wish it."[66] Flagrantly misusing national land policies, companies like the Dilworth outfit managed to control a vast territory around Red Lodge for a decade after the open range ended, thus, according to town builders, delaying the Turnerian evolution from cattleman to farmer, Wild West to civilized countryside.

More infuriating to local boosters, cattlemen actually allied with that other despised Wild West figure, the Indian, to gain access to even more land around Red Lodge. Ironically, cattlemen expanded their rangeland by twisting provisions of the Dawes Allotment Act of 1887, which was supposed to transform reservation Indians into independent farmers. Under the Dawes Act, individual Indians could claim 160 acres of reservation land for cultivation. A paternalistic provision of the act, meant to shield naive Indians from ruthless speculators, prohibited individuals from selling their allotted land for twenty-five years. However, Indians *could* lease their land. After the federal government redrew the boundaries of the Crow Reservation in 1892, ranchers such as Tolman, who had connections with the reservation agent, contracted with Crow Indians to lease both individual parcels of allotted land and tribal acreages within the reservation itself. Indignant town merchants and promoters assessed the situation and hotly denounced the Crow agreement (arranged in 1890, but not ratified until 1892) as "one of the most unjust and pernicious treaties ever made" — not because it abrogated earlier promises made to a loyal American ally but because individual Indians (and through them, area ranchers) managed to hold on to some of the better lands during the negotiations. Reluctant to acknowledge Indian agency in the process, boosters painted the Crow as simple dupes of wily ranchers. "Through the interests and manipulations of a lot of interested cattle owners," the Red Lodge *Picket* fumed, "most of this land amounting to some 54,000 acres, and the choicest for agricultural purposes, was reserved for the Indians as allotments in order that the cattle barons could use it for grazing and hay purposes."[67] Thus allied, these two Wild West figures could deny Red Lodge entrepreneurs their rightful slice of the region's promised wealth.

Red Lodge boosters furiously insisted that by monopolizing choice parcels of land, ranchers perpetuated an older, less efficient use of local resources. More important, the cattleman — who might use five or more acres to feed a single cow — kept that land out of the hands of hundreds or thousands of farm families. The greater population density created by numerous small farms would generate not only customers for local entrepreneurs but also many of the markers of civilization that boosters so wanted in the area: schools, roads, churches, and fences.[68] Determined to replace ranches with farms and the open range with picket fences, Red Lodge entrepreneurs waged a vicious propaganda battle not only against Indians but also against ranchers and their control of land and resources.

Red Lodge boosters despised both of these Wild West figures, but, significantly, they made important racial distinctions between them. The ranchers' unpardonable fault was that, in maintaining their business interests, they denied Red Lodge merchants their own chances to grow rich from the opportunities presented by the development of the West. Townsmen blasted the ranchers in print and fought to force them to give up illegal land claims. But Red Lodge boosters never dehumanized the ranchers as they did Indians. The Red Lodge *Picket* freely labeled Crow Indians as "barbaric," "worthless," government "pets." A headline in 1893 even declared one Crow, killed by a white settler, "A Good Indian! Because He Has a Bullet Through His Heart."[69] Articles denouncing the cattlemen rarely used terms any harsher than "Cattle Baron." In a state dominated by "Copper Barons" who ran much of Montana's economy and politics, the term was a slur, but nothing like the "good Indian/dead Indian" references to Crows. Ranchers were part of a much-despised Wild West, but they were also rich, powerful, and *white*. Racist assumptions lay at the core of the westward movement in all of its mythological manifestations, and once stripped of the bulk of their landholdings, ranchers metamorphosed into respected members of the community. Indians permanently remained outsiders, racialized others with no place in the town.

Whatever form their attacks took, however, Red Lodge boosters could do little about the presence of Indians and ranchers in the early 1890s. These local Wild West figures were close at hand and their offenses easily comprehensible, but they also lay largely outside the influence of Red Lodge boosters. Like the federal government, corporate officials, and the land itself, these Wild West figures — even though they made convenient targets for vicious propaganda attack — stood outside local control. In this phase of the battle between the Wild West and the agrarian one, local entrepreneurs did not have the power to take direct action. They produced scathing articles and allied with other businessmen around the state to lobby the federal government for help in reallocating Indian lands, but townsmen could not simply force Indians to give up allotments or demand that ranchers abide by the letter and spirit of the Desert Land or Dawes Allotment Acts. The federal government enforced (at least nominally) the rights of the Indians, and the stockmen formed powerful state organizations to protect their own privileged status in the West.

Unlike the rancher and the Indian, a third Wild West figure, the cowboy, invaded the public spaces of Red Lodge itself. The cowboy brought the Wild West into the community, posing a physical danger to residents and marking the town as "unsafe" to outsiders. Since the cowboy controlled no land, had no powerful protectors, and acted within the town, local entrepreneurs could more easily and readily regulate his behavior than they could that of the Indians and wealthy ranchers out on the prairies. In fact, Red Lodge entrepreneurs took advantage of the danger posed by cowboys and other "ruffians" to tighten their control over the town's development and public image. Boosters used the cowboy as an excuse to push residents into establishing a town government with ordinances designed to impose middle-class morality on the local population. The Wild West within Red Lodge died a quick death, stifled by an entrepreneurial class determined to create a respectable, safe, and profitable community.

Briefly, Red Lodge had played the role of a western boomtown. When the coal mine started operations in 1889 and the miners' payroll began to flow through eager hands, Red Lodge went a little wild. Although perhaps it was never quite as rowdy as later residents would like to boast, few social controls existed in the town's first years to keep the mostly single, male population in check.[70] Saloons operating out of tents opened up almost the moment the town existed; prostitutes followed as quickly. Gamblers wandered into Red Lodge ready to make a quick buck off a naive miner or a drunken cowhand. Hoodlums and cowboys (local entrepreneurs did not distinguish between the two) openly carried firearms, delighting in disrupting the church services (and the sleep) of decent citizens. Life and property seemed constantly endangered. In 1891, cattleman J. N. Tolman dismissed the town as a den of horse thieves, the headquarters of a "gang of very suspicious characters."[71] There simply was no one to stop any of these wild characters from doing what they liked. As an unincorporated town, Red Lodge had no city tax funds to hire police officers, and the sheriff lived over one hundred miles away in the county seat of Livingston; in 1891, Red Lodge did not even have a deputy sheriff in residence to deal with either Tolman's horse thieves or drunken cowboys on their shooting sprees. Of course, some businesses — most obviously the saloons and brothels — profited from the wildness of local cowboys, but they were outnumbered by other entrepreneurs whose dreams of expansion depended more on peace and respectability than in permitting dangerous activities within town limits.[72]

Although many different characters contributed to the vice and violence in the new town, cowboys epitomized (or at least were blamed for) much of the wild behavior in early Red Lodge. In the early 1890s, cowboys constituted an unemployed "hobo" population in Red Lodge during a large part of the year. Many of the cowhands who drove cattle to the railhead of the Rocky Fork Railway line were fired from their ranch jobs during the winter months; they wandered in and out of town, taking odd jobs here and there, often rustling livestock to keep from starving.[73] With no police force or town government to enforce codes of behavior, the cowboys freely carried and fired weapons, relieving their boredom through smoke, noise, and fear.[74] Montana cowboy Billa Gallagher typified the wild behavior of these cowboys. He swaggered into Red Lodge in late 1892, boasting of being a "desperado" and swearing to make the town "smoke." After loading up on whiskey, Gallagher and his friends let loose, firing off their guns in one of the local saloons.[75] Each shot they fired drove home to local residents the need for a local governmental structure to control legally the Billa Gallaghers of the world.

For middle-class westerners in the 1890s, the physical presence of the Wild West — drunken, obnoxious, smelly Billa Gallagher — seemed far from romantic. The cowboy in Red Lodge was an often unemployed, often inebriated nuisance, not some idealized hero of the plains, who, like Owen Wister's Virginian, bashfully asked the new school marm for a dance before riding out to rescue settlers from savage Indians.[76] Up close, men such as Gallagher simply did not fit Theodore Roosevelt's description of cowboys as "hard-working, faithful fellows" who constituted a proud, spirited, Anglo-Saxon class on the plains.[77] To many townspeople in the West, cowboys were working-class men who threatened the lives and property of their betters while making little or no contribution to the local economy. Invading public spaces and tying up town business with "wild and reckless abandon," cowboys like Billa Gallagher represented exactly what local elites were determined to eliminate from their town.[78] Such people, Red Lodge boosters insisted, needed to be controlled so that "the impression will not go abroad that we are a community of border ruffians who shoot and kill for the mere pleasure that is supposed to afford the bad man to spill blood."[79]

Suppression of the cowboys marked the tightening of local entrepreneurial control over Red Lodge society and the town's public identity. Eager to make Red Lodge an attractive and safe place for themselves and prospective settlers, town and company officials implemented controls to discourage undesirable people and behavior. They sought to remove the "wild" from this western town in their quest for prosperity. In the first step toward this goal, the entrepreneurial class led a successful vote for incorporation in 1892, which was followed a few years later by the town's victorious bid to become county seat of the newly formed Carbon County. The Red Lodge *Picket* justified the expense of creating local government by warning that this was the only way to "put an end to the lawlessness and all-around foolishness of the hobo element of the town."[80] The town then hired the famous old trapper John "Liver-Eating" Johnson as constable. A remnant of an older West himself, Johnson had earned a reputation for not carrying a gun while enforcing the law in nearby Coulsten (Billings) a few years earlier: "I just beat hell out of the ones that should be arrested," he once claimed, "and turn 'em loose, and I've never had to arrest the same man twice!"[81]

Despite Johnson's reputation, city officials thought it prudent to vote funds for the construction of a city jail. They, unfortunately, skimped on the project, and neighboring towns delighted in poking fun at the Red Lodge jail for being as easy to get out of as into.[82] The state of the city jail notwithstanding, town leaders took further measures to control wild behavior. The city council prohibited the discharge of weapons within the city limits and made it a crime to carry a concealed weapon in town.[83] Billa Gallagher and his friends found that Red Lodge was no longer a "wide open" place by the end of 1892. Constable Johnson arrested Gallagher and threw him in jail (which, fortunately for the town's crime-busting efforts, managed to hold him); town officials then imposed a fine so high that his friends could not raise the bail. Townsmen drove home the point that Red Lodge was no longer a wild town. "In future," announced the local newspaper, "cowboys, or others who indulge in the practice of firing their pistols within the corporate limits had better go slow. . . . Red Lodge is incorporated and the pistol must go."[84]

Social control in Red Lodge only began with cowboys like Billa Gallagher. The town's suppression of wild cowboy antics symbolized a larger movement to control public appearance and behavior in the new community that extended to women, miners, prostitutes, children, and even pets. Since the proper public behavior of women, in particular, marked a town as orderly and progressive, the town council took pains to regulate female activities in Red Lodge according to middle-class standards, stipulating what women could wear and how they could speak in public. In 1894, for example, the town decided that "Mother Hubbard" dresses violated local sensibilities and were thus forbidden. These loose-fitting garments, worn by a few daring women at the turn of the century, eschewed the structure of corsets and bustles, making them more comfortable but also more likely to reveal the real shape of a woman's body.[85] Such freedom from social restraints could not be allowed in the newly incorporated town. Hereafter, warned the Red Lodge *Picket,* "it will not be in 'good form' to wear these garments on the streets of Red Lodge."[86] The local constable also arrested women for swearing in public, arguing that this behavior disturbed the peace and offended "good order and morals."[87]

Other ordinances extended beyond women. By 1893 one could not sell alcohol to minors or drunks or peddle goods in town without a license. Rocky Fork Coal Company officials reinforced these municipal efforts in 1892 by threatening to lay off workers who failed to arrive promptly at the mines the day after payday.[88] This policy curbed the tendency of miners to make the monthly payday into an explosive day of celebration punctuated by drunken brawls and lewd behavior. And town leaders even regulated dogs. Every unlicensed hound that did not look valuable was subject to capture and extermination by order of the town council.[89] Acting together, local elites sought to impose "moral order" on the working-class element of the town (and its pets), thus making the town, as a whole, appear more regulated, efficient, and worthy of investment. The Red Lodge *Picket* hopefully asserted in early 1893 that "Red Lodge is now a quiet and orderly town. You don't hear any shooting on the streets any more because the marshal is around to put a stop to it."[90]

Creating a "quiet and orderly town" remained, however, a complicated procedure. Some of the elements of the "wild" West were not as easily (or as willingly, in some cases) controlled as others. The question of prostitution, for example, created dissension within the ranks of the town council. When brought up at a council meeting in early 1893, the issue of regulating "bawdy houses" generated a lively discussion. Opponents of the original bill to outlaw the brothels argued that it would be a "dead letter" if adopted. One alderman went so far as to acknowledge that humanity was "so low that bawdy houses were necessary in a community." The shocked mayor ended this discussion by referring the measure to a ways and means committee, which eventually declared the houses "public nuisances" to be fined from five to fifty dollars for each conviction.[91] The town would periodically crack down on prostitution (especially at the beginning of World War I), but the local brothels were well-known institutions that operated much of the time with little official interference. The town newspapers reflected the type of smug indulgence with which many residents regarded the working girls. Writers felt free to joke about a married alderman called upon to "prove that the defendants were bad girls" or the young man who "in the kindness of his heart" would bail out particularly attractive members of the demimonde.[92] As long as they paid their fines, prostitutes continued to work with little interference or official condemnation.

Regulating prostitutes rather than running them out of town made perfect sense to town leaders, especially those less shocked than the mayor about the morality of the profession. Many established communities around the nation practiced similar controls at the turn of the century. By keeping track of the bawdy houses, fining the inhabitants, and routinely jailing some of them, city officials practiced and expanded their new municipal powers. When brothel owners paid their fines and kindhearted young men bailed out their favorite "bad girls," that money went straight into the coffers of the new city's treasury, lightening the tax burden on more respectable citizens. Historian Anne M. Butler has argued that this "dual status" of the prostitute as both "criminal and citizen" made her a "stepping stone for the building of social institutions."[93] Through her marginal status, the prostitute helped the town's middle classes secure control over the community's remaining wildness. The town council took measures, however, to mute the public presence of local brothels. Prostitutes might be "necessary in a community," but there was no need to flaunt the fact. In 1905 town leaders effectively "zoned" for prostitution, restricting the "denizens of the badlands" to a "more secluded part of the city," where they would not disturb "moral citizens."[94] Properly regulated, the members of the demimonde did not detract from the overall image of a modern, orderly community no longer connected to the wildness of the open West.

Public attacks on the Wild West within Red Lodge lasted only as long as these wild figures seemed to present a real threat to the town's prospects for prosperity. When the immediate danger of wildness faded — when cowboys no longer threatened life and property, Indians stayed within their reservation borders, and prostitutes paid the appropriate fines — local residents gained the distance needed to reimagine these characters as somehow glamorous and appealing, or at least tolerable. Later celebrations of these once-despised figures showed that the local crackdown on the representatives of the Wild West was only a prelude to residents' mobilization of these characters as symbols of the town's ties to a romanticized view of the West. This change came quickly enough. By the last years of the 1890s, Indians and ranchers had lost control of much of the land around town. As ranches contracted or disappeared, many cowboys lost their jobs; they either gave up cowboying or left the region to find work elsewhere. As his numbers in Red Lodge diminished and his national fame increased, the cowboy became colorful instead of dirty, heroic rather than dangerous. By the 1920s, Red Lodge entrepreneurs would establish both the cowboy and the Indian as prominent symbols of the town's Wild West heritage, and local histories would make frequent, winking allusions to dance hall girls and prostitutes to add some verve to tales of past wildness.[95] In 1930 local leaders even established a highly successful annual rodeo to showcase the town's connection to the once-despised cowboy and his mystique. The war against the wildness associated with the cowboy, Indian, and rancher lasted

only a few short years; the period of proudly proclaiming the town's association to such a past would last much longer.[96]

In fact, even while local boosters attacked the Wild West of cowboys, Indians, and ranchers, they were actually starting the process of tying Red Lodge's
public identity into some fringe elements of the Wild West mythology. In the
early 1890s, although still focused on the farmer as the most appropriate icon
of western progress, alert local businessmen recognized that an older, safer
strain of the Wild West narrative might actually help the town's image and
economic opportunities. They seized upon the imagery of the "mountain
man," the valiant loner who trapped and hunted the high mountain wilder-
nesses. In its early years, Red Lodge actually possessed a few remnants of this
older breed of Wild West hero, the antecedent to the cowboy. Boosters
embraced these local figures (figuratively — they tended to dress in smelly
buckskins), presenting them to the outside world as proof that, in spite of its
hard-won respectability, Red Lodge was, indeed, a thoroughly masculine,
muscular western town — at least on the fringes.

The promotion of the mountain man was only a minor effort compared to
the later, vigorous attempts to associate Red Lodge with Buffalo Bill's Wild West
imagery, but it revealed a significant exception to town builders' determination
to control the Wild West in the 1890s. It illustrated the beginning of certain local
trends in the creation of public identity. First, local pride in the "mountain man"
showed how the concept of immediate "danger" influenced townspeople's
acceptance of certain western associations. The mountain man was part of the
Wild West, but he posed no immediate danger to Red Lodge entrepreneurs. Second, promotion of the mountain man marked the town's very earliest efforts
to attract visitors — tourists — into the community. Through the 1910s, tourism
was never much of a consideration for local leaders, but these early flirtations
with both Wild West imagery and tourist dollars created a foundation of sorts
upon which later generations would build.

The town's romantic Wild West associations began with boosters' modest
efforts to make the mountain man a local symbol of western masculinity
according to the national mythology surrounding this figure. The mountain
man represented an older version of the Wild West: Natty Bumppo and Jede-
diah Smith made popular again in the 1890s by Theodore Roosevelt's stirring
stories of western hunting expeditions. Roosevelt, a firm believer in the outdoor
life, focused much of his later works on the benefits of hunting to a society

grown soft from overcivilization. In the late nineteenth century, as T. J. Jackson Lears has shown, middle- and upper-class Americans like Roosevelt were long-ing for "physical, moral and spiritual regeneration."[97] Confronted by an increas-ingly industrialized and urbanized society, Americans experienced a "spreading sense of moral impotence and spiritual sterility — a feeling that life had become not only overcivilized but also curiously unreal."[98] Big game hunting, Roosevelt believed, could rejuvenate men whose lives were increasingly spent indoors managing businesses and shuffling papers.

Overcivilization found its antidote in the rugged and masculine West. The future president wrote a series of books and articles detailing how hunting in the wilds of the mountains forced men to test themselves against the natural world; in these works the "masculine" West contrasted favorably with the per-ceived "feminization" of East Coast cities. When Roosevelt named the hunting club he cofounded in 1887 the Boone and Crockett Club, he displayed this ven-eration of masculine confrontation with the wilderness. Naming the club after two of the most idealized frontiersmen in American history suggests the ex-perience of confronting and conquering raw nature that Roosevelt and his cohorts sought to re-create.[99] Elite easterners, according to this credo, could (and should) imitate their frontier forefathers. Of course, due to pressing business and social concerns in the East, they could confine the imitation to a few weeks in the West. And hardship in the wild should be pressed only so far. Many east-erners who took inspiration from Roosevelt's descriptions of hunting in the West often chose to confront nature in as much comfort as possible — bring-ing with them chefs, personal servants, wagonloads of provisions, and trained guides.[100]

Alert Red Lodge boosters quickly picked up that these eastern sportsmen who venerated frontier figures readily spent money in pursuit of their mas-culine adventures. So, while "taming" the cowboy and the Indian, local busi-nessmen also advanced a kind of milder Wild West image of Red Lodge in the form of the masculine hunter/trapper figure who could guide wealthy east-erners into the wilds of the surrounding mountains. Mountain men presented a variety of desirable attributes. Unlike the cowboys who could overwhelm the town during certain seasons, the remaining "mountain man" figures in the region tended to be more solitary, thus less dangerous and more exotic. Nor did they monopolize large tracts of land or threaten settlers. And their activities did not taint the town with a negative form of violence. Roosevelt's contemporary version of the "vigorous" West of tracking and hunting big game was just as violent as other Wild West narratives, but he channeled its violence into activities Red Lodge entrepreneurs could appreciate and benefit from. The vigorous West encouraged rich easterners to vent their "masculine" passions against big animals, not against other human beings or private property. And while pursuing this acceptable activity, the wealthy hunters traveled through the West, spending money and making themselves fair game (so to speak) for western boosters intent on turning every new visitor into an investor in their vision of the region. In the 1890s, Red Lodge boosters rejected Buffalo Bill's Indians and cowboys, but they seized upon the masculine trapper as a thoroughly acceptable hero whose appearance and activities lent a colorful, but safe, western edge to the town's newly won respectability.

Two particular local mountain man figures — John "Liver-Eating" Johnson and E. E. VanDyke — connected the town of Red Lodge to the western virility that wealthy easterners looked for in the West. Solitary men who did not threaten the orderly townscape that local leaders were trying to create, Johnson and VanDyke, nevertheless, wonderfully symbolized the perceived gulf between the strong, masculine West and the effeminate East that Red Lodge boosters sought to use to their own advantage.

E. E. VanDyke was the most prominent hunting guide in the region and a favorite character in Red Lodge newspaper stories. Operating out of Cooke City, about sixty miles south of Red Lodge, VanDyke traveled often to the Coal Metropolis over the trail he blazed across the Beartooth Mountains to the Northern Pacific line where he met most of his clients. There the grizzled hunter greeted each newcomer with a personal guarantee that the veteran mountain man would put the greenhorn in the path of big game animals; if necessary, he would even shoot the beast himself, so that the client could take home a worthy trophy. According to local rancher Malcolm Mackay, a wealthy eastern transplant who once hired the well-known hunter to guide a bear-hunting expedition, VanDyke's clients by the turn of the century included celebrities from large eastern cities as well as some "titled gentlemen from foreign lands."[101] VanDyke even guided Theodore Roosevelt himself on a big game hunt.[102]

The Red Lodge newspaper followed the actions of "the live hunter and trapper" with obvious enthusiasm, taking pride both in the clients he brought West and in his rough physical appearance. One account described him as a man who "wore a crop of hair which reached to his shoulders, and with his trapper's dress and big gun, would present a startling aspect in the effete east."[103] Malcolm Mackay, a somewhat less boastful observer, noted that the mountain man was amazingly slovenly, with offensive manners and an even more offensive odor emanating from his (exotic) buckskin clothes. This description was exactly what so delighted the Red Lodge boosters. Gruff, smelly, and taciturn, VanDyke seemed to embody a life in the rugged mountains that was to many the epitome of masculine adventure and hardihood. To Red Lodge boosters, he was a double blessing. They could use him not only to emphasize their own manly qualities — *they* were not startled at VanDyke's dress and big gun — but also to take advantage of the wealthy clients he brought into the area, all of whom were potential investors in the Coal Metropolis.[104]

Although not in the business of guiding greenhorn hunters from the East, old Liver-Eating Johnson generated local admiration as the living embodiment of the wild and woolly (and safe) past of trapping and scouting. Johnson, who had hunted and trapped in the Beartooths for over four decades, was a well-known Montana figure by the 1890s, primarily, perhaps, because of his gruesome nickname. A startling figure, over six feet tall with shaggy black whiskers and long hair (a biographer called him "a magnificent specimen of physical manhood"),[105] Johnson had reputedly killed dozens of Indians in various dramatic encounters. The story of how he acquired the name of "Liver-Eating" became a kind of Montana legend around the turn of century, and local historians still argue over the origin of the nickname. The most widely accepted story is that he held up the liver of an Indian he had just killed outside of Fort Mussellshell and pretended to eat a bite of it; at its most sensational, the legend is that he ate hundreds of livers from the Indians he killed avenging his wife's death.[106] His was the kind of name regularly dropped in memoirs, like Teddy Blue Abbott's, of life in early Montana, in contemporary newspaper stories about frontier life, and in national publications such as *Field and Stream*.[107] Red Lodge boosters delighted in their possession of this real western hero and highlighted his activities around town in a number of promotional stories.

Johnson actually encompassed two versions of the Wild West. Red Lodge promoters sold the old Liver-Eater not only as a rugged hunter but also as a more genuine version of the frontier scout hero made popular by showmen like Buffalo Bill Cody, Frank Miles, and Yellowstone Kelly. The U.S. Army had employed such scouts as guides, hunters, and Indian contacts; their national

fame soared in the late nineteenth century as Cody, Miles, and others portrayed themselves as the real heroes of the Indian wars. Dressed in tight-fitting
breeches with long lovelocks streaming from beneath their broad-brimmed
hats, these scouts toured the nation telling of their adventures.[108] Although
Johnson belittled the "three months men who wear their hair long and hunt
up a crowd in order to tell of their experiences," he and Red Lodge boosters
benefited from the notoriety that these men generated.[109] Local entrepreneurs
certainly recognized that "poet-scouts" such as Captain Jack Crawford, who
catered to audiences eager to believe in western heroes, helped to create the
frontier scout as an American icon, thus boosting Johnson's appeal as a local
promotional tool.[110] Johnson never toured the continent as the more famous
scouts did in the 1890s, but he told his own stories and enjoyed an audience
of appreciative listeners. Despite his rough appearance, he was a favorite
among the children of the town, and he would regale them and any adult
bystanders for hours with tales of life in the mountains and among Indians.
In the 1890s, however, Johnson was wearing down. By the time the old Liver-
Eater settled in Red Lodge, he was already in his sixties. Apart from his police
work, he spent most of his days tending to his garden and traveling to the
Wyoming hot springs seeking some ease for his aged, aching body.[111] His presence in town provided local color safely displayed in a tough old man who
told stories about the good old days and tended to his own business.

The western "edge" of the town's image served local promoters well.
Boosters packaged local residents according to national images of hero trappers and scouts and then sold these residents to the nation (at least those who
received Red Lodge booster materials) as more "genuine" than the showmen
who created those very images from which they had drawn. In their view, a
certain touch of the "Wild West" — descriptions of VanDyke, the "live trapper," and references to local hero Liver-Eating Johnson — made the town
interesting enough that wealthy tourists might stop by and take a look. It also
suited the townsmen's egos to contrast their masculine environment, embodied in the mountain man, to the "effete" conditions and residents of the East.
All that boosters really wanted was to be the Wild West at the fringes. Plung-
ing into the Wild West was exciting, but only in very small doses — and only
if remunerative.

Local efforts to control and exploit Wild West imagery in Red Lodge
demonstrated the shifting nature of public identities in this community. In

The solid brick buildings of Red Lodge's main street — worthy of a picture postcard — boasted of the prosperity created by industrial coal mining at the beginning of the twentieth century. (Carbon County Historical Society photo)

the 1890s, middle-class boosters spent much energy creating an image for the town that distanced the community both from the realities of surrounding Montana life and also from many of the popular images of the Wild West. They endorsed only a minor, "fringe" element of the Wild West — the mountain man — as a safe, exotic addition to the town's public identity. These efforts changed significantly in the early twentieth century when town leaders began to incorporate the imagery of cowboys, ranchers, and Indians into the town's public identity. Soon enough the western "edge" would take over much of the town's image. The positive associations of Wild West characters overwhelmed the negative as the figures themselves became physically harmless to the entrepreneurial pursuit of western prosperity.

In fact, boosters soon found that these characters could even improve the town's image and business opportunities. The popularity of western novels and movies reinforced the positive connotations of figures like the cowboy and rancher so that local elites actually became eager to identify with these men. They would work the region's cowboys into the town's public identity as they had already done with the town's remaining mountain men. Successful use of such images reinforced the townspeople's own identification with these symbols, which gradually became part of the town's public identity apart from specific promotional efforts by boosters. Instead of seeing these images simply as creations for the benefit of outsiders, local residents reinserted the figures into their town's history, thus using the past to serve modern needs. The local middle classes that once argued for the expulsion of cowboys and Indians from the community would begin to argue that their town's unique and proud history depended, in large part, on these once-despised figures.

Meanwhile, buoyed by improved economic conditions in the late 1890s, Red Lodge launched into two decades of prosperity by the beginning of the twentieth century. Coal mining boomed, and local farmers built extensive irrigation systems to create fields of oats, hay, and sugar beets. Some of the entrepreneurs who had pinned their hopes on Red Lodge saw their dreams fulfilled. As the town grew, so did the fortunes of the downtown business owners, lawyers, and real estate developers. The hierarchical underpinnings of the boosters' western mythology began to become clearer, however, in the new century as labor tensions shook the community and workers began to demand a bigger share of the West's fortunes.

As for young Johnny Southward, he quickly dropped out of the town's historic record after his romantic flight to Billings — probably because his father soon moved on from Red Lodge in pursuit of his own dreams of "the West," which apparently had not been fulfilled in this little progressive mining town.

2

"Nothing Up Here but Foreigners and Coal Slack"
The Industrial West

The full-throated bass of the steam sirens now carries fulsome, satisfying suggestions of a steady stream of coal tumbling over tipples at both the Sunrise and Sunset mines and a harmonious accompaniment is rendered by the groaning and grinding of fuel laden trains jockying around for a start toward the main line and the big centers of industry.
    —Red Lodge *Picket-Journal*, 24 December 1919

We was raised on coal dust and steam.
    —J. H. "Pat" Patten Oral History, p. 32, Montana Historical Society

As little girls, Lillian and Loretta Jarussi grew up, quite literally, beneath the shadow of the Northwestern Improvement Company's West Side Mine. They were so close, in fact, that on windy days the two girls sometimes feared that the three 150-foot-high smokestacks towering over the mine works might fall down and crush the small house into which they had moved in 1908. On cold winter days, the youngsters stood vigil to watch for the miners ascending from the depths of the coal tunnels. Black with coal dust, little lamps burning on the tops of their heads, the miners emerged onto the freezing surface in a cloud of steam as the sweat from their bodies hit the frigid air. Immediately upon surfacing the men would race down the hill toward home, warmth, and a washup as the two Italian girls gazed on sympathetically. Lillian and Loretta's father never worked in the mines himself— their mother refused to allow it after hearing from other local women about deaths in and around the mine works — but the two young Italian immigrants grew up surrounded by the sights, smells, and sounds of coal mining and coal miners. To them, as to most residents of the little town, coal and the work of coal mining was what Red Lodge was all about.[1]

For its first four decades, Red Lodge was a town whose public identity centered around industrialization, workers, and immigrants — all coated in the dust and grime of coal. Coal, quite simply, dominated the town's early years from the built environment and economy to the population composition and life patterns of local residents. In 1900, 65 percent of the adult males in this town of 2,152 people worked in the mines.[2] In September 1905 alone, the Northwestern Improvement Company (a subsidiary of the Northern Pacific Railroad and successor to the Rocky Fork Coal Company) pumped fifty thousand dollars in wages into the town as its six hundred employees put out about two thousand tons of coal a day from its two Red Lodge mines.[3] The mines shaped the boundaries of working-class neighborhoods, the influx of foreign workers, and the development of local union activism. Coal physically marked the town with its distinctive black powder. Tall smokestacks spewed the mine's product over Red Lodge so that the black dust coated houses, trees, people, and even the waters of Rock Creek, which sometimes ran black with mine runoff. Twin mountains of coal slack — waste particles too fine for use in most furnaces — towered over the west and east sides of town. Coal also connected Red Lodge to the avenues of national capital and industry, which turned the black rock extracted from under the town's streets into brick buildings, fine houses, and modern sidewalks.[4] Even the name of the county, Carbon, reflected the area's overwhelming connection to the products of the underground mines.[5] People moved to Red Lodge, stayed there, and left because of coal. Here lay a modern West full of immigrant miners and industrial pollution, very different from the world of farmers, cowboys, and ranchers who populated the mythic West of stories, pictures, and Wild West tableaux.

Indeed, Red Lodge boosters' efforts to create the "appropriate" western image for their town was only one facet in the creation of local public identity in the town's early years. Even as entrepreneurs waged their battles to push forward their own version of the popular West — the West of farmers, not cowboys — they actually lived amidst a West that on the surface had very little to do with the kind of western townscape made popular by eastern writers and artists. Red Lodge was not a farm town or a cow town. Its creation lay in a modern West of machinery, technology, and corporate capital. Initially, of course, some tension existed between the actual physical world of Red Lodge and the constructed public image that boosters tried to sell. Western salesmen and boosters with visions of an industrial/pastoral utopia ran hard into some of the grittier realities of industrialization and industrial workers. W. A. Talmadge, owner of one of the biggest mercantile stores in Red Lodge, was only one of the entrepreneurs who complained bitterly about his town's emerging public image. "Down there at Billings," he groused in 1909, "they say that we have nothing up here but foreigners and coal slack."[6] Talmadge, like other boosters, still clung to a vision of Turnerian farmers with neat fields and fences filling out the landscape around Red Lodge; in fact, Talmadge lobbied hard for a statewide dry-land farming effort that might help farmers find ways to work the arid land around Red Lodge. But beyond the frantic rhetoric and wishful hopes of local town builders, the twinned narratives of Buffalo Bill's "Wild West" and Frederick Jackson Turner's agrarian West had little place in the physical world of Red Lodge at the turn of the century. The dream of a diversified, farming-centered economy died hard, but Red Lodge, quite simply, represented a different kind of western development with a different kind of public identity than that put forward in the popular mythology about the region.

Even though most Americans of the 1890s (and 1990s, for that matter) regarded the West as the most remote and backward region of the country, historians have recently argued just the opposite — that the West of the post–Civil War years was in many ways not the least but the *most* modern part of the nation.[7] In the late-nineteenth-century West, after all, modern centralized government flexed its muscle most fully: managing Indian reservations, governing territories, and using the army to assert its will. Here the new, huge corporations wielded their greatest power: running rail lines that tied the nation together, controlling mineral resources in places like Butte, and chopping down entire forests to meet their industrial needs. Steel-edged plows made it possible for farmers to cut through the deep sod of the prairies, and mechanized combines and threshers from modern factories sheared swaths through endless fields of wheat on Dakota bonanza farms. Mass-produced barbed wire permitted the survival of cattle kingdoms in the settling West. Farmers in the Pacific Northwest sold their crops to an international market through steam trains and steamships. The West was a region of cities and towns, railroad lines, and the machinery of modern industry.

Red Lodge existed as a vibrant community apart from, yet also entangled with, regional and national images of the West and industrial development. Try as they might to proclaim Red Lodge the "Coal Metropolis" through fiat, middle-class town builders were forced to recognize other visions of Red Lodge that inexorably intertwined themselves into the town's developing public identity. From ethnic parades, labor strikes, and personal gardens to political rallies, fancy mansions, and, yes, propaganda publications, residents from across the community's social spectrum negotiated public images of the town that reflected both the dreams of the community's aspiring entrepreneurial class and the very real power of Red Lodge's hundreds of industrial workers.

Red Lodge, with its public identity of coal slack and immigrant workers, grew up as part of the modern West. In the first few decades of its existence, Red Lodge emerged as an industrial mining town, coated in coal dust and peopled by a mixture of European immigrants, native-born Americans, workers, entrepreneurs, and managers. Coal slack and foreigners — the work and workers of the modern West — defined the public appearance of the little town built on coal and dependent on the machinery of an industrial economy.

In order to understand Red Lodge's developing public identity in the industrial cauldron of the early twentieth century, one must return, at least briefly, to the work of the town's entrepreneurial boosters before moving on to the physical world of the town and its inhabitants. It is the public activities of local boosters that illustrate how perceptions of industrial workers combined with the growing strength of workers themselves to create a community whose public identity by the early twentieth century centered around both business and labor.

The town builders, as we have seen, began boosting Red Lodge almost as soon as they started constructing their merchant houses and law offices. And while cowboys and Indians posed significant challenges to the town's emerging public identity, there was an even more intransigent barrier to building a positive, progressive image for the budding coal metropolis than the lingering presence of the Wild West: the physical presence of the miners who actually built and maintained the economy of the small town. After all, Indians and transient cowboys laborers remained, at most, peripheral to the daily business of doing business in early Red Lodge. Miners, on the other hand, were essential to the very production upon which the town depended. And if cowhands and Crow Indians had wild reputations in the late nineteenth century, they could not even begin to compete with the terror generated among respectable middle-class Americans by the image of a radical immigrant union laborer.

So, in the game of selling Red Lodge's image to outsiders, the town's middle-class boosters from the beginning ran smack into a basic tension within their industrial economy. The industrial wages that supported the town came along with industrial wage workers whose very presence at the end of the nineteenth century could strike fear into the hearts of potential settlers and investors. Local town builders themselves did not so much fear the *actual* eruption of labor violence in Red Lodge, though; they feared a more general national apprehension about industrial workers that permeated the United States at the turn of the century. Middle- and upper-class Americans in the late nineteenth century (to whom Red Lodge boosters aimed their propaganda) feared the eruptions of violence that seemed necessarily to accompany industrial development. In the railroad strikes of 1877, the Haymarket Riot in Chicago in 1886, and the bloody strike at the Homestead steel plant in Pennsylvania in 1892, workers had proved their violent potential. The West seemed particularly vulnerable to labor unrest, especially following the Coeur d'Alene, Idaho, miners' strike of 1892, which was crushed by the mine owners using federal troops, and the Leadville, Colorado, miners' strike in 1894 in which the Western Federation of Miners (formed out of the Coeur d'Alene strike) fought back against repressive mine owners.[8]

Red Lodge seemed ready for just such a violent outbreak. Coal mining, after all, was a tough life that, even more than other industrial occupations, produced severe bust conditions and often violent struggles between miners and operators over working conditions, pay, and health issues.[9] Miners and their families lived daily with the threat of death or crippling injuries. They had to contend with new machines that dug coal more quickly without the skills that had once guaranteed workers at least some job security.[10] They also lived with the realities of economic fluctuations in an industry where a full paycheck one month might be balanced with only a few days of work in the next. When the trains ran less frequently or when the weather warmed up and people stopped putting coal in their furnaces, miners' work slowed down and sometimes stopped.[11] This dangerous, uncertain industry produced conditions that seemed ripe for explosions of worker frustration and anger. By the late nineteenth century, miners, like other workers around the nation, were erupting into what T. J. Jackson Lears called "periodic social upheavals [that] kept bourgeois hysteria at white heat."[12]

As an apparently inassimilable foreigner, a member of a potentially violent laboring class, and a symbol of the growing class differences in the United States, the miner was the figure most in need of social and cultural control in Red Lodge at the turn of the century — especially in the difficult operation of shaping Red Lodge's public image. Miners embodied a type of Wild West even more frightening than that which had been presented by cowboys or Indians. The miners' wildness threatened not only the local community and the town's image as a progressive, safe American place but also the very fabric of national society. Controlling the miners was more subtle, difficult, and frustrating than dealing with the other western figures of the area. Unlike their efforts with the Indian, town leaders could not just dehumanize the miners or make them disappear; the town depended on their work and wages. And unlike the occasional cowboy, the miner's wildness could not be solved by the combination of Constable Johnson's fists and town ordinances. Ordinances and company policies sought to impose some order on the physical behaviors of local miners, but as an essential component in Red Lodge's continuing prosperity, miners could not simply be run out of town because they damaged its image. Instead, boosters had to focus on ways to control the *imagery* of the coal miners to make them as safe or distant as possible. Initial efforts to control this imagery took two forms. One was to ignore the *physical* miner and focus instead on the product of his work; the other transformed the potentially radical industrial laborer into a kind of "yeoman" worker — strong, industrious, wholesome, and safe.

The most pervasive early tactic was to simply ignore local miners. In many 1890s promotional stories, miners lost their physical presence in the town; they became disembodied. Red Lodge boosters drew attention away from the miners as flesh-and-blood, potentially violent workers by describing these men as simply part of the local industrial machinery and economy. In one lengthy story extolling the virtues of the town, the Red Lodge *Picket* summarized the value of the mine workers quite simply: "The army of men employed therein consume a large quantity of the products of the soil, and so the wage of the miner finds its way into every channel of trade in and around the county."[13] In the 1890s, the local paper ran a series of stories on the new farmers in the area and painted dramatic word portraits of the progress of agricultural expansion; these booster articles personalized Red Lodge by naming the proprietors of stores and giving bits of information about the progressive entrepreneurs of the area.[14] But in almost all of these elaborate efforts to describe and sell Red Lodge, the miners and other laborers were little more than statistics of tons of coal loaded, numbers of men employed, and wages paid out: "The mines give employment to three hundred men, and when worked to their full capacity yield sixty carloads of coal per day."[15] In such stories, miners were not men with

The Northwest Magazine *created these idealized depictions (above and opposite) of local workers (yeoman miners) and their homes for its August 1892 feature selling Red Lodge as a progressive, safe place for settlement and investment. (Montana Historical Society photos)*

families, solid residents with hopes about the future; neither were they radical laborers with fire in their eyes, clutching copies of the *Communist Manifesto*. They were simply objects that facilitated the production of a never-ending flow of coal and capital. Prospective settlers need not fear the industrial coal miners, these articles assured the reader, for the miners were invisible — except, of course, when spending their wages.

In opposition to the systematic obscuring of physical bodies, other town promoters sought deliberately to reshape the image of the miner so that he became, essentially, a farmer with a pickax. Stripped of their class and nationality, the miners in these images became workers who lived and acted according to middle-class standards of behavior. In 1892, the Northern Pacific booster publication, The *Northwest Magazine,* presented this portrait of idealized Red Lodge miners:

> The men are an orderly and intelligent class and there have been no labor troubles of too serious a nature to be settled by the tact, kindness and good sense of the manager. Some of the men live with their families in neat and

comfortable houses built by the coal company and others live in little log cottages of their own. They support churches and are eager to secure for their children as good an education as the graded public school of the town affords. The troops of rosy-cheeked little ones that flock to the school every morning leave no room for doubt as to the healthfulness of this mountain climate.[16]

According to this promotional tactic, Red Lodge's laborers embodied the basic middle-class virtues of home, hard work, and education — they were nothing less than "yeoman workers." In covering the 1900 Labor Day festivities, the *Picket* even used that term. Introducing a story on the miners' celebration, a reporter pointedly lauded the efforts of "the sturdy yeomanry of Red Lodge and Carbonado, the men who earn their bread in the sweat of their faces."[17] The Carbon County government's earliest stationery provided a visual image of these idealized workers. A small picture at the top of the paper displayed two miners who, working with pickax and wheelbarrow, their lights shining forward, resembled nothing so much as healthy, robust farmers earning an honest living through skilled labor in the mines before heading back to the fields.[18]

The ideal miners were not meant to lure people into Red Lodge, but instead to reassure them that these men were honest laborers, not the troublesome "savage" workers of the Haymarket Riot or the Coeur d'Alene strikes. Such detailed descriptions and illustrations were the exception, however, to the more pervasive early depiction of the miners as simply disembodied, wage-earning, consumer entities. Both types of efforts represented the dreams of the local entrepreneurs to remake the miner or somehow to cause him to physically disappear without diminishing the flow of coal and capital running through the town.

By the early 1900s, however, the local newspapers had switched their coverage of area miners to reflect the reassuring, yeoman imagery. Although promotional editions and special advertising pamphlets still did not highlight (or often even mention) the town's working class,[19] the weekly newspapers began to include more personalized portraits of some of these individuals. In reports on mine accidents particularly, the *Picket, Gazette,* and *Republican* began to make a point of mentioning the miner's marital status, any children he may have left orphaned, and his length of residency in Red Lodge. Most stories also managed to include some description of the man as a good citizen and solid worker. The *Republican,* for example, lamented the 1906 death of miner J. E. Bracey, remembered as "a straightforward, industrious man [who] enjoyed the respect of all who knew him."[20] The *Gazette,* in a 1905 story, described miner Anton Kivistokoski as a longtime Red Lodge miner "respected by all who know him."[21]

Although some local business leaders, like timber contractor B. M. Rogers, continued to dismiss Red Lodge's workers as "a bunch of anarchists,"[22] the community newspapers preferred to paint a more benign, comforting public portrait of the local working class. Newspapers continued to be one of the town's primary organs of boosting; stories that touted the family habits of miners (many of them immigrants), their pattern of home buying, and their thrift could only help to reinforce a positive identity of the town as a stable, safe, comfortable place to live and raise a family. This version of local conditions, printed weekly and mailed across the country, created a reassuring image of Red Lodge as a thriving town with few of the disturbing problems that plagued the rest of industrial America.

Positive coverage of workers, of course, achieved more than just positive publicity for the town. Since rival newspapers in the small town had to compete for local readers beyond the entrepreneurial class, stories sympathetic to miners might draw these workers to a particular newspaper. Increased readership equated to both immediate subscription revenue as well as higher advertising rates for that publication. Although no figures of local newspaper readership exist, some evidence suggests that these publications began actively to solicit immigrant working-class readers by the early 1900s. The *Picket*, for example, published news stories from Finland, while the *Republican Picket* actually began to print a page of news in Finnish in 1909.[23] Before they finally merged under common ownership, the *Picket* and *Republican* even waged a bitter feud in their pages over, basically, which paper was more supportive of unionism in general and local unions in particular.[24] The national and local reception of these images of the working class reflect both a continuing desire on the parts of entrepreneurs to present a favorable public perception of the small town and also the very real and important role that laborers had assumed in the day-to-day business of living and working in Red Lodge. Workers had, by the early twentieth century, established themselves both in the town's printed imagery and its physical townscape.

Indeed, it was in the actual, physical presence of the town itself that the domination of Red Lodge by industry and workers was overwhelmingly and immediately apparent. The newspapers were in part simply reflecting a local world that revolved around the work of mining coal and the larger national business of industrial capitalism. This was no romantic West of farmers and cowboys; here lay the gritty, bustling, dirty, exciting modern West that Red Lodge boosters simply had to deal with. Red Lodge's public identity was visible to anyone who ventured into the community — here was a coal mining town conceived and born out of the modern West of machines, corporate capital, and mass production.

A bird's-eye view of Red Lodge is a good place to start to get the feel of this developing industrial town and its public persona. Such views were very popular in the West at the turn of the century. Almost any community worth its salt made the effort to hire a painter or photographer to capture the whole picture of a new or growing town. Seen from above, the town could display all of its best attributes (including some invented ones) and its potential for expansion in one glance. Looking down on industrial Red Lodge in the early 1900s — only about a mile square, nestled into the narrow valley of Rock Creek — one could easily spot the influence of modern mass production and industrial labor on the townscape. Twin mining operations dominated the southeast and southwest ends of town. Clearly visible because of their tall smokestacks and large tipples, these mines seemed to brace the little town, providing support to the neighborhoods of small houses clustered around the mine shafts. Red Lodge, with about 4,860 people in 1910, spread out away from these mines in the typical American grid pattern with a single downtown district packed tightly for five blocks or so on either side of a wide main street. The small homes and large boardinghouses of working-class residents clung closely around the mines, while to the northwest — the point farthest from the dust and smell of mine work — a street of large homes marked off the town's upper-class neighborhood. A single railroad track ran into town from the north, cutting diagonally across the obstinate north-south regularity of the platted streets. These tracks split into smaller branches near the middle of town, leading toward the coal tunnels and tipples to the south. On these rails, the town shipped out tons of coal and brought in factory-made goods, imported foods, and other products of modern capital.[25] Small, compact, and clearly industrial, the little community might have fit easily into any mining state from the East Coast to the Midwest. On a cursory view, only the characteristically western false fronts on the downtown buildings and the towering peaks of the Rocky Mountains to the south and west indicated the "westernness" of this productive mining community.

Refocusing down from the heights to street level, the observer could notice other signs of industrialism just a bit less obvious than those shouted out by the heavy mining machinery and impressive steam engines seen from the bluffs above town. In fact, all of Red Lodge, if one looked attentively enough, spoke eloquently of the ties that bound this community to a larger industrial network.[26] Many of the downtown buildings, for example, while constructed primarily out of locally quarried stone, sported cast-iron fronts or pressed-metal ceilings, mass-produced in Illinois or Indiana factories and shipped via rail to the developing town on the edge of the Rocky Mountains. The name of the Mesker Brothers Iron Works of Indiana imprinted on the front of Red Lodge's Budas block and on the sheet-metal cornice of the Pollard Hotel marked the modern manufacturing that defined much of the trans-Missouri West. Red Lodge, like many other small western towns of this period, combined the building products of the local place with ideas and materials supplied along the routes of modern industry.[27] Discerning eastern architects might disdain the "impatient West's" efforts as an attempt to look impressive through the use of manufactured materials such as ornamental cast-iron

*Busily churning out coal, smoke, soot, and slack, the East Side Mine marked the industrial
and economic heart of early Red Lodge. (Montana Historical Society photo)*

storefronts and mass-produced ceilings. As one old architectural don was
known to sniff, "It serves, for the time, to confer upon the newly built streets
of the West a delusive aspect of metropolitan completeness and finish, until,
after a few years, the paint wears off, the wooden sham begins to decay, and
the galvanized iron to betray its hollow mockeries."[28] But the "sheet iron elegance" dismissed by eastern elites possessed a variety of advantages to westerners, who favored it because it was fireproof, sanitary, and relatively cheap.[29]
And it provided the town with the illusion of modernity now available
through mail-order catalogs, mass production, and expanding railroad
routes — all made possible for local entrepreneurs because of the corporate
wages moving through the town's economy.[30] The NPRR paid workers to dig
coal for the railroad; workers spent that money in local stores; Red Lodge merchants used their profits to buy "eastern-style" facades for their expanding
businesses.

Likewise, the town's upper-class residential district, off to the northwest,
known locally as the "Hi Bug" area, reflected both local industrial wealth and
national mass production. In the Hi Bug, mine managers, bankers, merchants,

This Hi Bug home with its expansive lawn and comfortable veranda stood far away from the smoke, noise, and smells of the mines (and the miners). It was a physical marker of the class distinctions that divided the community in its early years. (Carbon County Historical Society photo)

lawyers, and doctors turned the fruits of the area's coal resources into elaborate homes, fancy furniture, and expansive lawns. The homes and furniture themselves came to Red Lodge via the nation's developing transportation and communication networks. Like hundreds of thousands of people around the nation, wealthy Red Lodge residents selected houses, interior designs, and furniture from the pages of mass-distributed "pattern books," design magazines, and catalogs.[31] Lawyer and banker William F. Meyer's beautiful Queen Anne house (built from a pattern book design) included parquet floors and an ornamented oak staircase. Banker John Chapman's spacious Hauser Avenue home featured intricately leaded and beveled glass windows, a golden oak staircase, and imported tile sheaths for the fireplaces. Coal flowed out of Red Lodge and returned as pressed-metal ceilings, wooden floors, and architectural designs.

Proceeding south along Rock Creek, the visitor could see how industry also shaped the physical spaces of the working-class sections of Red Lodge. Workers' neighborhoods, first of all, lay physically alongside both the West Side and East Side mines, as miners and their families oriented themselves toward the industrial workplace. Boardinghouses and company-owned saltbox duplexes intermingled in these neighborhoods with smaller single-family dwellings. These varied dwellings reflected the differing status of mine workers. Single, male workers tended to favor the boardinghouses, where they could eat and sleep between shifts. Married miners often rented a company house or tried to save up to purchase a home. Some of these houses were little more than shacks, hastily constructed for sale or rent to men and families who crowded into Red Lodge to find work at the mines. Others were quite substantial, neat little places owned by miners or other laborers who made ends meet by taking in boarders and relatives who helped out with living costs.[32] The shacks displayed the working poverty of the mine's least skilled workers, while the solid houses indicated the moderate success some workers found in the labor of industrial mining.

The yards of these houses and the number of people crowded into them also pointed toward the hardships of the mining business, which was tied so closely to a larger, fluctuating economy. In contrast to the expansive lawns of the Hi Bug, workers' yard spaces were filled with vegetable gardens, currant bushes, chickens, pigs, and even cows (at least until ordinances in the late 1910s imposed restrictions on livestock within town limits) — anything that might bring in some extra food or money for these working families. That cow, pig, or garden could ensure a family's survival when low coal prices or a warm winter slowed down work — and wages — at the Northwestern Improvement Company mines. The built environment, thus, reflected the town's industrial center in a variety of ways. Through its buildings, yards, and neighborhoods, a close observer could actually *see* the web of industrialism that spread over and around the little town.[33]

To identify some of the most pervasive markers of industrial identity in the town, however, one would have to listen instead of look. As a writer for the Red Lodge *Picket-Journal* noted in 1919, the *sounds* of industry permeated the town when the mines were working and identified Red Lodge's productive place in the national economy. The grinding of cars running out of tunnels, the rumble of coal dropping from the tipple into waiting railcars, and

This fine jewelry store, like many other structures along Broadway Avenue, boasted pressed-metal ceilings that gave the "impatient West" an aura of immediate refinement at the turn of the century. The stuffed elk head on the far wall reminded shoppers that, in spite of the fancy jewelry, this was still the rugged, masculine West—at least on the fringes. (Carbon County Historical Society photo)

the continuous rhythm of steam trains running in and out of town told the story of the town's life business.[34]

Of all these sounds, the mine whistles stood out as the most vivid marker of Red Lodge's urban, industrial identity. The mine whistles punctuated the townscape, signaling not just the ending and beginning of shifts but also the very pulse of the extractive labor that gave life to the little town. Residents lived by the sound of those mine signals, which split up the day according to the precise dictates of the mechanical clock. The whistles not only told miners when to be at work but also informed boardinghouse keepers when to have supper ready and let children know it was time to head down to the local pub to fetch father a bucket of beer.[35] When work was slow, especially in the summer, a double whistle in the evening was a welcome signal that miners would work the next day, or at least part of it; men listening for the sound knew to prepare either for work or for an evening at their favorite saloon. The regular whistles comforted a town dependent on the mines. But friends and family of underground miners dreaded the heart-piercing scream of the off-schedule siren. That sound would clear out the town's streets, schools, and business houses, drawing residents toward the mine to help victims of a fire or cave-in or, more often, simply to watch and wait to find out what had happened: who had been injured, who came out alive, and who had not survived. The sounds of industry could terrify as well as comfort.[36]

Industrial connections, in fact, stretched into every part of the town's life, including not only buildings and sounds but also the very people who lived and worked in the mining town. In this workers' community, the very bodies of the residents reflected the industrial nature of the labor that built Red Lodge. The gender composition of Red Lodge, first of all, featured the kind of imbalance that characterized extractive resources economies.[37] Red Lodge, like so many western mining towns, was very masculine in its early years. In 1910, men made up 61 percent of the population.[38] Although many miners had wives and families, the fluctuating work of the mines attracted to Red Lodge large numbers of young, single males, many of whom worked in the tunnels for a few months in the winter before moving on to jobs in other of the West's seasonal extractive industries. Businesses that catered to men thrived in the small town. Numerous boardinghouses sprang up in Red Lodge's working-class neighborhoods, particularly Finn Town. Male workers also found comfort and companionship in the saloons strung along Billings Avenue. According to popular legend, at one time this town of fewer than five thousand residents boasted twenty-one saloons serving drinks and food almost around the clock until local ordinances began limiting their hours in the mid-1900s. And a thriving red-light district operated just outside the downtown area. Regulated through fines and payoffs to local officials, Red Lodge brothels were a prominent part of the town's public identity until the combined forces of progressive reformers and company managers closed them down during World War I. But in the prewar years, the saloons and brothels lent an air of wildness to the streets of the little town. On most weekend nights, the downtown area would be punctuated by the raucous sounds of fighting in and around these places of male leisure.[39]

Red Lodge often seemed even more overwhelmingly male than it actually was in the early twentieth century because masculine work and pleasure dominated so many of the town's public spaces. Blackened miners heading home from work, raucous drinkers at the town's male-only saloons, and town meetings of male voters reinforced the masculine image of the mining community. The town's women, especially those from the working class, ventured into these downtown public spheres far less often than did men.[40] Most, quite simply, did not have the time to leave the housework that dominated their lives and enabled their families to survive the hard times that so often defined the mining economy.[41] Working-class women usually had to combine family work with paid household labor of some sort, usually caring and cooking for boarders or taking in sewing. The mines paid well when they ran, but families also depended on the work of women.[42] Some, like Ida Kallio, a Finnish immigrant, helped to run the family business, in her case a public sauna. In addition to other chores, Kallio cleaned the bathhouse, washed towels, prepared soap, and handled the crowds who showed up for the Wednesday and Saturday saunas. In her rare moments of free time, she might visit friends around the neighborhood but never went far from the safety of the places, people, and language she knew.[43]

A large number of immigrant women lacked the language skills to negotiate their way comfortably around town; unlike the men who picked up some English while working, many immigrant women had few opportunities to learn the language.[44] Children, whose English skills had been improved by attending local public schools, often ran the household errands for these families, sometimes eliminating the need for immigrant women ever to leave the safety of their neighborhoods. Kallio's children delivered milk around town and ran to the butcher shop to get meat for meals.[45] Not all women, of course, stayed so close to home. Lillian Jarussi's mother, an Italian immigrant, ventured into the commercial area to do her shopping, although she limited her movements around town, going only into those places where the clerks spoke Italian. Other mining women acquired enough English to take jobs cleaning house for the "English" women in Hi Bug or to advertise to take in sewing and washing.[46] Nevertheless, for many, work and language limitations narrowed their public lives significantly and contributed to the very masculine appearance of downtown Red Lodge in its early years.

If the work of mining influenced both the gender composition of Red Lodge and the town's masculine atmosphere, it also physically marked the very bodies of the people who lived there.[47] A visitor entering Red Lodge in the early twentieth century would see not only a town of robust male workers but also a place of cripples — men left too weak or disabled from accidents, black lung disease, or gas poisoning to function fully. Missing limbs, eyes, and fingers, limps, and crooked backs told the physical story of the hazards of underground mining.[48] A visitor did not have to look hard to find such evidence. Longtime police constable James McAllister provided only the most prominent example of the mines' physical toll on its workers. Patrolling Red Lodge's streets from 1903 until 1954, McAllister always wore a large patch over his face to cover the hole where his left eye had once been. The eye had been torn out by a loose machine handle in 1900, leaving McAllister, who had never known any job other than mining, unemployed and owing over two hundred dollars in medical bills. Like so many other stricken miners, McAllister could no longer dig coal after his accident; with no insurance or workers' compensation — such progressive reforms would not pass in Montana until a decade later — he was fortunate to find a lower-paying job with the city to scrape by.[49] Although he eventually rose through the ranks to a position of stability and respect, McAllister, along with many other Red Lodge workers, bore the visible mark of the mines for the rest of his life. In this mining town, even those men without visible injuries often walked more slowly and looked older because of years in the dank tunnels breathing the stale air that coated their faces and lungs with black dust.[50] These men, battered and crippled though they may have been, at least had survived the coal mines. Not everyone was so lucky.

The grimmest testament to the town's industrial heart lay in the all-too-frequent funeral processions winding their way from various fraternal lodges and union halls to the cemetery on the west bluff above the town. The mines that gave the town its substantial payroll also took the lives of many of its workers. Most residents of the town's working-class neighborhoods had lost a brother, father, son, or uncle to the mines, sometimes multiple family members.[51] Coal mining was a bloody industry made even more dangerous by the lack of safety regulations and by the contract system favored by the mining companies.[52] At the turn of the century, mine operators, including the Rocky Fork Coal Company and its successor the Northwestern Improvement Company (NWIC), paid most of its miners not by the hour but according to the number of tons of coal they removed each day. The system invited miners to disregard safety in order to get out as much rock as possible — especially since mine operators were notorious for underweighing coal.[53] The combination of haste, negligence, and dangerous conditions yielded predictable results.[54] Men died in the mines, sometimes only two annually (as in 1891, 1895, 1896), other times as many as eight in one tragic accident (1906).[55] And these figures do not account for those permanently disabled in nonfatal accidents.

The "bloody coal mines" of Red Lodge crippled and killed men every year of their operation. The NWIC entered the figures in cold numbers: from 1 November 1919 to 31 October 1920 there were 203 accidents, 3 fatal, 3 others resulting in permanent injuries, and 29 disabling workers for four weeks or more; one wife was made a widow and two children were rendered father-less.[56] These numbers, though, were men with names and identities, like Nestor Maki, killed by an explosion of powder in 1896, probably as he returned to the site to check on a delayed fuse — a common accident among miners who had to rush through these operations to get out enough coal to make their pay.[57] A fall of rock crushed Nestor Puumala to death in 1905 while he tried to clear away an obstruction of overhanging coal in a room inade-quately timbered for such an operation. In 1906, a seven-hundred-pound rock fell on Andrew Hill, killing him immediately.[58] Reports of accidents and deaths in the tunnels became almost routine in mining towns like Red Lodge, creat-ing a monotonous refrain in local headlines: "Fatal Accident in Mine," "Miner Loses His Life," "Rock Crushes Out His Life."[59] Townspeople in this coal min-ing community lived with the presence of death just as they lived off the prod-uct of the coal mines. The industrial coal mining that dominated the town's public identity took many of the town's residents also.

But if "coal slack" defined early Red Lodge, so too did the "foreigners" who did much of the work of bringing that coal to the surface and loading it into the locomotives that continually roared in and out of town. Wandering along the streets of Red Lodge in the early 1900s, one could not help but notice the diversity of the town's immigrant population. Slovenians, Finns, Italians, Rus-sians, Austrians, Germans, Norwegians, Croats, and Greeks all intermingled under the towering stacks of the NWIC mining works. The discordant hum of conversations in various languages, shop signs in Finnish and Italian, and the powerful smell of garlic coming from some residences (and residents) gave the town a decidedly international flavor. By 1910 almost three-quarters of the town's residents were immigrants or the children of immigrants, many of whom spoke little, if any, English.[60] Neighborhood names like Finn Town and Little Italy imprinted this foreignness on the town's nomenclature. Interwoven with the town's coal slack identity, Red Lodge's foreigners created a distinctive element of the community's public image as they negotiated their own identities as ethnic Americans in the town's early years.

Much of the West itself in these decades was a region of foreigners. Pushed out of the Old Country by debt loads and limited farmlands and drawn to the American West by stories of good jobs and cheap land, immigrants flowed into the region in the late nineteenth and early twentieth centuries. By 1890, 30 percent of California's residents and 32 percent of those in the Dakotas were foreign born; in 1900, over 25 percent of those living in Montana had been born outside the United States.[61] In some mining camps and lumber towns, the numbers soared even higher. Although many immigrants who made it that far west often tried to take up homestead land, others had neither the money nor the inclination to do so. Mostly young men, they flocked to places like Red Lodge, Butte, Bisbee, Coos Bay, and other communities that had jobs in extractive resources industries. Some lumber and mining companies actively recruited European immigrants to perform the strenuous physical labor required to turn the trees and rocks of the West into commerce and capital. Some, indeed, hoped that hiring workers with different backgrounds and languages might prevent laborers from joining together into potentially dangerous unions. Often these immigrants ran up against the hard wall of prejudice and job discrimination. Cripple Creek, Colorado, for example, was a "white man's camp"; entrenched workers there thwarted employers' attempts to divide and conquer workers by forcing out Slavs, Italians, Greeks, and others so that they would not undermine the wage structure for white (i.e., native-born or Anglo) workers.[62] The Red Lodge area, however, settled early on by Finnish and Slavic miners, had no such exclusions, and southern and eastern European immigrants eagerly headed there for the opportunities offered by the town's coal mines.

In Red Lodge and elsewhere in the West, people from specific regions of Europe often piled up in certain areas, creating particularly Finnish or Irish neighborhoods in cities and towns. These clusters of immigrants, with their concentration of alien language and customs centered in one area, reinforced a given community's "foreign" appearance. This phenomenon developed out of the common and understandable practice of "chain migration." Immigrants tended to follow each other in chains; one or two people would head out to a new site and send word to friends and family if things looked promising. Once in a place, friends and family tended to stick together, sharing homes and taking comfort from the presence of familiar voices, music, and jokes.[63] In Red Lodge, for example, Finnish miners often followed a well-worn trail from the mines of Pennsylvania to the Masabi Range of Michigan to the coal fields of Wyoming and finally to Red Lodge. From Red Lodge, many moved on to the copper mines in Butte or the coal mines at Roslyn, Washington.[64]

The very names and geographical locations of Red Lodge neighborhoods told much about the town's waves of migration, social mobility, and work, even while they imprinted a very public foreignness on the town's identity. Finnish immigrants were among the first workers in the town, and they clustered near the entrance to the East Side Mine. This working-class neighborhood, which gradually took the name of "Finn Town," assumed a long and narrow shape, hedged in by Rock Creek to the east and the rigid line of Billings Avenue's business district to the west, but as close to the East Side Mine as these other boundaries would permit. New arrivals crowded into the homes and boardinghouses on the town's east side, conveniently close to work, downtown businesses, and the reassuring sound of the Finnish language. Later waves of immigrant workers — particularly Italians and Slavic peoples from the Austro-Hungarian empire — arrived as the NWIC opened up the town's second mine, the West Side Mine. These newer people congregated in particularly, though not exclusively, Slavic and Italian neighborhoods on the west side of Billings Avenue (renamed Broadway Avenue in the early twentieth century) toward the tipple of the West Side Mine. A second grouping of Italians, "Little Italy," lay on the northeast end of town near Red Lodge's only other industry, the beer brewery, and also close to downtown where many of the Italian immigrants developed small businesses and shops catering to the miners. Immigrant workers chose to live near the town's industrial jobs but also close to those who could help them find housing, work, and a place in the community. The creation of these small neighborhood clusters lent a foreign nomenclature to the community as residents learned to identify the town by the groups of people who lived in specific areas.

Significantly, there was no "Irish Town" in the local geography at the turn of the century, even though Irish miners had been a large part of the mining company's original workforce. Unlike the Finns, the Irish were native speakers of English and often had some skill at mining; they quickly moved up the social and economic ladder — and away from the immediate proximity of the

Many Italian immigrants started their own businesses in Red Lodge. This is the Sconfienza Bakery and Grocery Store in 1908. (Montana Historical Society photo)

mines. The Irish, for the most part, ensconced themselves in and around the Hi Bug area on Hauser Avenue, a district marked by both nationality and wealth.[65] Also known as the English area of town, Hi Bug residents, with few exceptions, were native speakers of English born in the United States, Ireland, or England. In a town teeming with Finns and Italians who spoke little if any English, Irishmen like D. G. O'Shea, William O'Connor, and Roger Fleming could rise rapidly in the town's social and economic hierarchy.

O'Shea, who arrived in the United States from County Cork in 1881, started as a clerk in the Rocky Fork Coal Company in the early 1890s. By 1900 he had moved up to become the company's resident manager and into the grand Hauser Avenue home originally built for Rocky Fork's first manager, Maurice Fox.[66] William O'Connor, another Irish immigrant, was Red Lodge's first elected mayor and one of the original superintendents of the Rocky Fork Mine. Irish immigrant Roger Fleming, a prominent liquor merchant, built one of the biggest houses on Hauser Avenue. His wife, Kathryn, was a member of the Red Lodge Woman's Club and a leader in the movement to create the city's library association. In the new town, Irish immigrants quickly assumed positions of leadership in the mines and in the town's business and social communities.[67] Although numerous Irish continued to work in the mines, many assumed the most highly paid positions there. In the town's geography, "Irish" blended easily into the Hi Bug's "English" designation.

Non–English speaking immigrants and their children, on the other hand, tended to live and socialize within their own specific ethnic groupings, creating prominent "nationality" identities in Red Lodge through the 1910s. Immigrants not only chose to live close to each other, but they also created fraternities, businesses, and cultural groups that introduced "foreignness" into the town's social and cultural life. Places like Finn Hall, Italian Hall, the Roman Theatre, Paolo Pracca's Mining Shop, and the Kaleva Cooperative Mercantile became part of Red Lodge's downtown identity. Specific nationality saloons also popped up along Billings Avenue, readily identified by residents as the Finnish bar, the Slovak saloon, or the Italian place. More formally, each sizable immigrant population in Red Lodge organized its own fraternal group, usually mutual-aid societies that provided accident insurance and funeral expenses for members. These societies often featured specific uniforms for their members. The Finnish Kalevan Ritarit Society, for example, decked themselves out in blue tunics, white sashes, and dashing plumed hats. Gathered together in full uniform for funeral processions, sometimes two hundred strong, these immigrant societies made bold public statements about their identity within the town.[68] And nationality bands, like the Finnish orchestra, the Serbian tamburitza orchestra, and the Italian band — much in demand for community events — provided further opportunities for local immigrants, surrounded by others of similar background, to perform in public. Ethnic celebrations would also break through the ordinary routine of daily life, creating an even more visible foreignness in Red Lodge. For Croatian Christmas, celebrants would sing as they wandered from house to house, eating and drinking and dancing. Slovenians gathered in the long summer evenings to play guitars and sing in the grass meadows along Rock Creek. Finnish wedding parades danced their way through the side streets to raucous receptions at Workers' Hall or Finn Hall.[69]

But although Red Lodge looked and sounded very diverse in the early twentieth century, that diversity had some strict limitations. If Red Lodge was defined by foreignness in its early years, it was also marked very much by a shared European heritage — and skin tone. Red Lodge was and would remain throughout the twentieth century a decidedly white town. Biological racialists of the day, of course, categorized Finns, Italians, Slavs, and other "new" immigrant groups as "non-white" peoples, but a modern-day observer would readily note the absence of people of color in Red Lodge.[70] Neighboring Crow Indians sometimes wandered into the community, the town had a Chinese laundryman in the early 1890s, some African-American prostitutes worked in the red-light district, and an African-American man worked as a shoeshine boy at the local barber shop.[71] Otherwise, this was a strictly European place. According to the 1900 census, only forty-eight "colored" people ("Negro," Chinese, Japanese, and Indian) lived in the entire county. When the *Carbon County Republican* listed in 1906 the "Conditions that Make Red Lodge Famous as a City," it started off with, "There is only one negro in the town — and that's a-plenty," adding that "there is not a Chinaman within the boundaries of the city — and none are wanted."[72] In 1910, the census counted five "Negroes" in Red Lodge and no other "colored" residents.[73] In 1920, there were only two "Negroes."[74] Red Lodge's public identity was certainly foreign and diverse in the early twentieth century, but that diversity stayed within very European boundaries.[75]

Finally, Red Lodge's workers imposed a very *union* identity upon the small town. The image of the peaceful, prosperous workers' town projected in the weekly newspapers reflected, in large part, the increasingly prominent place of the unions in Red Lodge by the turn of the century. After some initial violent blowups — most particularly the murder of a mine manager by a union organizer in 1898— class-based tensions in Red Lodge subsided to a great extent as workers and their unions negotiated a stable, even powerful, position in the town's mines, businesses, and public life. Red Lodge became a solidly union town. As early as 1894, the Knights of Labor established the first union lodge in town with eighty-seven members; they held Red Lodge's first Labor Day celebration several months later.[76] Within a few years, many of the town's workers had unionized and gained important concessions from their employers. Union members were not only digging coal at the NWIC mines; they worked the switchboard at the town's Bell Telephone exchange, constructed the buildings along Billings Avenue, and ran the print works on at least one of the weekly newspapers.[77]

The biggest group of workers, the miners, made the biggest advances. Working first (1898–1903) with the radical Western Federation of Miners (WFM) and then with the larger, more conservative United Mine Workers of

Red Lodge's unionized miners pause for a picture before starting work. (Carbon County Historical Society photo)

America (UMWA) beginning in 1903, miners obtained guarantees from the Rocky Fork Company that included a union-paid checkweighman to ensure that the company weighed coal accurately, improved safety conditions, and set prices for work supplies. The town's other workers, including carpenters and joiners, also formed locals mainly through the American Federation of Labor (the parent organization of the UMWA), gradually winning some wage and hour concessions from their employers.[78] Through their different unions, workers carved out an increasingly important space for themselves in Red Lodge's public sphere, moving beyond immediate workplace concerns to shape the town's identity through parades, boycotts, buildings, and sheer financial clout.

Red Lodge, first of all, looked like a labor town by the turn of century because of the structures workers built for themselves. Union organizers, in fact, made sure that anyone entering the town could not miss the power of labor in Red Lodge. Although some union members grumbled at its location so far from the saloons of downtown, labor leaders in 1909 deliberately constructed a three-story brick Labor Temple almost directly across from the NPRR depot, right where it would confront (and impress) everyone who came into Red Lodge by rail. Built by the local miners and carpenters unions and financed in part by loans from the UMWA, the Labor Temple stood like a brick sentinel at the northern entrance to Red Lodge, one of the tallest and most imposing structures in the community.[79] Less impressively, the smaller, wooden Workers' Hall, one block off Broadway Avenue, imprinted the power of labor on Finn Town, while several cooperative stores that catered to workers also dotted the townscape.[80] These buildings made labor a prominent visual part of Red Lodge's public identity even as they became centers of the town's social and cultural landscape. The Labor Temple, for example, quickly became an integral part of Red Lodge social life, housing dances, club meetings, and other public events. Residents could shop at the Finnish Kaleva Cooperative on the street-level business space, browse through the library on the second floor, or wear down the heels of their dance shoes at the top-level dance hall. And Workers' Hall hosted Finnish-language dramas as well as English-language speeches, movies, and concerts.[81]

Labor's public presence extended beyond these structures and businesses. Periodic celebrations of labor also punctuated the town's public sphere, creating vivid, lively markers of the significance of workers in the little community. Red Lodge and Bearcreek miners and other workers celebrated a variety of labor holidays including Miners' Union Day (June), International Labor Day (1 May), American Labor Day (September), and the anniversary of the eight-hour day (April). Although workers did not celebrate each of these holidays every year, they took advantage of all of them at various times between 1895 and the 1920s.[82] These festivities swept up the entire town in the fun and excitement of parades down the main street, sports, orations, and fireworks. Sometimes owners closed the entire downtown area to honor the town's workers.

In 1900, for example, the local unions put on an especially splendid production for the September Labor Day holiday with the full support of the town's business class and politicians. Merchants swathed the downtown in patriotic red, white, and blue bunting while politicians prepared speeches of support and congratulations for the workers. Alex Fairgrieve, president of the

Red Lodge Miners Union, assumed the honorary marshal's position and led the parade down Broadway Avenue followed by a procession of workers, the Miners' City Band, the Rocky Fork Band, and the mayor riding in a carriage. Mercantile houses, the local dairy, and Hart's Barber Shop sponsored floats that added festive touches to the parade — the W. A. Talmadge Hardware float, for example, featured a mock-up of a mine entrance complete with a tin miner — while also making clear that these businesses cared enough about workers to support this celebration of labor. After the (relatively) long-winded but expected speeches honoring workers, residents headed out to the ball field to catch the traditional baseball game.[83] Certainly as big as Red Lodge events got in those days, the Labor Day celebrations made very public the prestige that workers held in this mining town.

The influence of local labor power ran even beyond the public spectacle of parades and baseball games. Red Lodge's prominent labor strength influenced such aspects of public life as political speech, proclamations about phone service, even the hanging of circus posters. In 1907, for example, union workers strode around town demanding that business owners remove circus posters because a nonunion shop in Erie, Pennsylvania, had printed the placards; the men met with little opposition from merchants anxious to comply with union policies.[84] In that same year, the Red Lodge Board of Trade passed a public resolution in support of "girl operators" on strike against the Rocky Mountain Bell Telephone Company. The strongly worded proclamation denounced the company's attitude and low wages and urged all who had not done so to remove their phones in support of the striking workers.[85] Only a year earlier, when the Red Lodge Miners Union and the local of the Carpenters and Joiners Union put the Billings Mutual Telephone Company on its "unfair" or "antiunion" list, half of Mutual's Red Lodge customers — including most of the town's business houses — requested disconnection of service within a week. The Billings company accurately summed up the workers' power in a formal complaint against the unions' action. Local merchants, the company's lawyer argued, had to withdraw from the phone exchange because "a large number of members of said Miners' and Carpenters' Unions in Red Lodge trade with and buy goods of a large number of merchants and other business men at Red Lodge who are patrons of the plaintiff, and that their trade is of great value to said merchants and business men, and that the loss of such trade to said merchants and business men would be a great detriment and injury to them."[86] Mutual and the Billings businessmen's association eventually gave in to workers' demands, and the Red Lodge unions, acting in the interests of worker solidarity, effectively and publicly demonstrated their strength within the local community.

Local politicians (often the same people as local businessmen) also understood all too well that public sympathy toward labor issues mattered. Political rhetoric, too, in this little town reflected general support of workers and their concerns. State senator W. F. Meyer, for one, made sure to announce publicly his support for progressive labor reforms that directly benefited the workers of Red Lodge. Meyer, a partner in the Chapman-Meyer Bank of Red Lodge, spoke of labor issues even at nonlabor celebrations; in his patriotic Independence Day oration in 1910, for example, he focused on the need for legislation on workplace safety and workers' compensation. To a crowd of locals deeply invested in these issues, Meyer pointed out that such legislation was vital: "We who live in coal mining camps know the many frightful injuries sustained by the miner, resulting in death and cripples and leaving behind destitute families to mourn and suffer."[87] Likewise, District Judge Frank Henry, whose court handled a series of wrongful death suits against the NWIC in the early twentieth century, made it a point to state publicly in 1906 his support for the eight-hour day for all those who labored with their hands.[88] Such political rhetoric, while motivated, perhaps, by personal convictions about labor reforms, played well to workers and became an integral part of the town's public identity in these formative years. Red Lodge not only looked like a workers' town; it sounded like one too.

Not all western towns, of course, embraced labor and unionism quite so fully as Red Lodge did, which only emphasizes the prominent role of labor in this community. In parts of the West, indeed, antiunion employers summarily ran suspected union organizers out of town, maintaining tight company control over workers and their wages. John D. Rockefeller's coal mines in southern Colorado, for example, were strictly company towns — houses, stores, and utilities run by the mining corporation — until miners finally exploded into violence that ended in the Ludlow massacre of 1914.[89] In Cripple Creek, Colorado, where union miners won a significant victory in 1893, vehemently antiunion mine owners managed to gain the support of town merchants who took up arms to arrest and deport organizers for the Western Federation of Miners.[90] Unionism had a mixed record in the West, strong in some areas and despised in others.

Red Lodge emerged as a union town for several reasons. Most significant, perhaps, the town was just a long way from everywhere else, especially from the centers of power that owned and operated the Rocky Fork mines. Forty-two miles off the main line of the NPRR with only once-daily passenger service, Red Lodge never attracted workers in the kinds of numbers that would permit operators to fire readily large numbers of miners; they could not be sure of finding enough workers to replace them. And although Red Lodge coal played an important part in maintaining the NPRR's rail service, the town itself was just one small cog in a much larger empire. Railroad officials in Tacoma and St. Paul sympathized with local managers who had to negotiate with unruly workers, but they could offer little substantive help. Mine managers whose responsibilities focused on maintaining a steady supply of fuel for the company's locomotives made the compromises they had to in order to keep the coal moving. Although intricately connected to the avenues of corporate industrialism, this remote western place was also far enough away to maintain some degree of autonomy.[91]

Equally important, labor's prominent position in the local landscape also built upon the town's entrepreneurial aspirations. Although a single mining company dominated Red Lodge's economy for over thirty years, the place was never a "company town." A strong and vibrant business class flocked to the city as soon as work started on the mines, and capitalist investors like Samuel Hauser and Frederick Billings actually encouraged these smaller entrepreneurs. Hauser and his partners, who owned the land around the Rocky Fork Mine, knew that they could make a lot of fast, easy money through the sale of town lots to business owners.[92] As part of the NPRR hierarchy, they also recognized that the railroad's long-term profits depended on settling and building the area's economic infrastructure; independent businesses in Red Lodge meant more business for the NPRR.[93] A strong entrepreneurial class thus emerged in Red Lodge, which gradually lent its support to the town's workers, whose purchasing decisions made them a vital part of the town's growth and development. Merchants liked steady workers such as Mikko Marttunen, who bragged in 1912 that after nine months in the Red Lodge mines he had "paid my debts, sent $50 to Finland bought clothers [sic] for $32, and have $200 in my trunk." Unable to resist the temptations of Red Lodge's saloons and other diversions, Marttunen soon spent the money in his trunk savings account also.[94] That kind of spending kept the cash registers of downtown Red Lodge busy and the merchants happy.

Finally, Red Lodge's labor establishment remained fairly conservative. Labor power, not labor radicalism, marked the town's public identity during these early years of the twentieth century. Indeed, only one short strike in 1912 marred the otherwise peaceful record of the UMWA in Red Lodge between 1907 and 1917, and although management frequently complained about labor demands, over this decade wages generally increased, work safety improved, and workers kept spending their money in local stores.[95] This was, in short, the kind of unionism most residents of Red Lodge supported. As a *Picket* reporter argued in a story on the 1900 Labor Day oration, local people did not want flamboyant attacks on the capitalist system, but rather evidence of the "best side of unionism, with good will and patriotic fraternalism as the watchwords of the hour."[96]

The "patriotic fraternalism" that defined Red Lodge's public labor identity developed dually from the leadership of skilled, English-speaking miners in the local unions and from the increasing conservatism of the national and state UMWA organizations. First of all, the union hierarchy reflected the ethnic divisions that marked the town itself. English-speaking union leaders, skilled workers with conservative tendencies, early on took control over the locals and did much to negotiate a powerful yet still nonthreatening position for labor in the town in the years before World War I. English, Scottish, and Irish names dominated lists of Red Lodge labor leaders in the early twentieth century to the extent that the town's Labor Temple was also known locally as the English labor hall. These same English-speakers dominated the most highly paid and skilled positions at the town's mines as well.[97] As Erika Kuhlman found in her study of Red Lodge Finns, native-born Americans and English-speakers overwhelmingly held the highest paying jobs at the mines — engineers, blacksmiths, electricians, machinists, motormen, and foremen — while the eastern European immigrants (Finns were considered "eastern") worked at the lowest-paying and most dangerous positions.[98] Thus, although Red Lodge unions, particularly those affiliated with the WFM and the UMWA, seem never to have denied entrance to any of the town's so-called "new" immigrants, an entrenched labor elite did control much of the locals' activities and influenced the demands made in negotiations with management. With a greater investment in their skilled positions, these English-speaking workers were more likely to accept moderate concessions from coal operators than would more transient, less-skilled miners.[99]

Moreover, the UMWA also helped to moderate local unions by negotiating basic improvements in miners' wages and working conditions that blunted the edge of workers' radicalism. Beginning in 1903, the UMWA started to negotiate working conditions and wages at annual conventions held with the Montana coal operators. Early agreements set the workday at eight hours for underground miners, provided that local operators would make doctor and hospital arrangements for workers, and established prices for powder and blacksmithing.[100] Eager to preserve these gains and anxious to forestall potentially violent confrontations with managers, UMWA officials developed increasingly cozy relationships with coal operators. As historian Michael Nash argues, the UMWA leadership around the nation gradually distanced itself from the rank and file of union members, becoming more concerned with keeping management happy than with listening to the concerns of the workers.[101] Montana coal operators even came to depend on the UMWA's district representatives as a sort of workers' disciplinarian, the party responsible for making sure miners kept in the tunnels and away from the strike lines. Northwestern Improvement Company Superintendent C. C. Anderson, for example, observed in 1917 that Montana miners "are restless and in a humor to strike, if they have a good excuse to do so, and it may take the District officers all their time to hold the mine workers to the agreement made. I think however, they can do so for the present." Union leaders, as Anderson predicted, controlled their workers and prevented the possible strike.[102] This kind of control marked the conservative unionism that imprinted itself upon the public identity of Red Lodge in the prewar decades.

The moderation of Red Lodge's union hierarchy becomes clear in contrast to the much more aggressive, class-based demands of radical labor activists whose voices grew increasingly strident in the West in the years leading up to World War I.[103] In mines and lumber camps around the region, socialists and members of the Industrial Workers of the World (IWW) cried out for a change in the very structure of the country's capitalist economy. Bitter over harsh working conditions in the region's mining and logging camps and infuriated by the heartless treatment of laborers by operators, these radical voices refused to be silenced even in the face of violent opposition from capitalists, managers, and townspeople in surrounding communities. Believers to various degrees in the need for worker control and solidarity, western socialists sought, generally, to dismantle the practice of private ownership of major industries with class-based demands for more equitable distribution of wealth and resources.[104] The IWW was even more ideologically amorphous.

As historian Phil Mellinger describes it, the IWW was a mélange of left-wing ideologies that was at once "syndicalist, and also slightly Marxist, anarchist, American Socialist, definitely egalitarian, very anti-capitalist, revolutionary, and even reformist."[105] Or, as the IWW constitution put it, the group believed that "there can be no peace so long as hunger and want are found among the millions of the working people and the few, who make up the employing class, have all the good things of life."[106] In contrast to other unions that accepted laborers only from certain occupations or with specific skills, the IWW welcomed all wage workers into its "One Big Union." These Wobblies (as members of the IWW were called)[107] waged a variety of very public battles across the West, gaining fame, especially, for their sometimes violent clashes with conservative citizens' groups and for their struggles on behalf of free speech in cities and counties where officials jailed anyone daring to advocate socialist programs.[108] Never a dominant force in regional labor in terms of numbers, the IWW's radical positions, nevertheless, made the group a specter of sorts among western industrialists and town builders who feared any kind of disruption in the smooth path of capitalist expansion.

Socialists and Wobblies both created niches for themselves in Red Lodge, especially among the town's substantial Finnish community where various socialist organizations took root in the prewar years.[109] Although an important force among Red Lodge Finns, these radicals played a lesser role in the town's overall labor identity, which ran more toward the trade unionism of the Labor Temple than the syndicalism of the IWW. Perhaps one of the key roles of socialists and Wobblies in the town's initial years was to make the American Federation of Labor locals appear conservative. Over time, though, socialists did make some imprint on the town's public identity. Moderate socialists, for example, won several city election races in 1906, including mayor, but implemented few reforms before being voted out of office in the next election. Finnish socialists initiated a townwide crusade against gambling in 1913 that drove gaming underground and made Red Lodge a bit less publicly wild for a few years. And periodic scraps among the different factions of Finnish socialists created some public excitement from time to time.[110] Wobblies had even less impact than the town's socialists, except that they became a favorite target for mine operators and local business owners who feared the growing strength of local labor. A vocal minority in the mine workforce, IWW members drew more attention than their numbers seemed to warrant, becoming a convenient scapegoat for managers to place the blame for any labor troubles.[111] If, as in 1917, workers seemed restless, it was easy for mine mangers like J. M. Hannaford to point the finger at "I.W.W. radicals who have secured a foothold among the miners."[112] Overall, however, socialists and Wobblies maintained a fairly moderate profile in this union town, tolerated, at least publicly, by many of Red Lodge's business and union leaders, but not much of a presence in the daily lives of most residents whose existence centered on the steady productivity of the Northwestern Improvement Company mines and miners.

By early 1917, Red Lodge's public identity revolved smoothly around the industrial work of miners, the wealth they produced, and the immigrant communities that sustained and nurtured them. Middle-class entrepreneurs no longer had to fight against the wildness of western imagery or the perceived violence of coal miners. The town had settled into a period of prosperity and calm that marked the boom days of Red Lodge. The modern town, with modern conveniences and modern labor relations, had entered the twentieth century gracefully. With few disruptions, business moved along and everyone seemed to benefit from the industry of the miners and the output of the coal mines. The town's brick downtown buildings announced with pride that even if it had never become the "Coal Metropolis," Red Lodge was, indeed, a place of plenty, while the Labor Temple and Workers' Hall stood watch over the comings and goings of the bustling community. Two huge piles of coal slack towering over the edges of the town announced its public identity as a community dependent on coal, while the multitude of foreign languages and odors of exotic foods displayed a seeming tolerance toward the various immigrant groups who had made Red Lodge their own. Red Lodge's public identity stood outside the popular Wests of farmers, ranchers, and cowboys and had instead fully embraced an industrial vision of itself as a place of coal, immigrants, workers, and business.

Nothing lasts forever, though, especially peace and prosperity. In 1917 Red Lodge's carefully constructed public identity as a diverse, industrial, union community would start to crumble. In the tumultuous years of World War I and its aftermath, Red Lodge residents would face new challenges to the town's ethnic and coal mining identities that would necessitate the construction of new identities for themselves and their community.

3

The End of an Era

Well, you're always supposed to work to produce as much as you can. The more you
produce, that means the more money for the big boys to put in the pocketbook.
            —Ollie Anderson Oral History, pp. 19–22, Montana Historical Society

There are plenty of competent men [not Finnish] who would be glad to get
employment and who have the welfare of this country at heart and hold our laws
and customs inviolable.
                              —Red Lodge *Picket,* 10 March 1894

In 1919, Red Lodge businessmen set to work mining the town's only public
monument. In this little coal town, that monument was, appropriately
enough, a huge chunk of bituminous coal — sixty-six hundred pounds' worth
dug out of the extensive mine tunnels that honeycombed the earth beneath
the town's straight, sidewalked streets. For over six years, the giant monument
had stood proudly on Red Lodge's main street, a symbol of the town's thriving coal industry. Red Lodge miners had placed the massive hunk of coal
downtown after parading it up Broadway Avenue on 4 July 1913. Pictures of
the parade depict the miners posing proudly next to their contribution to the
patriotic demonstration; with pickaxes over their shoulders, the laboring men
showed off their masculine strength and skill before residents and visitors
alike. That block of coal marked not only the industrial wealth of the town
but also the power of its workers.[1]

In the bitterly cold winter of 1919, though, when the United Mine Workers
of America (UMWA) went on strike, Red Lodge merchants started hacking
off nuggets from that monument to heat their homes and businesses.[2] Bit by
bit, as the strike went on, the hunk of coal disappeared. Like that block of
coal — quickly chopped up and carted away — mining itself would soon van-
ish from Red Lodge, a victim of mechanized strip mining in other parts of the
state and increasing competition from newer and more efficient fuels such as
electricity and diesel. When the Red Lodge mines stopped working in the
1920s and 1930s, no official public monument remained to commemorate the

industry that had created the town and shaped its early public identity. Only the persistent coal dust, the broken bodies of workers, and memories of better days would linger on to remind residents of the people and resources that had generated the community's founding identity.

Into the spring of 1917, Red Lodge hummed busily along, oblivious, it seemed, to what lay just ahead. Coal remained the key to the town's identity and survival. Never mind the dirt and dust, what was important was the wealth, the stability, the labor. As long as the trains needed coal, the wages kept flowing in and Red Lodge's "foreigners" and "coal slack" kept working together to create the public appearance of a prosperous, industrial, workers' community. Suddenly, however, the bitterness of World War I cracked that public image, and then the postwar years shattered it completely.

Coal dust and foreigners — the most prominent early markers of Red Lodge's public identity — would both give way to new community identities in the middle years of the twentieth century, victims of shifting corporate needs and national Americanization programs. Red Lodge, like much of the United States, underwent fundamental transformations as the war forced residents to readjust their sense of themselves as Americans, as workers, and as members of a coherent community. The cohesive and often insular ethnic communities came under attack in the years of World War I, forcing residents to negotiate their immigrant identities in new, often defensive ways.[3] Even more important, local and national attempts to repress workers during the war resulted in postwar upheavals that ended in a series of strikes and ultimately in the closing of Red Lodge's mines.

The industrial, foreign, workers' town of the 1900s and 1910s did not disappear overnight, but as the nation plunged into the fanaticism of World War I, its light was fading.

In April 1917 President Woodrow Wilson read his war message to Congress, and America was suddenly a nation at war. The government then had to rally public opinion in favor of a foreign conflict that seemed only peripherally important to real American interests. A virulent propaganda campaign ensued that defined the war in black and white terms: good versus evil, democracy versus tyranny, America versus all that was bad in the world. Since any red-blooded, "true" American would of course support a war to save democracy, anyone who could oppose the war effort, it followed, could not be a "real" American. World

War I propaganda revolved around the concept of "100% Americanism" — that in order to win a victory over tyranny, all Americans had to give total support to the government's efforts. These "100% Americans" did not speak foreign languages (our enemies spoke foreign languages, after all), they did not go on strike (that would hurt the war effort), and they did not criticize anything the government (national, state, or local) did in time of war. Basically, "100% Americanism" meant acting like middle-class, white capitalists. Or it meant not being a foreigner or union supporter, which, of course, were the most prominent public identities in Red Lodge at the time. Red Lodge's shifting public identity in the late 1910s and 1920s had everything to do with changing public attitudes toward Americanism in these turbulent years.

Interestingly, questions of Americanism and who was an American had not played much of a role in Red Lodge public life since the town's very early days. Only in the troublesome years immediately following the Panic of 1893 had local residents really wielded the rhetoric of Americanism as a weapon. In that case, entrepreneurs used "American" to attack foreigners who fled the town during its economic downturn or, even worse, sent what earnings the town still provided back to the Old Country rather than spending these wages in Red Lodge. The language employed was typical of that coming from other towns and cities grousing about who was to blame for each community's tough times. Some places blamed African Americans, others attacked Chinese or Japanese immigrants. In Red Lodge, boosters targeted eastern European workers.

"These people," the editor of the *Picket* argued in 1894, "are just precisely the kind that have brought poverty and distress to the workingmen of this country and until congress passes a law to prohibit them from landing here we can expect to see American workmen remain in their present condition."[4] Local merchants became enraged, for example, at news that the Finnish community was forming a cooperative mercantile business that would take business away from established downtown stores. The *Picket* fumed against the Finlanders, who received American wages and yet tried to confine their trade within their own nationality group. "This is not just," the editor stated flatly, "or in accordance with the principles of this government." He urged the mining company to deny the Finns employment if they persisted in this heinous pursuit, since there "are plenty of competent men who would be glad to get employment and who have the welfare of this country at heart and hold our laws and customs inviolable."[5] Americanism, at least according to the *Picket*, meant supporting the interests of the town's business class. The language of Americanism, thus, divided the town between good and bad, investor and transient, American and foreigner.

After good times returned, however, local demonstrations of Americanism tended to be inclusive rather than exclusive. The newspapers no longer used "American" to attack immigrant workers. Indeed, town and union leaders began to use Americanism to draw the community together rather than drive it apart. Workers, for example, draped their various Labor Day celebrations in the Stars and Stripes to emphasize the Americanness of labor organizations. Invariably, Italian and Irish immigrants waved dozens of American flags as they marched en masse in main street parades. And Swedish-born Albert Budas, running for county treasurer in 1906, sold himself as the epitome of the American dream — a poor immigrant boy who rose to prominence nurtured by the freedom and capitalism of the United States.[6]

Significantly, though, this kind of Americanism did not seem to exert much real pressure on residents to conform to an established public rhetoric. Unlike the Italians and Irish, for instance, most Finns and Slovenians chose not to demonstrate American patriotism at public celebrations, and their choice not to participate drew little overt criticism. Patriotism, while voiced and celebrated publicly, did not take on the sharp edge of passionate conviction. Even in the town's most prominent public expression of Americanism — the annual Fourth of July celebration — patriotism took a backseat to an overriding emphasis on boosterism and fun. Red Lodge, like many working-class towns across the nation, used this holiday less as a solemn commemoration of grand national ideals than as a chance to indulge in parades, baseball games, fireworks, and fun field sports.[7] Indeed, the day often seemed more about the economics of selling the town than about Americanism. Event organizers simply wanted to create an enjoyable community event that would prove that Red Lodge was a "live" town, a place on the move.[8] (A more sanctimonious generation in 1919 dismissed these early celebrations as too commercial, held simply to "pry the visitors loose from the largest amount of loose change.")[9] Patriotism, in the prewar years, remained a relatively minor consideration in the town's public life.

World War I dramatically altered this rather lax commitment to patriotism and Americanism in the public sphere. With the nation plunged into war, Red Lodge residents quickly adopted a much more aggressive public definition of Americanness that did not allow groups like the Finns to just "sit out" patri-otic language and displays. Like the rest of the nation, local residents embraced an Americanism that demanded public conformity to an idealized version of "American." This conformity pivoted around public performances: always speaking positively about the war, ostentatiously buying war bonds, harass-ing those who did not ostentatiously buy war bonds, working for the Red Cross, and laboring diligently to provide the wartime nation with essential products. Not engaging in these rituals of patriotism was tantamount to being a traitor, "un-American." Residents had to talk the talk and walk the walk — as publicly as possible.[10]

Ethnicity, interestingly, had little to do with this kind of Americanism, whose zealots targeted labor radicals and those critical of the war more than they harassed those with foreign accents. In fact, for many local immigrants, the war's emphasis on making everyone good Americans actually permitted greater inclusion in nonimmigrant community affairs. As John Higham has pointed out in his classic study of American nativism, *Strangers in the Land,* to "a remarkable degree the psychic climate of war gave the average alien not only protection but also a sense of participation and belonging."[11] In the inter-ests of community participation, Red Lodge civic leaders for the first time began to invite members of immigrant groups to participate in community activities, making them part of events like Liberty Loan drives and patriotic rallies. Foreign-born entrepreneur Albert Budas, for one, took charge of the county's Liberty Loan program, and at least three dozen Finnish businessmen and workers and a sizable number of other immigrants signed on to the new Liberty Committee formed in the fall of 1917 to ferret out disloyal townspeo-ple.[12] Some immigrant groups also seized the wartime opportunity to make their own community-wide statements in favor of America. Serbian Ameri-cans, for example, staged several dramatic parades and rallies to display pub-licly their support for the American war effort, and an Italian fraternity publicly expelled a member for criticizing the war, publishing its justification *in English* in the local newspaper.[13]

Significantly, though, for much of 1917, Finnish-American residents of Red Lodge as a group made little effort to announce publicly their "Americanness." Their lack of effort stands out not only because Finns were the largest immi-grant population in the city but also because of the contrast with Serbians and Italians, two other sizable ethnic groups who made very prominent assertions of American loyalty as soon as the United States joined the war. Individually, Finnish Americans helped out the Liberty Loan drives or joined other patriots in the Liberty Committee, but as a group they did not really alter their prewar apathy toward public displays of Americanism. Of course, the Finnish homeland, unlike Italy and Serbia, was not clearly an ally of the American side. Russia, one of the Allied Powers, had, after all, occupied Finland by force; Finns hated the czar more than they disliked the kaiser and could not really be expected to embrace the war as joyously as did the local Serbs (who hoped for an independent Serbia) or Italians (anxious to prove Italian manhood on the battlefield).[14] So Finns made no public group effort to announce local Finnish-American support for the war. There simply did not seem to be a need to do so in the early days of the conflict, when the campaign for public Americanism appeared fairly benign. By the end of 1917, though, the actions of the Liberty Committee would change all that.

Red Lodge's Liberty Committee, formed in late 1917, represented the most concerted local attempt to impose a very public "100% Americanism" on the community. This group, like most of the Americanism effort in Red Lodge, emulated a larger, national movement. From Maine to California, such organizations bullied or terrorized anyone who seemed to threaten the war effort, focusing particularly on socialist and Industrial Workers of the World (IWW) "agitators" who actually dared to disagree publicly with America's involvement in the conflict. In Montana, almost every county and major city had its own Liberty Committee to take care of these dangerous, antiwar radicals.[15] Some of their efforts, as noted by historian K. Ross Toole, were laughable. Committees, for example, investigated numerous reports of black German dirigibles floating over the mountains of western Montana spying, apparently, on the state's sheep and cattle herds. Other groups denounced as German agents any residents who failed to contribute to Liberty Loan drives or pressed charges against those who conducted church services in German. Ridiculous as some of these allegations were, these groups and other, less formal vigilante-type organizations had darker sides that rightfully frightened local residents who might be suspected of any kind of un-American wrongdoing. In Butte, for example, anonymous vigilantes seized IWW agitator Frank Little from his boardinghouse, tied him to a car, hauled him far and fast enough to take off his kneecaps, and then summarily hanged him from a bridge, leaving a message warning other radicals of similar treatment.[16] This "100% Americanism" was serious, even violent, business.

In Red Lodge, as in Butte and much of the rest of America, ultranationalism translated largely into attacks on radicals, particularly members of the IWW, rather than on members of specific immigrant groups.[17] Indeed, the Red Lodge Liberty Committee took pains to assure the community that its efforts were not directed against immigrants. Their work, according to one spokesman, was not against "any particular race. The action of the committee will be directed against any man of whatever race or creed who is reported or thought to be a German sympathizer."[18] Wobblies, since they spoke out most stridently against the war, were clearly "German sympathizers" who needed to be crushed and driven out of Red Lodge. Committed to a vision of working-class brotherhood, these Wobblies insisted that the war was simply a capitalist ruse, nothing, certainly, that need draw workers into a death struggle with each other.

Driven by their faith in world socialism, Red Lodge Wobblies, most of them Finnish Americans, publicly defied the demands of wartime Americanism. Standing on street corners they handed out brochures denouncing the war and protesting the arrest of national IWW leaders; they even ventured onto the main streets of smaller towns in the county, spreading their message against conscription.[19] Although their numbers in Red Lodge were never great — perhaps a few dozen active IWW members lived in Red Lodge at any one time — the Wobblies' public stance infuriated patriotic Liberty Committee members, particularly retired newspaper publisher Walter Alderson and former sheriff Fred Potter (who wildly estimated the number of local Wobblies at over nine hundred, or about three-quarters of the local mine workforce). Alderson and Potter, who assumed the leadership of the local committee, focused the group's efforts specifically against these agitators, vowing to drive them all from Red Lodge.[20] Their actions, though, had much wider implications for the town and its residents.

Determined to quash the public presence of the IWW in Red Lodge, the Liberty Committee went to work in October 1917, striking a series of blows against the town's "German sympathizers." Significantly, in spite of early assurances that ethnicity was not an issue, the committee almost invariably targeted Finnish-born workers for "questioning" and punishment. The group's actions started out simply enough; the Liberty Committee ordered a public boycott of the Finnish-owned Workers' Hall, reported to be the headquarters of the town's IWW faction. But the committee's activities quickly moved beyond such benign actions. Perhaps imitating the terror tactics of the Butte vigilantes, the Red Lodge Liberty Committee started to verbally then physically threaten local Finnish Americans. According to at least one Wobbly report, members of the Liberty Committee rounded up suspected IWW leaders one at a time, subjecting them to threats and abuse until they confessed their allegiance to the One Big Union and gave up the name of least one other member of the organization. When one man, Jalmar Winturri, refused to give in under verbal threats, a selected committee took him to the basement of the Elks Lodge where they strung a rope around his neck and hauled him up three times before he finally admitted that he was a Wobbly and provided names of other members. Three of the men so interrogated by the Liberty Committee — Winturri, Jack Ollila, and Jacob Lindquist — fled Red Lodge within the week; all three, according to IWW reports, were family men who had lived in Red Lodge for ten to fifteen years.[21] Their forced confessions initiated a new round of Liberty Committee harassment of supposed IWW radicals with tragic consequences to one family and significant consequences for the town's immigrant populations.

Angered by a continuing Wobbly presence in the town, the Liberty Committee gathered up a new group of suspected subversives in late November 1917, among them Finnish-born miner Emile Koski. After a night of threats and questioning, Koski, who had lived in Red Lodge for fifteen years, returned home to his wife and two children, shaken and frightened and unsure what would happen to him next. Scared, defensive, and armed, Koski would not answer the door when Liberty Committee men arrived at his house late on the evening of 28 November. In the aftermath of the violence against Red Lodge Wobblies, including his own "questioning," and the vicious lynching of IWW activist Frank Little in Butte, Koski's fear was understandable. When committee members forced the door down, Koski drove them back by firing his shotgun into the ceiling. In the ensuing gun battle, the intruders fired at least two weapons at the house. Kaisa Kreeta Jackson, who rented several rooms from Koski, returned home late and walked into this scene. Koski, believing her to be one of his attackers, shot and killed her. Then, distraught over his act, the weeping Koski surrendered to authorities.[22]

Public reaction to the shooting was immediate and widespread with long-lasting ramifications to Red Lodge's public ethnic identity. Violence against suspected Wobblies spread fear among many residents, especially those in the working class and particularly Finns. Overnight, immigrant residents re-adjusted how they and their children moved and acted within the town. Any-one, it seemed, could become the next victim of the crusade against radicals. Senia Kallio, whose Finnish-born parents ran one of the town's public saunas, recalled that the family quickly cleared everyone out of the bathhouse upon hearing the shots fired, and "for a long time we couldn't go [out]. The minute it got dark, my folks put the drapes down, the shades down."²³ Parents were afraid to let their children out of the house or even to talk to outsiders, for fear of what the Liberty Committee might do next. Steve Blazina, a Croatian-born resident, told his son to just ignore any tormentors, to come straight home when he was taunted about being a "Hun" or a "Hunky." "Just don't say anything," Blazina instructed. "Keep quiet."²⁴ Residents remembered this sense of pervasive unease long after the war ended. For the first time, these ethnic community members feared for their welfare, even their lives, *because* of their ethnic identities.

The shooting finally shook the local Finnish-American community and other nationality groups into a new and long-lasting public stance on Amer-icanism. Finnish-American leaders, especially, took decisive and immediate public action. They used the local newspapers, town meetings, and the court system to assert themselves as patriotic, loyal American citizens. Instead of condemning the actions of the vigilance group, local Finns strove to meet the committee's loyalty requirements, to prove to everyone that Finns were real patriots. In public, at least, the Finns did all they could to create themselves as "100% Americans." Finnish community leaders readily and publicly announced their cooperation with the Liberty Committee. "We have no other purpose," stated one prominent Finn, "than that of the Liberty Committee, to find out who is and who is not loyal to our country, and to pledge the rest in an obligation that is binding."

Finns planned a giant rally to "demonstrate by words and deeds our fidelity to the government in its present important work of war, and its ultimate aim of peace." Organizers put a full-page advertisement in local newspapers announcing, in both English and Finnish, the "Meeting of the Loyal-to-Amer-ica Finnish People." Over four hundred "Finnish born patriots," all of them naturalized citizens, attended the meeting, made public pledges to support the American government, and denounced the "small minority of our race, that have been misled by agitators so far as to forget the fulfillment of their duties to their adopted country."[25] And almost immediately after the shooting, moderate Finnish socialists ("respected citizens of the community, loyal and patriotic") initiated legal proceedings to remove title to Workers' Hall from the more left-wing socialists who had taken over its management and "permitted disloyal and unpatriotic meetings" to be held there.[26]

Out of the fear created by the Koski shooting, Finnish residents created new and public avenues of ethnic expression that conformed as much as possible to the "100% Americanism" demands of the Liberty Committee and other patriotic organizations. The war, thus, changed public expressions of ethnicity in Red Lodge, altering how the town's "foreignness" looked and sounded. Nationality groups like the Finns, often for the first time, felt compelled to voice publicly their allegiance to America and to take part in community activities and performances that would reinforce and prove that loyalty.

Significantly, however, these changes were not as sweeping as they might at first have seemed, for the town's hyphenated Americans (as the foreign-born and their children were called) articulated an Americanism still rooted in the strong ethnic bonds of Red Lodge's Finnish, Italian, and Serbian neighborhoods. Although these immigrants and their children voiced a public Americanism, they tended to do so as part of a specific ethnic group: the Italian *fraternity* declared its support of America, *four hundred* Finnish Americans rallied to show their patriotism, the local Serbians marched *together* to prove their loyalty. This approach fit with larger, national trends. As historian Gary Gerstle has pointed out, Americanism of this period tended to center around public rhetoric. Those groups interested in any form of public power (or protection) in their community had "to couch their programs in the language of Americanism."[27]

In Red Lodge, as elsewhere, immigrants and others learned to speak in new ways as they publicly defined themselves and their actions in reference to Americanism. Although no officials went into ethnic neighborhoods to drive out foreign customs, clothes, or music, the war caused immigrants to rethink their public attachment to these traditions. Fear added impetus to some immigrants' adoption of the language and symbols of Americanism, as in Red Lodge, where immigrants and their children created a new American identity as a defense shield against the terror of "patriotic" organizations. Importantly, though, the larger community accepted and even encouraged this kind of attenuated Americanism.[28] It was all right for these immigrants to declare their Americanism as a group, as long as they declared it loudly and publicly.

The Italian and Finnish auxiliaries of the Carbon County Red Cross provide one example of this process of group adoption of sanctioned "American" rhetoric and activities. After the Koski incident, foreign-born women wanted to prove their loyalty through direct action by joining the Red Cross. But in many ways, the local Red Cross was as much a social club as it was an aid organization — women gathered in the library basement to knit socks and stuff packages while chatting about neighborhood scandals and children's marriages. To sidestep the difficulties of working and socializing with people who could not communicate across language barriers, the Italian and Finnish women — with the blessing and support of the nonimmigrant county organization — arranged to have their own separate, ethnic chapters. They worked for the patriotic cause, but they continued to speak Italian or Finnish while doing their own stuffing and knitting.[29] They made public their support for America even while remaining within the ethnic group.

World War I and the actions of the Liberty Committee, then, jolted local immigrants into announcing a public American identity and forming groups that, while separate from nonethnic committees, initiated some of the first steps toward greater community cooperation and discourse. The Italian and Finnish women, after all, did associate with a traditionally Anglo group when they affiliated with the Red Cross — an important move toward integrating into the larger public life of the town. Another product of World War I, the Italian Girls Victory Club, a charitable and social organization composed of Italian-born women and their daughters, would stride even further. This group, devoted to raising money for cross-ethnic community causes, survived the war years to take the lead in forming ever stronger public alliances between immigrant groups and the rest of Red Lodge. Their work contributed to the formation of several multicultural festivals in the 1930s and eventually to the town's Festival of Nations in 1951, in which residents celebrated the unity of community purpose among the town's varied nationality groups. Through the Festival of Nations (as discussed in Chapter 5), local people would try to recapture a taste of the town's immigrant identity that was so tangible and pervasive in the pre–World War I years but that was already beginning to evolve into a more general Americanness by the 1920s.

World War I, thus, marked a key transition point in the development of Red Lodge's public ethnicity. Through the process started in the war years, combined with immigration restrictions and the maturation of second-generation ethnics, Red Lodge would start to lose its very visible, audible, and olfactory identity as a vibrantly multiethnic community.

The program of "100% Americanism" initiated during the war would also set in motion another transformation of public identity in Red Lodge. Within a few years of the war's end, Red Lodge's identity as a coal town began to slip away as workers' smoldering resentments against wartime repression destroyed the stable labor/management relationship of the town's earlier years. Starting in 1919, workers erupted into a series of strikes that ended, eventually, in the closing of the Red Lodge tunnels. The industrial workers' town of the early twentieth century would be gone forever.

World War I prompted this transformation in several ways. First of all, the war provided the Northwestern Improvement Company (NWIC) with a golden opportunity to impose greater control over its workers than it had been able to attain through close relations with the UMWA. The company started the process by freezing or even reducing workers' wages, citing a patriotic need to produce coal more efficiently for the war effort.[30] Since the federal government had banned strikes in vital industries such as coal mining for the duration of the war, this unilateral decision by management left workers simmering with frustration but unable to retaliate while the country was engaged in its great struggle. Then, the operators went even further.

Company officials pressured local leaders into restricting working-class amusements in Red Lodge because the war demanded fit and able workers. The NWIC had long complained of men failing to show up for work "on account of certain places of amusement," specifically brothels that served alcohol. Spurred by the demands of the NWIC, town and county officials closed down places of prostitution and arrested all "vagrants and women of ill-fame" within the town limits.[31] When the NWIC requested that all saloons close at 10 P.M. so that miners would show up for work on time, local authorities jumped to attention, ordering not only the 10 P.M. closing but also shutting down all saloons and clubs that served alcohol (the Elks Club as well as the Workers' Club) from Saturday night until 1 P.M. on Sunday.[32] Measures of social control that could not have passed earlier now swept through the town and county councils under the rationale of "war work" and "necessary coal production" and with the strong encouragement of the area's coal operators. Limiting workers' rights and pleasures—and thus making them more efficient laborers—was in the best interests of "Americanism," according to mine managers. And the workers, legally forbidden to strike and socially constrained from protesting against these restrictions, had to bide their time and wait for the chance to regain their former position of power.[33]

Local workers recognized the hand of the coal operators behind the anti-radical activities of the local Liberty Committee, which also became fuel for the fire of resentment and disquiet that spread through the Red Lodge coal tunnels in the years after World War I. It did not take much to connect mine officials with the Liberty Committee's drive to terrorize the community's Wobblies or to see it as a first step toward silencing all labor protest at the mines. William Haggarty, the NWIC mine foreman, for example, led the Liberty Committee faction that dragged suspected IWW members to inquisitions at the Elks Lodge. Liberty Committee cofounder Fred Potter, a former sheriff, was widely known locally as someone with strong procompany sentiments. The other cofounder, Walter Alderson, actually published in the local newspaper a letter from the NWIC superintendent that praised the Liberty Committee for purging the mines of Wobblies.[34] And a year after the war ended, the NPRR provided one thousand dollars to support Liberty Committee members defending themselves against a civil suit brought by a Finnish Wobbly.[35] Local people readily noted these links between management and the patriotic organization. Daniel S. McCorkle, for example, a minister who lived in nearby Chance, Montana, fingered a "a few of the worst labor hating employers" for sponsoring most of the violence in their desire to destroy labor organizations.[36] The coal operators' public crackdown on workers' pay and pleasures combined with their behind-the-scenes endorsement of the Liberty Committee created a new, dangerous tension among local workers that would snap almost as soon as the war ended. The miners had to fight back against the owners because, as Red Lodge miner William Glancy put it, "See, the coal miners really got the book throwed at them during the First World War."[37]

And in the postwar years, local miners saw their chance to fight back. Between 1919 and 1922, Red Lodge workers' strikes closed down the local mines three times, with one strike lasting almost half a year. In this action, local miners actually joined in a national wave of strikes after the war ended. In 1919 John L. Lewis, a towering figure in union leadership, assumed presidency of the UMWA and led the union on a long, often contentious struggle against the nation's coal operators.[38] Red Lodge workers, many of whom idolized Lewis, readily followed the UMWA leadership, sometimes going even further than the national union thought necessary.[39] In the 1922 strike, for example, local workers, outraged by the hiring of a nonunion man, stayed out of the NWIC mines almost two weeks longer than their counterparts in other parts of the country.[40] The men seemed eager to strike back against the "coal barons" who had deprived the workers of rights and wages during the war years. Ollie Anderson, for example, weathered all three strikes and spoke bitterly against the operators who kept pushing workers to produce more for less so the "big boys" would have more money to put in their pocketbooks.[41] And miner Mikko Marttunen called the prolonged 1922 work stoppage "a splendid strike" against "owners [who] want to break the union and lower wages by half."[42] Red Lodge, the stable union town, became a war zone of sorts, a place of almost continual fighting between management and workers.

In the end, though, the miners' radicalism and united strength backfired on them. Marttunen's joy in the miners' victory in 1922 did not last long. A relatively minor player in a much larger national operation, Red Lodge miners had clout only so long as they provided a needed material for the operation of the Northern Pacific Railroad. Frustrated by workers' demands and the high cost of taking coal out through underground tunnels, the Northern Pacific decided to shift part of its operations in the early 1920s to Colstrip in southeastern Montana. Coal near the surface there yielded more easily to mechanized strip-mining techniques that required fewer workers. Also, in this new operation the railroad company could subcontract for the coal through a separate firm, skirting union agreements and establishing Colstrip as a firmly nonunion operation.[43] In 1924, then, the Northwestern Improvement Company closed down the West Side Mine, and Red Lodge lost a large chunk of its corporate payroll. Some miners found work at the East Side Mine or over the hill at the Bearcreek and Washoe operations; many had already given up after the prolonged series of strikes. Red Lodge, the Coal Metropolis, began to shrink and draw in upon itself. The East Side Mine held out until 1932, but then the NWIC pulled out of the little town completely. The coal identity that had marked Red Lodge for over four decades was gone, leaving residents to work out new ways of defining themselves and their town in the middle years of the twentieth century.

By the 1930s, Red Lodge, though still surviving in part through the work of mines in Bearcreek, was no longer a mining town. Company employees removed working equipment, razed some remaining buildings, boarded up mine entrances, and moved out of Red Lodge. The company left behind a town of workers and businesses that had depended on the mines' payroll. It also left two towering piles of coal slack, a maze of tunnels beneath the streets of Red Lodge, coal miners with broken limbs and black lung disease, and the memory of a time when the town had boomed, wages were high, and times were good. For much of the twentieth century, town leaders would strive to replicate the corporate industrial complex that had built and maintained Red Lodge for over forty years. Such efforts remained futile, however. Plans for new coal mines, a chromium mine, a coal crude plant, and oil wells would fall through one after another, leaving local businesses and workers increasingly dependent on tourism and the functions of being a county seat.

But in its first four decades, Red Lodge's identity was, indeed, grounded in foreignness and coated in coal dust — dirty grime that enveloped the city and all its inhabitants. In the boom years of coal, few had minded the visible dirt of the industry or the obvious foreignness of the workers who brought the coal to the surface. While coal ruled Red Lodge, the grimy coating marked the town's industrial heart; only when that heart stopped pumping capital through the community would residents look at the soot as something dirty and undesirable. As boosters turned to tourism — the next golden economic hope — they would gradually begin to erase the physical remnants of the town's industrial past, adopting instead a Wild West heritage of rustic log cabins, cowboys, and ranches and a public ethnicity of peasant skirts, *kolas*, and *krumkaka*.

Everyone's a Cowboy
The "Wild West" in the Twentieth Century

Tourists coming into Red Lodge expect to see a certain amount of western atmosphere in keeping with the true western setting of Red Lodge. By looking the part, you are advertising the city to the ultimate benefit of the entire population.
—*Carbon County News*, 6 June 1941

In 1961, John Barovich, a Montana insurance man born in Niksich, Yugoslavia, returned to the land of his birth to reacquaint himself with relatives he had not seen for forty years. Barovich's father had moved his seven-year-old son to Montana in 1921. There the older Barovich dug coal in the Bearcreek fields outside Red Lodge for twenty years while young John grew up in the modern, industrial world of mechanized, unionized mining. As a teenager, Barovich played basketball in coal dust–laden air, took it for granted that everyone's father was a miner, and learned to distrust the greed of coal operators. A graduate of Montana State University, a high school history teacher, and eventually a full-time insurance salesman, Barovich's adult life, like his childhood years, had everything to do with the modern West of technology, innovation, and salesmanship. His background lay in a much different West than that embodied in the mystique of the cowboy and rancher. Yet, when he returned to Yugoslavia as a middle-aged man, Barovich wore not a miners' cap or a fashionable fedora, but rather a broad-brimmed cowboy hat — a physical symbol of his claims to the West's pastoral, ranching heritage.[1]

The immigrant coal miner's son in the cowboy hat raises some interesting questions about how public western identity developed in the twentieth century. Why did westerners with no clear roots in the pastoral heritage of ranching begin to adopt visible symbols of the cowboy and rancher? When did modern industrial towns in the region start to acquire the trappings of log cabin frontier villages? Why by the mid–twentieth century did so many westerners dress like cowboys? The answers to these questions are wrapped up in a national obsession with the mythic West, westerners' own desires to embrace that mythology, and the developing demands of regional tourism.

Like westerners in hundreds of other small towns in the 1920s and 1930s, Red Lodge residents, including John Barovich, plunged feetfirst into the modern game of acting "western" — that is, assuming a public identity of "westernness" defined not so much by the West itself as by the nationally created, mythic West. Of course, westerners always were western just by living in the west. But Americans who lived west of the Missouri River in the mid–twentieth century learned how to look like the kind of westerner *other* Americans expected them to be. This new regional identity pulled the imagery of popular Western movies and novels into specific western places.[2] Towns like Red Lodge, and their residents, began to take on some of the physical trappings of the Wild West so admired by Americans like young Johnny Southward — the boy who had been greatly disappointed by Red Lodge's lack of "westernness" in the 1890s.

The developing tourism industry produced the most immediate impetus for this very public assumption of cowboy westernness by local westerners. In many places around the region, westerners began to dress like cowboys and cowgirls in the 1920s and 1930s because town boosters noticed that the "Wild West" — cowboys in particular — "sold" well to tourists. As small towns in the West began to lose their economic base in extractive industries, local leaders sought, almost desperately, to buoy up sagging economies through infusions of tourism revenue. Most visitors, however, did not really care about seeing a West of immigrant miners, corporate industrialism, and insurance salesmen. Tourists preferred western places that met their expectations — shaped by movies and novels — of what the West *should* look like: log cabins, horses, Indians, and cowboys. So, catering to the demands of tourists, westerners began to re-create their towns and themselves to appear appropriately western for their visitors. They constructed log cabin facades for brick buildings, held rodeos, and dressed themselves up in neckerchiefs, blue jeans, and cowboy hats. The same "wild" figures that residents had driven out of town in the 1890s became the new heroes of a twentieth-century interpretation of the nineteenth-century past.

Tourism became the new western industry. In Red Lodge, as in other communities, increasing numbers of visitors from the outside presented a kind of golden hope as local residents found their older, extractive industries closing down or moving away. After the Northwestern Improvement Company closed down its coal mines and stripped away much of the town's industrial identity, Red Lodge survived in part through seasonal jobs in a local pea canning factory and the business of being a county seat. More and more, though, townspeople came to depend on the dollars brought into the community by outsiders coming into and through town searching for excitement, entertainment, recreation, or just something different to look at. As many as seventy-five thousand visitors a year streamed through Red Lodge by 1934, and local business developments reflected the growth of this new industry. By 1924 Red Lodge boasted its first filling station — essential to the motor touring public. By 1939 the town had nine overnight facilities, including a municipally built "tourist park," and eight service stations, and almost one-quarter of all local work was classified as service sector.[3] Red Lodge residents were transforming their little town into a new type of community; instead of selling coal to outsiders, local people were now selling Red Lodge itself. And in the 1920s and 1930s, what sold best was being "western" — or, more accurately, looking like the kind of West depicted in popular novels and movies, the kind of West visitors wanted to see.

Although not the only impetus for looking western in the early twentieth century, tourism promotion pressured many residents into remaking their local worlds (including themselves) into the kind of West most appealing to tourists. The West itself became a production in the western United States. Indians in full-feathered headdresses erected tepee camps next to highways, charging fifty cents for guided tours; women in calico sunbonnets drove buckboards down main streets behind stagecoaches full of local dignitaries dressed as "rollicking cowboys and cowgirls"; and town buildings acquired a coating of cedar shakes to make them appear appropriately rustic and western.

But this drive to adopt the mythic West into modern western identities never revolved completely around tourism. Local westerners drew from their own pasts — or their neighbors' — to affirm their claims to an Old West history because this heritage seemed to represent the very best of America. In Red Lodge, residents could look to old-time cowboy Packsaddle Ben Greenough and his stories of Liver-Eating Johnson and Calamity Jane to confirm the reality of the town's connection to the real Old West, the West of popular myth that reaffirmed the residents' place in the heroic struggle to settle and conquer the continent. Rejecting (for the moment) the town's vibrant industrial mining heritage, local people reached back to grab at any tenuous relation they could find to the pastoral ranching heritage that epitomized the values, morals, and freedoms Americans treasured.

At the heart of this drive to appear "western" stood the powerful image of the cowboy, a deceptively simple figure with a variety of modern-day representatives in the West. By the mid–twentieth century, the cowboy stood unchallenged as the quintessential hero of the American West, and indeed of the entire nation. He, more than any other national figure, represented American fortitude, independence, and initiative. Easterners and westerners alike strove to borrow some of the glamour of this national hero, dressing in cowboy hats, boots, and pearl-buttoned shirts to emulate the western icon. But in the process of adopting the cowboy as a regional and local symbol of westernness, westerners had to address the complicated contradictions of this working-class drifter who had come to represent the twinned values of freedom and responsibility. Was a real cowboy a rodeo rider, rancher, wrangler, movie star, or poorly paid cowpuncher? In Red Lodge and other western places, residents chose between a variety of local and national figures to select the most appropriate modern representatives of the idealized nineteenth-century cowhand. Westerners essentially transferred the glamour of the working cowboy onto capitalist ranchers and eventually — through their own performances as cowboys and cowgirls in annual rodeos and Wild West parades — onto themselves.

Through various public performances — most prominently rodeos, dude ranches, and parades — westerners created what Richard Slotkin calls "mythic spaces."[4] Residents carved out arenas of performance and exhibition in which they reproduced selected historical narratives, grounded in the local past but drawing from larger myths of the West and the frontier, particularly the strains of Buffalo Bill Cody's theatrical "Wild West." As residents acted out mythic roles in these productions of "westernness," they gradually expanded the stage upon which they performed — adding more background, enlarging certain roles, and pulling some of these theatrical acquisitions into their own lives. Log cabins and rustic storefronts began to dot western townscapes, movie-inspired cowboy drawls crept into local accents, and the son of an immigrant coal miner (who might never, ever, have contemplated chasing a cow) made the cowboy hat part of his own claim to a western identity.

Of course, local people in places like Red Lodge did not simply "forget" about the very real industrial past that had created so much of the modern West. Coal mining remained an essential part of residents' sense of themselves — a point made all too clear in the oral histories and memoirs that continued to center around the work and products of mining. Indeed, some residents were still traveling over the hill to mine coal in Bearcreek and Washoe into the 1950s, so the physical reminders of the mining past remained strong. But Red Lodge lost the vibrancy, the immediacy of the coal identity that had so marked the town into the 1920s. As local people scrambled to find new ways to sustain the community, they moved beyond their mining, unionized history to find a different public identity that would be more appealing to the tens of thousands of tourists Red Lodge residents now hoped to "mine" for new kinds of wealth. For the moment, westerners like those in Red Lodge looked past the modern, industrial West that had shaped the community in its first three decades to find a more suitable version of a western heritage — one that would better fit the demands of the day.

By the early 1940s, then, a western patina had descended over towns like Red Lodge. Clothing, building styles, advertising images, even the style of local speech, reflected the "westernization" of these places as local people created a westernness that readily mixed myth with modernity or, as an area dude rancher put it, "reality" with "unreality." In towns around the region, westerners began to acquire a new public identity based on the formerly despised symbols and characters of the Wild West and particularly around the multi-layered imagery of the greatest of all American heroes, the cowboy.

In Red Lodge, as in other western towns, the process of becoming "western" did not have an exact starting date. As early as the 1890s, after all, town leaders sought to make Red Lodge western at the fringes through the promotion of local links to the masculine mountain man figure. In the early years of the twentieth century, however, the desire to celebrate Red Lodge as a modern and progressive mining town clearly overwhelmed any efforts to associate the community with the mythic Wild West. Some popular "westernness" crept into the town — local leaders invited nearby Indians to perform at a Fourth of July celebration in 1909 and a local paper used a mounted Indian as a masthead in the 1910s — but in the boom years of coal mining, local residents embraced modern technology, unionism, and the image of an eastern-style city rather than the symbolism of a rough and wild frontier.

By the early 1920s, however, conditions had changed, both nationally and locally. The Northwestern Improvement Company closed down the West Side

Mine in 1923 at the same time that an extensive drought devastated local farms and ranches.[5] Nationally, travel restrictions during World War I, improved transportation, and a large-scale propaganda campaign to "See America First" persuaded many easterners to tour the West in ever greater numbers.[6] These new tourists arrived eager to experience the "real" West of horses, cowboys, Indians, and ranch life. So, just as towns like Red Lodge began to see their economic base in extractive resources slip away, tourists arrived at their doorsteps with money to spend on experiencing the Wild West. The money these new visitors brought to western communities promised hope for a new type of industry to replace the old, familiar work that no longer filled the demands of the nation's economy. A new opportunity beckoned; residents simply had to learn to "mine" tourists as effectively as they had done coal. Effective mining in this case meant recognizing and exploiting the region's most valuable resource: being western.[7]

Easterners, it turned out, loved "the West" and were more than willing to pay to acquire a little bit of it for themselves. And nothing marked the increasing fascination of easterners with all things western — and westerners' willingness to give these ripe new tourists what they wanted — like the remarkable growth of the dude ranching industry in the 1920s. Dude ranchers spearheaded twentieth-century efforts to fashion the West according to cinematic and literary visions of the area. The dude rancher created a personal fantasy West: a three-dimensional replication of the mythic West full of "real" western experiences in beautiful, rugged settings. And visitors ate it up.[8] Of course, westerners had run dude ranch operations for decades, but the postwar demand for guest ranching spurred more and more ranchers and businessmen to create romantic, rustic lodges and cabins on working ranches and leased Forest Service lands. By 1930, there were over one hundred dude ranches in Montana alone, four of them headquartered out of Red Lodge.[9] Guests, or "dudes," typically stayed at these ranches for at least a week, working themselves into a cozy routine of communal meals in the lodge and outdoor activities that ranged from "just loafing" to weeklong pack trips into the mountains.[10] It was the Wild West of the gentleman rancher made simple and comfortable, even "picturesque."

Dude ranches assumed such great popularity in the 1920s because dude ranchers hit upon the ideal combination of image, ambiance, and comfort. To achieve this effect, proprietors and promoters easily mixed history and movies, myth and modernity. As western dude ranchers showed, the "real" and the "fantasy" did not necessarily have to contradict each other; rather, one could see them as two sides of the same coin. Fantasy simply served to make the real more, well, real. Dude ranch buildings and clothing illustrated this mixture. The cabins and lodges, for example, even if constructed only last year, had to look as if they had been built by pioneers who had only "native materials" to work with. Take Red Lodge's Al Croonquist, who assured guests that his new ranch, Camp Senia, was "so wild and rugged . . . that everything that went into the building of the picturesque log cabin tucked away among the lodge pines had to be packed in on horseback."[11]

Here was western as dudes wanted to see it. No matter that modern westerners in Red Lodge, Cody, and Billings were building bungalows of stucco and wallboard; dude ranches had to eschew twentieth-century construction materials and machines to capture the nineteenth-century illusion of a rustic West that visitors demanded. Playing to this illusion, dude ranchers also dressed up in movie-star western outfits — big hats, fancy boots, and loud shirts — instead of the blue denim overalls worn by working cowpunchers. As one dude ranch promoter admitted, the costume was necessary: "We have to do a little advertising and have to carry on the heritage of the movies in respect to having a little unreality."[12] Reality and unreality intertwined in the world of dude ranching where participants spurned the modern West to create an idealized past in the service of a modern industry. And it succeeded tremendously. By 1926, Red Lodge's four dude ranches continued to expand to accommodate the growing demand for Old West living.[13]

As these dude ranches expanded their operations, they not only pumped dudes' cash into the local economy, but they also held out the possibility of increased investment and development in the areas around the ranches. In terms of actual business, dudes infused about a million dollars a year into Montana's economy in the 1920s. Smaller ranches like Camp Sawtooth naturally saw less of that money, but larger outfits around Red Lodge such as Camp Senia, which could accommodate up to one hundred guests by 1926, brought in a larger share of the dudes' bounty.[14] And, of course, all of these dudes needed to at least pass through Red Lodge on their way up into the mountains, giving them a chance to drop a bit of cash in the tills of local establishments. Dude ranching was never mass tourism, however, and its real promise was never simply the money dudes happened to spend in a few weeks or months in the Beartooths. More significantly for local townspeople, dude ranches seemed to attract just the right kinds of people into the West. As one editorialist explained, many summer visitors were really home seekers "in the guise of tourists in search for the land of promise." Enterprises like dude ranches that lured visitors thus ended up enticing to the area "new and substantial citizens who will make the fertile prairies bloom like garden spots."[15] The old dream of creating a garden around Red Lodge lingered on but was now tied more fully to a tourist trade based around western imagery. Westerners enticed visitors into the region by promising to fulfill their western fantasies in the hopes that more than just transitory trade might result.

Rodeos presented a more fast-paced, thrilling version of the Wild West than did the dude ranch. But, like the dude ranch, the rodeo established itself as a distinctively western form of entertainment that played upon the popular images of the mythic Wild West. Rodeo developed out of the cowboy's work of roping cattle and breaking wild horses but added some of the glitter of nineteenth-century Wild West shows. The great western showman Buffalo Bill Cody himself took credit for "inventing" the rodeo in 1882 when he presented a show of "Cow-boys' Fun" that included "Bucking and Kicking Ponies" and "Roping, Tying, and Riding the Wild Texas Steers."[16] Cody's show attracted thousands of viewers, and soon towns throughout the West were hosting rodeos with events ranging from saddle bronc riding and bulldogging to trick riding and "Roman racing" (riding two horses by putting one foot on the back of each).[17] Women excelled at these competitions; they rode broncs, raced horses, and attracted viewers fascinated by their skills as well as their cowgirl outfits of bloomers or split skirts.[18] In the early twentieth century, more and more towns around the West held rodeos. Small community competitions drew mostly local cowboys and cowgirls, while larger events — the Pendleton Roundup, Calgary Stampede, and Cheyenne Frontier Days — attracted competitors and fans from around the West. The excitement soon moved east. In 1926, Madison Square Garden began holding an annual rodeo, and in 1932, Boston Garden introduced its own rodeo championships.[19] Rodeos gained in popularity because promoters gave American spectators what they wanted: cowboys, cowgirls, horses, and excitement without danger to spectators.

Together, the rodeo and the dude ranch adapted Cody's Wild West performances to the modern tourist's West. By reinforcing the popularity of the Wild West among easterners and showing its potential profitability among westerners, dude ranchers and rodeo promoters blazed a wide path for others to follow. Many towns tagged along. Not all westerners, of course, took part in these efforts to redefine themselves and the local townscape as western. Some refused to participate in the rodeo activities or cooperate in efforts to appear western for tourists. Others, however, especially a business class anxious to cash in on the growing tourist economy, vigorously embraced and encouraged the development of this new "old western" identity. Under the guidance of an enthusiastic middle class and with the help of old-timers eager to share memories and memorabilia, local communities reshaped themselves, at least on the surface, into "Old West" towns.

Cody, Wyoming, which entered the rodeo business several years before Red Lodge, seemed especially adept at this creation of western mythology in a living townscape. Of course, as the former home of Buffalo Bill Cody, the town had a natural lead-in into the business of selling the mythic West. In the 1920s, Cody businessmen actually initiated a concerted campaign to turn the entire downtown business area into what was essentially a giant dude ranch complete with all the props and characters that dudes might expect from the Wild West. Businessman Jacob M. Schwoob summarized the Cody efforts at a 1929 meeting of the Dude Ranchers' Association. His message: Give the dudes what they want — the "big hat, the old stage coaches, the relics of the trapper and trader, the Indian things with cowboys and cowgirls at hand and the horsey air of a western town everywhere." When the dudes stepped off the train, Schwoob told his audience, "they should step into a western atmosphere" that embodied the "days of the range, the cattle and the wild life of the real west." Why should the West provide these things? The answer was simple: money.[20] To succeed in the modern world — to tap into the wealth of the eastern tourist — the West needed to turn itself into a popular version of the Old West.

Much of the local staging of the Old West revolved around money. Most Red Lodge boosters readily admitted that they instituted their first annual rodeo competition in 1930 to keep up with merchants in other towns. They wanted to be as successful at attracting tourists as Cody was. Town leaders jumped on the rodeo bandwagon when they noted the effects of rodeos in other communities, particularly on the summer's biggest holiday, the Fourth of July. In 1927, the *Picket-Journal*'s editor observed that hundreds of locals had gone to Cody over the Fourth for its annual stampede festivities,[21] and by 1929 the town was clearly losing holiday business to the "Rodeo exhibitions, stampedes, celebrations and Fourth of July pageants" held in outlying communities from Bridger and Absarokee to Livingston and Cody. On the defensive, the *Picket-Journal* contended, "No rodeo spirit in the world could compete with the fishing which impels hundreds of local folks to seek the stream bank or the lake shore today."[22] But by the next year, local citizens conceded that rodeo was the wave of the future and laid the groundwork for a Red Lodge rodeo, which the paper optimistically predicted would be "one of the most successful public events held in this community in years."[23]

And, indeed, the rodeo proved to be a great success. Hundreds of visitors flocked to Red Lodge to watch what the local newspaper dubbed a re-creation "of the great West which still lingers in recollections of the romantic and blood-stirring past."[24] The rodeo committee made sure the day was packed full of fun and excitement. After an early morning baseball game, a grand rodeo parade entertained residents and visitors alike with the colorful spectacle of rodeo riders, Indians in "all the variegated regalia of olden days," and dozens of local businessmen and women dressed up as cowboys and cowgirls. When the parade had looped back up Broadway Avenue for a second time, a steady stream of people followed the "great West" procession up the low bluff overlooking Red Lodge. Some walked, a few rode horses, but most motored up the hill in cars and trucks. They knew where they were heading; the marker was hard to miss. Under a massive seventy-five-foot-tall mound of glistening coal slack topped by a forty-two-foot flagpole flying the Stars and Stripes stood a raw, hastily constructed arena with bleacher seats. While most fans climbed up into the stands of the brand-new rodeo arena, others simply drove to a reserved "auto stall" to enjoy the town's Old West competition from the comfort of their Chevy or Ford. From there the entire family could watch local cowgirl Alice Greenough taking on one of the meanest broncs around, Crow Indians from Pryor competing in relay races, and a stunt plane dropping parachuters into the dirt arena. Cowboys wrestled steers, got bucked off broncos, and tied up calves. The gorgeous Beartooth Mountains formed a stunning backdrop to the West's "most scenic rodeo grounds" (although those parked right next to the giant slack heap missed out on the view of real mountains). As the competition drew to a close, residents gave a last cheer for their favorite cowboys and headed down to the Labor Temple, thrown open by the local miners' union for postrodeo music and dancing (cowboy boots optional). Thus ended the first day of what boosters would soon call Red Lodge's "truly inspiring reincarnation of the early days of the old west."[25]

Ride 'em cowgirl! Local icon Alice Greenough in her trademark oversized hat strides across the Red Lodge rodeo grounds after a ride. The immense pile of coal slack looming up behind her did not detract from the town's boast that it had the "most scenic rodeo grounds" in the country. (Carbon County Historical Society photo)

All in all, the event confirmed the appeal of Wild West entertainment. The town almost burst with visitors who filled up not only the local hotels but all the nearby campsites as well. Instead of just passing through town en route to mountain hikes and picnics, cars from Billings paused in town for a day or even two as visitors soaked up the fun of the rodeo, parades, baseball games, and dances. Boosters' chests swelled with pride as regional newspapers congratulated Red Lodge residents on the fine and crowd-pleasing spectacle.[26]

The annual rodeo brought the western imagery made popular by the dude ranches directly and very publicly into the local community. Rodeo boosters found that the Wild West sold well. Townspeople struggled in the first few years of the depression to finance the event, but the rodeo always drew crowds and it quickly became the town's major vehicle for boosting its other tourist attractions, primarily the Beartooth Mountains.[27] According to Rodeo Association figures, the event attracted as many as seven thousand spectators for three days of entertainment in 1931, an impressive figure for a town whose population hovered just over three thousand in 1930.[28] Although attendance figures dipped in the early years of the depression, by 1937, the rodeo gained financial stability, and boosters rejoiced at the thousands of visitors swarming to the event.[29] In that year, officials estimated that five thousand people showed up for the Sunday installment of the multiday extravaganza. Indeed, the town attracted more visitors in some years than it could accommodate; in 1936, rodeo officials began to encourage residents to open up their homes to tourists so that the town would not lose business because of lack of public accommodations.[30]

Even without enough hotel space, the crowds could never get big enough for rodeo promoters who continually pushed townspeople to work harder at making Red Lodge more "western." If a little Wild West got such good results, then a whole bunch must be better, and Red Lodge boosters soon sought to expand the Wild West atmosphere of the two- or three-day rodeo into a summerlong affair. In 1934, the Rodeo Association announced its intention to keep the rodeo at the forefront of the town's attention throughout the year, so that "every citizen will do nothing but think rodeo, talk rodeo, eat rodeo, and sleep rodeo next June and July."[31] In that way, residents could convince visitors that the town's summer entertainment really did mark a "revival of the early range and roundup days of the cattle country here."[32] Like the Cody businessmen, rodeo boosters tried to create within Red Lodge the kind of western fantasy world they believed tourists would pay for.

As the popularity of the rodeo grew, the Wild West facade of the dude ranch and rodeo expanded to include not only local residents but also the very buildings in which they lived and conducted business. First of all, starting in the 1920s, the Red Lodge townscape gradually acquired a rustic veneer — a smattering of log cabins and rough-wood storefronts meant to convince observers of the town's western identity. Not coincidentally, dude rancher Al Croonquist took the lead in establishing this Wild West architecture within the town borders. Employing skilled Finnish craftsmen, Croonquist built several log cabin–style homes throughout the town, modeled after the dude ranch cabins at his Camp Senia. Croonquist's own Red Lodge residence exemplified the incorporation of rusticity into the contemporary townscape. Perched against the town's western bluff, the Croonquists' winter home boasted a log frame, rock fences, wide veranda, and massive chimneys. Looking like a novelist's description of a cattle baron's abode, the log cabin–style house stood in stark contrast to the elaborately trimmed Victorian and Queen Anne mansions from the mining boom era, located just two blocks away. Croonquist's architecture caught the notice of the Red Lodge town council; when the town built a camp for tourists in the early 1930s (with New Deal funding), the council chose to use this same rustic, log cabin–style construction, complete with rock fences and chimneys.[33] Gradually, other business and home owners would begin to incorporate Old Western features into local buildings: covering brick walls with cedar shakes or adding a rubble of moss rock to a storefront to achieve an appropriately rugged look.[34] To the despair of later historic preservationists, residents masked much of the town's elegant, turn-of-the-century brickwork with the facade of a more popular version of the Old West — wood rather than brick, rustic instead of industrial. They covered the modern with an illusion of the old.

Like the "rugged" cedar shakes over industrial brick, what westerners actually produced in places like Cody and Red Lodge was not so much a re-creation of the Old West (hardly surprising), but a fascinating mélange of myth and modernity, commercialism and nostalgia, salesmanship and pride. Residents' efforts to turn Red Lodge into a real western town reflected not just a desire to attract more tourists but also a deeper need to valorize their own sense of belonging in the American West. To many residents, the Old West meant pride, heritage, and roots; they participated in the local rodeo and parades because they wanted to display and share a vital part of their lives and their history. Westerners adopted and promoted the national mythology of the West because it told a story they wanted to believe.[35] According to the myth, westerners built America and maintained its democratic institutions by settling and taming a wild land. Such people had to be tough, resourceful, and fiercely independent to conquer the West. Westerners, then, represented the best of a strong, courageous people. That's not a bad way to remember your grandparents, parents, or indeed yourself. Even recent transplants might cloak themselves with the glory of the myth that only special, hardy people survived in this hard, beautiful, wild place. Celebrating the Old West through rodeos, parades, dude ranches, and rustic storefronts reinforced the glamour of that mythologized past and made people proud of themselves and their place.

This meeting up of local history and economic needs with national mythologies and economics revealed some interesting, vital tensions about the Wild West and concepts of "authenticity," especially those surrounding the images of the western cowboy and Plains Indian. Locals insisted on a production of westernness that met the national expectations of the West. If that westernness could be grounded somehow in real characters or events, great. But the "authentic" in local Wild West celebrations increasingly came to be defined not on historic or present conditions, but rather against nationally produced images of the West. Like the new, rugged facades on downtown buildings, the quest to celebrate the Wild West tended to cover up the real West while creating a new authenticity in its place.

This process of creating authenticity can be seen most clearly in Red Lodge residents' efforts to incorporate authentic representatives of cowboys and Indians into the annual rodeo celebration. As residents struggled to re-create the Wild West in Red Lodge, they laid bare the complications and contradictions at the heart of the national myths enveloping the most popular regional characters. Determined to people their landscape with authentic (mythic) western figures, local residents consistently rejected working-class or Indian cowpunchers as adequate representatives of the cowboy hero. "Real" cowboys and Indians — whose lives were substantially more complicated (and interesting) than those of, say, the Virginian or Tonto — simply would not do. While publicly celebrating, even venerating, the romanticized cowboy and Indian, local residents gradually moved away from identification with the flesh-and-blood representatives of these groups, who were too modern and complicated to fit into the simple categories of the Wild West mythology. Instead, local people created paper and neon images of Indians (or their tepees) and invested rancher/capitalists with the mystique of the independent cowhand. They stripped away the complexities of history and modernity to create simple, easily comprehensible versions of these popular figures. As authenticity butted up against the myth, local townspeople redefined "authentic" so that it matched the expectations of the mythology.

Perhaps the deepest irony in Red Lodge's embrace of the Wild West lay in its twinned celebration/rejection of the mythology's most representative figures: the cowboy and the Indian. Indians, especially, had many modern and historical identities other than the mythic roles of "brave," "chief," and "squaw." Crow Indians, for example — to hit at the heart of western contradictions — were also cowboys. Indeed, some Crow had more legitimate claims to a cowboy past than most Red Lodge residents did. By the time of Red Lodge's founding in 1887, many of the cowboys in the area actually were Indians — a historical fact not recorded by Frederic Remington or Theodore Roosevelt, who championed the image of the heroic Anglo cowpuncher. Photographs from the 1890s show several Indian cowboys who worked the range around Red Lodge. An 1897 photo of the Dilworth outfit delivering cattle to Miles City included at least two Indian cowboys, each with long braids but otherwise dressed in "typical" cowboy fashion — long-sleeved shirt, neckerchief, vest, broad-brimmed hat, and six-gun strapped to the hip.[36]

Twentieth-century Crow Indians continued that cowboy tradition, raising cattle and horses on the expanses of the reservation. In the 1930s, tribal leader Robert Yellowtail began building up the reservation's cattle herds even further, taking back up to forty thousand acres of leases from white ranchers so that even more Indian cowpunchers could work the land.[37] The Crow also possessed a proud history as rodeo cowboys dating back to 1903, when Sam Bird-in-Ground won a world championship in bronc riding at Miles City. Indian rodeo champions like Bird-in-Ground and Nez Percé cowboy Jackson Sundown had a great influence on Indian youngsters who admired and emulated these heroes. Bird-in-Ground's legacy lived on among his family, including his grandson, Dan Old Elk, who in his early years "went to rodeos, broke horses, and did all the things an Indian boy would do."[38] Cowboys were Indians and Indians were cowboys in the American West.

Red Lodge residents, like other Americans, rejected much of this intertwined western world of Indian cowboys/cowboy Indians. In the first few years of the Red Lodge rodeo, however, some of this fascinating mélange of modern western identities pushed through more studied displays of the mythic Wild West. When the rodeo organization was new and its structure more fluid, Indians participated more fully in the entire production, and their performances reflected this more complicated western history that Wild West shows and popular movies rarely addressed. At the 1930 rodeo, contestants were somewhat scarce so Indians participated in a variety of events that two years later they would not take part in. At the rodeo itself, for example, Sampson Bird Hat won not only the Indian relay on 5 July but also placed second in the Roman Race on the Fourth and won the wild cow milking contest on 6 July. Other Indians placed in the cowboy race, calf roping, and the half-mile free-for-all. Outside the immediate rodeo activity, Indians also assumed important "non–Wild West" roles at the 1930 celebration that would not be repeated in later years. Most prominent, the Indian team from Hardin took on the Red Lodge and Bearcreek baseball teams with Chief Russell Whitebear (a Haskell Institute graduate) filling the dual roles of umpire and war dance performer.[39] Further muddying distinctions between Indian and non-Indian, an anonymous "Indian boy" won first prize for being the "Best Dressed junior cowboy" at the 1932 parade and two "local boys" received honors as "Toughest dressed junior cowboy" for running through the parade wearing nothing but Indian makeup.

This fluidity between all-American sport and Wild West performance, cowboy and Indian costumes, Indian and non-Indian rodeo competition, soon gave way, however, to more clearly set distinctions between Indians in feathered headdresses and white cowboys roping calves. Although Red Lodge's rodeo board made no public proclamation about Indian roles and events, there is no evidence of other Indians dressing as cowboys in later parades, non-Indian boys playing at being Indian, or Indian baseball teams playing the local nine. According to local newspaper coverage, Indians did not exist after the first few rodeos except as participants in specific "Indian" events and as exotic additions to the Fourth of July parade. The boundary-shifting cowboy Indian faded from the rodeo's public identity, replaced by the more familiar imagery of the Plains Indian "warrior" and "squaw."[40] Indeed, rodeo boosters consistently emphasized the point that the visiting Crow Indians would dress "appropriately" for the occasion, that is, in the "feathered head-dresses," buckskins, and moccasins that would lend "color and vividness to the early picture which this annual event presents."[41]

In fact, Crow Indians themselves often catered to this more mythic vision of "Indianness." As historian Philip Deloria points out, Indians by the 1920s and 1930s had become quite adept at "imitating non-Indian imitations of

Indians."[42] Modern Indians, just like Red Lodge boosters, recognized the economic value of playing to the expectations of tourists. This practice of Indians "playing Indian" actually had a long history dating back to Buffalo Bill Cody's Wild West show. Since the late nineteenth century, American Indians had contracted with showmen of various types to perform as "Indians." These professional performers, called "show Indians" by reservation agents, accepted money and other forms of compensation for acting the role of wild or primitive Indians. Most show Indians took roles in productions like Buffalo Bill's Wild West, playing out the dramatic Indian attack scenes for which the Wild West became famous. Others traveled to events such as Chicago's 1893 Columbia Exhibition and the 1909 Alaska-Pacific-Yukon Exhibition in Seattle; there they set up camps displaying "primitive" Indian cultures. Indians who did not get positions in the grander shows often agreed to attend off-reservation fairs and Fourth of July shows in return for food and other items.[43] Many Indians actually competed for the privilege of performing at such events. As historian L. G. Moses has shown, these shows and celebrations provided Indians, whose cultural practices were actively suppressed by well-meaning reformers and agents, the opportunity to "play" at being Indian — dressing like warriors and performing war dances. Even though their performances perpetuated stereotypes of Indian behavior, show Indians took advantage of Wild West shows and small-town fairs to express part of their cultural identity.[44]

By the 1930s, the Crow Indians around Red Lodge certainly knew the value of "playing Indian" for tourists in search of the "authentic" Wild West. Crow member Max Big Nose (who once gave a seminar on tourism promotion to the Red Lodge Commercial Club) even established his own Indian camp at Laurel, Montana, about forty miles north of Red Lodge. There he and his wife demonstrated Indian crafts for curious (and paying) tourists and let them poke around the couple's buffalo-skin tepees. Dressed in an imposing full-feathered headdress, Big Nose used his own "Indianness" as a source of income. Like Red Lodge rodeo promoters, Big Nose and his followers understood the economic value of reproducing the mythic Wild West for the inquisitive tourists who thought they touched a part of the Old West when they opened the buffalo hide door of a "genuine" Crow tepee. They played the roles that tourists wanted to see. Red Lodge boosters and Max Big Nose alike advanced an image of the traditionally "Indian" Indian, not the boundary shifting figure of the cowboy Indian.

So when Red Lodge started its rodeo, local Crow Indians had long practice in "acting Indian" for outsiders and readily contracted with the Red Lodge Rodeo Association to provide these services for a set price. Under the contract with the rodeo association, Indians agreed to dress "authentically," ride in the daily rodeo parades, compete in specific Indian events, and establish a tepee camp alongside the arena that was essentially an open museum for curious observers. Unfortunately for local rodeo organizers, though, "authentic" Indians were in high demand in the 1930s. The Crow Indians, in fact, became so adept at playing "Indian" for tourists by the end of the decade that Red Lodge boosters began to have trouble luring them into town for the annual rodeo. Local histories have often assumed that Red Lodge leaders chose to stop including Indians in the celebration, but in fact the opposite took place.[45] Year after year in the 1940s, rancher and rodeo promoter Lou Tunnicliff sought to bring Indians into Red Lodge for the rodeo, hoping to add Indian "color" to the show, but the Crow spurned his efforts, preferring to perform at Cody, Laurel, and other communities where, apparently, they received more remuneration for their performances as "authentic" Plains Indians.[46]

Red Lodge rodeo promoters, then, had to look elsewhere to obtain the validating presence of "authentic" Indians for their annual celebration. Discouraged, perhaps, by the Crows' intransigence (and costly demands), townspeople solved the problem, in part, by turning to symbols and images to create an Indian "presence" in Red Lodge. The symbolic Indian — whose authenticity lay in the town's claim to an Indian prehistory — proved a suitable alternative to the capitalistic, expensive Crow. Although not as aesthetically satisfying as actually seeing (and maybe touching) a "real, live Indian," Indian images proved much more convenient and manipulable, and town leaders readily adopted them. Residents especially favored the Indian tepee, which by the late 1930s became recognized as the symbol of Red Lodge, "the land of the red tepee."[47] "Red Lodge," as local promoters pointed out, referred to Indian dwellings or tepees. Thus, businesses and organizations began to use the red tepee as shorthand for Red Lodge, putting it on bumper stickers, pennants, and Chamber of Commerce brochures. The town, in this way, secured an "Indian" presence without having to negotiate with the Crow. (Nearby dude ranches, like Richel Lodge, settled for labeling cabins with "Indian names" or at least, as wrangler Marcella Littlefield put it, "English names that sound Indiany." Guests could have their choice of such cabins as "Mishe Nahma" [King of the Fishes],

"Singing Arrow," or "Shadow of the Forest" — all meant to give dudes a feel for being in Indian country without the trouble or expense of actually bringing Indians onto the ranch itself.)[48]

Significantly, Red Lodge residents chose to emphasize Indian *objects* — particularly the tepee — rather than images of human Indians. The Red Lodge tepee, as usually depicted in the 1930s and 1940s, stood empty. Although occasionally occupied by a "buck" and his "squaw" (especially in the 1920s), more often the tepee remained vacant but with the flap door open as if someone had just left. Some pictures even included smoke rising from the top of the dwelling, signaling that someone (presumably an Indian) was nearby but just out of view.[49] Figures of Indians remained around town — on store signs and advertisements — but the empty tepee developed into the Indian symbol of choice for area merchants. The vacant tepee stood for Red Lodge, the town named after Indian houses, not Indians themselves. The name "Red Lodge" meant that Indians had once inhabited the area, *not* that Indians actually still lived in the town. Local people, indeed, enjoyed the joke of outsiders inquiring after the town's nonexistent American Indian population: "What, No Red Men in Red Lodge?" the *Carbon County News* teased after one visiting salesman expressed disappointment that the town had no Indian inhabitants.[50] Historical blurbs in local pamphlets in the mid–twentieth century reinforced the idea of the disappeared Indian. These accounts of the past, meant for visitors passing through, rooted Red Lodge history in the area's original Indian occupants; according to these stories, however, the Indians had simply (and conveniently) vanished, leaving Red Lodge and the symbolic tepee behind. As a 1930s pamphlet phrased it, the Crow moved on to let "the pale faced successors to the red skin ferret out the underground riches in the mountains near Red Lodge and Cooke City."[51] In the frozen image of the abandoned tepee, Red Lodge residents found a satisfying, uncomplicated representation of the Wild West.

Channeling the appropriate imagery of the West's other major figure — the cowboy — would prove somewhat more challenging. But if local boosters could simply make Indians "disappear," they could also figure out a way to make cowboys "appear" in Red Lodge. As with the Indians, the major difficulty would be to make the "right" kind of cowboy materialize for the annual rodeo and Wild West festivities. Like the Indian, the cowboy represented a complicated, somewhat troublesome figure for rodeo promoters, although on the surface he seemed just as simple as the image of the Plains warrior. Red Lodge promoters could not simply trot out local cowboys to enhance their summer celebration because these real cowboys did not exactly live up to the nationally venerated image of the heroic rider of the plains. The root of the cowboy's problem lay in his one essential contradiction: the mythic cowhand who symbolized American independence was a paid employee, and not very well paid at that. Real cowboys were working-class men whose only independence, as historian Robert G. Athearn put it, "was the right to quit at the drop of a hat."[52] "Real" cowboys simply could not assume the heavy cultural weight heaped on them by western mythology. America's most beloved hero, the cowboy presented a paradox that most modern observers simply chose to ignore and that Red Lodge leaders controlled by transferring the cowboys' glamour to other, safer figures.

The cowboy, of course, was a hero in Red Lodge as he was nationally by the 1930s.[53] People around the world readily recognized the cowboy as the symbol not only of the West but of America. Squinting into the sun, clad in leather chaps and vest, the figure of the cowboy evoked masculinity, freedom, and love of open lands; he was the man that other men wished they could be and women wished they could have. In movies and novels, the cowboy embodied the ideal hero. Owen Wister created the mold in *The Virginian* (1901), which other writers and filmmakers tirelessly re-created. Zane Grey's immensely popular books, like *Riders of the Purple Sage* (1912), painted cowboys as honest, forthright men who recognized right from wrong and commanded the knowledge of the natural world to ensure that right triumphed. In a world where men and women felt themselves increasingly confined by walls, cities, and social structures, the cowboy riding across the sage represented independence and wholesome, simple values. No matter that cowboys were actually paid employees of corporate enterprises, their celebrated aura of freedom was more important than mundane realities. Image overwhelmed the physical cowboy.

The national mythology of the cowboy swept up westerners as well as easterners in its powerful embrace. Even real cowboys were not immune to the mythic figure of "the cowboy." Carey McWilliams witnessed firsthand the "mimicry and imitation" that made up much of "Western spirit, so-called." He recalled that "my father had no end of difficulty, as a pioneer cattleman in northwestern Colorado, in keeping his cowboys from playing the role of Cowboy. They spent long hours in the bunkhouse on dull days devouring cheap romances of the West and insisted on dressing and acting and talking like the characters in their favorite romances."[54] Indeed, many cowboys as early as the 1890s had taken up the profession because they dreamed of living like their heroes from Wild West stories. Inspired by dime novels, fifteen-year-old Art Wahl headed out to Montana from Norway in 1907 to "become a cowboy and kill Indians." With typical youthful confidence, he did not worry about taking up a strange new profession because "I knew all about it through those books."[55] Western town builders, too, accepted and reinforced the media-generated image of the romantic cow handler. In fact, to many westerners movie cowboys were more "real" than the actual cowpunchers who worked the region's ranges. When town leaders in Billings (about sixty miles from Red Lodge) decided to commemorate their city's connection to a ranching past with a statue of a "range rider," they did not choose a specific local cowboy or even an anonymous cowhand; their statue actually depicted William S. Hart, the man whose movie characters seemed best to epitomize the heroic, noble cowboy.[56]

In local, western places, the stigma attached to the rough, working cowpuncher of the 1890s never faded away entirely, which is why movie cowboys like Hart proved much more appealing than their real-life counterparts. Cowboys in the West remained paid employees, seasonal workers whose place in local society was unclear. Some ranch hands stuck to a single ranch for several years, but many others moved on at the end of the season, looking for employment farther south when snow closed off the ranges in Montana. These "real," drifting cowboys retained a rough image in places like Red Lodge. In 1937, for example, a Red Lodge judge summed up one unsavory character as "more or less of the cowpuncher type, the Western type, that sometimes gets boisterous or maybe even mean."[57] The cowboy was a tough, potentially dangerous character who, indeed, may have cultivated some of that "boisterous" image. McWilliams blamed much of the wild antics of his father's cowpunchers on their desire to imitate the free ways of Western romance heroes. Such behavior, however, even in the 1930s, still played better in fiction than in a "civilized" community. Boosters and residents valorized the cowboy-hero of the movies and paperbacks — fictional figures brought to life mostly by easterners — but remained suspicious of the rootless drifter of the cattle range.

Fortunately, however, westerners soon learned how to create appealing, local representatives of the "authentic" (mythic) cowboy by the 1920s and

1930s. Western dude ranches and rodeos, especially, worked to build up the romanticized, Hollywood vision of the cowboy. Dude wranglers, first of all, helped to perpetuate the image of cowboys as clean, polite, helpful figures — romantic in the way of summer vacation heroes. Wranglers, or horse handlers, helped dude ranch guests live out their fantasies of life in the Old West. Although some purists would insist that wranglers were not cowboys because they did not work cattle, dude wranglers readily assumed the aura and costume of the cowboy, helping to tie the dude ranch to the romance of Hollywood and fictional Westerns. These "cowboys" soon found out that being courteous to guests, telling then yarns around the campfire, or even learning to play the guitar would enhance both their job security and their pay. They were a far cry from the rough and dirty working-class hooligans who had terrorized decent Red Lodge residents in the early 1890s. A whole romance eventually developed around the cowboy wranglers at dude ranches. They became heroes in popular novels like Mary Roberts Rinehart's *Lost Ecstasy,* Caroline Lockhart's *The Dude Wrangler,* and Gene Hoopes's books on Jim Dawson, a former cowhand and army scout turned wrangler. According to historian Lawrence R. Borne, Dawson epitomized the ideal of the dude ranch wrangler: "He was an expert horseman, cook, guitar player, singer, and storyteller; he possessed excellent health, loved wide open spaces and disliked cities, was a crack shot with a pistol, and, of course, was exceedingly attractive to women."[58]

Rodeo riders, even more than the dude wrangler, self-consciously combined the worlds of the "real" cowhands with the imagery of the popular cowboy hero to create the kind of western figure that tourists wanted to see. Red Lodge's first and most famous rodeo cowboys and cowgirls, the Riding Greenoughs, grew up working cattle and horses, but they learned how to dress from movies and Wild West shows. Marge, Alice, Turk, and Bill Greenough, like other rodeo riders, had to do more than just stay on a bucking horse; they had to cater to a public that expected to be entertained. Anxious to draw an interested, paying audience, rodeo riders and promoters played with the same extravagant western imagery that had made Buffalo Bill's Wild West so popular. Cowgirls, especially, cultivated a fanciful western image in eastern cities. In the 1930s, rodeo women relied on contract work. Rodeos hired them to perform trick-riding stunts and compete on broncing horses and steers. As Mary Lou LeCompte has pointed out, women quickly recognized that flashy, exotic outfits would get them more contracts. Cowgirls like Marge and Alice Greenough found sewing deftness almost as vital to their success as their roping and riding skills. Traveling with their sewing machines, these women whipped up glamorous costumes with billowing silk sleeves and flowing neckerchiefs to emphasize their femininity along with their western identity.[59] Like Little Annie Oakley of the Wild West show and Calamity Jane of Edward L. Wheeler's Deadwood Dick series, women riders made exotic "western" clothing a vital part of their personas.

The worlds of Hollywood and rodeo had actually intertwined for years by the time Red Lodge held its first rodeo. Rodeo riders not only dressed like movie cowboys, but they also played cowboys and cowgirls in many of the early Western movies. Turk and Alice Greenough, for example, both actively sought work in Hollywood in the 1930s and 1940s. Alice played some small parts in a variety of movies, including *The Californians* in 1937. Her Hollywood work also included teaching Dale Evans, Roy Rogers's new cowgirl love interest, how to ride. The most famous cowgirl in movies, as Alice found out to her disgust, had never even been on a horse.[60] Alice's brother, Turk, a world-champion saddle bronc rider, also got a few small parts in films, mostly performing stunts. In movies like John Wayne's *Angel and the Badman*, Turk played any number of good and bad guys shooting at each other and falling off horses in countless chase scenes. Turk made an even bigger splash in the nonrodeo entertainment world with his 1942 marriage to fan dancer Sally Rand, whose nude "bubble dance" had been the sensation of the 1933 Chicago World's Fair. Turk's marriage captivated Red Lodge residents, some of whom kept scrapbooks of the couple's courtship and wedding, recording every event in their public life.[61] Like most fairy-tale marriages, this one lasted only briefly, but long enough to reflect the glamour associated with top rodeo riders in the 1940s. Although rooted in the world of real ranch work, these local cowboys and cowgirls did their part to glamorize the image of the rodeo rider and create the rodeo cowboy as one of the most popular local versions of the nation's beloved hero.

The alluring call of the rodeo, however, took these performing cowboys and cowgirls away from the very West that the rodeo seemed to celebrate. Most rodeo performers in these early days, like the Greenoughs, came out of ranching families, but their profession took them out on the road for much of the year; they became professional wanderers. Except for the very top riders, few cowboys and cowgirls made much money on the rodeo circuit, which kept performers continually on the move in the hopes of earning a stake at

Playing cowgirl during her short marriage to rodeo rider Turk Greenough, fan dancer Sally Rand seems to be enjoying her stay at Ben Greenough's rustic western ranch house. In the 1940s, Packsaddle Ben kept an Old West collection of Indian arrowheads and other memorabilia at this ranch, which he readily showed off to curious visitors. His family later donated the collection to the county museum. (Carbon County Historical Society photo)

the next show down the road. Even top moneymakers like the Greenoughs spent much of the year living out of trailers, traveling around the nation trying to catch as many rodeos as possible. And after so many years away, many of these riders never settled back into the small-town life of places like Red Lodge. Marge and Alice Greenough frequently visited Red Lodge, but they eventually chose to live permanently in Arizona; Turk decided to retire in Nevada. Local residents claimed these exciting, attractive rodeo riders as their own, but such performers no longer seemed completely rooted in Red Lodge or the real cowboy's ranching life.

So, although the glamorous rodeo cowboys and wranglers assumed the role of "authentic" cowhands for the touring public, westerners themselves had to look elsewhere for a satisfying representative of the golden days of the Old

West.[62] They found this figure in the person of the established rancher, the man with ties to the free and easy ways of the cowboy but with solid roots in the national ideals of capitalism and private property. These were men like Ben Greenough and Malcolm Mackay, stable scions of the local community who also happened to be living representatives of the town's ranching and cowboy history.

Ranchers such as Greenough and Mackay, more than wranglers or rodeo riders, reconciled the contradictory symbolism of the American cowboy. Ranchers, whether they worked cattle or dudes, combined the cowboy's outdoor work — the freedom of the range — with the responsibilities and independence of capitalistic land ownership. An employer rather than an employee, the rancher enjoyed, theoretically, the independence that Thomas Jefferson had believed to be the basis of a democratic society (although debts owed to local banks often compromised that vaunted independence). Possessing most of the physical glamour of the cowboy — horse, hat, boots, jeans, belt buckle — the rancher added steadiness and responsibility. As Robert G. Athearn has pointed out, the rancher was actually much more appealing to most Americans than the cowboy. If one looks closely at the Marlboro Man, the most ubiquitous "cowboy" in mass media in the late twentieth century, Athearn argues, one will notice "that in most of these advertisements he is no mere cowpoke. He is a stockman, a mature American with the proper wrinkles around his eyes to prove that he has been out of doors, but his dress is that of an owner, not of an employee — a businessman with roots, with property; and he is not a drifter. He is solid and conservative; and beyond all doubt he votes the straight Republican ticket."[63] Even cleaned up and presentable, the cowboy remained a wage laborer or an athlete competing for prize money. In the twentieth century, local ranchers took on the role of the settled cowboy, the organizer who stayed in one place and assumed responsibility for making sure everything worked; he was the "sticker" who invested his time, money, and heart in the community; he was the "real" cowboy.[64]

Local ranchers actually did much to promote this connection between themselves and the romantic imagery of the cowboy and the Old West. Enthusiastic about using the Red Lodge rodeo as a celebration of Wild West imagery, Mackay and Greenough assumed leading roles in the creation and support of the local production. Mackay served as the first president of the Red Lodge Rodeo Association and donated hundreds of dollars to the event. Greenough, meanwhile, channeled his energies into promoting the rodeo: marching in regional parades with a string of packhorses bearing signs and placards reminding people to attend Red Lodge's big celebration. Neither profited much from the transference of the Old West into the modern town, but both remained convinced that this kind of living history played a vital role in maintaining a proud heritage not only for Red Lodge but for the entire country. These two former cowboys did not want the nation to forget what the Old West stood for: freedom, democracy, opportunity.[65] The Old West — and the cowboy/rancher — represented the best of America, the most prized values of an energetic, masculine nation.

Significantly, Mackay and Greenough represented two different types of cowboys who came out West in the late nineteenth century — one the heir to a huge eastern fortune, the other an impoverished orphan. Both, however, were determined to share their Old West memories, to make sure that the younger generation would not forget, as Mackay put it, "the folks that 'fought it through.' "[66] Their stories of life on the range provided the kind of grounding local civic leaders needed for their annual Wild West pageant. The presence of these two old cowpunchers validated Red Lodge's claims to a cowboy heritage. Although their lives as Carbon County ranchers could not have been more different, Greenough and Mackay shared a love of the grand mythology of the cowboy West, a mythology that they wrapped around their own tales of ranching and cowpunching in the early days of Carbon County.

Of all the "pioneer" cowboys still in Red Lodge in the 1930s, Ben Greenough did the most to keep alive the Old West "spirit." The bearded and grizzled patriarch of his rodeoing family, Greenough reveled in his role of old-time rancher and pioneer, and he possessed all the stories, connections, and memorabilia to support his position as Red Lodge's most popular old cowpuncher. An orphaned newspaper boy from New York City, Ben moved to Montana in 1886 to work as a cowboy and eventually settled down on a homestead. While working the range at the end of the nineteenth century, he ran into such well-known figures as Calamity Jane and Liver-Eating Johnson, encounters that would later establish his claims to represent the real Old West. A teetotaler who swore to whip any of his kids who took up drinking or smoking, Greenough had no part with the antics of wild cowhands. Instead he struggled his whole life to hang on to the ranch he established at the foot of the Beartooths and on which he and his wife, Myrtle, raised their eight children.[67]

By the 1930s, though, with four of his offspring established as rodeo luminaries, Ben had some time to enjoy his local notoriety as a remnant of the Wild West. He did all he could to keep his vision of that West alive in the community, playing the role of "cowboy" much as area Crow played "Indian" at the annual rodeo. With his full beard and wide-brimmed hat, Ben *looked* like an old-time cowhand and he relished the nickname of "Packsaddle Ben," which he had acquired from Liver-Eating Johnson in the 1880s. And he gleefully recounted lively stories of all-night horse rides, fleeing from Indian warriors, and working for Calamity Jane — tales worn smooth with repeated telling, but that continued to captivate audiences to the end of his life.[68] An active member in several regional pioneer and cowboy associations, in 1939 Greenough was elected "wagon boss" at the organizational meeting in Billings of the Montana-Wyoming Cowboys' Association of the '80s and '90s. He also organized a local Carbon County pioneer society with membership criteria that a person had arrived in the county by 1900 and lived most of his or her life in the area.[69] Packsaddle Ben was a permanent feature not only at Red Lodge rodeo parades but also at Billings's annual rodeo and "Go West Days." Parade watchers could count on seeing Greenough leading a team of mules in these events, cheerfully conversing with the crowd in between cussing at his animals. He also welcomed visitors into his log cabin–style home, eagerly showing off his growing collection of western relics — Indian arrowheads, old tools, plows, guns.

An appealing, friendly old coot, Packsaddle Ben charmed New York City reporters when he visited his children at the Madison Square Garden rodeo in 1939. The *New York World–Telegram* followed his visit to his old family home, his participation in the rodeo parades, and the hit he made at a local children's hospital, where he regaled young patients with stories of the wild characters of the Old West.[70] A local radio station, enchanted by the colorful old westerner, even offered to make him a permanent guest on one of its shows.[71] New Yorkers apparently liked the interpretation of the Old West cowboy that Packsaddle Ben brought to the East. Like his stories of the Wild West, Greenough's portrayal of the old-time cowhand grew ever smoother and more appealing the more he played it out for public consumption.

If Ben Greenough personified the solid, gruff, working-class cowpuncher turned small rancher, then Malcolm Mackay typified the fun-seeking, noble cowboy of the vanishing range turned grand rancher and scion of elite western society. Son of a prominent Wall Street banker, young Mackay headed out

West in the late 1890s, arriving in Red Lodge in 1901. He was one of hundreds of young adventurers from the East, often wealthy men from established families who came west to take part in the "wild, free life" of the vanishing cattle frontier.[72] Texas cowpuncher Teddy "Blue" Abbott recalled that the Montana range was crawling with this type by the 1890s — young men seeking to live out the western adventure stories of Theodore Roosevelt and Frederic Remington.[73] And Mackay found in the West what he had expected to find.

Buffered by money, connections, and respectability, Mackay led a carefree life of hunting big game and riding the range, where he met "picturesque" folk and lived through the type of ranch adventures that his friend Charlie Russell, the "Cowboy Artist," later captured in sketches and paintings.[74] He delighted in witnessing "western" events such as a bank robbery and shootout in Red Lodge, a dramatic episode that "added a zest and charm to things for us, for we were full of longing for real adventure in any of the western molds."[75] But although Mackay relished the wild life of the western range, he was not wild himself; he readily settled into the comfortable life of rancher and big game hunter once he had had enough fun playing cowboy. With money inherited from his family, Mackay eventually established one of the largest ranches in Carbon County, maintained a winter residence in New Jersey, and served as president of the Red Lodge Rodeo Association in the 1930s.

With their wealth and gentility, "gentleman cowpunchers" like Mackay fit readily into Owen Wister's romanticized image of the Virginian, the aristocrat of the prairies. And they had the money and time to cultivate that imagery. Mackay embedded his vision of the West in his 1925 memoir, *Cow Range and Hunting Trail*, a firsthand account of his cowboy adventures. Written to widen Americans' "conception of the cattle country and enhance . . . respect for the folks that 'fought it through,'" the book recalled a West of hardworking women, rugged men, and enough colorful characters to provide sidekicks for dozens of B-Western heroes. Mackay's cowboy (himself) lived a life filled with "happiness and hardihood [and] a great love for the open places, and the folks I met there."[76] His firsthand account of Red Lodge's cowboy heritage never strayed very far from the established mythology of the heroic cattle frontier. Charlie Russell illustrated Mackay's book, grounding the work even more fully in the popular Wild West.[77]

Mackay's and Greenough's vision of the ranching heritage of Carbon County, so similar to that described by Theodore Roosevelt and his compatriots, became an important source for the developing western pageant of the Red Lodge rodeo in the 1930s when the demands of the tourism industry called for the resuscitation of the cowboy as hero. Ranchers like Greenough and Mackay self-consciously created themselves not only as ranchers but as successful and romantic cowboys. But they were the cowboys who had become property owners and respected members of the community. Secure in their positions, both men could afford to embellish the exploits of their youth and use their connections to the cattle frontier to establish their authenticity as representatives of the Old or Wild West. And through these men — living representatives of the golden years of the West — Red Lodge residents laid claim to a Wild West past that they actively tried to stage within the town itself as a way to attract and please tourists. Mackay donated money and time to making the Red Lodge rodeo a success and in so doing established the idea that area ranchers should take a lead in creating and maintaining this annual event. Greenough's own children grew into top-flight rodeo riders who carried old Ben's name around the country and brought the glamour of the modern rodeo into Red Lodge on an annual basis. Both men served to tie Red Lodge into an idealized vision of the old-time cowboy, who was rapidly becoming the symbol of choice for town boosters.

Unfortunately, though, such "authentic" representatives of the Old West were few and far between by the 1930s. Red Lodge had many more miners, clerks, and housewives than it had rancher/cowpunchers. Ranchers like Mackay and Greenough provided vital validation of the town's ranching heritage, and they developed into convenient receptacles of the nation's reverence for cowboys. But tourists wanted to see more than just two old men, no matter how colorful and authentic they might be. Red Lodge boosters valued the participation of local ranchers in the annual western celebration, but they needed much, much more obvious westernness around town during this summer celebration.[78]

All the complicated unraveling of layers of the "authentic" cowboy aside, the town simply needed more *visible* cowboys in order to please the paying tourists. Remember that through the 1920s Red Lodge remained a town identified more with industry and corporate capitalism than with cows and lassos. So where was this town of immigrant miners and shopkeepers going to find more cowboys? The solution, which boosters pounced upon quickly, was to turn Red Lodge's industrial and white-collar workers into convincingly "western" westerners (i.e., cowboys and cowgirls) by clothing them in appropriately western attire. To be convincingly western, the entire town would have to dress up like cowboys and cowgirls.

So, in the 1930s, Red Lodge civic leaders initiated a strident, persistent campaign to cajole, browbeat, and shame residents into looking like cowboys. Ironically, like much else about Red Lodge's "re-creation" of the authentic Wild West, this "cowboy" fashion that boosters began to press upon residents had much of its roots in eastern perceptions of westernness. Indeed, eastern influence on western-style clothing dated back at least to the turn of the century. Several sources suggest that cowpunchers around the West self-consciously modeled themselves after the cowboys from popular fiction and movies. Cowboy aficionados have made much of the practicality of "cowboy" clothes, but, according to Laurel Wilson, photographs of cowboys actually at work in the late nineteenth and early twentieth centuries showed only occasional use of such "typical" cowboy attire as chaps, bandannas, and revolvers. She argues that cowboys learned to emphasize certain distinctive types of clothing, modeling themselves after descriptions of cowboys in dime novels and the cowboy performers in Buffalo Bill Cody's Wild West shows. An astute showman, Cody gave his audiences what they wanted to see — exaggerated woolly chaps, guns, and big neckerchiefs that identified the Wild West cowboy of the popular imagination. In their formal pictures, working cowpunchers drew upon these popular images of the cowboy, often tricking themselves out in their best and finest, deliberately adorning themselves with holstered guns, bandannas, chaps, big hats, and other attire readily recognized as cowboy wear by Americans.[79] For many cowpunchers, these clothes become part of a costume, a way to set themselves off from other, lesser workers. Early-twentieth-century cowboy actors such as Tom Mix, who wore finely tooled boots, ostentatious hats, and elaborate vests both on and offscreen, made this look even more famous.[80] Mix and rodeo riders who dressed to please the crowds established the flashy "western" look that easterners expected to see from all westerners. The cowboys' fancy-dress outfits entered the national and regional imagination as an identifying feature of westernness that westerners themselves would eventually begin to adopt as their own.

The "western" fashion adopted by westerners in the 1930s and 1940s was even refiltered through eastern tourists and fashion houses before landing on the heads, feet, and torsos of local residents in places like Red Lodge. Many

items on the approved list of western clothing checked off by rodeo boosters —
"Loud shirts, handkerchiefs, 10 gallon hats, cowboy jeans, leather jackets and
cowboy shoes" — were the same items that easterners wore during their stays
at dude ranches.[81] Dude ranchers, indeed, had done much to convince Americans that true westerners had to dress in a certain way. The process began simply enough. Dude ranchers advised guests to bring comfortable, warm
clothing — "outing togs" — with them to the West.[82] What started out as sen-
sible "outing togs" and "democratic" dressing down, however, quickly became
a fashion trend of its own, a popular mixture of romanticized western clothing and eastern chic. Dude ranchers' own fancy, dress-up duds (the bit of
"unreality" indulged in for visitors) set the tone, and by the early 1930s, dude
ranch guests who shucked fashionable city clothes for the trip out West ago-
nized over choosing the most fashionable and attractive dude clothes for their
rustic vacation.

Anxious to achieve the right western "look," easterners found advice in magazines like *Vogue*, which in 1936 compiled a list of appropriate clothes for dude
ranching that ran from silk neckerchiefs to practical underwear. Although rec-
ommending that dudes buy some of the "logical and necessary" attire from
merchants in western towns, *Vogue* also listed New York City stores that carried dude ranch clothing in a "better selection of colors" than was available in
the less-refined West.[83] The magazine also offered such invaluable tips as to
avoid shirts "with the inside white collar band; you wear them with the neck
open, and it's unsightly." Color, too, was important: "Clear yellows, blues, and
white are especially handsome with jeans," *Vogue*'s fashion advisers decreed,
but "pastels look feeble." The result, considered dressing like "the local cowboys" by *Vogue,* often astounded westerners. One unsympathetic Red Lodge
high school student scoffed that a "dude is first recognized by his elaborate costume, very unsubstantial for the rugged life on a Western ranch."[84] But not
everyone laughed. Where *Vogue* and Hollywood met at the western dude
ranch, there sprang up a ready market for a new style of western clothing that
westerners themselves would eventually learn to wear.[85]

Town promoters, who understood that eastern tourists expected to see
westerners dressed like cowboys, worked with merchants to sell these "western" outfits to townspeople. Latching onto Schwoob's advice and the Cody
experiment with western appearances, Red Lodge boosters tried almost desperately to get local residents to look like real "westerners" — to make them

over into fantasy cowboys — for they were simply too disappointingly modern to suit the tastes of visitors. One "prominent visitor" in 1931 expressed dismay that instead of the "skirts and trousers, the spurs and boots, the hats and kerchiefs, the jackets and riding habiliments which distinguished the old day," he confronted "the most incongruous sight [of] the presence of parlor pajamas in the grandstand and on the streets." Anxious to please the paying tourists, the local newspaper editor warned residents that unless everyone worked "to restore here the atmosphere of the carefree west of a generation ago, without that atmosphere the annual western entertainment will wither and die."[86] Parade organizers routinely gave prizes for "best-dressed" cowboys and cowgirls and sometimes handed out free rodeo passes to children who rode horses up to the rodeo gates. In 1935, the Rodeo Board even formed a specific committee on "cowboy regalia" to encourage western-style dress during the summer. This committee sponsored not only a "kangaroo court" to fine those not dressed western during the summer months but also beard-growing contests to encourage businessmen to add a grizzled look to their faces.[87] Pressed by the need to generate a real Wild West atmosphere about Red Lodge, boosters set out on a campaign to make everyone in town dress like a westerner from a Hollywood movie or maybe an eastern dude loafing around at Camp Senia.

Westerners, however, did not eagerly adopt this "western" look for themselves. Modern lifestyles, poverty, or sheer reluctance to dress up for boosters led many residents to resist the call to cowboy clothing. Although some Red Lodge locals eagerly participated in the parades and took home trophies for best-dressed something, others attended the rodeo in their most stylish attire or in the clothes their parents got for them from the town's relief office.[88] Into the 1940s, the chair of the Rodeo Regalia Committee continued to plead with residents to wear "western duds" because "tourists coming into Red Lodge expect to see a certain amount of western atmosphere in keeping with the true western setting of Red Lodge."[89] As a committee member explained, visitors "from the east expect to see western garb, and it is not a policy of the city to disappoint their guests."[90] Residents needed to cooperate so that the town would be "attractive to tourists."[91] By 1948, though, organizers who urged residents to "show our visitors a real western time in a true western atmosphere" were content if people would wear only *one* article of western regalia, "either a scarf, boots, shirt, or frontier pants."[92] Although some townspeople plunged into the rodeo's Wild West celebration with gusto, others obviously resisted boosters' concerted efforts to transform them into "westerners."

Gradually, however, many residents adopted at least some of the boosters' suggestions about dressing western. Business owners, especially members of the Chamber of Commerce who were desperate to promote the rodeo, most readily embraced the effort to make townspeople look more like cowboys. These middle-class men and women ran the kangaroo court and participated most actively in the various beard-growing and costume contests. They became the most visibly "cowboy" of the town's residents. Ironically, then, by the 1930s and 1940s, the imagery of the cowboy in Red Lodge was transferred from the dangerous, transient cowhands of the 1890s to not only established ranchers but also to the respectable, bourgeois elements of the little coal town. The settled proprietors of the mid–twentieth century — townspeople and ranchers alike — appropriated the (adapted) clothing and proud wildness of the formerly detested cowpuncher.

This incongruous appropriation of cowboy imagery by bourgeois westerners produced, of course, some fascinating inconsistencies that residents smoothed over as well as they could. Most significant, the settled proprietors of downtown business houses had to find ways to mix the "wildness" of the Wild West with their own comfortable stability and desire for modern conveniences. Most residents and tourists wanted the pleasures of the rustic West but without its messiness, odor, inconvenience, and even danger, for much as westerners might want to recapture the Old West — for themselves as well as for tourists — no one really wanted to (or ever did) go back to the "good old days." It took a week or so, after all (and usually a heavy rain), to clean all the horse manure off the main street after a good-sized rodeo parade. And who actually wanted real hooligans firing off weapons within the town limits? Town leaders had to balance their wild westernness with their own place within the established order.

A 1926 Radiola advertisement beautifully illustrated this American attitude toward wildness and comfort. The ad shows a man stretched out against a fallen log in front of a crackling campfire in a beautiful western location; alone in this wild place, he is comforted by the presence of his Radiola radio — conveniently small enough to carry anywhere, even into the woods, and "sealed against summer heat and moisture." "There is no loneliness where there is a Radiola," the manufacturers assured a nation poised to head into the wilds for summer camping trips.⁹³ The forest without the radio, this ad suggests, was boring, inconvenient, old-fashioned. The West, like the woods, needed a boost of modernity to make it come alive, to make it interesting and appealing to outsiders and locals alike. What residents and visitors wanted was an appealing staging of the mythic West in at least some of its splendor and glory, but without sacrificing the modern conveniences and comforts upon which the new "leisure class" depended. They wanted the "Wild West" without any real "wild" in it.

Local ambivalence about wildness in the modern West highlighted the tension between myth and modernity in the presentation of the Wild West within the community. Wildness proved a double-edged sword to Red Lodge residents in the 1920s and 1930s. Unlike the 1890s, when boosters feared the very real wildness that surrounded Red Lodge, there was not much wild about the town by the early twentieth century. Once wildness was controlled, it became appealing. So instead of reassuring newcomers and visitors that the West was "safe," as they had in the 1890s, local people actually began to emphasize its dangers, highlighting any possible wildness. In 1934 a young Red Lodge student, Helena Warila, described the delight dude ranch wranglers took in "razzing" guests, relating wild tales that only confirmed the easterners' "already distorted ideas of massacres, Indian raids, and outlaws." Instead of shrinking from such stories of danger, however, the dude drank it all in gleefully. "He is so elated at actually being in the midst of this wilderness," Warila related, "that he goes about with mouth open, eyes staring, soaking up all the preposterous stories told him."⁹⁴

Aware of the appeal of wildness in the modern age, rodeo boosters worked even harder than local teenagers to convince outsiders that the West remained wild enough to be exciting. Business owners, for example, sought to convince outsiders of the "wildness" of Red Lodge's western celebration through a raucous publicity campaign. In the mid-1930s, boosters organized car caravans that carried "lusty cowboys and cowgirls" through the region to advertise the Red Lodge show. By letting off "pistol shots and cowboy shouts," Red Lodge civic leaders disguised as a "grizzled band of howling westerners" tried to create a feeling of wildness, if not quite danger, around the annual rodeo.⁹⁵ And the rodeo itself became not just an afternoon's entertainment, but a life-or-death struggle between man and beast. Instead of Indians, modern cowboys battled animals. As the *Picket-Journal* announced breathlessly, Turk Greenough and the other riders "engaged in [a] struggle with the outlaw horses,"[96] pitting "their strength and skill against some of the toughest, most wiry, twisting, sun-fishing outlaws that ever bolted from a rodeo chute."[97] All this took place before an audience that sat safe in the stands, observing but not participating, taking in the spectacle of wildness without the accompanying danger.

Indeed, if most tourists preferred to experience their western wildness from a safe distance, so did westerners themselves. However much they might relish the fun of wild rodeo imagery and teasing dudes about savage Indians, many westerners bristled at the implication that the West might *really* be dangerous in some way. Playing at the Wild West was fun, but the prestige of wildness — feeling superior from living in a rough place — had to be balanced against not only the modern realities of the West but also the resentment against being labeled as "backward" by a superior easterner.[98] Although she thought telling tall tales to easterners was funny, for example, Helena Warila insisted that the West was not "uncivilized and barbarous as it was in the days when first set-tled."[99] And dude ranchers who lauded their rough and natural accommoda-tions and surroundings were also quick to assure guests that "comfort" was an essential feature of dude ranch life. Dudes always had plenty of blankets, good food, and hot water; the West, after all, was a civilized, settled place.

Accordingly, boosters seemed to object only to *certain* types of modernity in Red Lodge during rodeo time. Although promoters lamented that residents' refusal to dress appropriately distracted from the Old West flavor of the rodeo, in many other cases "modernity" — like the slack pile that made such a con-venient flagpole site — only seemed to enhance the town's celebration of the Wild West. Ironically, the same Red Lodge Rodeo Association that rebuked locals for wearing "pajama outfits" saw nothing contradictory in combining parachute jumps, remote-control automobiles, and golf tournaments with their "characteristic revival of the Old West."[100] Like the ancient Roman sculp-tors who combined mature heads with youthful bodies to create the perfect male image — the wisdom of age joined with the vigor of youth — so too did Red Lodge rodeo promoters mix the best of the old West with the modern technology and conveniences of the new. Visitors jarred by modern attire in the rodeo stands made no similar objection to the presentation in 1935 of a "phantom car" driven around the arena "without driver or passenger, honking its horn and obeying all the dictates of a man in the grandstand holding a radio key."[101]

The residents of Red Lodge incorporated modern technology and modern pastimes into their celebration without hesitation. Golfing, for example, quickly became an important part of the rodeo program, and by 1931 a golf committee was a permanent fixture of the Red Lodge Rodeo Association. The rodeo arena featured auto stalls in which spectators could watch events from their parked cars. Publicity for the show also noted the modern movie theaters in town with "two of the best sound-equipped stations in the northwest." And one of the big features of the initial celebration was the stunt flying of a Sheridan pilot, who would also give adventurous people aerial tours of Yellowstone Park in his plane.[102] Later rodeos included carnivals with mechanized rides, boxing contests, and an airplane parachute jump. Although the Red Lodge Rodeo Association never ventured so far into the future to attempt aerial bulldogging (a failed experiment from a 1920s Wild West show), for several years in the 1930s Bill Greenough wrestled steers from the running board of a speeding car.[103]

In the mythic space of the twentieth-century Wild West, nothing made more sense.

Like the facades on downtown buildings, the Old West spread a thin coat over Red Lodge in the middle years of the twentieth century. By the 1940s and 1950s, that veneer had settled, becoming deeper and harder through repeated coatings. Log cabin–style structures, like that belonging to Al Croonquist and the new tourist camp, joined with the cowboy hats and neckerchiefs of rodeo supporters to mark the expanding mythic spaces of the Wild West in Red Lodge. The "western" veneer extended from the rodeo grounds to include much of the town, especially its businesses, which began to add items such as Indian jewelry and moccasins to local gift shops' inventories and frontier jargon to advertisements.

Perhaps the most painful indicator of the pervasiveness of western imagery in the modern West was the reinvention of the cowboy drawl. Although some southern-born westerners may have spoken in a slow drawl in the nineteenth century, this speech pattern had mostly faded from the region by the twentieth century — until relearned from movies and books. Returning to the West in 1946, Bernard DeVoto lamented the revival of this drawl as "the West began to succumb to the most damaging of its illusions, the notion that it is universally a race of cowpokes." Westerners, he observed, no longer used the

A 1953 advertisement from a Red Lodge promotional brochure urges locals and visitors alike to "Go Western in Red Lodge!" "Western" here equals "cowboy" (or "cowgirl") — the Indians are just for decoration. (Carbon County Historical Society collections)

assumed drawl simply as part of a joke, but as part of their desire to "drama-tize themselves to strangers."[104] The assumed "westernness" of the dude ranch and rodeo began to move into the everyday lives of western residents.

From the 1920s through the 1950s, Red Lodge promotional booklets read-ily mixed a kind of cowboy drawl with corny Indianesque phrasing. The effort produced incongruous results like the following description of the town from a Red Lodge Cafe menu in 1949: "Maybe you hone for local color that smacks of the old time West. Waal now, Podnah, our atmosphere ain't laden with powder smoke any more and lead isn't the common malady it used to be. Our best citizens claim that packing six guns interferes with their golf swing but we have local color, lots of it."[105] Or this passage, from a 1949 Fraternal Order of Eagles booklet for a state convention in Red Lodge:

Welcome to the land of the Shining Mountains and the Old Red Tepee! It's shore been many a moon since we've seen you around our wigwam, and we are more than proud to have you stop in at our diggin's. We've cooked up a few pots of stew and laid some extra bedrolls around the village to make your stay comfortable. . . . So climb off your hoss, toss your saddle on the cor-ral fence, and we'll have a pot of coffee brewing for you right soon. Wel-come, Podner, you're no stranger here after you sit once.[106]

Local residents designed these pamphlets to appeal to grown men and women. The Red Lodge Cafe, amazingly, even received a national award from the Chicago Advertising Club for its "Howdy Folks" menu.[107] And this kind of pseudo-western schlock appealed to more than just Chicago ad men. The Eagles targeted their "Welcome to the land of Shining Mountains" pamphlet at men and women *from Montana* — fellow westerners who knew that Mon-tanans didn't really talk like that in the mid–twentieth century, if they ever had. This sort of down-home drawl came out of movies and cheap cowboy novels, not the typical greeting of one middle-class fraternal brother to another. Westerners had adopted the persona created by Hollywood and writ-ers of Westerns to the extent that they were even using it on themselves as a fun kind of game or promotional gimmick.

Popular "westernness" had so imbedded itself into the physical West by the mid–twentieth century that westerners themselves adopted its markers to claim their place in the region. What started out as a marketing program turned into something much more personal and pervasive than a Chamber of Commerce "Go West" promotion. Westerners who had no roots in a ranching past incorporated the speech, clothes, and memories of that past — filtered through popular movies and novels — and turned them into a modern western identity. They began to dress, talk, and "act" like cowboys in their everyday lives. Motivated by the expectations of visiting tourists and bolstered by the presence of authentic "cowboys" in the region (capitalistic ranchers), western residents convinced themselves that they were, indeed, the heirs of the nineteenth-century mythic West.

Like John Barovich, the immigrant coal miner's son in the cowboy hat, western identities in the mid–twentieth century abounded with ironies and contradictions. Repeated public performances, however, smoothed out these ironies or made the contradictions seem humorous rather than significant. Brochures, such as the "Howdy, Podnah" booklet, deliberately played on the incongruities of modern western identity; contrasting six-guns with golf swings was funny and effective because such a pairing flew in the face of eastern expectations about westernness. Of course, the brochure itself presented and reinforced the very "westernness" that it poked fun of, and that reinforced westernness established a hold on many of the region's residents. When Barovich was a young man, cowboy hats became a popular symbol of westernness at local rodeos and Go West parades; as he grew older, such hats, which evoked the strength of the self-reliant rancher, became an accepted part of a Montana businessman's attire. By the time he was a middle-aged man, Barovich had worn his cowboy hat so often that it became part of his identity as a Montanan and a westerner. Where the scrutinizing outsider might find irony in the coal miner's son assuming the heritage of a long-gone era, Barovich, and others like him, saw simply a statement of who he was: a westerner.

5

"Hardy Pioneers, American and Foreign"
Public Ethnicity in the West

The Festival has been very important to the development of Red Lodge. Many years ago we had many little small ethnic groups that sort of kept to themselves, but with the Festival it started bringing us all together and appreciating the wonderful cultures that we had here.

—Bob Moran, 11 August 1996

In August 1951, when the dust from the annual Fourth of July rodeo had completely settled, Red Lodge residents took off their cowboy hats, boots, and Levis to go public with a different interpretation of local heritage. From 18 to 26 August, the town transformed itself from a remnant of the Wild West into a model of international harmony and American multiculturalism. Residents pulled out old German lederhosen and Norwegian *bunas,* dusted off accordions and bagpipes, learned ethnic folk dances, and re-formed ethnic choirs and orchestras. Guided by a particularly energetic set of community activists, townspeople produced and performed a nine-day festival of dancing, singing, free food, and craft displays. Finns, Scandinavians, Britons (Irish, Scots, and English), Italians, Yugoslavians (Serbians, Croatians, and Montenegrins), Germans, and Montanans each took charge of a given day to present their particular ethnic traditions (to fill up the nine days, Montanans had two days in the first years, and everyone participated in the final day's events).

Each group emphasized the colorful and entertaining aspects of its nationality, handing out free samples of *leftsa* and ravioli, playing accordions and harps, and dancing *kolas* and *lendlers* before curious onlookers. In the evenings, the Civic Center filled with ethnic dancers and singers for an hour of free entertainment. On the first night, the Finns, "in a blaze of colorful costumes," displayed not only singers and dancers but also "elderly ladies [who] worked at the home crafts of spinning, carding, and churning." Montanans arranged a community campfire, Yugoslavians performed a "Slovenian pillow dance," and the Italians "presented a picture of an out of door polenta party complete with wine, song and dancing."[1] Enthusiastically received by locals and visitors alike, the Festival of Nations quickly established itself as a permanent feature of Red Lodge life. Residents began what would become a half-century-long tradition of public celebration of the community's (Christian) European immigrant roots, an annual nonprofit venture designed "to help bring a closer understanding among people of all nationalities."[2]

The story of the Red Lodge Festival of Nations began, as did most of the town's major public events in the twentieth century, with considerations of tourism. Red Lodge in the early 1950s had survived the troubling years of the 1930s and 1940s, but just barely. The tourism push that had begun with the Red Lodge Rodeo and accelerated with the construction of the Beartooth Highway in the 1930s explained, at least in part, the town's persistence through some very trying years. The town's population had plummeted during the 1920s, from 4,659 in 1920 to only 3,026 in 1930. Between 1930 and 1940, the community's population dropped by only 76 people, to 2,950, despite that decade's sharp decrease in coal mining operations.[3] In 1950 a further decrease of 220 residents brought the town's total to 2,730—not terrific compared to the boom years of coal mining, but not too bad considering that nearby communities like Bearcreek and Washoe simply did not survive the relocations and readjustments of the war years.[4] Red Lodge *had* endured where others had failed and died away. Dazed but undaunted by the turmoil of the depression and war years, residents pushed ahead to reinforce the one remaining industry that seemed able to ensure the community's continued survival: tourism. A community ethnic festival seemed one way to make Red Lodge even more appealing to visitors, a way to bring essential tourist dollars into the local economy.

Tourism, though, is not the whole story of Red Lodge's survival and public identity in the twentieth century. Although tourism was (and is) an essential part of annual performances like the rodeo and Festival of Nations, these celebrations were never simply productions for tourists. The Festival of Nations, like the rodeo, became an annual staging of local heritage that provided an important "narrative structure" around which residents fit stories of the town's past and through which they presented local identity.[5] Like the rodeo, the Festival of Nations proffered a powerful and appealing interpretation of a past very much grounded in *real* history and *real* people, a past that made sense to the residents who performed in this ceremony year after year.

Unlike the rodeo, however, the festival drew from historical events that did not seem particularly "western" in the way of cowboys and Indians. By the 1950s, for various reasons, local people had become ready to publicly portray a different aspect of the local past — one that, interestingly enough, coexisted quite readily with the already popular and successful Wild West rodeo. Although they seemed quite different, even contradictory, on the surface, both celebrations presented significant public interpretations of local history and heritage that residents then integrated into their own sense of themselves and their place in Red Lodge.

To some residents, of course, the festival was mostly an event that filled up their motels or restaurants with paying guests. But the celebration's influence on the community ran much deeper than that. Residents who developed the festival in the 1950s created a powerful sense of modern and historical ethnicity as one of the key factors in the town's development and identity. This sense of ethnicity continued to shape the ways in which local people thought of their town and their past. Through the festival, local people learned to regard their town as peculiarly "ethnic" — different from other places because of its immigrant heritage and because of the festival itself, which publicly celebrated that ethnic background every year.

Fashioned variously out of cold war tensions, community pride, perceptions of the past, and the demands of a tourism-based economy, the festival grew into one of the defining features of Red Lodge life.[6] Through the festival, residents incorporated into their public sphere an appealing, classless, cleaned-up version of European ethnicity without reference to socialism, racialized discrimination, or labor strikes. Like the cowboy, the Red Lodge ethnic became a local symbol with somewhat tenuous connections to actual historical conditions. Red Lodge, through the Festival of Nations, presented ethnicity as a kind of timeless peasant culture, full of brightly embroidered dresses, exquisite pastries, and pretty songs about edelweiss. The immigrant miners' messy work, so evident in the huge slack piles on either side of town, became, like the class tensions that had divided the community, a muted background to the larger celebration of sauerkraut, saunas, dirndls, and tourist revenue.

Beyond the present-day awareness of ethnicity, the festival produced a popular interpretation of local history centered on the divisions between early immigrant populations.[7] By focusing on past ethnic differences now overcome, residents forged a comforting, celebratory story of local unity. In 1996, on the last night of the nine-day event, the festival coordinator (the local librarian, who had held the position for over forty years) gave a succinct version of the celebration's historicized message of community harmony. "The Festival has been very important to the development of Red Lodge," he informed the audience with obvious emotion. "Years ago we had many little small ethnic groups that sort of kept to themselves, but with the Festival it started bringing us all together and appreciating the wonderful cultures that we had here. . . . We have such a wonderful community here, and such wonderful people, and in the diversity that we find here and the appreciation of cultures we just are very fortunate."[8]

The festival, performed over decades, helped to create and then reinforce a particular version of the local past. But histories, including public pageants such as the Festival of Nations, themselves have histories, and the history of these histories can reveal much about how local, western identities are created.

Public celebration of Red Lodge's ethnic diversity developed in fits and starts in the 1930s, when Americans as a whole became more interested in immigrant cultures and more willing to celebrate ethnic contributions to the nation. Immigration policies, national demographic shifts, and reactions against the frightful xenophobia of the war years all influenced the acceptance of American pluralism. World War I and the new immigration laws of the 1920s drastically reduced the numbers of new aliens in the country, alleviating many of the tensions produced by millions of newcomers streaming into the nation every year. At the same time, the number of second-generation immigrants in the United States swelled to over 26 million by 1930, creating a new population of European "ethnics" much more acculturated into American society than their parents were.[9] In Red Lodge itself, the proportion of foreign-born residents dropped from 43 percent to 29 percent of the total population between 1920 and 1930, while the number of residents with foreign or mixed parentage increased from 31 percent to 40 percent.[10] National and local leaders noted these changing demographics and responded to them. Hollywood and the federal government, both intent on diffusing nativist sentiments, teamed up in the 1930s to foster positive national images of European ethnicity. Movies like *Black Legion* villainized phobic native Americans, while Franklin D. Roosevelt's Office of Education radio broadcasts stressed the "rich heritage" of the nation's immigrants.[11] A significant segment in the public school community also worked to include cultural diversity in education training and curriculums, while an ethnically diverse national intelligentsia promoted pluralism through its plays, articles, and books. Although the acceptance of America as a nation of immigrants would not really take hold until U.S. entry into World War II, European ethnicity was less threatening to most Americans by the 1930s than it had been a decade earlier.[12] Immigrants — like cowboys and Indians — could become a prominent part of the town's official public heritage when they no longer seemed much of a threat.

Driven by these national cultural changes as well as by local conditions, Red Lodge residents began to incorporate selected aspects of immigrant culture into the town's public identity from the 1930s into the early 1950s. "Unity" was the byword for this process of incorporation. Significantly, as townspeople struggled to keep their town alive through the closing of the East Side Mine in 1932 and the ongoing national depression, they began to think differently about what unity meant. While the local business classes continued to ground their concept of community identity in assumptions of the sanctity of American culture and government, public definitions of "American" and "Red Lodge" expanded to include not only the "cowboy" identity of the rodeo (where everyone was encouraged to indulge in a general "western" imagery) but also selected, safe facets of immigrant cultures. Through festivals and other performances, residents began to display European crafts, dances, costumes, and music as vital parts of Red Lodge's public culture.

This expansion of public identity met several immediate needs. Concerned residents who dreaded further emigrations from the shrinking town recognized that public displays of ethnicity might bolster commitment to the community among Red Lodge's large first- and second-generation immigrant populations. Public ethnicity, others argued, might also boost the area's fledgling tourism industry, providing the town with some cultural interest that could draw curious visitors. Organized ethnic groups, especially those with large second-generation memberships like the Italian Girls Victory Club,[13] facilitated this process of incorporation to help secure their own cultural and social positions in the town. Working closely with nonethnic community leaders, these groups helped to redefine the role of the "nationalities" in the town's public sphere through public displays of certain Old World cultures and traditions. In the process, Red Lodge residents began to establish the parameters of "appropriate" public ethnicity in the community.

Public displays of ethnicity, like public displays of "safe" Westernness, could be a community asset, but only if presented properly within an established context of Americanism — the kind of public American identity adopted by residents during the tense years of World War I. Two depression-era festivals made this point clearly. The 1932 Red Lodge Woman's Club Community Fine Arts Festival started the process of drawing the "nationalities" into the town's public image in ways that complemented rather than threatened American values. Designed to demonstrate the depth and breadth of Red Lodge's cultural resources, the Community Fine Arts Festival showcased the town's diversity, producing an interesting mélange of local cultures and interests that highlighted, in particular, the "foreign born residents of the community."[14] In the festival's crowded showroom, displays of fossils and minerals from the Beartooths sat next to family heirlooms from Finland and Slovenia; the Italian Girls Victory Club performed alongside the Finnish Orchestra and the Red Lodge Ladies' Glee Club; community members read essays and poems about George Washington and skiing; and local craftspeople exhibited handmade furniture and jewelry. The festival, which attracted almost a thousand attendees, presented Red Lodge as a place rich in resources and culture, with at least part of the town's strength lying in its diversity of ethnic heritages.[15]

A second ethnic festival, Dr. J. C. F. Siegfriedt's 1939 Beartooth Highway Opening Day Ceremony, made clear not only the past contributions of nationality groups to Red Lodge but also the present-day potential of ethnic celebrations to lure tourists into the community.[16] The event, held in late May on a grassy meadow just outside of town, featured costumed residents performing Old World folk dances and songs against the backdrop of the magnificent Beartooth Mountains. A sprawling carnival of sorts, the celebration combined presentations by the Slovenian chorus, Finnish choir, Italian Girls Victory Club, and Austrian string orchestra with boxing matches and food booths. The deliberate combination of ethnic music groups, sporting events, and beautiful scenery created a pleasing spectacle of diversity and strength rooted in the American landscape.

The display of cultural diversity in these shows assumed a set of shared values. Nothing strayed very far from middle-class American convictions. All performances and presentations became part of a larger structured whole established by the Woman's Club and Dr. Siegfriedt. Ethnicity was colorful and entertaining, but largely decorative. It enhanced the town's image and became a source of community pride. The Finns, for example, played music and displayed embroidered dresses for the assembled audiences; they did not discuss Finnish ties to socialism or the arrests of local Finns who had supported the radical Industrial Workers of the World during World War I.[17] Performances and displays constructed a depoliticized version of Finnish ethnicity that, apart from clothing styles and some specific (and harmless) traditions, looked and sounded very American. It was a display of foreignness that continued the movement toward attenuated ethnicity seen during the war years when Finns and other groups declared their Americanness in group forums. Siegfriedt himself argued that his event — billed as a celebration of cooperation between the "nationalities" — was really about maintaining American community values. Community celebrations such as his, he proclaimed, were the only way "to keep alive the old country mores and traditions, and learn to link them with *our own* customs for better cooperation and understanding between groups."[18] Siegfriedt valued immigrant cultures, but only so far as they fit with mainstream beliefs. "Cooperation" and "understanding" meant linking the nationalities ("them") with "real" Americans ("us").

Of course, Siegfriedt and the Woman's Club could never simply impose these notions of "acceptable" performances on the community. Ethnic residents had their own reasons to present depoliticized Old World traditions like folk dancing, songs, and crafts as representative of their immigrant cultures. Not surprisingly, members of the "nationalities" who chose to participate in community cultural events preferred to present their ethnicity in ways that would gain them applause and acceptance from the larger society.[19] Folk dancing, for example, a popular American pastime in the early twentieth century, was a favored form of public ethnic expression for second-generation immigrants.[20] Through dance, these young people could find joy both in participating in their parents' culture and also in the admiration they received from onlookers. Positive response from outsiders, in turn, often reinforced the performer's own sense of ethnic group attachment and desire to continue performing traditional dances.[21]

Similarly, the increasing popularity of ethnic music, particularly polkas, in the 1930s and 1940s created a ready audience for Red Lodge's various ethnic bands, whose repertoires featured a mixture of American and Old World tunes. Nationality choirs in Red Lodge chose to present easily comprehensible songs, sometimes in English, at these public events. At the Woman's Club festival, for example, the Finnish girls sang "Among the Trees" and "A Song of Kuijalo" to an appreciative audience, while the Finnish mixed quartet added the eminently respectable "A Song of Finland" and "Our Country."[22] Finns played Finns in the same way that Indians played Indians at the 1930s rodeos and ranchers like Ben Greenough and Malcolm Mackay played the heroic cowboy/rancher. The process of public performance reinforced the presentation of safe and popular aspects of immigrant cultures; ethnic residents presented what they and their visitors wanted to hear and see, and the audience encouraged this selection of performances with applause and admiration.

Even the "nationality" costumes worn by ethnic residents at public performances reflected a process of cultural negotiation, a drive to present an appealingly picturesque vision of European nationality. Early immigrants to Red Lodge had rarely if ever worn these fancy-dress outfits. Indeed, many of the "folk" costumes that would be put on display in Red Lodge in the twentieth century were not even invented until the nineteenth century when the leaders of emerging European countries — engaged in their own quests to develop cohesive national identities — began to adopt certain local kinds of peasant dress as "national costumes."[23] Some immigrants brought various versions of these elaborate folk costumes with them to the United States but wore them in public only infrequently. Photos of immigrants in Red Lodge from the 1890s through the 1920s and 1930s show only the very rare individual clothed in what might be called "traditional" or "national" dress. When dressing up to pose for carefully arranged group photographs, ethnic residents inevitably chose to dress in "American" suits or shirtwaists; even formal wedding and family portraits would include almost no hint of "nationality" clothing.

In Red Lodge's photographic history, "Old World costumes" began to appear only in the mid–twentieth century as public ethnicity gained acceptance through local ethnic festivals and as adaptations of picturesque folk outfits — particularly dirndls and "peasant" blouses — made their way into popular fashion at a national level.[24] A growing American fascination with European ethnicity thus led Red Lodge ethnics to adopt publicly a version of Old World folk culture created to meet the nationalistic needs of a European bourgeoisie and popularized by a mass fashion industry. This process followed the pattern of local adoption of western rodeo attire in the 1930s; once eastern tastes sanctioned this style of dress, local people began to incorporate such costumes into the town's public identity. Soon colorful nationality costumes became one of the most prominent markers of Red Lodge's public ethnicity as local civic leaders set out to put this popular version of ethnicity to work for the community. And Dr. Siegfriedt, the town's most energetic booster, led the effort to promote a picturesque version of Red Lodge's costumed ethnicity as a tourist attraction.

Connected explicitly to the town's major visitor attraction — the Beartooth Highway to Yellowstone National Park — Siegfriedt's 1939 festival marked not only the opening of the summer tourism season but also the beginning of efforts to use Red Lodge's ethnic identity to lure tourists into the community. Siegfriedt pointed out that ethnicity, properly presented, might join the cowboy of the Wild West as a tool of community promotion. Alert to any possibility to enhance the town's business, he argued early on that Americans' increasing interest in their own and others' ethnic backgrounds could be put to good use locally. Siegfriedt told Red Lodge residents much the same thing that sociologist Dean MacCannell would later write about tourists: they would take interest in anything that stood out "from the others in their class for reasons of being foreign, old fashioned, weird or futuristic."[25] Tourists might stop for an extra hour or day to look at beautiful costumes or listen to tamburitza music that was familiar enough to be nonthreatening but different from the everyday routine at home. Those extra hours spent in Red Lodge could add thousands of dollars to the local economy each year.

Even if Siegfriedt's festival did not evolve into the annual spectacle he hoped to create, his event proved an important turning point. Siegfriedt showed that local people would willingly perform as "ethnic" for special events much in the same way that residents already performed as "western" for the annual rodeo. In fact, he managed to get locals to perform both identities at his gala event. Although the festival highlighted ethnic performances, Siegfriedt included "western" as a type of ethnic identity for nonethnics; he stipulated that all local residents had to wear "old country . . . or western costume" to gain entrance to the festivities.[26] The requirement served dual purposes. First, the western outfits rooted this ethnic event in a familiar cultural practice of donning fancy dress to please tourists. Siegfriedt used the already established pathway of the annual Wild West rodeo to introduce European ethnicity as a tourist attraction. Second, the addition of western attire ensured that all residents could participate in the gala regardless of ethnic background. For the benefit of tourists, everyone had to play at dressing up in idealized versions of the past, be it the romantic westerner or the romantic European peasant. The brightly clad "immigrant" thus began to assume a public place in the town's identity alongside the sanitized "cowboy," both of them welcoming tourists to Red Lodge in the warm sunlight of a May afternoon.

Ethnicity began to work itself into the town's public identity in the 1930s as residents adapted certain Old World traditions to the current needs of a changing community, in effect inventing a new kind of ethnic identity in Red Lodge. Public displays of ethnicity drew community members together in common celebrations of town unity, allowed second-generation immigrants to present part of their cultural heritages to admiring audiences, and promised to boost the local tourist industry. Celebrations of public ethnicity, however, faded into the background in the 1940s, as Red Lodge residents found themselves pulled into the national patriotic fervor of World War II and the cold war.

In the cauldron of this patriotic decade, European ethnicity actually became less important in the public lives of most Americans, including those living in Red Lodge.[27] But, ironically, dramatic shifts in population and economic resources in this turbulent period left local residents clutching at public ethnicity as a way to secure the town's cultural and economic survival in the postwar years. By the late 1940s, local people needed something to hold their town together; they found their "glue" in an annual Festival of Nations that celebrated not only Red Lodge's ethnic diversity but also a new interpretation of the town's past that fit comfortably into emerging national narratives about ethnicity in America. In the process of making public ethnicity a community asset in the 1940s, residents reimagined their local history to reflect contemporary interpretations of the role of ethnicity in the town. Through the Festival of Nations, invented in 1951, local people constructed a powerful interpretation of local history that privileged ethnic differences over any other divisions, particularly racial and class, that had marked the town's past. The message of the Festival of Nations — annually reinforced through printed brochures, public addresses at performances, and published accounts in the local newspaper — created an appealing history of local pluralism: Red Lodge had been a town once sorely divided by ethnic factionalism, in which, *through their own efforts*, local people overcame their differences to embrace diversity and find peace, happiness, and success in a prosperous, shared community. At once a cultural performance of community unity and history, an assertion of the town's identity in a cold war world, and an entertaining program for tourists, the Festival of Nations tied together a variety of local concerns. It became an ongoing celebration that annually would reaffirm the town as a unique and special place.[28]

World War II played a key role in creating the conditions that would shape the town's creation of the Festival of Nations as a public expression of local ethnic history. The war had united the community more completely than craft shows and town picnics could.[29] It brought Americans together and further diminished any negative associations about European ethnicity that may have lingered through the depression years.[30] In popular culture, writers and movie producers emphasized the bonds that united Americans across ethnic lines. John Hersey, for example, in his popular 1944 novel *A Bell for Adano*, explained to his readers that "America is the international country. Our Army has Yugoslavs and Frenchmen and Austrians and Czechs and Norwegians in it, and everywhere our Army goes in Europe, a man can turn to the private beside him and say: 'Hey, Mac, what's this furriner saying? . . . And Mac will be able to translate.'"[31] War movies also routinely depicted American platoons as ethnically diverse, with various characters representing the Jew, Irishman, Hispanic, and other ethnic "types."[32] America, in these patriotic depictions, typified the classic melting pot in which people might retain some ethnic traits (like speaking a foreign language), but where European ethnicity no longer overwhelmed the Americanness of acculturated immigrants and their children.

Local conditions reflected and reinforced national culture. In Red Lodge, families from all ethnic groups sent sons and daughters to Europe and the Pacific to fight for America. Joined together in a patriotic cause, residents cast off some of the public markers of ethnic difference that had stuck with the community through the 1930s. Most noticeably, people less often made note of ethnicity in public forums. Newspapers less frequently described residents according to their heritage as "a daughter of Finland" or "the Italian." The large posters in downtown windows displaying the photos of local men and women in the armed services offered no commentary on ethnicity.[33] When servicemen with names like Tony Zupan and Willie Zaputil sent letters home from Italy or France boasting of their affection for Red Lodge, the local newspaper readily published these epistles — without pausing to make reference to the authors' background as second-generation immigrants. Newspaper stories, indeed, proudly played upon the men's "Montana" identities rather than their ethnic heritages. Zupan's army buddies from Brooklyn, the *Carbon County News* joked, had "never even heard of Montana, much less Red Lodge" until Zupan, the "one-man commercial club," set them straight with grandiloquent descriptions of Red Lodge with its "26 streets. Mind you, man, 26." Zupan, the hometown boy, overwhelmed Zupan, the son of Croatian immigrants. As with Hersey's fictional GIs, ethnicity no longer marked these local second-generation immigrants as "furriners."[34]

Economic crises in Red Lodge further shook up local notions of ethnicity and community membership. When Zupan, Zaputil, and other local soldiers returned to Red Lodge's "26 streets" in the mid-1940s, they might well have been shocked. The home these American soldiers bragged about to their eastern buddies had changed dramatically during the war years. The town was smaller and poorer than it had been since the early 1890s. Like many other little mining towns around the state, Red Lodge's economic infrastructure was collapsing. Increased use of natural gas and strip mines and a devastating fire at the Smith Mine in 1943 all but closed down the remaining Bearcreek mines. By 1950 only eighty-nine men and three women in Red Lodge continued to earn their living from mining. Local businesses foundered as corporate wages disappeared, and improved highways led rural shoppers away from Red Lodge to bigger and less expensive stores in Billings and Laurel. The median annual income per family in Red Lodge plummeted to $1,580, or roughly half that of comparably sized towns in the state. The number of town residents had dropped more than 40 percent from the 1920 level, and significant gaps appeared in the population as those between the ages of fifteen and twenty-five fled the community for urban areas that beckoned with promises of jobs and educational opportunities.[35] As the price for local houses dropped to three hundred dollars or less and businesses boarded up windows on Broadway Avenue, Charles W. Stevens, owner of the Red Lodge Cafe, groused that the town's motto was "No future here!" "Most of our young folks," he complained, "say the same thing — no future — no opportunity here! Our younger generation is migrating to greener fields." Frightened by the loss of jobs and population, Stevens posed the question that hit at the core of local anxieties in the immediate postwar, postmining years: "Are we to become a ghost town? A city populated by old people?"[36]

Red Lodge was not alone. To the despair of small-town inhabitants and concerned social observers, broad demographic and economic changes swept the nation during the war and its aftermath, transforming America into a more fully urbanized nation by the late 1940s. Over fifteen million Americans moved during the war, most of them to cities where they could find jobs in war industries or stay close to family members in the armed services.[37] The end of the war slowed this trend, but the nation remained a people on the move, mostly away from small towns and rural areas in search of economic opportunities in the cities. Many small towns simply could not survive this national mobilization. In Bearcreek — the example closest to Red Lodge— the few remaining residents in the early 1950s put their houses on wheels and rolled them to Red Lodge and Billings or simply burned them down and moved on. Bearcreek practically ceased to exist, even as a ghost town. Little towns like Bearcreek and Washoe (both of which had once rivaled Red Lodge in terms of population) continued to wither and disappear in the 1940s and 1950s, victims of a changing world that made little effort to respond to the needs of these dying communities.

Red Lodge survived the 1940s and 1950s through luck, location, and the grit of local people determined to keep the town alive. Buffeted by national, even global, demographic, economic, and social forces, Red Lodge residents chose, out of necessity, to focus on *local* projects and people as they negotiated a path of community survival in the postwar years. Community activists fixed their attention on the local manifestations of national trends and local solutions to those problems.[38] When, for example, McCarthyism-inspired "wild" rumors about local communist organizations swept through the community, civic groups held Americanism programs to promote patriotism at the grassroots level; residents sought to secure themselves against the global "menace" of communism through sing-alongs and skits exposing the lie of Russia's "class-less society."[39] Rather than simply resigning themselves to the inevitable trans-ference of industrial jobs from rural to urban areas, the Red Lodge Chamber of Commerce regeared its boosterism machine, reaching out to area ranchers for local support while setting out to convince any company it could to extract every mineral conceivable — oil, gas, chromium, gold — from the Beartooth Mountains.[40]

Merchants also redoubled efforts to build Red Lodge's tourism industry, hosting two successful statewide conferences in 1949 and trumpeting the Beartooth Highway as the "pre-eminent approach" to Yellowstone National Park.[41] And fearing that the town was losing money and population to cities like Billings that had hospitals and large recreational facilities, town leaders in the late 1940s obtained federal and local funding to build a new hospital and community center for Red Lodge.[42] Boosted by the symbolism of the "fine New Civic Center," local merchants, like the owner of the Ford dealership, began once again to invest in the town, modernizing businesses "to keep abreast of Civic Progress in Red Lodge."[43] The editor of the *Lewistown Daily* heralded Red Lodge as "a city that refused to die."[44] Red Lodge was not the "coal metropolis" envisioned by 1890s boosters, nor was it the thriving coal town of the 1910s. But shrunken and battered though it may have been in the early 1950s, the town survived while other communities dried up and blew away. The Festival of Nations emerged out of this frenzied period, when community members fought to ensure the survival of their small town in a world that seemed to be running out of places for rural communities.

The first Festival of Nations, in fact, evolved out of the popular celebration marking the opening of the town's new Veterans' Memorial Civic Center in late 1950. The key part of this celebration, a historical pageant of Red Lodge, vividly illustrated the focus on local initiative and ethnic cooperation that would undergird the developing Festival of Nations. Thousands of people from around the area packed the domed building in mid-November to participate in the grand pageant of Red Lodge performed through a series of tableaux. Homesteaders, cowboys, and mountain men placed the town firmly in the triumphant narrative of the Old West, scenes of miners and farmers showed the work that built the community, and folk dances by ethnic performers highlighted the diversity of the town's immigrant community. At the pageant climax, a one-hundred-voice community choir burst into song. With many of its members in ethnic costume and at least one song sung in four different languages, the choir posed an attractive picture of local harmony.[45]

The 1950 historical pageant presented entwined narratives of progress. First, townspeople who had been historically divided by language and ethnicity had overcome their differences to build a common "roof," the new Civic Center. Named after all the men and women who had served their nation during World War II, the Civic Center (like the pageant itself) symbolized local unity across ethnic lines. At the same time, the performed history insisted that local people through their own *local* efforts had not only created this remarkable ethnic harmony, but they had simultaneously invented, maintained, and saved Red Lodge. In this story, the local people did everything themselves, from exploring and settling the land to building the local ski area. The events depicted stood by themselves, without references to larger trends of capitalism and modernization that had influenced what happened in Red Lodge. Tellingly, pageant directors chose *not* to include depictions of mine officials, federal bureaucrats, or eastern capitalists. These larger forces did not fit into a historical narrative that explained local progress as the result of people of different backgrounds learning to work together. To deal with the forces that seemed to be tearing their community apart, local residents turned in upon themselves, creating a performed history in which they, not powerful outside forces, were in control. Inspired by this triumphant performance of local initiative and cultural diversity, town activists made plans for a separate festival of ethnic harmony to be held during the summer tourist season.

From the beginning, a small group of people gave form and direction to the Festival of Nations, shaping the celebration to reflect their ideas about the community, its past, and the nature of "ethnicity." Significantly, several of the most energetic festival organizers — Congregationalist minister Don Scanlin, newspaper columnist R. S. Davis, and high school art teacher Lucile Ralston — were not particularly "ethnic," or even "local." Some organizers, like John Lampi, a Finnish immigrant who directed Finnish-language theatricals, were longtime residents actively involved in "ethnic" activities, but most members of the original festival steering committees had Anglo-American names and backgrounds.[46] Scanlin, who served as the original general coordinator and festival master of ceremonies for several decades, had only moved to Red Lodge in 1948.[47] In a way reminiscent of the 1930s multiethnic events, Anglo-Americans took charge of the broad direction of the festival. The various ethnic groups played large roles in the Festival of Nations, but originally they focused more on their individual "nationality" day performances and exhibits, while the steering committees and coordinators (Scanlin and Ralston) set the broader parameters of the celebration.

The presence of so many Anglo-Americans on the committees served to imprint a certain understanding of ethnicity and multiculturalism on the celebration. The festival became not so much about *European* immigrants as a celebration of *American* success at integrating so many different types of peoples into a harmonious national community. Like the 1932 Woman's Club event, the first festival focused on presenting the resources of Red Lodge, which included ethnic diversity, in order to show its strength and resilience.

But ethnicity only served this larger purpose. Ralston, for example, emphasized the cultural aspects of the Festival of Nations. She organized a series of
art shows during festival week and encouraged local people like eighty-year-
old "Grandma" Webber to demonstrate "crafts in action" behind the windows
of downtown shops. Although enthusiastic about the idea of a multiethnic
event, Ralston saw it more as a backdrop that provided "something a little different" to intrigue passing visitors and make them want to look at the paintings and pottery produced by local residents.[48] By insisting that ethnicity was
simply one part of the town's cultural landscape, organizers like Ralston
helped to shape a consensus message for the festival: the message that European ethnic diversity symbolized the best of American freedom, egalitarianism, and justice for all.

Significantly, though, organizers like Ralston never had the kind of control
that the Woman's Club or Dr. Siegfriedt had over earlier ethnic productions;
by 1950, immigrants and their children were more fully intertwined in the
social fabric of the town than they had ever been before. Nonethnics assumed
important leadership roles that shaped the theme and structure of this grand
community production, but they could not control how the festival would
develop and the meanings local people would give it. Ralston and Scanlin could
not maintain control over the festival as residents made it part of their lives
and local identity. Nor could organizers completely manage the influence that
tourism would have on the festival and its message of international harmony.

The Festival of Nations had much deeper roots and motivations than just
tourism, but from the beginning, tourism intertwined with the event and the
meanings given to it by local residents. Festival organizers in the early 1950s
recognized the validity of Siegfriedt's assertion that ethnicity, like coal and
cowboys, could be a community resource if packaged correctly. Residents realized that they could use ethnicity to strengthen the town's economy in much
the same way as they had used the rodeo and the Wild West. Performed ethnicity might attract a whole different set of tourists into town. Festival plan-
ners, like newspaper columnist R. S. Davis, had noted the success of other
ethnic events around the nation, especially the annual Dutch Tulip Festival in
Holland, Michigan — a celebration, one organizer argued, that brought visitors and newsreel teams to that town each year. Americans, it seemed, were
willing, even eager, to plan trips around displays of ethnic folk dances and
crafts. If Holland drew so much attention by featuring just one ethnic group,

what might a festival of eight different nationalities do for Red Lodge?[49] As the local newspaper editor pointed out, "The idea of festival draws attention." The Festival of Nations, he predicted, "can develop into an annual attraction if our first year is a good one."[50]

Driven by the desire to make the festival both culturally and financially successful, residents self-consciously adapted the event's structure and content to the perceived needs of the traveling public. They presented the Festival of Nations as a product for outside consumption. Organizers, for example, chose to hold the event over two weekends during the notoriously quiet month of August when motels and businesses most needed a tourism boost.[51] They adjusted the hours when residents would present active crafts in downtown windows so that they would be seen by as many visitors as possible, who might then pause to purchase local products. In ways very similar to the "Go West" costume campaign of the July rodeo, participants and organizers alike strove to dress up residents and the town in as many bright colors as possible to catch the interest of those passing through. Local activists continued to emphasize the moral and social benefits of the community festival, but they also grew increasingly focused on what they might do to bring more tourists into Red Lodge. In 1955 some participants even suggested restricting the free samples of ethnic food to tourists only (it seems that local youngsters were helping themselves to too many of the goodies). Indignant festival directors insisted that the festival was not just for tourists. But the suggestion itself showed how centered organizers had become on the tourist industry, which provided not only some financial support for the event (through donations) but also hearty encouragement for this community project and the public ethnicity it celebrated.[52]

The directors were right; the festival was not *just* for tourists, but the publicity of the event, which was directed at tourists, made Red Lodge regionally renowned for its ethnic diversity. In promoting their community's nationality celebration, town leaders achieved some measure of outside recognition for their festival and the town's immigrant heritage. For years, the Festival of Nations received a coveted place in the official state highway map's "Points of Interest" section; the blurb directed visitors to Red Lodge in August to participate in the town's annual celebration of ethnic harmony. The festival's publicity machine (a fairly modest mechanism) churned out leaflets and brochures that gained the event mention in various magazines and travel

"Active crafts" displayed in downtown windows brought the first Festival of Nations to pedestrians strolling along Broadway Avenue. (Carbon County News)

guides as well as in newspapers ranging from the Spokane *Spokesman-Review* and *Great Falls Tribune* to the *New York Times.*[53] Buoyed by the positive reception of the festival, business leaders started to include pictures of ethnic performers in local visitors' guides, often displacing the ubiquitous cowboy in favor of full-color shots of international flags and residents dressed up in fancy ethnic costumes. Visitors, state residents, and locals alike learned to associate Red Lodge with ethnic diversity. Through the festival and its publicity, "ethnicity" became part of the town's public identity. Other Montana towns — particularly mining communities like Belt, Stockett, and Roundup — also had large numbers of immigrant groups, but Red Lodge's early publicity about the Festival of Nations secured its reputation as Montana's "ethnic city," behind only Butte, which had always been a much larger and more prominent player on the state's economic and cultural stage.

Festival directors deliberately shaped Red Lodge's ethnic celebration for consumption by a touring public, and tourism played a vital role in the development of the festival and its place in the local culture. Tourists affected not only the existence of the festival but also its content and the meanings given to it by local people. Scholars of tourism have long noted its ability to influence local people and their cultural practices.[54] As locals learned to meet the needs of tourists, they began to "commodify" their culture, to produce it for sale to tourists in pursuit of "authentic" experiences and objects.[55] Thus, in the process of their interaction with the "authentic" cultural practice, tourists necessarily influenced that practice and what it meant for local performers. But as cultural products like the Festival of Nations became more commodified for tourists, they did not simply lose meaning. For local people these commodified practices could become, as Erik Cohen has argued, "a diacritical mark of their ethnic or cultural identity, a vehicle of self-representation before an external public."[56] In Red Lodge, performance before tourists made residents more aware of their ethnic heritages while also marking the town itself as a special place *because* of these ethnic performances. Tourism reinforced ethnic associations, not only for individuals but also for the whole town.

The emphasis on Red Lodge's "unique" ethnic harmony developed largely out of the success the festival had in attracting tourists from around the state and eventually around the world. The numbers of people flocking to the shows and exhibits and the positive comments about the pretty dances and costumes elevated residents' views about the importance of the Festival of Nations and their own ethnic identification. The local newspaper and Chamber of Commerce brochures contributed to this process by reprinting only the most positive praise from visitors, such as that repeated by exhibitor Ben Greenough, who observed in 1951 that tourists "were plumb amazed that a town this small could produce such a show," or the 1955 assertion by the festival coordinator that several persons had told her "that the Festival restored their faith in humanity because they didn't think people did things like that any more."[57] Local residents became convinced that their festival was less a celebration of what made their town and themselves special than the *source* of their uniqueness. Encouraged and flattered by the large and positive response to the celebration — many of the shows were standing room only by the second year — organizers and participants presented increasingly grand pronouncements about the event and what it represented. In the first three years, the theme of the Festival of Nations quickly evolved from being about community talent and cooperation (1951) to "an adventure in friendship" and American multiculturalism (1952) to an event meant to "help bring a closer understanding among people of all nationalities (1953)."[58] The hyperbole built upon itself until by 1974, the local newspaper could readily state that the festival should inspire world leaders with the "stunning realization that a melting pot of people have been celebrating their differences and living so peacefully — for 25 years!"[59]

But, Red Lodge, of course, was not the unique example of ethnic harmony that enthusiastic residents and newspaper editors might want to proclaim. The very narrative of "nationalities" uniting in the New World (the "melting pot" metaphor from the 1974 editorial), in fact, lay at the core of consensus-era American immigration history. Cold war Americans displayed and preserved ethnic differences, in part, as a way of celebrating and reaffirming the nation's cherished traditions of freedom and egalitarianism against the looming specter of international communism. Conveniently obscuring other deeper tears in the national social fabric, particularly divisions of class and race, Americans pointed to ethnic integration as proof that the United States indeed exemplified democratic pluralism and opportunity.[60] By the 1950s, Americans accepted and celebrated themselves as a nation of Swedes and Italians and Finns and Irish. According to consensus historians, this diversity had made the nation strong and vibrant and rich. If the United States could successfully incorporate so many diverse ethnicities into its body politic, then American democracy must be working.

In Red Lodge, the Festival of Nations wove this selective version of ethnic adaptation into a triumphant historical narrative of American superiority rooted in a specific place. Residents created themselves as "*über*-Americans" by celebrating their community's ethnic heritage. In true consensus fashion, the festival emphasized what made America, and the community, strong, not what really divided them. In spite of the display of international flags and European costumes and ethnic performances, a conviction in American superiority permeated the Festival of Nations. Americanism shouted its presence at every turn, never letting visitors or residents forget that *Americans*—and, more particularly, local Red Lodge residents—had achieved this amazing display of international harmony. Each evening performance began (and still does) with a salute to the American flag and the singing of "The Star Spangled Banner" or "America the Beautiful." The international flags along Broadway included an American flag prominently placed in the center of each cluster of five. Hints that other nations might be treated with more respect than the United States could draw immediate criticism. In 1962, a local woman complained that the American flag had not been positioned prominently enough in the flag display at the Civic Center, and the flag chairman agreed that it would be "unfortunate" if visitors left the festival thinking that the U.S. flag had been neglected.[61] In a similar manner, festival organizers gradually reduced the prominence of the United Nations flag in the 1960s, until, like the other international flags, it too was overwhelmed by the omnipresence of the Stars and Stripes.[62] The Red Lodge festival's celebration of diversity could not threaten even the symbolism of the superiority of the American way of life. In fact, diversity itself had to be contained within some fairly strict boundaries in the postwar years to ensure its compatibility with the dominant consensus paradigm.

Cold war American pluralism, as presented by the Festival of Nations, showcased timeless, classless, raceless ethnicity. The festival organizers' neat arrangements of nationality "groups"—"Yugoslavian," "British Isles," "Finnish"—presented ethnicity as something easily grasped by American viewers. Stripped of race, class, and historical change, ethnicity became an inviolate concept; it was a kind of core identity brought pure and good from the Old Country and eventually accepted as good by other Americans. Ethnicity, in this view, had always been the same; what had changed was people's ability to understand, appreciate, and celebrate the different traditions and customs of these groups. Americans, and Red Lodge residents in particular, were special because they had learned how to do this. Easily comprehended and presented, static ethnicity fit readily into assumptions both of personal ethnicity and American pluralism.

This notion of "timeless" ethnicity shaped much of the town's preconceptions about the meaning of the Festival of Nations and its place in local history.

In this juxtaposition of Red Lodge public imagery, the dancing Indians of the Red Lodge Cafe share space with some of the international flags flying along Broadway Avenue for the Festival of Nations. (Yes, that's the Papua New Guinea flag in the middle; note also that an American flag always flies in each cluster of international flags.) (Author's photo)

Like other Americans, Red Lodge residents by the 1950s preferred to imagine ethnic groups, in Werner Sollors's words, "as if they were natural, real, eternal, stable, and static units."[63] They wove this belief in authentic ethnicity into the festival itself, continually insisting on the authenticity of the celebration's dances, foods, costumes, and crafts. Organizers assured residents that " 'authentic' is the watchword and on that basis the Festival is growing."[64] "Genuine" or "authentic" suggested a graspable ethnicity, something readily verified against a presumably stable, historical model — and more significantly, something that could be learned or, if need be, purchased. Authenticity came from ancestry, but also from information from older members of the ethnic group and through costumes, recipes, and dances obtained from those with trusted claims to knowledge. One could even buy "genuine" ethnicity, as festival organizers did, from European or American costume and craft shops that catered to an international interest in Old World folk traditions.[65] By wearing the right costume, dancing the correct steps, or shaping the *polenta* in some "traditional" way, Americans believed they could recapture vital pieces of their parents' or grandparents' Old World culture. One could find and communicate a Yugoslavian ethnicity, as it were, by playing polka music composed in the Balkans on an accordion brought over from Europe by a grandparent or uncle. Insistence on authenticity denied the negotiated nature of American ethnicity, smoothing out the tangled strands of shifting immigrant group identification through a mutual agreement that a real, core ethnic identity existed to be purchased, learned, performed, sold.

Ethnicity was, however, a much messier concept than the simplified structure of the Red Lodge festival and the broader pluralistic narrative implied. Neatly compartmentalized nationality groups like Yugoslavians were, in fact, very recent inventions still in the process of definition and redefinition in the 1950s. Rather than the timeless construction presented in the festival, ethnic creation, as scholars such as Kathleen Neils Conzen have shown, had always been (and still was) very much an untidy *process* of individuals and groups figuring out what it meant to "be Finnish" or "be Croatian" in a race- and class-conscious America.[66] At the turn of the century, when most of Red Lodge's immigrant population came to the United States, national identifications were not even fixed in much of Europe, let alone among immigrant groups living in America. The nineteenth century had witnessed a burst of nation-making movements in which victorious nationalists forced political unity on diverse groups whose members identified more with local surroundings than with larger creations such as Italy or Austria. When these Italians and Austrians immigrated to the United States, they did not necessarily define themselves according to broad political or national designations.

Some of the shifting boundaries of immigrants' national identification could be seen in the 1910 Red Lodge census data. In this enumeration, Finns were sometimes Russians and sometimes not; Poles divided themselves (or were divided by the census taker) into Russian and Austrian; Austrian included Servians, Croatians, Slovaks, Bohemians, Slovenians, and Montenegrins; and Italian encompassed a disparate group of northern and southern immigrants who could barely understand each other's language or culture.[67] Gradually, these immigrants began to negotiate new ethnic identities in the United States, created in part by outside conceptions of who they were. To Americans, as Conzen points out, the "provincial and village identities, so

There's not a dirndl or scarf in sight in this Finnish wedding portrait from turn-of-the-century Red Lodge. (Carbon County Historical Society photo)

important to the immigrants, were meaningless; these were lumped together into ethnonational categories, Irish Catholics, Italians, or Poles (or more likely, Micks, Wops, and Polacks)."[68] This "lumping together" meant that diverse groups of people often ended up as "ethnic" brothers and sisters in the United States. These imposed labels, of course, required some adjustment before members began to accept them as comfortable or natural.[69] But eventually, third- and even second-generation immigrants accepted ethnic identities like Yugoslavian as meaningful, even authentic, designations.

Ongoing tensions within some of the ethnic categories created by the Festival of Nations point out the shifting nature of these constructed identities. "British," for example, originally combined Scots, English, and Irish into a single category. Although not divided by high passions (as their Old World compatriots were), the local British always separated their performances at the festival instead of attempting a unified presentation. At the 1951 program, for example, the Scots began with bagpipes and the Highland fling, the English followed with madrigal singers, and the Irish closed the show with a demonstration of the Irish jig.[70] Combining these divergent cultural practices did not seem to make sense; "British Isles" had more meaning as a geographical and political designation than as a cultural category. In the 1960s, the Scots, their numbers boosted by the participation of Caledonian societies from Billings and Miles City, finally demanded and received a day of their own that focused on Highland games, bagpipes, kilts, and Robert Burns — without the distractions of Irish step dancers and English heraldry.[71] Although a handy term for grouping together residents for performance, "British Isles" made less sense to people who had not learned to think of themselves according to this broad title.

The Yugoslavians had even more difficulties creating themselves as a unified ethnic group. Croatians, Montenegrins, and Slovenians all came from countries that were once part of the Austrian-Hungarian empire, which were later combined into Yugoslavia by international fiat after World War I. Following this larger model of inventing nations, festival directors designated a single Yugoslavia Day to encompass the big, diverse group. Cultural distinctions within this designation remained prominent enough in the first festivals that the Yugoslavians had to create separate programs on their day. The Croatians and Slovenians, especially, simply could not work together to produce a unified program; they performed separately not only on their own night but also at All Nations Day, which was created in 1960 specifically to celebrate the "amazing" harmony evidenced by the cooperation of all these different nationality groups in a single festival.[72]

Such tensions gradually faded, however, as the various groups grew accustomed to the shared nationality designation and as ties to Old Country cultures grew fainter with time and distance. The description of Yugoslavia Day in the official 1971 Festival of Nations program did not even mention Serbs, Croats, and Montenegrins; from the original immigrants to the present-day performers, all had become simply Yugoslavian.[73] In the four decades since the first Festival of Nations, Red Lodge Slavs forged a benign public definition of Yugoslavian ethnicity — centered around tamburitzas, *kolas,* and pig roasts — that obscured previous distinctions between these immigrant groups and presented "Yugoslavian" itself as a timeless, natural ethnicity. In 1997, though, the group changed its name to "Slavic," reflecting the years of brutal warfare and ethnic cleansing in the Balkans that had destroyed any international fiction of a united Yugoslavia. Significantly, however, group members did not consider splitting up their own local pan-Slavic designation. In fact, Red Lodge Slavs publicly chided their Old Country brethren for not learning how to get along as well as the Festival of Nations' Serbs and Croats did.[74] Glossing over the bitter ethnic divisions within the former Yugoslavia, Red Lodge residents blithely pointed to themselves as proof that Slavs really were brothers, capable of harmonious reconciliation.

What Red Lodge Slavs and other Festival of Nations participants overlooked, of course, was race, which played a critical, though rarely acknowledged, role in the construction of European ethnicity in the United States. By the mid–twentieth century, most Americans recognized European ethnics as "white." In a racialized society, "whiteness" mattered. As "not black" and "not Indian," white ethnics secured their positions within the dominant culture, even if they chose to ignore (as most Americans did) the importance of what George Lipsitz calls their "possessive investment in whiteness."[75] Midcentury conceptions of timeless ethnicity assumed the common whiteness and middle-class aspirations of European immigrants — assumptions that served well the middle-class descendants of these immigrants. Established themselves as white Americans, Red Lodge's ethnics assumed the whiteness of their ancestors, weaving this racial construction into their histories, including the Festival of Nations. Later-generation ethnics preferred, perhaps, not to investigate too deeply their own historic claims to this racial designation.

In the first two decades of the century, however, Slovenians, Italians, and other "swarthy" immigrants from eastern and southern Europe could not take their "whiteness" so much for granted. In the heyday of biological racism, white was not just a skin color, but a reflection of culture, social behaviors, and even the shape of one's face. Sociologist Edward A. Ross, one of the most prominent academics in the country in the early twentieth century, maintained, for example, that the newcomers from southern Europe were "subcommon" stock. Framing his argument in the language of scientific sociology, Ross concluded that these immigrants — whose numbers included many of those who settled in and around Red Lodge — were "hirsute, low-browed, big-faced persons of obviously low mentality."[76] Other educated observers agreed.

Social reformer Jacob Riis, a champion of the lower classes, noted a variety of traits, both good and bad, among newer immigrant groups that he attributed to their "blood" rather than to learned cultural behaviors. Riis described the "Italian," for example, as "hot-headed" and a "born gambler" but also "gay, lighthearted and, if his fur is not stroked the wrong way, inoffensive as a child."[77] Other Americans took a much less benign stance toward the influx of "swarthy" newcomers. Artist Frederic Remington, a popular and vociferous champion of the Anglo-West, readily added southern Europeans to his list of inferior peoples worthy only of extinction: "Jews, Injuns, Chinamen, Italians, Huns — the rubbish of the earth I hate — I've got some Winchesters and when the massacring begins, I can get my share of 'em."[78]

No one in Red Lodge echoed such racist blatherings in the public record, but many early residents clearly saw southern and eastern Europeans as a race apart. Rocky Fork Coal Company manager Daniel O'Shea, for instance, an Irish immigrant himself, informed disgruntled stockholders in 1913 that the town site company made less money that year in part because of the "change in the type of coal miner employed in the mines in this vicinity." "There has been," O'Shea argued, "a large influx of the Slavonian, Serb and other southern European races to these coal fields, and such people do not build, do not improve real estate; rather are they disposed to herd in large numbers in cheap places."[79] Where later residents would see simply white ethnics, earlier inhabitants observed racialized, even bestialized, distinctions in the town's immigrant populations.

Racialized arguments about immigrant groups dropped out of celebratory local histories such as the Festival of Nations, though, overwhelmed by the subsequent creation of these immigrants as white. Gradually, as historian Noel Ignatiev has shown, European immigrant groups learned to identify themselves as white, creating "a new solidarity based on color" by setting themselves off against African Americans and others whose skins were more clearly darker than their own.[80] White workers in the East defined themselves as "not Blacks," while immigrants in Red Lodge set themselves off against the few Chinese, Mexicans, and African Americans who dared attempt to find opportunity in the mines and businesses of the burgeoning town. Immigrant miners, with the assistance and encouragement of workers' organizations like the Western Federation of Miners, fought to secure their own position in the mines and in the local community through a racialized construction of themselves as white workers. From the town's earliest years, the local miners' unions enforced restrictions against Chinese workers at the Rocky Fork mines and issued statements in support of legislation ending Asian immigration entirely.

During the frequent boom periods, the mines freely hired almost any man whose back could bear the work, but invariably those employed were of European background. A few Mexicans worked around the mines in the early years but not for long, and the town's only longtime African-American resident found employment shining shoes, not digging coal.[81] The mines became the province of white workers, and the town's European immigrant laborers increasingly defined themselves as white.

The overwhelming presence of foreign-born residents in Red Lodge — 43 percent of the population in 1910— aided this process. The sheer number of "Italian" and "Hunky" miners ensured that merchants and other professionals dependent on mine wages could not blatantly discriminate against these workers and their families as "non-white." The immigrants' whiteness grew ever more accepted, especially in the 1920s as Red Lodge adopted its Wild West imagery and business leaders encouraged all residents to don the costume of the white conquerors of the West — leaving, one assumes, Frederic Remington spinning in his grave at the picture of these "rubbish" races staking a claim to his idealized, defiantly Anglo, cowboy hero.

Significantly, though, "swarthy" immigrants dressed in cowboy boots and hats stood in marked contrast to the "red-skinned" Indians who participated in the seasonal western pageantry clad in their own Wild West costumes of breechcloths and feathers. In comparison to the obviously not-white Indians, European immigrants and their descendants began to blend into the whiteness of the rest of the rodeo celebration. By the 1950s, the process of "whitening" had proceeded so far that race, even historically, no longer seemed to touch the town in a public sense. Descendants of the "hirsute, low-browed" immigrants readily constructed consensus narratives, like that embodied in the Festival of Nations, that let racial distinctions drop away entirely, leaving, as one Red Lodge historian put it, simply "strong-willed Americans [and] ambitious and determined immigrants" to people the community's celebratory local history.[82]

The addition of Montana as a nationality equal to all the other ethnicities underscored the assumptions made in the festival, and at the national level, about the place of European ethnicity in American society and culture. Decked out in cowboy boots and spurs, Montana Day offered the same kind of western imagery that local residents had known for over twenty years of rodeo performances. Montana Day was, in effect, one day of this adapted Wild

West heritage incorporated into the festival's nine-day celebration of ethnic differences. For decades, the rodeo's Wild West imagery had generously wrapped up any resident who agreed to dress up and play along with the town's energetic rodeo promoters, so by the 1950s everyone could play along on this day. Ethnic background had never precluded participation in rodeo events; local business leaders did not care where residents were born, just that they dressed up for the tourists. The more people who went western — beards, loud shirts, cowboy boots and hat — the better for the town's Old West image. Encouraged by boosters and the demands of tourism, local ethnics had already gained entrance into the public Montana identity by 1951, and they readily took part in the Festival of Nations' version as well; names like Matt Sironen, Paavo Huovinen, and Olavi Kainu showed up regularly on Montana Day programs.[83]

Identification with the whiteness of Montana Day, however, ran deeper than the simple act of pulling on a pair of jeans or growing a beard for the annual rodeo. "Montana" marked an investment in a "West" of American conquest and domination. By the 1950s, European ethnics were well entrenched as beneficiaries of westward expansion. They lived and worked on land that had sustained thousands of Crow Indians before a succession of broken treaties pushed the original inhabitants out of the area. Red Lodge itself was predicated on the 1887 dislocation of the Crow from their established reservation. European immigrants had claimed this inheritance of racial conquest as they set pick to coal in the black tunnels of the Rocky Fork mine, hewed the trees of the Beartooth forests, or served customers at the local merchant cooperative. Even though only a fraction of the area's wealth passed through their hands, Red Lodge immigrants established themselves as rightful inheritors of what Patricia Nelson Limerick has called the West's "legacy of conquest."[84]

A little tidbit in the local newspaper points out how pervasive the assumption of immigrant inclusion had become in the dominant narrative of the West. In 1950, columnist Roger S. Davis, a third-generation immigrant, lavished praise on the town's grand Civic Center opening gala. In his regular *Carbon County News* column, Davis gushed that the show was an "excellent example of the type of entertainment that is possible in a multi-cultural society. It defied an 'impossibility.'" A few paragraphs later, however, Davis launched into a racist story about the Crow Indians. He suggested that instead of painting Indians around the tepee in a new town mural, the artist should

Red Lodge's ethnic identities merged easily with its western identities as shown in the red tepee used to spruce up the drum for the Yugoslavian band. (Author's photo)

just wait until next Fourth of July and "he may have some genuine ones around it. If the Redmen get some firewater, there may be three or four resting near the mural after several attempts at running headlong into the tepees door flap."[85] This weak little anecdote, common enough in a western culture that perpetually ridiculed American Indians, stands out mostly for the juxtaposition between the celebration of "multiculturalism" and the continuing derogatory attitude toward Indians in public forums. "Dumb Finn" jokes, doubtless, still made their way through the community, but not into the local newspapers' coverage of the town's ethnic festivities. These events, especially the Festival of Nations, were somehow too special, sacred even, to permit so much as a hint of bigotry against European ethnics. Indians, however, stood outside the town and outside the local definition of multiculturalism. Although their ancestors had lived in the region longer than anyone else, Indians were not Montanans. They were the conquered, not the conquerors. Their continued exclusion from public assumptions of "Montanan" only highlighted the successful incorporation of European immigrants into the culture of white conquerors.

Residents whitewashed Red Lodge's ethnic past in the Festival of Nations and other local histories, blurring or eliminating the very real racial distinctions that still shaped local culture and identity. In much the same way, residents chose to ignore the deep class distinctions that had defined community life during the mining years and that continued to mark local society. Focusing on safe and attractive ethnic traditions, the festival's historical message obscured the town's history of socialism, unionism, and bitter strikes, class-driven movements that had divided the community more completely than differences of clothing or cooking styles. For a variety of reasons, residents preferred not to remember publicly what had divided them most deeply.

Like race, class was a national problem best ignored in the 1950s when the rhetorical battle of one-upmanship raged between the United States and the emerging Communist bloc. Attacked by communists for the great disparity of wealth in their nation, Americans began to stress a pluralistic model of American society that denied the persistence of class divisions. According to this model, the United States did not have fixed classes that determined a person's identity and destiny. Refuting studies done in the 1930s that suggested the presence of a real, vital class system in the nation, sociologists in the early 1950s argued that class, if present in communities, was fluid, and Americans were continuously moving upward.[86] These ideas, which tended to ignore or gloss over the connections between race and opportunity, assumed popular form. As early as 1940, a *Fortune* magazine survey found that 47 percent of Americans considered themselves "middle class," while 10.6 percent thought of themselves as "working, laboring," 2.9 percent as "upper," and only 4 percent as "lower."[87] In 1949, *Life* magazine published a story on Rockford, Illinois, that defined and examined the town's six classes, but with an emphasis on the advancement between classes. Most of the representative figures from each class had moved up at least one rung ("upper-lower" to "lower-middle" or "upper-middle" to "middle-upper") in his or her lifetime. Even the "lower-lower" class resident, Sam Sygulla, who lived in a trailer court and had not graduated from high school, saw himself on the move. As the reporter put it, "Sam is at the bottom of the ladder. But he has dreams. He is excited about an air-conditioning training program in Chicago which he may join."[88] The only thing standing between Sam and "upper-lower" — or even "lower-middle" — status was hard work and determination.

Red Lodge's Festival of Nations embraced this pluralistic model at the local level. Residents publicly denied the town's very real class divisions — past and present — to emphasize, instead, their triumphant tale of ethnicity united. This erasure of class as a community division showed up clearly not only in the Festival of Nations' performances of timeless ethnicity but also in the printed and spoken histories of the event.[89] The best example of classlessness as a historical creation was provided by local author Leona Lampi's 1961 article, "Red Lodge: From a Frenetic Past of Crows, Coal and Boom and Bust Emerges a Unique Festival of Diverse Nationality Groups," published in *Montana: The Magazine of Western History*. A Red Lodge native and second-generation Finnish immigrant, Lampi made ethnicity the key point of historical community division. Relying on wishful booster literature about the town's turn-of-the-century working class, she painted a portrait of Red Lodge laborers that fit exactly with the messages conveyed by the Festival of Nations. Describing local miners at the turn of the century, for example, Lampi quoted directly from an 1892 article in the Northern Pacific Railroad's *Northwest Magazine*, designed specifically to create a positive portrait of Red Lodge for potential investors:

The miners are an orderly and intelligent class and there have been no labor troubles of too serious a nature to be settled by the tact, kindness and good sense of the management. Some of the men live with their families in neat and comfortable homes built by the coal company and others live in little log cottages of their own. They support churches and are eager to secure for their children as good an education as the graded public school of the town affords. The troops of rosy-cheeked little ones that flock to the school every morning leave no room for doubt as to the healthfulness of this mountain climate.[90]

Class lines barely mattered in early Red Lodge; everyone in the community shared the same basic middle-class values of home, church, and school. The only divisions that counted, in Lampi's history as in the Festival of Nations, lay within the "often-seething melting pot" of the town's various "nationality" enclaves. Immigrant groups maintained their boundaries so thoroughly, Lampi maintained, that "if there was crossing of the 'line,' at dances and other gatherings, contact would almost invariably end in fist fights and brawls."[91] By the 1940s, however, these divergent groups finally broke down the walls dividing them and joined equally in claiming a sense of place and roots in this western town. The story, like the festival, ended triumphantly — with local people eliminating prejudice and intolerance from the community through the agency of a public festival. Even history became inclusive. In Lampi's story all Red Lodge residents could be proud to call themselves the "descendants of our hardy pioneers, American and foreign, who found their way to the banks of a rocky stream at the foothills of the Beartooth Mountains."[92] By depoliticizing class and ignoring race in their local history, residents like Lampi proudly claimed their immigrant parents and grandparents as Red Lodge "pioneers" — peers of the town's original business class, who in the 1890s had implicitly denied this title to miners and immigrants.

But, much as Americans might deny its presence, class *had* mattered in the late nineteenth century, and it still mattered in the middle years of the twentieth century. Red Lodge residents had woven class into the town's nomenclature as surely as they had ethnic distinctions. If there was in Red Lodge a "Finn Town" and "Little Italy," there was also a "Hi Bug," the small-town equivalent of a Nob Hill. Business people, doctors, professionals, and mine officials made their homes in Hi Bug at the north end of town, on a stately tree-lined street away from the smoke of the mines and the garlic-scented homes of the immigrant miners.[93] Although local histories might lightly touch on Hi Bug as simply the place where "affluent native Americans clustered," longtime inhabitants understood the neighborhood in more personal ways.[94] In an industrial mining town marked by the struggles between corporations and labor unions, class distinctions ran deeply enough that residents could still recall them with bitterness after fifty or more years. If the Festival of Nations created a specific public memory that ignored class, it did not supersede or eliminate *personal* memories of this local hierarchy.

Miners, not surprisingly, remained most emphatic in their memories of local class differences. For many miners, in fact, class stood as the key social division in the 1920s, 1930s, and 1940s. Against the perceived inhumanity of the industrial system, workers formed a sense of class that subsumed ethnic differences. Interviewed in the 1980s and early 1990s, former coal miners who had grown up in Red Lodge's small ethnic enclaves continued to structure their memories more around work and class than along ethnic lines.[95] Their working lives had not followed Leona Lampi's tale of happy, contented laborers, and they made clear distinctions between management and labor, capitalists and workers. Miners united across ethnic lines to work, create unions, and face down the operators who, as one miner's son noted, did not care about nationality and language, only that laborers "were over here and they could make them do the hard work."[96]

Looking back at the heyday of Red Lodge mining from the distance of the early 1980s, retired miners like Tony Persha still insisted that mine operators always found good jobs for their own family members but would willingly sacrifice other workers' lives in the name of profit: "They don't care about a man's life; they can always replace that man; a lot of men looking for work."[97] Persha, like other old-time miners, continued to structure his personal memories around class divisions decades after the local mines had closed down. These miners insisted that the multiethnic unions were the only protection the workers had against the power of mine managers. Even when questioned specifically about ethnic differences in the community, miners like John Kastelitz, whose parents were both born in Austria (Slovenia), emphasized class instead. The miners were different nationalities, he admitted, "but we were all 'brothers' and worked together."[98] As another retired miner insisted, "nationality made absolutely no difference" in the working-class neighborhoods, where all would "come to help" a neighbor building a house or putting up a garage.[99] Ethnicity played a great role in these men's lives — many of them, like Persha and Kastelitz, had grown up speaking "Austrian" and other Old World languages — but as industrial laborers they had formed such a strong sense of themselves as workers that class cohesion overwhelmed memories of ethnic differences.

Ethnic differences mattered in the lives of working-class immigrants and their children, but class mattered also. Ethnicity intertwined with class to create boundaries, both real and imagined, in the town's social and cultural life. Indeed, for many long-term residents, class has stood out as the most painful marker of difference in their memories of the town's early days. Not all felt the pain equally, of course. For many ethnic boys in the 1920s and 1930s, for example, class was evident but not that important. Tony Zupan, who graduated from Carbon County High School in 1939, recalled few problems getting along with boys from different ethnic groups or from Hi Bug. A talented athlete, Zupan, like many other second-generation immigrant boys, built alliances on the ball field, where athletic prowess overwhelmed ethnicity and class. Even the Hi Bug boys recognized the leveling of the baseball diamond, where the "rough" boys from the south end of town often held the upper hand. Zupan recognized class divisions, but insisted that sports eliminated such distinctions. "We were on teams together. We were team mates through the high school years, and we just liked each other."[100]

Some girls, though, saw things differently, for gender also shaped how residents perceived social divisions. Red Lodge did not have any girls' sports teams in those years, and even if the boys all played together, the girls, such as Zupan's sister Liz, were always "acutely aware" of differences between their family and the residents of Hi Bug who wore nicer clothes and hired the poor girls to do their work.[101] In the 1920s and 1930s, Slavic, Finnish, and Italian girls, dressed in the outcast clothing their families received from the local relief office, walked daily from "Lo Bug" to the more affluent homes of the town's north end to clean house and do laundry. Little social interaction took place between the daughters of the Hi Bug and the "foreign girls" who cleaned their houses.[102] Some, like Rose Jurkovich, harbored resentment for decades against the better-off townsfolk who thought "they could get the foreign people to work and slave for them for absolutely nothing."[103] Although the festival and printed local histories may have ignored the class dimension of past community divisions, these young women could not. Almost a half century later, these now middle-class women continued to feel the residual humiliation of having once been forced to play the role of servant, inferior to the town's upper crust.

The most vivid class distinctions faded as the mines closed and the population shrank, but they did not disappear. Even into the 1950s, as townspeople celebrated their annual festival of unity and friendship, county leaders continued to publish in the Red Lodge newspaper the names of all those receiving general relief payments from the state welfare system. In defiance of established state policies, local civic leaders insisted that those getting assistance should be publicly shamed.[104] American pluralism, after all, presumed that people would work their way up the ladder on their own, not take government aid to get by. Other signs of continuing class divisions manifested themselves over time. In the 1970s, middle-class residents mobilized against the presence of inexpensive mobile and modular homes in certain neighborhoods, requesting that mobile homes "and houses that look like trailers" be restricted to a tract of land near the local landfill.[105] Inexpensive housing had its place — out by the dump. Likewise, a federally funded low-income housing project was acceptable only on the fringes of town, beside the local "See 'Em Alive Zoo."[106]

The Festival of Nations, organized and promoted by a concerned group of middle-class activists, ignored these lingering class issues, creating instead a joyous celebration of classless immigrants united in a story of American progress and success. And immigrants and their children, many of whom considered themselves "middle class" by the 1950s, supported this interpretation of local history that privileged benign ethnicity over painful memories of deference and service to a local upper class. Through the Festival of Nations, Red Lodge residents constructed a vision of classless, raceless, timeless ethnicity that they used to create an appealing local heritage; they celebrated diversity to create and commemorate local unity.[107]

Of course, too much unity could be a problem if it threatened to turn into homogeneity. Festival promoters needed *difference*, lots of it, in their annual public display of diversity. The Festival of Nations, after all, was not simply an expression of local cultural values; it also had developed into a major tourist attraction by the mid-1950s. Ironically, however, just as the organizers began to promote the Festival of Nations as a living model of international brotherhood, the examples of international harmony supposedly embodied in the festival were visibly fading from the community. By the 1950s, ethnic differences were safe enough for public celebration, in part because Old World customs and flavors had ceased to be part of the visible everyday life of the town. Fewer and fewer residents spoke the old languages on the streets of Red Lodge, the trainloads of grapes for homemade wines had long since stopped arriving, and "Finn Town" had become a geographic rather than an ethnic designation. Within the first few years of the celebration, some festival tourists began to complain that the people of Red Lodge appeared disappointingly American (remarkably similar to the earlier complaint by rodeo attendees that residents were too "modern" to be convincingly "western"). And, unfortunately, the town's homogenous American identity grew only more pronounced over the years, as the original immigrant generation inevitably continued to age and die. As one observer noted in the 1980s, a large percentage of the population claimed Italian descent, but the local grocery stores did not carry olive oil in anything other than small, specialty containers.[108] Residents proudly announced their ethnicity to strangers, but their accents, clothes, customs, and even foods seemed to be generically white western American. The town no longer needed a festival to unite residents across ethnic lines; it needed the festival to reinforce those lines publicly.

Even as festival promoters presented an increasingly grand message about their celebration by the mid-1950s, they had to work harder to produce visible displays of ethnic difference. In order for the festival to demonstrate harmony among different peoples — and remain successful as a tourist attraction — it had to display to visitors and locals the differences among town residents that life in Red Lodge had gradually erased. This contradiction in presentation and message meant that local leaders had to plead continually with residents, especially those who worked downtown, to appear ethnic for the tourists. Appearing ethnic usually meant wearing costumes but also included playing instruments like the accordion or learning and performing Old World folk dances. Festival leaders tended to emphasize costumes as the easiest way to convey ethnic differences. Almost anything would do. "A simple gathered skirt and dirndl blouse, or a vestee, bonnet or sash will do wonders to make your ordinary clothes look like a costume," begged the organizers in 1955 as they sought to please visitors who wanted residents to appear at least a little exotic.[109]

Every year festival organizers publicly praised the great community spirit and deep ethnic heritages that embodied the all-volunteer Festival of Nations. But for many residents, as indicated by the ongoing pleas for people to dress up, ethnicity did not necessarily mean putting on a costume and performing in public. Hundreds of residents took part in the festival every year, proudly showing off the costumes, dance steps, and recipes that made them feel particularly Finnish or Norwegian or Italian. But other first-, second-, and third-generation immigrants simply did not see the point of buying or sewing European peasant outfits, learning folk dances, or cooking food for crowds of tourists. Ethnicity had certainly shaped the lives of most Red Lodge residents — the town was still 21 percent foreign-born in 1950[110]— but, except for the nine days of the festival, that ethnicity took more private forms of expression. The local undertaker read Finnish prayers at funerals, and residents spoke Slovenian or Italian to their parents, visited family in Norway, or longed for the good Finnish bread the local bakery used to supply.[111] *Public* ethnicity, however, was a burden that not everyone wanted to assume in the cause of trying to make tourists satisfied with their experience in the town. For festival workers desperate to make Red

Lodge live up to some idealized vision of a multicultural European peasant village, ethnicity was not what it should be.

As festival organizers struggled to make Red Lodge "look" ethnic, they found themselves increasingly dependent on the efforts of "symbolic" ethnics: residents whose connection to the ethnic group was not always strong, but who desired to express their ethnic heritages in public ways. Like many other Americans in the 1960s and 1970s, these local people continued to identify with certain ethnic groups long after cohesive ethnic communities had fallen apart. Herbert J. Gans called this "symbolic ethnicity." Looking at later-generation ethnics, he observed that ethnicity created no demands or restraints upon individuals, who felt free to choose attractive, easy, and convenient aspects of an ethnic culture to celebrate. Individuals chose to be ethnic, in part, to differentiate themselves from an American society that seemed increasingly homogenous and bland.[112] As a respondent in a study done by Mary C. Waters put it: "We feel uneasy before the prospect of becoming just Americans. We feel uneasy before the prospect of becoming as undistinguishable from one another as our motel rooms are, or as flavorless and mass produced as the bread many of us eat."[113] According to Werner Sollors, that blandness of American culture actually made possible such a notion as "symbolic ethnicity." "It is," he states, "ironically, because Americans take so much for granted among themselves that they can dramatize their differences comfortably."[114]

Symbolic or voluntary ethnics wanted their ethnicity to be comfortable and easy to put on, making no real demands on their lives but serving to make them feel special. Public performances, like ethnic festivals, provided easy ways for later-generation immigrants to retain a feeling of ethnicity. Such festivities did not make great demands on individuals but could be fun and interesting ways of setting themselves off against a homogenous American culture.[115] Unlike the downtown workers who had to be coaxed into donning "dirndls and vestees," some residents took great pride and pleasure in dressing up in Old World costumes and performing complicated dances or displaying family treasures from Norway or Serbia. The praise and encouragement that such performances received from admiring audiences only reinforced this sense of pride and enjoyment.[116] Spurred on by festival promoters and the ready audiences of the celebration, local residents formed ethnic bands, dance groups, and choirs, often practicing year-round for the annual summer event.

The festival became so successful in reviving certain types of ethnic per-

formances that Red Lodge actually began to export its public ethnicity. Red
Lodge bands and dance groups, resuscitated by the festival's annual presentations, gained some regional notoriety in the 1960s and 1970s. The Yugoslavian Tamburitza Band, a small string orchestra, attained the greatest success.
The eleven-man group cut two records after it officially reorganized in 1961
to perform at the Festival of Nations. Although labeled as "an outgrowth of
the early Yugoslavian musicians who came to Montana in the early part of the
20th century," the group admitted that it was not entirely of "Yugoslavian
descent" anymore. All members, however, shared "a familiarity with the guitar and mandolin-like tamburitza instruments," a rather vague definition of
"ethnic" affiliation.[117] Other groups found themselves in demand at cultural
events and festivals around the region. In the 1980s, a strong Scandinavian
folk dance troupe performed at various Oktoberfests and other autumn celebrations in Montana and Wyoming. Another good example of an invented
ethnic group — Scandinavians, after all, had fought each other bitterly over
the centuries — Red Lodge's dancing Norwegians, Danes, and Swedes traveled regularly to folk seminars in Colorado to learn new dances and brush up
on techniques.[118]

Individuals also sparked interest and excitement in certain nationalities.
Finnish-American singer Sue Maki faithfully performed year after year at the
Festival of Nations, a central figure at that nationality's evening program.
"Montana" Vera Buening, similarly, led the Montana Day entertainment for
decades; dancing around the floor in her hand-sewn cowgirl outfits, squeez-
ing out tunes on her accordion, Buening almost single-handedly kept Montana Day alive through the 1980s. Such dedication ebbed and flowed, however.
The Tamburitza Band dissolved in the 1980s, only to be reborn again in the
1990s (no records were cut this time around), and an aged Buening no longer
had the strength to perform by the mid-1990s.

As newcomers took the place of those who quit or moved on, the festival
retained the same structure and messages given to it by concerned residents
in the early 1950s. Each generation, however, added its own meanings to the
public ethnicity it chose to perform each August for the town and for itself.
Deeply felt ethnic affiliations did not necessarily have much to do with these
continuing performances. Rather than exemplifying the peaceful coexistence
of diverse peoples, the festival really showcased residents who had the time
and interest to learn about ethnic traditions, practice them, and present them

in public. One young participant in 1996 explained her varied performances this way: "I dance the Scotch-Irish because it's really peppy and upbeat. Also, my grandfather is Scotch. The Yugoslavian I dance just because I like it and I dance German because my great-grandparents came from Germany."[119]

The Red Lodge Festival of Nations, a cultural product of the anxious years of the early cold war, continued to exist largely through the efforts of a firm core of "symbolic ethnics," both from within and outside the community, who enjoyed their ethnic affiliations and relished the opportunity to show off costumes, songs, and dance steps to receptive audiences.

Red Lodge's public celebration of immigrant cultures played like a reversal of the famous Americanization pageant presented by the graduating class of Henry Ford's English School during World War I. In Ford's drama, immigrant workers marched on stage "dressed in their national garbs" and then poured themselves into "the Ford melting pot" from which they emerged "dressed in their best American clothes and waving American flags."[120] In the Festival of Nations, American descendants of immigrants performed the flip side of this ritual by symbolically reappropriating the "national garb" that the Ford workers had stripped off decades earlier. In this act of reappropriation, Red Lodge "ethnics" publicly reclaimed their parents' and grandparents' European clothing, dances, and foods — emerging from their own local melting pot as timeless, classless ethnics whose traditions and customs fit comfortably into American middle-class society. In so doing, they reflected current conceptions of Americanism and America as a land of immigrants.

The Festival of Nations quickly assumed a prominent place in Red Lodge's public presentation of itself. Ethnicity joined the cowboy of the Wild West as a marker of local identity. Like the cowboy, the symbolic ethnic was an ahistorical figure, stripped of class and racial context and remodeled into a representation of what modern residents wanted that figure to be. Inspired by national propaganda efforts and other international festivals, Red Lodge inhabitants created a public ethnicity that was both attractive to tourists and reaffirmed the place of immigrant forebears in the town's history. Drawing selectively from the town's past, residents generated a historical narrative to support this appealing vision of ethnic difference and progress. Tourists did not want to be confronted with messy race and class issues in Red Lodge's ethnic festival; locals wanted to include their families in the progressive story of American pluralism. In the best cold war fashion, organizers produced a festival of American pluralism, of differences combined into a joyous, peaceful celebration of democratic opportunity.

The simplicity and power of this message of triumphant ethnic diversity contributed to the appeal of the Festival of Nations for both participants and visitors. The festival was Red Lodge's embodiment of the national motto: *e pluribus unum*. From the many are made one. Its performance commemorated the conviction held by many Americans by the middle of the twentieth century that (European) immigrant history lay at the very heart of American identity. America was a nation of immigrants who came together, overcoming differences, in the pursuit of common dreams of liberty and democracy. From many different peoples was made one strong, vibrant nation. The Festival of Nations, locals believed, exemplified this harmonious development. They held up the festival as a model of success to which other nations should pay heed: the rest of the world should be more like Red Lodge, more like America. Like a set of mirrors, the festival reflected not only America in Red Lodge but also Red Lodge in the Festival of Nations. Through a display of European ethnicity and rhetoric about international cooperation, Red Lodge residents presented themselves as a living embodiment of what had made America great. And this ideal of ethnic pluralism in turn became part of the Red Lodge identity. Because European ethnicity has been displayed and celebrated so prominently every year, it has become an integral part of how residents think about their community and their own place within it.

6

Nature's West

Man's conquest of raw nature is the subject of all history.
—Montana Power Company advertisement, 1934

Red Lodge is a stunningly beautiful place. Although the town itself may sometimes seem run-down, shabby around the edges, or a bit ticky-tacky touristy, the scenery that surrounds the community more than makes up for any aesthetic untidiness in the town proper. Standing in the shadows of the Beartooth Range of the Rocky Mountains, which includes the highest peaks in Montana, Red Lodge is only a few miles from what many Americans consider the archetype of "beautiful nature." Soaring mountain peaks, vast forests, rushing streams, dramatic waterfalls, wild animals, and Yellowstone National Park itself lie in the backyard of the little mining town. In terms of physical beauty, Red Lodge stands in sharp contrast to the region's largest city, Billings, only sixty miles away. Travel less than a dozen miles east over the sheltering benchlands of Rock Creek and it's almost like dropping into a different world. In Red Lodge, mountain breezes carry the coolness of snowcapped, glaciated peaks. Billings, in contrast, feels more like part of the desert than the mountains, more prone to the chill Canadian winds in the winter and the shimmering stillness of scorching summer days. Billings is part of the high plains of eastern Montana, characterized by dry, brown prairies, winding coulees, and dramatic rimrocks that are intriguing but hardly as pretty as the green mountains and fields of wildflowers one finds around Red Lodge. That beauty ensured Red Lodge's survival. Americans, it turned out, would pay to vacation in a town like Red Lodge with its sweeping views, its trout streams, and its location at the end of a highway access to Yellowstone National Park.

From its founding to the present, the natural world has always been a prominent part of Red Lodge's image and identity. The mountains towering south and west of town, the rich coal carried out of its meandering mine tunnels, the mild summers and long winters, all shaped what Red Lodge looked like, what it meant to residents, and how visitors perceived it. In key ways, the natural world also became an integral part of the town's deliberate creation of its public identity. Coal, wild animals, and the beauty of the Beartooths all worked their way into the vocabulary, the townscape, the very definition of what it meant to be of Red Lodge. Coal, of course, dominated the town's initial identity, but in the 1930s, when the Northern Pacific Railroad closed down its last Red Lodge mine and the federal government constructed the spectacular Beartooth Highway from Red Lodge to Yellowstone National Park, the town's identification with the natural world would make a seismic shift. Red Lodge ceased being the "Coal Metropolis" and became instead a "gateway" to nature's "Wonderland." With the construction of the Beartooth Highway, the surrounding mountains and forests became an integral part of Red Lodge's public sense of itself. Even before the road, local promoters used "Beartooth" to mark the town's connection to the wilderness, and residents used the natural world for their own recreation and survival. But the highway, the increased popularity of national forests in the 1930s, and the demise of the local coal industry transformed local identity so that the natural world became an ever greater part of the town's image and reason for being.[1]

Of course, the transformation did not take place overnight. Many residents continued to mine in the Beartooth fields five miles out of town into the 1950s; even in the 1990s, some local people would still cling to the old hope that coal mining would return to Red Lodge. The change, however, was permanent. Mining was dead; long live scenery and fishing and camping and hiking. The natural world that used to provide sustenance through the wages of digging coal would now begin to provide economic well-being through the thousands of tourists and outdoor enthusiasts who would seek out nature in Red Lodge, the Beartooths, and Yellowstone Park. And as the economics of resource extraction in the community moved from coal mining to nature tourism, so too did local ideas about the very meaning of "nature" and the place of "the natural" in and around Red Lodge.

"Nature," as historian William Cronon points out, "is a human idea, with a long and complicated cultural history which has led different human beings to conceive of the natural world in very different ways."[2] In the twentieth century, Red Lodge residents became, quite literally, part of shifting national ideas about what nature was, how it should be valued and enjoyed, and whose conceptions of natural should take precedence in the West's millions of acres of federal lands. In many ways, local concerns and definitions of "the natural," or "wilderness," coincided with those of popular culture. In fact, Red Lodge residents made a living out of catering to the popular notions of enjoying "wilderness" experiences: creating dude ranches, highways, and motels to entice nature tourists into the community. Sometimes, though, local people created their own ideas about the place of nature, based on very intimate economic and personal concerns about work and quality of living. From the 1930s into the present, all residents had to adjust to a basic transformation in the role nature would play in the town's economy and identity as Red Lodge lost its mining industry and gained a highway into Yellowstone National Park.

So, even while residents negotiated multiple and shifting public images as a "western" and "ethnic" and "tourist" community, they had also to work through an essential economic shift that refocused the very sense of what Red Lodge was. No longer able to survive through the extraction and sale of one natural resource — coal — local people found other facets of the natural world that Americans were increasingly eager to purchase. In marketing the natural beauty around their little community, residents created a new public identity for Red Lodge. As the "coal metropolis" slipped away, "nature's town" emerged to take its place.

In the beginning, Red Lodge was defined by nature, but nature was seen as little more than the coal that created its economic infrastructure, its industrial population, its very reason for being. Industrial Red Lodge of the 1890s through the 1910s developed as a place focused on the *work* of finding and using the area's abundant natural resources. The town's initial public identity centered around the labor and profits of exporting rich, dark coal to the outside world. Coal, rock, and timber built the physical world of Red Lodge at the turn of the century, and thousands of local residents used their hands, backs, and sweat to dig, cut, and cart these natural resources from the earth. Most of Red Lodge's inhabitants in those early years knew the natural world through their work in it.[3]

Miners, most significantly, worked intimately with nature, digging rock hundreds of feet below the streets of Red Lodge. As much as 65 percent of the adult male population labored in the coal mines during the boom years of the early twentieth century.[4] The dark, dangerous mine tunnels had none of the aesthetic appeal of the region's picturesque alpine vistas, but they were just as much a part of nature as the mountains and trees up above. And knowledge of the natural world — the acquired skills of years of working with rock and dirt — conveyed power to experienced workers who took pride in knowing where to place explosives, how much powder to use to open up a coal vein, and when to flee from pockets of deadly gasses. They always, always respected the environment in which they worked. They could ill afford not to: those who did not respect the mines died in the mines. Mining was tough, demanding work that not everyone could do; miners knew this. When local coal operators called in the United States Army to dig coal during a prolonged 1922 strike, miners sat back and watched with amusement. They knew that unskilled workers — those who did not understand the underground world of dirt, rocks, and coal seams — would never be able to dig much coal out of the mines. And they were right. In a few weeks of work, the soldiers managed to extract only a carload or two of coal, or about as much as an experienced miner and his helpers could dig in several hours. Old-time miner Ollie Anderson chuckled that the soldiers "couldn't even mine enough coal, you know, to keep a stove hot."[5] An intimate knowledge of the natural world marked the skilled miner and gave him some economic stability in a volatile economy.

This working relationship with the natural world, like most relationships, was never simple or easy. Miners who labored in the tunnels both loved and hated what they did for a living. In their oral histories, old-time miners only rarely recalled their years of mining with the hazy fondness characteristic of many other reminiscences. The long, backbreaking hours of work, months without seeing the sun, and dust and danger of machinery seemed to overwhelm occasional stories of jokes, songs, or camaraderie underground. Mostly, the men remembered the hard work and the darkness. Leo Michelcic said he used to recite the same phrase every time he emerged from the tunnels: "I'm sure glad to see the sun again, I hope I see it again."[6] Miner Tony Persha swore that given the choice, "I wouldn't do it again. . . . It isn't worth it, crazy to work like we did."[7] But there remained among the shrinking cadre of former Red Lodge miners the lingering pride in work well done, in the labor and knowledge and luck that kept them alive and in Red Lodge during the hard years of the 1930s, 1940s, and 1950s. Loading coal, Daniel McDonald mused, was a "back-breaking job I'll tell ya . . . [but] she was a great life. . . . I ain't kidding ya, if I had my life to live over, I'd go right back." Mining, he concluded, just "gets in your blood or something."[8] The sweat, skill, and danger of mining bestowed a certain dignity upon the men who had survived and prevailed.

As machines replaced human skills and human contact with the coal seams, local coal workers gradually become more distanced from the natural world. In the late 1910s and early 1920s, mine operators began to bring in joy-loaders and other mechanized equipment that dug and loaded coal ever more quickly and efficiently. Steam and diesel engines replaced animal and human labor, and miners could no longer count on their skills as mule skinners, diggers, or powdermen to guarantee them work in the tunnels. Machines removed men from the direct contact and knowledge they had once had with the rock and coal; mechanical drills and loaders kicked up so much dust and made such noise that men could barely see where they worked or hear the creaking of support timbers. Eventually, the new strip mines at Colstrip in eastern Montana completely removed men from the coal tunnels. At Colstrip huge earthmovers dug away at the soil to expose seams of coal, which were removed by other big machines, without a man ever having to touch the coal itself. Red Lodge miner Daniel McDonald dismissed such operations as not *real* mining. "It wouldn't be a mine, would it?" he asked. "You're out in the open all the time, you're out in the weather, the sun shines, stuff like that."[9]

But real mining or not, Colstrip's nonunion operation sounded the death knell for the Red Lodge mines. As the Northern Pacific shifted its operations to these distant strip mines and away from the deep underground works of the Red Lodge field, labor in the natural world no longer defined the town or its people. This is not to say that Red Lodge residents stopped working in the natural world, or that the natural world ceased to provide the foundation of the local economy. Rather, in the mid–twentieth century, local residents' work with the natural world — and, thus, their identification with that world — shifted. Nature became more about play than about work. Instead of digging coal out of the earth or felling trees for mine timbers, workers started to create jobs out of helping outsiders *play* in and with nature. They became pack guides, hotel maids, bus drivers, restaurant waiters, soda jerks — all serving the needs and desires of the thousands of tourists who would start coming through town as Red Lodge created itself as a gateway to the "wonderlands" of Yellowstone National Park and the Beartooth Mountains. The town's industrial identity, centered around black-faced miners, corporate wages, and unionism, faded away as the mines stopped working. In turn, Red Lodge residents' sense of themselves changed as they distanced themselves from the work of mining and tied their town more closely to the mystique of the Yellowstone region and assumed the role of selling the beauties of the Rocky Mountains.

Although the shift toward Red Lodge "the gateway" town occurred rather quickly in the 1930s — when the East Side Mine closed down and left the town with only the Beartooth coal fields for its economic survival — the roots of local attempts to sell the area's natural beauties ran much deeper. In fact, almost since the town's inception, boosters and other residents had recognized the potential economic value of Red Lodge's picture-perfect setting, and some local people had always thought of the natural world less as a place of work than as a site for leisure. The same boosters who had promoted Red Lodge as a civilized urban metropolis in the 1890s and who had emphasized Red Lodge's connection to Liver-Eating Johnson's "mountain man" imagery had also worked hard to establish the beautiful outdoors as part of the town's public identity. By the time Red Lodge was founded in the late 1880s, after all, the notion of nature as a place for play and spiritual fulfillment had already swept through the upper and middle classes of the nation.

American elites in the years after the Civil War had embraced the ideas promulgated by eighteenth- and nineteenth-century Romantics that in nature human beings might find the "sublime" and "picturesque" — views and experiences that could uplift the soul and bring a person closer to seeing God. The increasing industrialization of the postwar years only reinforced this proclivity toward favoring nature. Machines and cities, it seemed, endangered the nation's founding masculine virtues: self-sufficiency, independence, valor. Feeling uneasy about a perceived overcivilization, upper-class Americans created a new mystique about the outdoors, turning to the natural world to cure many of society's ills. Wealthy urbanites built summer cabins in the Adirondacks to renew themselves and sponsored the creation of various youth camps to inspire the right kind of morality in the nation's youth. Nature enthusiasts started organizations such as the Campfire Club (1897), the American Boy Scouts (1907), and YMCA boys' camps to encourage youngsters to develop their own affinities for the natural world.[10] As part of this growing veneration for the outdoors, Americans also began to take an intense interest in the preservation of natural areas, promoting the establishment of Yellowstone National Park in 1872, Yosemite National Park in 1890, and the Adirondacks State Forest Preserve in 1892. By the turn of the century, nature had become something to be enjoyed, admired, and saved (at least certain parts of it) from industrial development.[11]

Red Lodge promoters and business owners quickly realized that the Beartooth Mountains region just southwest of Red Lodge was almost exactly what many Americans described as the ideal natural landscape: mountains, forests, lakes, streams, flowers, and lots of big animals. And although they always banked on the region's coal and agriculture to build Red Lodge, entrepreneurial town builders in the 1890s recognized the power of the picturesque and readily incorporated popular language about the natural world into their effusive descriptions of the town's surroundings. It is not surprising, in fact, that Red Lodge boosters and other residents used the same kinds of phrasing and images as the various nature writers whose work made its way into mass-produced books and magazines by the turn of the century. Even if they had not waded through the great Romantic works of William Wordsworth or Henry David Thoreau, many of Red Lodge's town builders had probably read some of the popular nature stories of Ernest Thomas Seton, the hunting exploits of Theodore Roosevelt, or the travel narratives of Mary Roberts Rinehart and Helen Hunt Jackson, some of which were published in such widely distributed magazines as *Ladies Home Journal* or *Atlantic Monthly* or were even serialized in regional newspapers.[12]

These authors not only helped popularize the scenery of the West, but they also gave Americans the language to describe this dramatic environment. In 1883, for example, Helen Hunt Jackson published this description of a sunset on Mount Rainier: "In many years' familiar knowledge of all the wonders which sunrise and sunset can work on peaks in the Rocky Mountain ranges, I had never seen any such effect. It was as if the color came from within, and not from without; as if the mighty bulwark were being gradually heated from central fires. . . . The spectacle was so solemn that it was impossible to divest one's self of a certain sense of awe."[13] She echoed the observations of Isabella L. Bird, published a few years earlier, upon viewing the sunset at Green Lake in the Rocky Mountains: "I had come up into the pure air and sunset light, and the glory of the unprofaned works of God."[14] These prominent writers' effusive descriptions of the area gave, as Earl Pomeroy put it, "a certain literary and historical sanction" to the mountainous West.[15]

Although Red Lodge would not aggressively enter the business of nature tourism until the 1920s and 1930s, as early as the 1890s, boosters recognized the power of the "picturesque" and eagerly endeavored to best the popular nature writers by distributing lavish descriptions of Red Lodge's own mountains and forests with the goal of attracting wealthy tourists, health seekers, and hardy recreationists to the area. In 1892, for example, a story about Carbon County invited readers (ideally, potential settlers or investors) to "imagine, if you can, the summer loveliness of this free, wide open country where no fences mar the face of the landscape, where every prospect is an outlook over a vast flower garden, where stately mountains suggest mystery and aspiration and where a vivid blue heaven bends over all."[16] One year later, another story praised the Beartooth region for being "as pretty a country for the tourist as there is in the world. It is all beautiful parks, lakes, and forest and a natural home for big game. This place will some day come into prominence as the finest place in America for tourists and others who are in search of health and recreation."[17] Picturesque scenery and sublime vistas showed up over and over again in booster descriptions of the land around Red Lodge. In 1907 the editor of the Red Lodge *Picket* painted this picture of a particular lake in the nearby mountains: "On the placid surface of this sheet of water are reflected the frowning outlines of the cliffs surrounding the amphitheater. Nature herself has appropriated this spot for castle building, and the dream castles she builds are focused on the retina of this lake in exquisite design and gradually merging into the dark shadows of the banks."[18]

More than the purple prose of boosters and newspaper editors, Red Lodge benefited from its very location on the edge of the newly established Yellowstone Forest Preserve and only fifty some miles (as the crow flew) from the border of Yellowstone National Park. By the turn of the century, Northern Pacific Railroad promotions had made "Yellowstone" synonymous with "wilderness" and "spectacular nature." Dubbed "Wonderland" by these early promoters, the nation's first national park quickly emerged as a cultural icon in America's growing fascination with rugged, beautiful wildlands. The park, remote though it was to much of the nation, drew nearly ten thousand visitors a year by the late 1890s.[19] Theodore Roosevelt himself toured Yellowstone National Park in 1903, celebrating the place as a bit of "the old wilderness scenery and old wilderness life."[20] Other visitors were more vocally ecstatic about the "marvelous formations of nature" and "vast collection of marvels" that made up the park.[21]

Yellowstone came to epitomize the spectacular natural world, and fortunately enough for local boosters, the Yellowstone Forest Preserve, set aside in

1891, extended at least the name "Yellowstone" almost to the border of Red Lodge. The little mining town practically touched Yellowstone itself, or so promoters would have one believe. Later designated as the Beartooth Forest Reserve and then the Custer National Forest, this vast expanse of government land running south and west of Red Lodge to the park's boundaries remained relatively untouched through the 1920s — too remote and mountainous to attract much development or exploration but ideal, according to local boosters, for adventurers seeking a touch of the "strenuous" life and the glamour of Yellowstone by hunting or camping in the wilderness.

From the town's earliest years, these images of Yellowstone and the Beartooths made their way into the public identity of Red Lodge as local residents formed their own attachments to these wildlands. Through pictures, articles, and advertisements, the surrounding landscape established itself in the local townscape. By the 1890s, professional photographers were taking pictures of the lakes, streams, and peaks of the Beartooth region, which businesses printed as postcards and published not only in the town's newspapers but also in the high school literary magazine and yearbooks. The 1909 Carbon County High School Annual, for example, featured photographs not of downtown buildings or mine works but of area waterfalls, creeks, and cliffs. Advertisers reinforced this identification with local forests and mountains by pitching their new outdoor merchandise to students and parents alike. "Take a Kodak and fishing rod and spend your vacation right," the Talmadge Mercantile Company advised readers about to enjoy three months of summer weather.[22] Such images became part of Red Lodge's identity, and part of what it meant to be of Red Lodge was seeing these kinds of photographs and advertisements in most of the town's public forums. It also meant taking Talmadge's advice to head into the woods for the summer, although maybe without the expensive camera and fancy fishing gear.

Indeed, from the early 1890s through the twentieth century, local people ventured out into the nature around Red Lodge with great frequency. Experiences with the natural landscape varied widely according to class and gender, but all reflected in some way Americans' increasing desire to move outside urban areas and enjoy contact with nature. Those wealthy enough threw themselves into nature for weeks at a time. In the early 1890s, the local paper made note of dozens of Red Lodge residents who packed into the Beartooth Mountains for a month or more, many of them journeying into Yellowstone National

Park to enjoy the scenic wonders. Known as sourdough tourists (as opposed to the Pullman tourists who came by train), these local vacationers — men and women alike — might camp for a week or more at some particularly amenable spot, fishing and hunting amid the splendor of nature's beauty.[23] By the early 1900s, residents on these camping tours carried their own cameras into the wild, capturing lakes, mountains, streams, and geysers on film and then carefully pasting them onto the heavy black paper of formal scrapbooks. Some even interspersed the poetry of Keats, Wordsworth, and Emerson with the photos, embellishing the still shots of sublime nature with the printed words that had helped shape Americans' understandings of the natural world.[24] As these residents went into the woods and carried stories and images away from their adventures, they helped to establish a connection between Red Lodge and the wonders of the surrounding mountains.

And the outdoors was not reserved for the well-to-do. Local workers also enjoyed nature, even if they could not afford to spend weeks exploring the far reaches of Yellowstone National Park. Rock Creek, which ran right along the east side of town, quickly became a favorite retreat for the community's laboring class. Many residents took advantage of any holiday from mine work to gather at picnic sites along the creek where they fished, gathered berries, and enjoyed the mild summer weather. Slovenians established the Happy Brothers Camping Ground for picnics and outdoor dancing, while the Finns set up their own Kaleva picnic area for group excursions. Women as well as men participated in these community events, even though the former often had to carry household chores such as cooking and cleaning out to the popular picnic grounds. Fishing, the other favorite outdoors pastime, was, however, much more of a male activity. Many of the miners spent the slow summer months fishing in the creek, wandering up and down the banks to find the best spots. And workers who wanted to stay out drinking past the midnight saloon closures often headed out to water's edge to share "funny stories" along with a bottle of wine.[25]

In some way or another, most local residents made the effort to leave the "urban" environment of Red Lodge to enjoy the beauty, resources, or privacy of the natural world. Although motivated by a variety of personal reasons to venture "into the woods," part of the appeal of the natural world probably came from the changing attitudes of eastern elites. Indeed, although some westerners preferred to think of these outdoor excursions as a legacy of their hard, frontier heritage, historian Earl Pomeroy has instead attributed the growing appeal of outdoor recreation in the West to influences from the East.[26] Even though some residents still feared the towering mountains and the raging waters of Rock Creek, local people picnicked and hiked and camped for enjoyment in the Beartooths not only because the woods were a convenient and close place for recreation but also because by the late nineteenth century Americans had learned to regard such places as appropriate vacation and recreation sites. In any case, local people went into these places and thus created connections between their town and the natural world around it.

Significantly, however, for most Red Lodge residents in the early years of the century, experiences with the great outdoors stopped at these pleasant excursions and daylong picnics or with an angry fist raised against piles of snow that blocked doorways and caused accidents on icy sidewalks. Aside from the miners who worked all day in the bowels of the earth, most local people lived lives that were increasingly separate from direct experiences with the natural world. These, after all, were modern folk living in a corporate, industrial town. Popular stories of the Wild West still extolled the hazards of mountain travel, the dangers of fighting bears, and the struggle to live off the land. In the modern, industrial West, though, people traveled by train when they really needed to get somewhere; they ate meat out of cans and bought clothes from the downtown mercantile. Packhorses, big game hunting, and buckskins were part of the fun of playing in the outdoors, not necessities for everyday life. Because they lived closer to rugged mountains and lovely meadows, westerners had easier access to the beautiful nature extolled by eastern writers, but that did not make much difference in the day-to-day grind of mining, boosting, and caring for boarders. Residents ventured into the natural world and brought some of it back in the form of pictures and stories, but the forested lands outside of town had not yet worked their way into prominence in the small town. Red Lodge's public identity remained much more about industry and mining than about mountains and wild animals.

As early as the 1890s, however, for a very few residents the wonderlands of the Beartooth Mountains and Yellowstone National Park translated into economic opportunity and survival. These few people — guides and packers like Liver-Eating Johnson and E. E. VanDyke — created a space within Red Lodge that celebrated the frontier skills of hunting and scouting through the sale of these skills to tourists. Eventually this space would expand as more local residents provided outdoor services to visitors and as the town itself transformed into a "gateway" to outdoor recreation. Like their later counterparts, these early wilderness guides translated their knowledge and skills of the outdoors into businesses, inventing themselves as stereotypical rugged westerners adept at surviving in an "uncivilized" landscape and sharing these abilities — for a price — with their more civilized clients.

Before the advent of automobiles and highways, expeditions into the Rocky Mountains were just that — expeditions. Residents as well as tourists who wanted to spend a month or so in the woods hired men and horse teams to pack their gear and set up heavy canvas tents and cooking appliances. Those trekking over the mountains had to know the land well or hire guides because there were few trails to lead them. The very earliest trappers and hunting guides, like VanDyke, definitely took pride in the way "effete" easterners depended on their tracking skills to bring down big game and to survive in the Beartooth Mountains. VanDyke, indeed, remained so convinced of the ineffectiveness of dudes that he routinely took his own shot at the big game his clients aimed at in order to guarantee a trophy even if the poor easterner could not shoot straight.[27] Such guides were very few in number through the 1910s, but by the 1920s, as playing in the wilderness gained ever greater popularity among urban Americans, a new industry — the dude ranch — began to offer even more local people the chance to show off their skills and prove themselves as the kind of outdoorsy westerners that easterners seemed to admire most.

Dude ranches spearheaded Red Lodge's growing identification with the natural world in the 1920s, even as they facilitated the community's appropriation of Wild West imagery in this same period. Through dude ranching — the *work* of facilitating visitors' play in nature — a growing number of local residents learned about the surrounding mountains and, more important, learned to compare their outdoor knowledge with that of visitors from back East. The dude ranches that became so popular in the late 1910s and early 1920s catered to people who wanted their leisure in nature to be more intimate than a few nights at a resort like Monterey's Hotel del Monte, but also more comfortable than just camping in the woods. So dude ranching depended on the skilled labor of area ranchers and wranglers who interceded between guests and the dangers (or discomfort) of wild nature. As hired wranglers, local workers thus gained a growing sense of themselves as special because of their understanding of horses, mountains, trails, and camping.

The new dude ranches — Camp Senia, Richel Lodge, Camp Sawtooth, and Camp Beartooth — worked their way into the local identity as Red Lodge residents took jobs as wranglers guiding "dudes" and "dudines" into the backcountry of the Beartooth plateau and Stillwater region. Interestingly, many of these wranglers were actually very young friends or relatives of the ranch owner (who apparently realized the economic advantages of hiring youngsters for summer jobs). These local youths, many of them "city kids" from Red Lodge who gained their own horse and trail skills working at the ranches, quickly found out that eastern dudes lacked even basic knowledge about nature and animals, a condition that reinforced their own developing positions as skilled western outdoorsmen and -women. It did not take much to stand out as more knowledgeable than the naive dudes who stepped off the air-conditioned express trains from Chicago or New York City. Edward Nordstrom, for example, a Red Lodge high school student and wrangler at Camp Sawtooth, quickly took it for granted that dudes would ask "dumb" questions like, "Doesn't it hurt the horse when you're shoeing him?" Outwardly patient with guests who refused to take advice on saddling horses, the teenaged Nordstrom inwardly reveled in his role as competent westerner who knew more about riding and fishing than any of the dudes he met.[28] Marcella Littlefield likewise enjoyed a sense of resigned superiority toward the rich dudes who made up her so-called "little white fleet" of followers who dared not venture out alone along the trails her uncle had cut into the valley of Rock Creek.[29]

The admiration, and dependence, of these dudes shaped the ways in which local wranglers understood themselves and their role in the natural world; pride in these outdoor experiences lingered for years after local dude ranches closed their doors. Esther Johnson, for one, readily recalled in later years how she used to guide dudes up the slide rock trail to the top of the Beartooth plateau before the federal highway made the area readily accessible.[30] The experience stood out as a highlight of her life. And young workers like Johnson, Littlefield, and Nordstrom did not keep these stories and experiences to themselves. Tales about dudes and dude ranches became part of local lore, to the delight of Red Lodge residents who seemed to enjoy the stories of local skill contrasted with dudes' ignorance of nature and animals.[31] Such personal pride in basic outdoor skills — wranglers, after all, followed well-marked trails and usually "camped out" at the ranch — would gradually broaden to a more general local pride and identification with the rugged outdoors.

But the significance of dude ranches in shifting the public identities of Red Lodge and other western communities should not be overrated. These establishments did play a key role in the early phases of the region's tourism business, but they only spearheaded what would become a much broader regional and local phenomenon of "Wild West" and wilderness identification. Dude ranches, after all, attracted only a small and select clientele, and only a few local people ever worked at them. And these ranches remained outside of towns like Red Lodge, actually in the "wilderness"; their relative distance from the community lessened their influence on the town. Red Lodge's growing identification with the natural world was nurtured in the atmosphere of the dude ranch but really blossomed only with the introduction of automobiles into the mountains of the Beartooths.

Through roads connecting the town to the Beartooths and Yellowstone, residents would actually begin to pull nature into Red Lodge. As automobile tourists started to explore the nation's forests and parks, Red Lodge responded by re-creating itself as a component of that natural world; townspeople opened businesses within Red Lodge that catered to nature tourists, took jobs serving these visitors, and even adjusted the physical appearance of the town to meet the expectations of those in search of beautiful vistas and scenery. Significantly, instead of residents actually going *out* into the wilderness to serve tourists, locals would increasingly serve these tourists *in* Red Lodge as they drove through on their way to and from "wonderland." Cars and highways, not horses and dude ranches, would fuel the town's developing affinity with the wilderness.

Roads and automobiles, indeed, reshaped much of the West in the 1920s and 1930s. The advent of the automobile and the accompanying effort to create new highways to accommodate the popular machines opened up the remaining wild areas of the West like never before. The machine created ever greater access into the nation's "gardens" of park and forest reserves, and local communities adjusted themselves to the new phenomenon of the auto tourist.[32] More and more, Americans did not have to content themselves with simply viewing the wonders of the West in photographs and paintings or experiencing the mountains through strenuous pack trips, dude ranch excursions, and hunting expeditions; they motored there with their families, taking along tents and other camping gear to make the journey cheaper and more convenient.[33] Towns along these new highways scrambled to provide amenities such as campsites and tourist camps that might attract these visitors (and their spend-ing money) into the communities.[34]

Even the national parks began to cater to the automobile travelers. Yellow-stone National Park held out against the automobile hordes longer than some other parks — officials argued in 1911 that cars and motorcycles on its roads would be "dangerous to persons passing over the roads on horseback or in vehicles drawn by horses" — but by the mid-1910s, tourists in cars had con-quered even the oldest national park, and they never looked back.[35] In 1926, of 187,000 visitors to the park, more than 140,000 came in private automo-biles, traveling over the park's three hundred miles of dirt roads, which were designated as one-way routes to control the growing streams of traffic. By 1928, so many cars clogged the Yellowstone Park roads that officials found themselves fighting a losing battle against the "ever-increasing dust devil" kicked up by these automobiles.[36] With cars entering the park at a rate of one per minute, Yellowstone had become, as park superintendent H. M. Albright noted in a 1928 understatement, "a very popular place for visitors."[37] National parks and forests truly became "national playgrounds" as millions of Ameri-cans and foreign visitors loaded up their cars and trucks to drive through one, two, or even a half dozen reserves in their tours of the West. And thousands of these auto tourists began to find their way to, and eventually through, Red Lodge by the 1930s.

Locally, Red Lodge's growing identification with the Beartooths and Yel-lowstone National Park in the 1930s had everything to do with the automo-bile and the new culture that developed around the personal motor vehicle, especially in the West. Although the entire nation embraced the automobile craze in the early twentieth century, westerners took the lead in buying cars. Automobile registration and ownership in the West soared in the post–World War I years at a rate roughly twice the national average. To accommodate this new form of transportation, westerners took advantage of federal highway funds provided under acts passed in 1916 and 1921; states also subsidized high-way construction to enhance travel around the vast expanses of the West. As a result, between 1919 and 1929, western states added almost a million miles of new roads to the region. Individual towns like Red Lodge lobbied hard for these funds, each community eager to reap the benefits of improved trans-portation. Good roads, after all, meant better access to markets, more oppor-tunities for expansion, and more travelers coming through town.[38] Like the railroads before them, highways offered hope for economic prosperity to communities with the good fortune — and political savvy — to obtain them.

In the Red Lodge area, the Beartooth Highway stands both as the great monument to this era of opening up the wilderness to cars and as the local marker of the town's switch from mining to nature tourism, from work in nature to serving those who played in nature. Authorized in 1931 and completed in 1936, this $2.5 million project ran through a section of land that had been all but inaccessible in prior years. Only the most athletic of visitors, accompanied by experienced guides, made the arduous, albeit stunningly beautiful, trek up and over the Beartooth plateau. After the official opening in 1936, thousands of tourists each year drove the zigzagging highway up the Rock Creek Valley, across the Beartooth plateau, almost ten thousand feet above sea level, down to Cooke City and into Yellowstone National Park. Upon completion, the highway became Red Lodge's greatest visitor attraction, the cornerstone of its summer tourism season, and a major reason why the town managed to survive through the hard years of the 1930s, 1940s, and 1950s. Although open only three months a year, the highway created a physical connection to the wonders of Yellowstone and the Beartooths that changed not only the town's economy but also the year-round identity of the little community, tying it more tightly into national ideas and concerns about nature, wilderness, and the place of human beings in both.

The Beartooth Highway, like Yellowstone National Park, was always more than just a local concern. The highway represented a variety of complicated, often contradictory, American and local attitudes toward the natural world in these middle years of the twentieth century. Unraveling the different arguments and attitudes about the highway, descriptions about its usefulness, and its place in local identity, one finds a complex mix of ideas about people's place in nature and nature's place in American and Red Lodge society. The Beartooth Highway marked an era of vast government projects in the western forests spurred on by the conviction that opening up the wilderness was an unmitigated good for the nation's inhabitants. It also revealed a certain arrogance toward the natural world prevalent in post-Enlightenment Western thought: the belief that human beings could tame or shape nature to meet their own needs. Finally, construction of the highway, and Red Lodge's new connection to Yellowstone National Park, showed how class continued to shape the ways in which Americans interacted with nature, for even though the type of work changed, many working-class westerners still survived through their labor in the natural world.

The Beartooth Highway, first of all, was a depression-era "make work" program justified by Americans' increasing demands for access into the national parks and forests. Although not technically part of Franklin D. Roosevelt's New Deal program, the highway reflected the philosophy that created such agencies as the Works Progress Administration (WPA) and the Civilian Conservation Corps (CCC). The national government had started building access roads and trails in the forests in the 1920s, but the New Deal greatly expanded these efforts, combining make-work construction with nature "enhancement" in programs like the CCC. The CCC, one of the most popular of the New Deal programs, hired young men to do conservation work on the nation's public lands. "Conservation" in this case meant not only planting trees and fighting fires but also constructing roads, clearing trails, and building new campgrounds that would make nature better and serve the needs of the nation's automobile tourists. Construction on the highway created jobs, while the road itself added a northeast entrance to Yellowstone National Park, or, as the *Picket-Journal* put it, a "new and thrilling scenic gateway to nature's wonderland."[39] To put it yet another way, human beings (through government agencies) *improved* upon nature through human effort and technology. A modern highway over a ten-thousand-foot pass made nature better by opening up the Beartooth Mountains and the park for the greater enjoyment of the American people who could now drive through this area in comfort.[40]

Agencies like the CCC, which used machines and human sweat to improve nature and make it more accessible, served local as well as national goals. Municipal leaders in cities all over the West fought each other to secure CCC camps in their areas. Town leaders saw advantages not only in selling supplies to the camps and their workers but also in the agency's campaign to make lands more accessible for recreational visitors: new campgrounds and roads, built with government funds, would increase an area's attractiveness to tourists. In Red Lodge, for example, the local commercial club lobbied relentlessly for a CCC camp in the late 1930s. As the club explained to Montana senator Burton K. Wheeler, a nearby camp could do much-needed work to help the region's developing recreational economy. "Work," the club suggested, "would consist of road building, to open summer home sites, building trails and public camp ground, and a general cleanup of this section of the Custer

Forest as a recreational area."[41] The Forest Service, although harassed by constant requests for new camps, saw its CCC work as valuable public relations as it competed against the National Park Service for the affection of the American people. As one ranger noted in 1938, projects in the Red Lodge area — roadside cleanup, campgrounds, recreational trails — would be "a wonderful chance to do a real piece of PR work" for the thousands of Americans who were turning to the mountains for recreation.[42] Americans wanted to enjoy the natural world, and the government (with the encouragement of local boosters) was making it easier and more comfortable for them to do so.

But the Beartooth Highway and the various other government projects in the national forests and parks were much more than just ways to get more Americans, and their cars, into the natural world. Like many of these other projects, the highway embodied the hubristic conviction that human beings could control and shape nature according to their own needs. Although sometimes voiced in the language of conquest, this reshaping of nature also reflected Ralph Waldo Emerson's conviction that human beings could "mimic" nature to improve upon it; that is, they could finish what nature had started to make the natural world the way it *should* be. The Brooklyn Bridge, the Panama Canal, and hundreds of other grand structures proved that human beings could overcome almost any natural obstacle to make the world a better place in which to live. Grand Coulee Dam, constructed in the early 1930s, stood as the epitome of humans' ability to improve nature — to use human ingenuity to "finish," as it were, the natural state of the world. As engineer Carl Magnusson reflected, the immense structure actually re-created the vast glacial lake that had covered the region thousands of years earlier. "After being dry and arid throughout almost all the history of mankind," he observed, "the Grand Coulee once more will be a waterway."[43]

More locally, residents of Red Lodge had long sought to "improve" upon nature, to reshape it to fit their own needs, although admittedly with far less dramatic results than the Grand Coulee Dam. For example, local people had in the town's early years substantially altered the animal populations in and around Red Lodge. In the town's first two decades, some area residents actually made their living killing wolves, coyotes, and other "pest" species; they drew their wages from state and federal bounties created to encourage this reshaping of wildlife populations to make the natural world safer for sheep and cattle herds.[44]

In addition to removing undesirable animals, residents also brought in favored species. Hunting and fishing became key features in the town's early identification with nature, but sportsmen needed the right kinds of game in order to enjoy fully this association with the natural world. So local hunting groups imported European pheasants into Carbon County to provide a better variety of game for sportsmen, while area sport fishers planted selected species of fish in Beartooth streams and lakes.[45] The Red Lodge Rod and Gun Club even helped the state construct a fish hatchery twelve miles above Red Lodge in 1922 to ensure the steady propagation of the right kinds of fish for local waterways. These sportsmen knew that the beautiful lakes of the Beartooths *should* have fish in them, so they brought in golden, rainbow, and brook trout to make these bodies of water even better than nature had created them.[46] They "finished" the work that nature had started. Improved technology made the process ever easier. By 1939, sport fishermen applauded the new technique of dropping young fish from airplanes into the more remote lakes of the region so that even when pack trippers ventured into the farthest reaches of the Beartooths, they could enjoy the "natural" thrill of catching and frying up fresh golden trout imported from California to enrich the Montana wilderness experience.[47]

The improvement of nature reached far beyond birds and fish, though, to touch almost every aspect of the "natural" in the area, and few had anything but praise for these sometimes dramatic alterations. Modern highways, dams, mines, and irrigation systems not only made life for residents more comfortable and convenient but even added grandeur to an already picturesque region. As a 1930s Billings booster magazine observed about the Shoshone Dam (just southeast of Red Lodge), "Man Creates Beauty in Harnessing Nature." For most Americans in these years, human technology and machinery did not detract from nature; these tools only made it better.[48]

Considering the proclivity with which Americans had dammed, graded, mined, and otherwise "improved" the western landscape, it is not surprising that from the early 1890s Red Lodge boosters believed that all they needed was enough money and machinery to build a four-season road over a ten-thousand-foot-high snowbound plateau to reach Yellowstone National Park. The natural world presented obstacles to human progress, but human technology (with enough capital backing) could easily overcome such barriers. The question of snow, for example, met with easy assurances from local boosters who believed that modern machinery could take care of any problem; men who were skilled enough to construct a ten-thousand-foot-high road were also smart enough to find routes that could be easily cleared year-round. Such arguments confidently assumed that nature had already provided a ready route between Red Lodge and Cooke City and that knowledgeable humans simply had to determine where that natural route lay and thus finish the connection between the two communities.

In 1893 boosters contended that they had found a way from Red Lodge to Cooke City so "natural" that there was "no point on the route where the snow piles up so as to block travel in winter."[49] Testifying before Congress over thirty years later, Red Lodge newspaper publisher O. H. P. Shelley reassured the Highway Committee that engineers had planned the roadway so that with just "a little bit of assistance" Red Lodge men could keep the road open year-round "because the very natural contour of the country there on the plateaus is such that the snow blows off."[50] Like the Grand Coulee Dam that re-created a long-vanished lake, the proposed Beartooth Highway would simply fulfill nature's original plan for a route over the mountains between Red Lodge and Yellowstone Park. All the engineers needed from the federal government was $2.5 million to find that route and build the road. Human beings tamed nature with machines and knowledge, and tamed nature — which actually "cooperated" in its submission — made human existence more comfortable, convenient, and leisurely.

But nature, of course, was never so easily "tamed" as Americans liked to believe. In the process of being reshaped, the natural world had an irritating tendency to stick out at odd angles beyond the boundaries set by progressive engineers, reformers, and boosters. As anyone familiar with high-elevation highways so far north might guess, the Park Service and Forest Service were never able to keep the Beartooth Highway open more than three months out of the year. Interestingly, however, Red Lodge boosters only reluctantly admitted that this limited highway season might reflect limits on human technology. Rather than accepting this setback, boosters in fact attacked the government for the road's problems — federal bureaucrats, according to local accounts, *chose* not to try harder to open up the highway earlier in the spring or keep it open later into the autumn. Modern machines *could* open the highway earlier if officials would only make the effort to do so. Thus, even while local residents had to admit that they could not shape the world exactly as they wished, many retained the faith that more money, and cooperation from the federal government, could create the highway they wanted.[51]

Even with its limited season, however, local residents and regional boosters celebrated the Beartooth Highway as a technological and engineering feat. Like Shoshone Dam, the highway harnessed nature and made it more impressive. The highway itself, in fact, became part of the wonders of the Beartooth region. Local, regional, and even national promotions of the highway sold it not only as a scenic entrance to Yellowstone but also as an impressive technological achievement in its own right.[52] A local high school student summarized this rhetoric nicely in a 1934 description of the new "Hi Road." The highway, he argued, did not simply open up a "new paradise" isolated for centuries but also invoked wonder at the people who had built it. Man's "extensive effort and ingenuity" had created a road that twisted itself "ever onward and upward to heights that excel that of any engineering accomplishment in the vast country that is ours."[53]

Significantly, the presence of the machine did not detract from the natural beauties of the world it altered. Machinery and nature combined into a pleasing aesthetic whole, a view exemplified in a 1934 editorial celebrating the new highway. In this article, the writer readily mixed enthusiasm for natural beauty with glowing descriptions of smoking smelters and mines. The roadway, "already acclaimed one of the most scenic in America," he gushed, would "open up a vast scenic and recreational area to the American public." At the same time, the road would also make accessible the rich fields of the New World mining district, leading to the construction of "mills, smelters and concentrators in this new bonanza mining area." Most important, the new "steel and chemical plants located here" (in Red Lodge) would guarantee that three to four hundred men "will find productive employment."[54] Smelters and smokestacks and factories at the edge of Yellowstone National Park and along the route of the scenic highway did not detract from the wonders of the natural world made accessible by the road. Instead — like the highway itself, which invaded hundreds of square miles of pristine wilderness — industry and nature worked together to make life better for everyone concerned. Human accomplishment and natural beauty mixed easily and readily in this vision of the Beartooth Highway: the machine that made itself a rightful part of nature's garden.

In part because the road was such a technological marvel (even though drivers could only marvel at its brilliance three months a year), Red Lodge residents immediately took a possessive pride in *their* highway, and even before it was officially opened the road became a prominent marker in the town's public identity. Townspeople readily appropriated the various nicknames for the road (Beartooth Highway, Hi Road, Top of the World) into the local culture and townscape. There soon popped up groups like the Red Lodge Highroad Ski Club, the Bear Tooth Boosters Club, the Beartooth Mountaineers band, and the Hi-Road Harmonizers.[55] Pictures of the road appeared everywhere, inevitably enhanced so that the highway would stand out clearly against the background green of pine trees: a snaking line of sharp switchbacks working its way up to the "top of the world," as boosters quickly dubbed the Beartooth plateau. Flash's Studio, the local photography store, advertised its collection of scenic murals of the "Spectacular Hi-Road" and pictures of sites such as Twin Lakes "as seen from U.S. Highway 12."[56] Pete's Riverside Restaurant Club featured pictures of the highway on its menus. Not to be outdone, the Red Lodge Cafe owners actually painted a mural of the highway on a wall of their restaurant. At the very first productions of the Festival of Nations, residents performed their *kolas* and waltzes in front of a large painted backdrop showing the mountains behind Red Lodge with the Beartooth Highway prominently marked.[57] Even the cover of the Carbon County High School annual magazine featured the highway switchbacks.[58] The Beartooth Highway, nationally acclaimed and promoted, quickly emerged as Red Lodge's claim to fame, and residents got used to using the highway as a marker, not only of the town's connection to Yellowstone National Park but also as part of Red Lodge's defining identity.

The new highway with its national appeal and publicity became, in fact, a vehicle for promoting the community's other public performances and identities. Rodeo promoters, for one, eagerly embraced the highway and the Beartooth Mountains as integral parts of the entertainment package they sold to tourists every Fourth of July weekend. From the first year, boosters had promoted the Red Lodge Rodeo as having "the most scenic Rodeo grounds in America." They urged fans to "make it a three-day vacation. Bring your camp outfit and enjoy our mountains, and camp anywhere on our 80 miles of trout streams."[59] Construction of the highway only accelerated rodeo promoters' determination to tie the two attractions — wilderness and Wild West — together into an attractive (and remunerative) package. As early as 1933, when the bulldozers had barely begun to make inroads on the massive project, the

Festival Picture Makes State Bulletin

News Staff Photo.

The above picture is the publicity shot that has been circulated about the state of Montana on the cover of the Montana Motorist, AAA publication, advertising the coming Festival of Nations. Appearing before the backdrop of the Hi-road are left to right: John Meyers, Mrs. Elmer Salo, Mrs. John Lampi, Miss Martina Gardetto, Milt Crawford, Mrs. Lawence Monahan and Mr. Monahan and John Sim, a Scotsman wi' out his kilties.

The ubiquitous Beartooth Highway switchbacks provide a scenic backdrop for the town's emerging identity as a multicultural community. By 1951, the highway was already well established as Red Lodge's most famous attraction; the Festival of Nations was just emerging as an important annual celebration. (Carbon County News)

rodeo committee predicted that the "opportunity to travel part of the new Red Lodge approach highway to Yellowstone park" would serve as a "magnetic attraction which will draw hundreds of motor cars to Red Lodge during the coming week."[60] To capitalize on the lure of the new highway, boosters made sure to include in the rodeo's official program an array of beautiful pictures of the Beartooth region. The 1934 program, in fact, had more photos of mountains, lakes, and streams than it did of cowboys, Indians, and horses. Wild West rodeo and auto tourism into the "wilderness" complemented each other beautifully in the game of creating and selling the appropriate vision of Red Lodge.

Likewise, the town's ethnic celebrants would explicitly link themselves to the Beartooth Highway. One of the town's first ethnic festivals, after all, centered around the annual opening of the highway in 1939. And publicity photos for the initial Festival of Nations in 1951 showed off costumed performers posed against (what else?) a backdrop of the highway switchbacks. The town's multilayered public identities did not compete against each other; instead, residents found ways to make these different personas work together in the common goal of presenting a positive, attractive, appealing image of the former mining town.

Of course, "former mining town" is the key phrase here. This promotion of cowboys and highways and nature had everything to do with the shifting economy of Red Lodge in the 1930s. Townspeople shifted their public identities in large part because they were trying to survive. For many Red Lodge residents, the highway meant jobs, both the immediate work of building the road and the longer-term opportunities that nature tourism promised. The highway represented simply another way of working with nature to generate a wage. The timing was important. Construction of the highway — approved in 1931, started in 1932, and finished in 1936 — coincided with the shutdown of the town's East Side Mine in 1932. Although some local miners continued to find work in the small mines of the Beartooth area, Red Lodge itself ceased to be a mining town. The town limped along as a trade center for farmers and as the county seat, but the economic mainstay of the community disappeared almost overnight, and town promoters sought desperately to replace mining with increased revenues from tourists who could be lured in by rodeos and Wild West days and the scenic grandeur of Yellowstone National Park. Red Lodge had to adapt to a new kind of labor system as its residents embraced the Beartooth Highway and the tenuous promises of a tourism economy. Attracting and serving tourists required a much different kind of labor than that done by skilled union miners, and when this work moved into Red Lodge by the 1930s, it created new problems, opportunities, and identities for local residents.

Quite simply, nature tourism and wilderness appreciation remained very much a middle- and upper-class phenomenon in the 1930s and early 1940s. Class, in fact, had much to do with the ways in which Americans, including westerners, experienced the nation's parks and forests in the years before World War II. Wealth, to a large extent, determined who drove through places like Yellowstone National Park and the Beartooth plateau and who made the beds and served the meals for these nature tourists. The new roads and auto-mobiles certainly democratized American tourism; many middle-class peo-ple who could not afford to stay at the grand Old Faithful Inn could afford to drive their cars into the park and camp out at the adjoining campground. But auto tourists were still people whose incomes exceeded the national average. Millions of Americans, and hundreds of local residents, simply could not afford to see places like Yellowstone National Park. They did not have the cars, leisure time, or money to travel even a hundred miles to see mountains and geysers and lakes full of (transplanted) fish.[61]

In spite of earnest assertions that public projects like the Beartooth High-way helped America's working class by "open[ing] up to tourists and campers a highly scenic region now reserved because of its inaccessibility to those of more than average wealth,"[62] the "public" remained a very class-defined term. Indeed, O. H. P. Shelley, one of the most strident supporters of the Red Lodge access road to Yellowstone Park, testified in 1925 that the park's entrance fee — set at a relatively high rate to fund needed road repairs — should not be low-ered to accommodate poor tourists. If they could not pay the price, Shelley stated coldly, "they ought to be at home at work, because I don't see how they can get through the park if they can't pay the $7.50 entrance fee. I don't see any injustice in that at all. . . . I would say that anyone that could not afford to pay the $7.50 had better be doing something else."[63] A well-off newspaper publisher, he epitomized the assumption held by many in the early twentieth century that the national parks were there to be enjoyed only by those who could afford them. (As an active booster for Red Lodge, Shelley probably rec-ognized that someone who could not afford the park's entrance fee also would not be spending much money on Red Lodge's new tourist services.)

It is not surprising, then, that many local residents ordered their memo-ries of the Beartooth Highway not around effusive descriptions of beautiful scenery and rich mining resources — the stuff of newspaper stories and booster publications — but around the jobs and money that construction of the new road and the connection to Yellowstone National Park brought to friends and family. Even fifty years later, many residents recalled construction of the highway not as something that improved the town's image or attractiveness as a tourist site but as something that gave work to fathers, uncles, brothers, neighbors. Highway jobs saved many families who might not have had the time or money to explore the Beartooths by car. Trying to work out the chronology of the town's economy, Tony Zupan, for example, recalled that the East Side Mine "had to close before the mid-thirties because my Dad worked on the Cooke City highway. He didn't have a job at the mine. The mines were closed."[64] Likewise, Red Lodge native Senia Kallio placed the construction of the highway around " '33, '34 something like that. I think Leo worked there. . . . Mrs. Paavola's brother worked up there and he got killed while he was working for Morris Knutsen."[65] Zupan and Kallio remembered the highway primarily through jobs because work was so important to their families' survival in Red Lodge. Zupan's family, even when his father did find work, was so poor in these years that he and his sisters had to get their clothes and some of their food from the local relief office.[66] Driving trucks and operating bulldozers on the government highway offered real work, money, and pride to these local residents. In spite of all the rhetoric about the beauty, accessibility, and spirituality of the national parks and forests, for many Red Lodge residents, nature and machinery still meant work and survival.

But the highway took only four years to build and the hoped-for boom in the Cooke City mines never materialized. After completion of the Beartooth Highway, local residents had to find other employment to keep them in Red Lodge. What they found was a series of jobs and businesses serving the tourists who headed into the region looking for fun, leisure, and recreation in the playgrounds opened up by the Beartooth Highway and the other new roads in the mountains around Red Lodge. Although the Beartooth entrance remained the least-used road into the park, this scenic highway drew up to fifty-five thousand visitors driving through Red Lodge by 1937. An additional two hundred thousand or so recreationists motored through town that year heading up into the Custer National Forest to enjoy camping, picnicking, and fishing — all much more readily accessible with the construction of the new highway.[67] Not everyone stopped in Red Lodge, but thousands did, bringing with them money to spend on gasoline, fishing supplies, and food. Taking that money from tourists in exchange for services became the goal of local business owners and their employees. For these workers, the new road and Americans' growing interest in outdoor recreation meant the development of a new identity far removed from that of skilled laborers. Service workers did not warrant the kind of respect that longtime miners achieved through their work. J. N. "Buck" Cornelio, who worked a few summers as a bus driver in Yellowstone Park, complained that he had to sleep in his bus at night because park concession operators threatened to fire any driver who entered one of the big tourist hotels. As Cornelio bluntly put it, "They didn't want employees mixing with the people who paid good money."[68] Local workers thus found themselves experiencing firsthand the nation's changing relationship with nature as they negotiated new positions as part of a *service* economy dependent on the whims and interests of those who had the money to travel among the beautiful areas of the West.

That service economy, in turn, necessitated changes not only in how local people worked but also in the very physical appearance of Red Lodge. The demands of tourism forced townspeople to assess what Red Lodge looked like and remake themselves and the community into what they thought tourists wanted. The town's built environment took on a new appearance, one centered less around coal mines and more around making visitors comfortable and well supplied with amenities. With tourists heading up the Beartooth Highway at the rate of over fifty-five thousand a year in 1937 and sixty-six thousand a year by 1946, residents responded by creating businesses to service these visitors.[69] The town soon boasted three service stations and several motels such as Harley's Cottage Motel, with small "cabinettes" that catered specifically to motorized visitors. Instead of working in mines or taking in boarders, residents now pumped gas into touring Fords and Chevys or dished out food at the Busy Bee Café.[70] Although not as visually extreme as the phenomenon of dressing up townspeople in chaps and spurs, this shift made a significant impact on the public character of Red Lodge.

More than just gas stations and motels, the highway prompted another key change in Red Lodge's public appearance: the town was, quite literally, getting cleaner. The highway, as it were, brought "nature" — or at least the tourists who sought out nature — through and into Red Lodge, and that made all the difference. Instead of exporting their raw materials to unseen consumers, townspeople were now in the business of importing customers into Red Lodge itself to consume the resources of scenery, mountain air, and fishing streams as well as the services of local people. Town leaders realized that re-creating Red Lodge as "nature's town" would take more than a few murals and singing groups named after the highway. In the 1930s, the town just did not *look* the part of a gateway to nature's wonderland. Years of mining had, quite literally, been imprinted on Red Lodge: coal dust, grime, slack piles, and dying vegetation attested to the long decades of smoke and pollution that had accompanied the town's boom years. And suddenly looks were starting to matter. Customers who bought Rocky Fork coal had never cared if Red Lodge was a dirty, dusty town. Indeed, most coal customers never even saw Red Lodge; coal arrived for their locomotives or home stoves without any acknowledgement that this resource came from a physical town with a public image. But nature tourism was a different business. In transforming itself into a service economy catering to recreational tourists, the *appearance* of Red Lodge itself began to matter. As a gateway to Yellowstone and the Beartooths, Red Lodge had to sell itself as a part of nature, as an "appropriately beautiful and distinctive" entrance to Yellowstone National Park.[71] Although local organizations like the Chamber of Commerce and Woman's Club had long urged residents to clean up and prettify Red Lodge, construction of the highway created a new impetus and focus for the work of making Red Lodge beautiful by "cover[ing] unsightly [*sic*] relics of man's handiwork."[72]

In a writing contest held in early 1933, local eighth graders neatly summarized the problems facing Red Lodge as its residents tried to make the transition from mining to tourism town. Responding to the topic "Beautify Red Lodge — Gateway to Yellowstone Park," students stressed the need to make the town worthy of the natural beauty that surrounded it. The challenges of such a feat, however, loomed large. "Tourists travel around to see beautiful things," one student pointed out bluntly. "Therefore, they would not care to travel through Red Lodge." Almost a half century of coal mining had made the town seem "dismal and dirty among such surroundings," observed another student. Smokestacks had spewed soot all over the community, destroyed vegetation along the streambed, and made the town, as a whole, look and feel too industrial for a proper gateway city. As part of its transformation to nature's town, students recommended that Red Lodge residents wash off the reminders of the mining past, plant greenery, and cater to tourists who expected certain amenities from the towns they patronized.[73] Shedding its older, industrial image, Red Lodge needed to "green" itself up to bring nature into the townscape.

The movement would take a long time — even into the 1970s and 1980s, the town looked a little seamy around the edges, especially where the two giant heaps of coal waste loomed up on either side of the community. Gradually, however, Red Lodge cleaned itself up. The closing of the mines helped, of course, as did the general switch to cleaner-burning heating fuels like gas and electricity. The coal dust that had perpetually coated the community began to wash away, leaving Red Lodge a little less "dismal and dirty" and a little more like a gateway to nature.

Nothing illustrated the newer, greener identity generated by the Beartooth Highway better than the See 'Em Alive Zoo, a tourist attraction that quite literally brought the wild into Red Lodge. Developed in the early 1930s as a curiosity for tourists driving along the highway, the zoo quickly turned into one of the town's big tourist draws: the "biggest" zoo in Montana and a physical marker of how Red Lodge embraced, displayed, and marketed the natural world. The establishment's founders, D. W. Columbus and Les Lyons, self-consciously set out to create a microcosm of the state's wilderness right in Red Lodge. They acquired a variety of Montana animals — elk, black bears, deer, antelope, beavers — placed them in "surroundings simulating the natural," and sold the experience to visitors for ten cents apiece.[74]

Situated at the south end of town right alongside the Beartooth Highway, the zoo, in effect, created a "natural" space within the town itself, and for over forty years Columbus and Lyons marketed it as something as good as (or better than) the wildlands around the town. The zoo would not have been possible without the new highway, which made all the difference. As Lyons pointed out, "We didn't have tourists before the Highway. This was a dead-end road. Of course they didn't come up here."[75] The highway and zoo, in fact, worked together. As the highway connected the town to the natural world of the Beartooths and Yellowstone, the zoo pulled the images and physical creatures of nature into the town where there were now tourists who would pay to see such re-creations of the wild. Cofounder Lyons even advertised the zoo locally as something that would improve Red Lodge's developing identity as "nature's town." The zoo, he argued, would "prove a valuable item in promoting the attractiveness of this region for tourists enroute to or from the Yellowstone Park."[76]

And he was right. People loved the zoo, which quickly became one of the town's defining features, drawing not only tourists passing through to Yellowstone Park but also repeat customers from Billings and Laurel who would drive up to Red Lodge for the day to gawk at the caged beasts. Americans were fascinated by wild animals; they loved to watch moose, bears, bighorn sheep, and almost any other wild creature found in the nation's forests and parklands. And looking at the animals in Red Lodge's zoo did not entail the chance involved in spotting wildlife along the Beartooth Highway or one of the park roads; there, seeing a bear or mountain lion was a hit-or-miss proposition. In Red Lodge, Columbus and Lyons provided easy, convenient, landscaped access to these animals. It was nature, but better, more reliable. Not that the establishment — which was really little more than a "trap zoo" — would necessarily seem so "natural" to modern observers. Pictures of the See 'Em Alive Zoo from the 1930s and 1940s show animals penned in cages with little room to move, let alone run. Some cages fit together like pieces cut into a pie; the animals had only a triangle in which to live with mesh fences between them and inhabitants on either side. To the operators and the visitors who flocked to the exhibits, however, such a display seemed not horrific but enlightening, even beautiful. Red Lodge mayor J. C. F. Siegfriedt, for one, declared that there was "really a veritable thrill to be enjoyed by being in close proximity to the wild life native to the State of Montana . . . in a beautiful setting perfectly contented with their surroundings."[77] The zoo, like the Beartooth Highway, became simply part of nature, improved, of course, by human ingenuity and machinery.

This mixture of nature and machinery, the acceptance of humans "finishing" nature, marked the initial phase of Red Lodge's transformation into "nature's town." In the 1930s and 1940s, as residents started to clean up their coal-dusted identity, the machine in the garden seemed to be the local ticket to economic survival. Very few voices emerged criticizing the efforts to open up the wilderness or to cage the wild within Red Lodge. Rather, as townspeople adapted to the town's new economy, they embraced these efforts to build into the Beartooths and to extract the scenery, wild animals, and other natural amenities that tourists wanted to see. Switching from coal mining to outdoor tourism, boosters now referred to Red Lodge as "Just What the Doctor Ordered": a place where people could find spiritual fulfillment amid the beauty and grandeur of the natural world. Never mind if the natural world were seen at a zoo or through the windshield of a speeding car.

In the second half of the twentieth century, Red Lodge's public identity as nature's town grew even stronger, especially as new residents started moving to Red Lodge just to be closer to the natural beauty of the Beartooths and Yellowstone Park. Ideas about nature, however, were changing significantly in

The Beartooth Highway zigzags showed up everywhere in midcentury Red Lodge. Here a postcard suggests that visitors could experience the animals of the Beartooth Highway region more immediately at the Red Lodge Zoo. (Carbon County Historical Society collections)

these post–World War II years. Although many Americans still preferred to see nature from their cars, a growing number of "wilderness" advocates refocused national and local arguments about the value of undeveloped lands. In Red Lodge, public identification with the Beartooth area and economic dependence on the business of being a gateway to nature caused residents to shift their public stance on the role of machinery in the wild and beautiful lands around their community. The town that so enthusiastically supported the construction of the Beartooth Highway in the 1930s took a very different stance on the development of nearby forestlands three decades later, as shown first in the public debates over the Absaroka-Beartooth Wilderness Area in the 1970s and later in arguments over the expansion of Red Lodge's ski area in the 1980s and 1990s. The town created out of coal dust gradually became a place where fewer and fewer people would accept intrusions into the forests and mountains now considered Red Lodge's premier natural resource.

Of course, many of the ideas about "pristine wilderness" that gained popularity in the 1960s and 1970s were even older than the Beartooth Highway. Some Americans had long spoken out against the use of machinery to open up and improve nature. In the first half of the twentieth century, foresters Aldo Leopold and Bob Marshall spoke and wrote for people across the country, urging Americans to value "roadless" areas where machinery did not distract humans from their peaceful interaction with the natural world. In 1921, Leopold explained this vision of wilderness areas: "By 'wilderness' I mean a continuous stretch of country preserved in its natural state, open to lawful hunting and fishing, big enough to absorb a two weeks' pack trip, and kept devoid of roads, artificial trails, cottages, or other works of man."[78] Leopold's arguments helped convince Forest Service officials to begin setting aside so-called "primitive areas" from the nation's forest reserves in the late 1920s and 1930s.

The formation of the Wilderness Society in 1935 marked another key step in the nation's developing interest in wildlands. Headquartered in Washington, D.C., the Wilderness Society's stated mission was "to integrate the growing sentiment which we believe exists in this country for holding wild areas *sound-proof* as well as *sight-proof* from our increasingly mechanized life."[79] With the support of Leopold and the Wilderness Society, the Forest Service had designated almost fifteen million acres of primitive areas by 1939, including the Beartooth Primitive Area outside of Red Lodge. Meant to appeal to wilderness recreation enthusiasts, the regulation authorizing creation of primitive areas restricted roads, settlement, and economic development in designated areas but was broad enough not to exclude potential industrial development in these places. The new regulations did establish, however, official agency recognition of the need to conserve "the values of such areas for purposes of public education and recreation."[80]

"Primitive" and "wilderness" did not mean much to most residents of Red Lodge in the 1930s, however. Townspeople in these years, after all, were busily constructing a public imagery centered around sixty-two miles of oiled road running smack through the center of one of the nation's most beautiful "wild" areas. Wilderness advocates in these early years attracted only a small constituency, a kind of lunatic fringe to the more appealing conservation ethic that promoted construction of roads, dams, and fish hatcheries designed to "finish" nature in appropriate ways. Like most other Americans of the period, Red Lodge residents focused more on making the wilderness accessible than in preserving nature from development.

Interestingly, there was one regional group that early on took a very public stand about the need to save roadless wilderness. In the 1920s and 1930s, dude ranchers, who had already established a certain economic niche in the Beartooth region, vigorously opposed the construction of the Beartooth Highway. The last thing a dude rancher needed was a two-lane highway carrying gawking tourists into lands that had once been accessible only through the services of his wranglers. Dude ranchers, of course, had always depended on a certain amount of mechanization — electricity, phones, mass-produced sheets and blankets — but they fought to limit the extension of machinery into *their* wilderness. Dude ranch promoters in the 1920s protested that the proposed highway would penetrate "the last virgin wild area reached by pack outfits in the United States." Further, they argued that Americans preferred to have some wilderness available for recreational activities like backcountry pack trips, which were becoming increasingly popular every year. The "interest of the public," industry representatives informed Congress, "will be best served in maintaining this area for that purpose."[81]

The interests of this little group could not compete, however, with the more strident economic arguments of Red Lodge and Billings boosters who insisted that a highway through this "virgin wild area" would increase regional tourism on a broad scale and provide automobile tourists (an important lobby group) with a convenient, scenic entrance into Yellowstone Park. The machine won, hands down, in this early contest over the place of roads and cars in the wilderness. Only gradually would local people start to adopt a new attitude toward the natural world. Significantly, like the early dude ranch protest, much of the new argument about wilderness would revolve around an already established niche into the greater Yellowstone area, specifically Red Lodge's very own gateway to Yellowstone: the Beartooth Highway.[82] In the 1930s, though, the dude ranchers were a lone voice against a deafening local call for construction of ever more roads and amenities in the greater Yellowstone area.

The 1950s and 1960s, however, witnessed some significant changes in how Americans in general, and Red Lodge residents in particular, viewed the natural world. Nationally, the Wilderness Society, the Sierra Club, and other environmental groups gained increasing popularity as Americans turned against industrial development of the nation's remaining wildlands. Even as the nation was vastly expanding its industrial base in the postwar years, Americans underwent a fundamental shift in how they lived and how they viewed the natural world. "After World War II," as historian Samuel P. Hays argues, "extensive changes in human values gave these intangible natural values far greater influence."[83] As Americans enjoyed higher standards of living and increased levels of education, they began to esteem wild nature more highly than developed nature. These changing attitudes came through in public support for the efforts of the Sierra Club and the Wilderness Society in 1950 to prevent the damming of the Green River at Echo Park near the Dinosaur National Monument.[84]

Opponents of development argued passionately about the need to restrict encroachments on public lands; they also began to develop powerful arguments about the value of wildlands for all Americans. George W. Kelley, for example, who represented the Colorado Forestry and Horticultural Association, contended that Americans needed "wilderness areas" as "a spiritual necessity, an antidote to the strains of modern living." And Bernard DeVoto, writing in the *Saturday Evening Post*, drew from the work of Aldo Leopold when he declared that Dinosaur was important "as wilderness that is preserved intact . . . for the field study of . . . the balances of Nature, the web of life, the interrelationship of species, massive problems of ecology — presently it will not be possible to study such matters anywhere else."[85] Environmental lobbyists brought the pressure of American public opinion to bear on the Echo Park decision, and in 1956 Congress finally squelched the proposal. In 1964, environmentalists followed up their Dinosaur victory when Congress passed the Wilderness Act, which established the mechanism for withdrawing millions of acres of pristine land from the National Forest system and preserving them as "roadless areas" — places where machines were not permitted.

Wilderness, however, remained a complicated idea that generated intense feelings in the late twentieth century. Americans battled each other over how to balance preservation of natural areas with public accessibility to what were, after all, *public* lands. How much, in short, should the government value roads like the Beartooth Highway that let thousands of people a year gaze upon spectacular scenery? And how much should agencies value the spiritual, ecological, scientific, and aesthetic worth of roadless areas that most Americans would never see?[86] In Red Lodge these questions struck very close to home. National ideas about wilderness that could remain somewhat ephemeral for urbanites in Boston or Seattle or even Billings had very real effects on local people's economic security, quality of life, and plans for the future. Red Lodge, after all, had come to rely on the tourism business generated by building roads and businesses in the Beartooth Mountains; it had a long history of using machines to get what local people wanted out of the natural world. Yet, by the 1960s and 1970s, the very definition of "local" had started to change, and so had the town's public position on machinery in the wilderness.

World War II and the closing of the region's mines had transformed the community, creating a new kind of "local" in the postwar years. Although a core of "old-timers" remained in the little town, Red Lodge lost many of its miners in an initial wave of migration after the East Side Mine closed, and even more when the war lured away men and women into the armed services and the war industries of the West Coast. The population dropped slowly but steadily, from 2,730 in 1950 to 2,278 in 1960 to 1,844 in 1970. And those who remained were getting older. In 1960, almost one-quarter of the town's population was 65 or older, and by 1970, Red Lodge had the highest median age, 51.5, of all the communities of its size in Montana.[87] Most of the town's residents into the 1980s were older, retired folks living on Social Security. But slowly at first and then more rapidly by the late 1970s and early 1980s, Red Lodge drew new residents. Between 1970 and 1979, 146 houses were constructed in Red Lodge, the biggest growth spurt that the town's built environment had seen since the 1910s.[88] By the 1980s, these new residents had finally started to reverse the decades-long population decline in Red Lodge and Carbon County. The new "locals," what historian Hal K. Rothman calls "neolocals," did not share the town's history of coal mining; they moved to Red Lodge not for high-paying jobs or the promise of prosperity, but because they wanted to live in a small community in a beautiful area near millions of acres of national forest and park lands. They came because of Red Lodge's identity as a gateway to nature.[89]

Dismissed by some as longhaired hippie types, these newcomers created an important new force in the town that strengthened Red Lodge's public identification with the natural world. The Brokedown Palace Project (BPP), a social justice group founded in the early 1970s, reflects the energy and direction some of these new residents brought into the community. Made up of a "roughly even proportion of indigenous [longtime] residents and recent immigrants" to the county (according to its literature), the BPP's goals included maintaining the rural character of Red Lodge and its surroundings. Far from endorsing a return to the "good old days" of coal mining, BPP members encouraged residents to "change our hardware and our habits" by investing in "clean" energy that would not pollute "this spaceship earth." While working to attract environmentally friendly businesses to town, organizers tackled a remarkable array of community concerns, from a "Green Thumb" gardening program to employ the elderly to writing proposals to obtain Department of Housing and Urban Development support for rehabilitation of local housing. "There is no better stage," they concluded, "upon which to begin this important work than on the local level, where, particularly in rural and agricultural communities, people mingle with the environment's interdependencies on a daily basis."[90] Although the Brokedown Palace Project lasted only a few years, these new ideas about "spaceship earth" and "environmental interdependencies" gained an important public forum among residents who viewed the natural environment as a primary reason for living in Red Lodge.

The prominence of these new voices started to come through in the debate over the creation of the Absaroka-Beartooth Wilderness Area in the 1960s and 1970s. Caught in the middle of a prolonged national and regional struggle between pro- and antiwilderness forces, Red Lodge residents negotiated an environmental path on regional wilderness that would have surprised prior generations of town boosters, although it made great sense considering how the community had changed by the early 1970s. When the National Forest Service and Congress began to hold public hearings in the early 1970s on the creation of a wilderness area in the Beartooth Mountains, it was hard to hear a dissenting voice in Red Lodge. For the most part, residents who voiced opinions not only favored creating a wilderness in the Beartooths but also supported environmentalists' efforts to more than double the Forest Service's proposed wilderness designation. Local rancher William R. Mackay Jr., for example, argued, "In this age of constant change and disruption, surely we can find room in the nation for preservation." Instead of 516,815 acres separated by two nonwilderness "corridors," Mackay and other local residents demanded a "unified" Absaroka-Beartooth Wilderness Area of over a million acres.[91]

Not that local opinions necessarily made much difference in this conflict. The fight over nearly a million acres of land in the Absaroka and Beartooth ranges — some of which lay only a dozen or so miles from Red Lodge — lay largely outside the purview of local residents. National organizations like the Sierra Club, the Wilderness Society, the Cattleman's Association, and the Inland

Forest Resource Council contributed lengthy statements about how much wilderness was too much or not enough. Private citizens from Illinois, California, and Pennsylvania added their voices. Across the nation, groups and individuals wrote letters, attended hearings, and talked to their representatives about the Absaroka-Beartooth Wilderness in Montana. Their arguments about wilderness rarely considered specific local concerns. Those in favor of wilderness created impassioned arguments about the scientific and spiritual value of wildlands; they made pleas for their children's and grandchildren's rights to see and experience "virgin" woods and mountains. Opponents made equally intense arguments about the values of free enterprise, the nation's need for timber and minerals, the dangers of "locking out" development in an economically strapped state, and citizens' rights to ride snowmobiles across federal lands.[92] Red Lodge voices were largely drowned out of this process; even so their position on the wilderness reflected some significant developments in the local community.

Timing had everything to do with local residents' reactions to the proposed wilderness area. First of all, not all residents who supported the unified Absaroka-Beartooth Wilderness Area were necessarily against all machinery in the nation's forests, but they were against new development in *this* particular forest. Why? By the early 1970s, Red Lodge residents who lived off the tourist trade coming through town on the Beartooth Highway — a federal project that could never have been built in a wilderness area — supported the concept of keeping machinery out of the Beartooth Mountains because *more* machinery and roads threatened the economic niche and association with wild places they already enjoyed. Their support of *unified* (i.e., bigger) wilderness made sense when one considered the purpose of the splintered wilderness proposal. One of the nonwilderness corridors that would break up the single Absaroka-Beartooth Wilderness had only one real purpose: to provide for the future construction of an access road between the town of Big Timber and Yellowstone National Park. As Red Lodge business owners and others quickly pointed out, any new park access road would divert traffic from the Beartooth Highway and cut into Red Lodge's tourism base. A unified Absaroka-Beartooth Wilderness Area would eliminate this corridor — and the competition of another gateway to the park.[93]

Looking out for their own self-interests, Red Lodge residents meshed the language of environmentalism and economics into their own, local argument about the wilderness proposal. The editor of the *Carbon County News* summarized this position in a series of articles in favor of wilderness written in early 1974. His argument easily combined an environmental defense of the wilderness with a practical economic appeal to local readers. A joint Absaroka-Beartooth Wilderness, he argued, was necessary to "preserve as much as possible of the remaining unspoiled land in the U.S., to provide adequate domain for migrating elk and other wildlife, and to safeguard the area's resources in event that some future generation may need them more desperately than we do." More significant, the unified wilderness would also help Red Lodge businesses. A three-part wilderness, according to the editor, would "be a severe blow" to the county's economy dealt by "shortsighted" Big Timber businessmen who would create a "corridor of pavement, hamburger stands, and litter-strewn campgrounds." The interests of the conservationists and the local businessmen, he argued, coincided in the push for a single, unified wilderness.[94]

Red Lodge's own highway to the park, built during the heady New Deal days of conservation construction, apparently did not damage the amenities of the region; it had the certain dignity that time (and a possessive interest) lent to such intrusive structures. Not that everyone, of course, saw the road as a splendid addition to nature: one (nonresident) supporter of the Absaroka-Beartooth Wilderness, after all, referred to the Beartooth Highway as "an insult, intruding inappropriately into the sensitive alpine tundra."[95] But the Beartooth Highway was an established fact, and the Big Timber road was simply a dream; assured of the permanence of their own machine in the garden, Red Lodge residents could readily accept and promote a wilderness designation that would prevent Big Timber from building a competing highway to the park and halt any other kinds of developments that might hurt Red Lodge's growing economic interest in nature tourism.[96]

This, of course, is not to say that all Red Lodge residents wholeheartedly supported the unified Absaroka-Beartooth Wilderness Area or even the idea of federally protected wilderness. Indeed, into the 1990s, some local people would argue that extensive coal mining and oil exploration in the national forests was the best solution to the town's economic woes.[97] But the voices that gained *public* notice — those with the time, money, or energy to testify before congressional committees, submit editorials to the local paper, and attend Forest Service meetings — overwhelmingly favored the creation of a large, coherent wilderness and grounded their arguments both in ecological and economic language. As Red Lodge's economy and identity grew ever more intertwined with recreational tourism, concerned residents voiced their conviction that certain kinds of development could not be permitted on federal lands. When the Forest Service in 1977 invited local people to vote on a forestry management plan for the Custer Forest, townspeople approved a proposal that emphasized "amenity values including wildlife, recreation, visual and water resources" over one favored by the Forest Service that stressed "balanced development" including timber, oil, gas, and livestock use. Many residents still viewed the natural world as something to be exploited for economic gain, but they no longer accepted all exploitation as equally beneficial.

By the 1980s and 1990s, Red Lodge had moved even further from its roots in mechanized mining. Residents had acquired an ever more strident public voice about the environment, and they no longer necessarily framed their arguments in the language of economics, as they had in the debate over the Absaroka-Beartooth Wilderness. In 1986, Phillips Petroleum, which was investigating oil and gas sites in the area, even labeled Red Lodge a "hot area" due to the number of "vocal complaints from local people" registered with the Forest Service.[98] By this time, most of the people who lived in Red Lodge had not known the old days of coal; they supported the town's identification with nature, but they did not understand its industrial, machine-driven past.[99] Red Lodge's population, while not exactly exploding, was increasing steadily in the latter decades of the century, from 1,896 in 1980 to 1,957 in 1990 and 2,177 in 2000. And many of these new residents were coming from outside of Carbon County. Almost 30 percent of the town's population in 1990 had moved into the community from outside the county within the previous five years, and half of these newcomers had arrived from outside of the state.[100] Attitudes toward land use changed because so many of these newer residents moved to the Red Lodge area because of its natural beauty and ambiance. And many of the established residents who still remembered the flush days of mining now depended on nature tourists for their livelihood. Increasingly, public opinion turned against the intrusion of the machine into the natural areas of the Beartooths, and residents made fewer apologies for their positions.

The creation and expansion of Red Lodge's ski area illustrated the town's increasing emphasis on the importance of "wild" nature. The controversy over enlarging the area's ski resort highlighted changing ideas about the appropriate roles of capitalism, the federal government, and machinery in the natural world. Built in the early 1960s, Red Lodge Mountain ski area (originally called Grizzly Peak ski area), like the highway, offered a technologically enhanced way to experience the natural environment; it, too, became a tourist attraction, although never to the extent of the nationally renowned Beartooth Highway.[101] Although residents initially embraced the ski area as an economic boon, that enthusiasm waned over the years as local people adopted a new public attitude toward "appropriate" uses of Forest Service lands. Unlike the highway, the ski area attracted a snowfall (so to speak) of criticism and condemnation from residents who by the 1980s challenged Red Lodge Mountain (RLM) on everything from water use and sewage disposal to disruption of vegetation and interference with wild animal migrations.[102]

Things had been much different in the late 1930s, when boosters first proposed construction of a ski area near Red Lodge. Then townspeople cheered the use of machinery to further develop the region's forestland; a ski run, after all, promised to enhance the town's growing tourism business by making nature more accessible and enjoyable in the winter months. Enthusiastic boosters from Red Lodge and Billings created ski clubs to promote winter sports, and the Chamber of Commerce readily pitched in money and volunteers to help the clubs construct lifts and buildings at a site on Willow Creek, about three miles southwest of Red Lodge. As skiing became more popular around the United States, ski boosters grew more and more aggressive and grandiose in their plans, especially as the numbers of skiers in Billings increased in the 1950s. The state's second largest city needed a nearby ski hill to satisfy the demands of affluent recreationists. In 1955 Billings and Red Lodge business leaders created Grizzly Peak and obtained a Forest Service permit in 1956 to start building the grand new ski area on a mountain just southwest of Red Lodge. In February 1960, the area opened with fanfare, billing itself as the "highest and sunniest" ski slope in the United States. Although it struggled for some years as dry winters and recessions dissuaded people from spending money on ski vacations, Grizzly Peak, renamed Red Lodge Mountain in 1971, gradually expanded its runs and became an entrenched part of the local establishment and an essential player in the town's winter tourism.[103]

The ski area almost immediately became part of Red Lodge's public identity. In the years right after the opening, for example, the local yearbook featured the freshman and sophomore class officers in various poses around the ski area, and residents promoted a winter carnival to showcase the new lifts and runs. Physically, the carved-out ski runs etched themselves, quite literally, on the local landscape — impossible to miss from the town below. But the ski area never integrated itself into the town's public identity like the Beartooth Highway did. Residents skied at the site and promoted it during the winter months, but they did not take RLM into Red Lodge. Mountain promoters tied themselves to Red Lodge with the slogan "A friendly mountain and a fun little town," but the town showed few noticeable signs of this association. No "Grizzly Peak Harmonizers" or RLM dance troupe ever graced Red Lodge's public arena. The Chamber of Commerce ran advertisements for Red Lodge Mountain in glossy magazines, but pictures of the ski runs did not pop up on local menus or on the sides of buildings.[104]

The town's relationship with Red Lodge Mountain was complicated by the fact that the ski area was a private business on public land and also by the town's growing identification with an idea of wilderness that increasingly denied the place of machinery in natural places. Even more than the Beartooth Highway, RLM represented the use of technology and machinery to enhance people's enjoyment of the natural world. From the bulldozers that ripped trees off the side of the mountain to create smooth runs to the engines that churned ski lift chairs up and down the slopes, machinery played an essential role in the creation, maintenance, and promotion of this recreational enterprise. Indeed, RLM promoters routinely reassured visitors that machines — snow grooming machines, snowmaking machines, bulldozers — were creating the best possible ski environment for its patrons. As one manager put it, the machines made Red Lodge "a more efficient mountain." Boosters, for example, assured skiers in 1986, "If Mother Nature doesn't cooperate that's just fine; the ski area is equipped with snowmakers and expert grooming crews keep the slopes smooth and slideable."[105] Without machines, skiers depended on the whims of nature to provide snow and smooth runs, but visitors did not have to worry about that at Red Lodge Mountain because the ski area had a huge snowmaker that daily consumed as much as 250 gallons of fuel and 200,000 gallons of water forced through guns that were actually "monstrous mechanical marvels of water lines, condenser, compressors, heaters, pumps and fans" to "magically" produce snowflakes or man-made snow — which actually lasted longer than natural snow.[106] The old idea of finishing nature still held true among RLM operators and the crowds of recreationists who descended upon the mountain every winter. The machine still made nature more accessible, more amenable, and more convenient.

By the 1970s and 1980s, though, many were questioning how best to situate and control that machine in the garden. Finishing, while retaining some adherents, was falling into disrepute among local residents, who, for various reasons, began to question the need for enhancing the natural world. How much more help, after all, did nature need? Did snow machines and floodlights and expanded trails really make the wilderness more enjoyable for all or just for some? By the late twentieth century, Americans, including many Red Lodge residents, were thinking differently about forests and wilderness than they were in the 1930s. Red Lodge had actually become *about* living near nature. Residents like Karen Kinser and Michael Madsen, for example, relocated to Red Lodge without any real plans for monetary gain; the economic wisdom of the move interested them less than moving to a beautiful, remote place.[107] They, like many other "neonatives," wanted to freeze Red Lodge in place to preserve the natural amenities that had lured them there in the first place. This was the kind of feeling voiced by Yvonne M. Unruh in 1992 when she urged all her neighbors to protest against any oil drilling in and around Custer National Forest. Such development, she argued, would create noise and pollution, disrupting area wildlife and destroying the "quality of life" in Red Lodge. The business of drilling oil "would be the ruination of the creative atmosphere" that Red Lodge's natural environment provided for local artists and writers.[108] And, increasingly, these residents spoke up against plans for development of the Forest Service lands that bordered the town. As resident John Clayton put it, "When business activities take place on Federal lands . . . we (the owners of the land) have both the right and duty to speak our minds" about how those lands will be managed.[109]

Thus, when RLM proposed construction of an expanded Alpine Village on their mountain in 1971 and again in the 1993, they could not count on the kind of booster support that had backed local efforts to construct the Beartooth Highway or the initial Grizzly Peak ski area. More often, developers found themselves fighting local residents on almost every point as they sought to expand and improve Red Lodge Mountain to make that part of nature "better" for visiting tourists.[110] Even though the Forest Service, through the local district ranger, vocally supported expansion of RLM into a resort facility, townspeople remained unconvinced about the viability of such expansion.[111] Locals who depended on the natural world for their livelihood or who had moved to Red Lodge for its scenic beauty were, quite simply, more wary of developers, environmental destruction, and the social consequences of development in the national forest. And federal regulations — especially the requirement for a lengthy environmental impact process before developing on federal lands — gave those opposing such development much more of a voice in what was happening on the lands around their town.

By 1996, when Red Lodge residents responded in hearings on the expansion of RLM, they expressed fears about almost every aspect of what expansion might mean to 1,288 acres of Custer National Forest land. One respondent argued that he did not want Red Lodge to "become just another tamed mountain area like Vail, Aspen, Jackson, Breckinridge."[112] Many locals questioned expansion of trails (which Forest Service officials argued would open up backcountry vistas to visitors) as compromising "the existing wilderness area" and threatening wild plants and animals.[113] Although some residents welcomed RLM's expansion, many others questioned its planned development from the specifics of septic system construction to the presence of lighted buildings on the mountainside that would "pollute" the night sky.[114] Red Lodge's residents no longer trusted, necessarily, the machine to enhance the garden; rather, they felt that the machine (and those operating it) had to be watched every minute. The environment — the mountains and forests around Red Lodge—had become an integral part of how residents defined their town and themselves. Economic expansion, particularly that which affected public lands, was no longer simply accepted as a public good. Red Lodge had a new identity, one that had everything to do with protecting the natural environment and that had very little in common with the large-scale resource development of the town's founding years.

By the early 1990s, the slack piles and tipples and dirty grime that had once marked Red Lodge's identity as a coal metropolis were long gone, removed by the NPRR, the state bureau of reclamation, and the efforts of the Woman's Club and other civic groups. Old miners were dying off fast and moving to homes in Billings even faster. Little remained as evidence of Red Lodge's history of industrial mining; instead, residents had remade the town into a Wild West environmental community. Although a few businesses like the Red Lodge Coal Company (a restaurant) clung to the old identity of mining, many more deliberately adopted the persona of the great outdoors. Stores like Mountain People and Sylvan Pass provided upscale Columbia clothing, Gore-

Tex raingear, and high-tech camp stoves for backpackers heading up into the wilderness (hikers, after all, needed some mechanical assistance to rough it in the Beartooths). An Outward Bound dormitory stood along Broadway Avenue. On the side of a downtown building, a huge map showed the most popular hiking trails within a twenty-mile radius of town. Red Lodge, it seemed, had completed its transformation from coal metropolis to nature's gateway.

This local transformation was repeated in hundreds of other small, extractive resources communities all over the West — those towns fortunate enough to survive the demise of mining, farming, and lumbering because of the beauty and appeal of their natural surroundings. As Anne F. Hyde argues, these communities moved from "traditional extractive industries that bored mountains out and tore them down . . . [to] the tourism that worshiped the mountains."[115] Guided by enthusiastic visitors who sought beauty, spirituality, and freedom in the national parks and forests, local westerners found themselves extracting new kinds of resources from the land around them and creating new identities out of those resources. Nature remained a resource even as residents found new ways of selling it to themselves and others. But the methods of extracting those resources had changed as the town adapted to its new identity as nature's town. At first very comfortable with using machines to "improve" nature — steam- and diesel-driven equipment had, after all, been ripping coal out of Red Lodge seams since the late 1910s — local people grew increasingly wary of large-scale intrusions into the lands whose health and beauty had become their livelihood. This switch, then — from mining to nature tourism — *did* change the public identity of Red Lodge. As the older, mining population aged and moved on and as newcomers became accustomed to dependence on a different type of resource use, residents created not only a new, cleaned-up townscape but also new ways of describing and valuing their community and its surroundings.

Interestingly, however, even as Red Lodge cleaned off the last of its coal dust, coal mining as a public identity for the town started to regain some popularity. Finally, when no visible reminders of the coal past remained beyond the brick buildings of downtown and the defunct chrome mine entrance on the east slope, some residents began to yearn for a greater connection to that misty past. After successfully reinventing itself as a cowboy town, ethnic community, and gateway to nature, Red Lodge finally was ready to have a go at celebrating a cleaned-up, nostalgic version of its mining heritage.

7

Preserving a Past

Montana has traditionally been a place of honesty and integrity, where people are friendly and sincere. This same code should apply to our image as projected by our buildings.
—*Red Lodge Commercial Historic District Revitalization Master Plan,* 1986

In the early 1970s, old Liver-Eating Johnson — what was left of him, quite literally — sparked a heated struggle between Red Lodge and Cody, Wyoming.

It all started when a junior high school history class in California suddenly took a keen interest in the remains of Red Lodge's first constable. The interest was predictable considering that Robert Redford had just come out with a movie, *Jeremiah Johnson,* which fictionalized the bloodthirsty exploits of the renowned mountain man. After taking in the heroic actions and beautiful scenery of the Hollywood film, the class was shocked when their teacher informed them that their hero was interred not in the Wild West they had seen in the movie, but in a VA cemetery in California surrounded by freeways and asphalt. The students immediately decided to take action — they must return Johnson to the "Big Sky Country" he had loved so much. They even formed a group, the Committee for Reburial of Liver-Eating Johnston, to accomplish the task. But where exactly should Johnson be returned to?

Uncertain where the seminomadic Johnson might prefer to rest, the concerned teenagers wrote to both Cody and Red Lodge asking if either town might be interested in paying for the return and reburial of the mountain man. While Red Lodge town officials dillydallied a bit over expenses and details, the more alert businessmen of Cody jumped on the opportunity to bring Liver-Eating Johnson "home." Bob Edgar, owner of Cody's Trail Town, a re-created Old West community, led the way. Edgar, who planned to create a whole showcase around Johnson's body, rallied the county historical society to chip in for the moving expenses, announcing proudly that "people here in Cody . . . see it as part of the growing trend to promote the history and heritage of this area."[1] Of course, once Cody made this bold move, Red Lodge residents had to take action. Local historian Harry J. Owens spurred community outrage at the idea that Cody could dare lay claim to Red Lodge's historical property. Owens founded Montana Friends of John J. Johnston, filed a federal lawsuit to prevent Cody from appropriating the body, and urged Red Lodge businesses to take a "long-range view" of the benefits of donating to the cause of reburying Johnson in Carbon County.

Owens and his followers had a tough campaign ahead of them. A step behind from the beginning, they simply could not compete with Cody. Buffalo Bill's namesake town had, after all, been wholeheartedly in the business of selling itself as the epitome of the Wild West for almost a century. Even if Liver-Eating Johnson had not spent much time actually *in* Cody, the town clearly understood the value of adopting the remains of the man whose image had been so nicely reglamorized through the star power of Robert Redford. Easily rebuffing Red Lodge's move to claim itself as the "authentic" home to the old trapper, Cody welcomed Johnson's body with a dramatic reinterment that drew nationwide media attention (having Redford as one of the pallbearers didn't hurt the town's publicity effort). "Mountain men" outfitted in fur caps and leather pants solemnly lowered the Liver-Eater's body into the ground before fifteen hundred onlookers while more "mountain men" fired off vintage muzzle-loaders to salute Johnson's return to "the lofty peaks and wind-swept plains that he had loved."[2] Edgar then erected a stone monument and plaque to mark the burial site for those who paid the entrance fee to visit Trail Town.

Red Lodge was not, however, left completely out of the Liver-Eating Johnson commemoration business. Even if Owens and his group couldn't secure Johnson's body for display, they did manage to hold on to his old cabin (Cody's Edgar had tried to obtain it for his Trail Town display), which the historical society moved to the outskirts of town, right next to the county museum (free admission, donations accepted). Local historians had at least kept some physical remnant of the famous mountain man. More important, though, Red Lodge residents had taken a significant step toward constructing a new (old) public identity for their town.

Apart from gaining Red Lodge a lot of unfavorable publicity — as the town that tried to steal Johnson's body from a well-meaning group of students — the brouhaha over the reburial marked a turn in Red Lodge's public presentation of itself. The struggle with Cody over Liver-Eating Johnson was a precursor of a local movement that would have important implications for

In the struggle over Liver-Eating Johnson's body, Red Lodge didn't stand a chance against the more aggressive and commercialized forces of Cody, Wyoming — ridiculed here in a 1974 cartoon. (Carbon County News)

the town's public identity over the next few decades. By the early 1970s, Red Lodge, like much of the nation, was taking a new look at itself and evaluating the presence of the past in what remained of old buildings, artifacts, manuscripts, photographs, and, yes, the occasional corpse. Ironically, the movement that started over Liver-Eating Johnson — a representative of the Wild West — quickly moved beyond this one prominent figure to embrace the industrial town and working-class miners over whom Johnson had once presided as constable. Unlike displays of heritage seen in celebrations like the Red Lodge Rodeo and Festival of Nations, this emerging concern with local history focused more fully on the gritty industrial past of workers, machines, and buildings.

Liver-Eating Johnson's body sparked a community-wide fascination with uncovering and displaying local history that came to fruition in May 1999 when the Carbon County Historical Society closed down its old museum at the south end of town and opened up a new one at the north entrance to Red Lodge. The move was almost poetic in its symbolism. The society packed up its possessions from a couple of wooden huts and a log cabin and moved them into the town's stately brick Labor Temple; the society moved from a museum that faced toward Liver Eating Johnson's rustic old log cabin into the former home of Red Lodge's once-powerful unions. The original museum had exhibited mostly artifacts from farming, rodeoing, and ranching (the "Old West"); the new museum featured an underground mining exhibit, a Finnish kitchen, and a display on the Beartooth Highway (the industrial, tourist West). In the move from rustic Red Lodge to industrial Red Lodge, the society seemed finally to rediscover for the town a coal-mining past worthy of public celebration.

Residents, under the leadership of the county historical society, imprinted this public identity not only through a new museum but also through a refurbished downtown district and Hi Bug area, where plaques proclaimed the areas' listing on the National Register of Historic Places. Downtown buildings regained some of their original colors and awnings, and Queen Anne homes were lovingly restored to their previous grandeur. Cleaned up, painted in "historic" colors, and stripped (mostly) of Wild West facades, the downtown and Hi Bug, like the museum, began to reflect the glory days when the coal mines pumped thousands of dollars a month through the little town, funding construction of solid brick buildings and wide sidewalks. A century after its founding the town had begun to look, in some ways, very much as it had in the 1890s. At the end of the twentieth century, Red Lodge's public identity once again showcased the industrial mining — the coal slack as well as the foreigners — that had created the little town. A new Coal Miners' Park on the north end of town even boasted a marker in memory of the miners whose work and lives had made the town possible. A movement that began with a controversy over a romanticized mountain man had turned into a more widespread effort to recognize, preserve, and display what was left of the town's industrial heritage.

But had Red Lodge, then, by the end of the twentieth century returned to a celebration of a more historically "honest" public heritage? Did the new museum and downtown area reflect a more "accurate" public presentation of local heritage than the community had generated through the rodeo and Festival of Nations? Not exactly. In its latest creation of public heritage and identity, townspeople created a new imagery that, like its other personas, was very much the product of what residents wanted Red Lodge to be. Although rooted more firmly in the town's real history of industry and miners, this new coal mining identity emerged from the same complex mixture of

This 1984 advertisement in a publicity brochure illustrates beautifully Red Lodge's overlapping and intertwining public identities. (Carbon County Historical Society collections)

national movements, local desires, and historical invention that had marked Red Lodge's other prominent public identities—the Wild West, ethnic community, and nature's town. Red Lodge's public identity was changing by the late 1990s, but not so much as one might think.

Like the mountain man, cowboy, Indian, and immigrant worker, coal mining could be celebrated only when it was distant enough to be safe and sanitized. Residents increasingly promoted their coal mining heritage, but few wanted that industrial past to be *too* present. Remember that the town had begun to solidify its identity as nature's town by the early 1970s, and many inhabitants had moved to Red Lodge for both its proximity to wildland and its small-town ambiance. By the end of the twentieth century, local residents actively sought to capture a certain vision of Red Lodge that included cleaning up historic buildings, obscuring human impacts on the landscape, and preserving the small-town "feel" of the former mining town. Modern residents would, as it were, seek to return Red Lodge to some of the prosperous grandeur of its early heyday of coal mining through the revitalization of brick buildings and the commemoration of miners in a new museum. At the same time, however, they would turn their backs both on the grand dreams of the town's early boosters and on the actual work of the old-time miners by halting natural resource exploitation in the surrounding area and attempting to severely limit the community's growth. Stripped of his historical context — transience, violence, class tensions, smells, dirt — the miner, like the cowboy before him, could be valorized, romanticized, and made to serve modern needs. The downtown revitalization simply continued a process begun a hundred years earlier when town boosters boasted of Red Lodge's connection to the exotic and masculine (but safe) mountain man. Like the mountain men in the 1890s, the cowboy in the 1930s, the immigrant in the 1950s, and the natural world in the late twentieth century, the industrial coal miner found a place in the town's pantheon of icons, but only after local leaders distanced him from controversy, dirt, and any threat to the town's well-being.

By the 1990s, Red Lodge was not only a Wild West rodeo site, an ethnic Festival of Nations community, and nature's town, but it was also a "historic" mining district. The forces started in the 1970s historic preservation movement would result in the revival and public presentation of a new/old public identity in Red Lodge, one rooted very much in the gritty, industrial work of coal mining while also tied very strongly to a decidedly nonindustrial vision of

As Red Lodge began to lose its physical connections to a coal mining past, the town built new monuments to that history, including Coal Miners Memorial Park, which lies on the reclaimed slack pile from the East Side Mine, just past the old brewery. (Author's photo)

what Red Lodge should be. The modern little coal town of the 1910s had become a postmodern community of the 1990s.

Like so much of Red Lodge's public identity, the resuscitation of the coal miner and industrial downtown area, while reflecting very local concerns, had much to do with larger national trends. The public celebration of the town's industrial heritage really began in the 1970s, when the Carbon County Historical Society was formed as a result of a nationwide surge of interest in local and state histories. Americans became increasingly concerned with history in the 1960s and 1970s for a variety of reasons, some positive and others less so. First of all, a growing excitement over the approaching bicentennial naturally caused people to look backward to assess how the country had developed; at the same time, state and federal agencies preparing for the big celebration began awarding grants to groups focused on researching, presenting, and preserving all aspects of American history. History became not only more interesting but also more accessible to more and more Americans.

Accessibility had much to do with the kind of subjects that local historians were exploring by the early 1970s. Instead of just the stories of great men and politics, investigators focused on the histories of everyday families. The enormous popularity of Alex Haley's book (and later television miniseries), *Roots* exemplified this trend. Haley's work made his own ancestors, many of them slaves and none of them famous, the center of a gripping narrative of American history.[3] This was what people wanted. Americans wanted to learn about who *they* were; they wanted to learn about the ordinary men and women — their own grandparents and great-grandparents — who had done the real work of building the nation. Local, personal, family, "real" history lured Americans into investigating their own roots, establishing town historical societies, and visiting history museums for fun and entertainment.

History existed not only in grand monuments and the exhibits of great museums, but also in the houses, downtown districts, and pioneer memorabilia of local communities. Under the guidelines of state and federal preservation programs, which focused on saving the "authentic" past, Americans received encouragement to locate and publicly display just this kind of history — the industrial, working-class stuff that previously might have been considered too dirty, ordinary, or boring for public presentation, but that now had become popular.[4] In towns like Baltimore, Maryland, and Lowell, Massachusetts, Americans in the 1970s and 1980s were actively engaged in reviving such industrial heritages for public consumption: designating factories as museums, putting tools on display, and setting up exhibits of working-class residences. In rural areas, communities established museums showing off farming tools and steam tractors. Rather than seeing the working-class past — both urban and rural — as pedestrian, preservationists insisted that this sort of "genuine" history could actually attract visitors while providing residents with a more accurate sense of their own complicated pasts.[5]

Behind the excitement over the bicentennial and unearthing family stories, however, lay some deeper concerns about America's past and future that also sparked increased interest in history and historic sites. As protests over civil rights and the Vietnam war gained stridency, a general fear about a loss of national identity swept the nation. America, observers pointed out, seemed

to be losing its sense of itself in these tumultuous and troubling years. The reassuring values and communities of the past appeared to be disappearing
more rapidly every day as traditional downtowns faced the wrecking ball of
progress and Americans fled the inner cities to the comforting safety of the
sanitary, anonymous, cultural vacuum of the suburbs. Malls and strip developments catering to a new automobile culture seemed to dominate the American landscape, replacing the idealized communities of the past. Americans
began to fear that that they were destroying not only buildings but also their
core traditional values as they bulldozed physical remnants of the past to create parking lots, fast-food restaurants, and impersonal high-rises. It was not
enough to preserve the past in museums and monuments in Washington,
D.C.; Americans felt the need to save their history at the grassroots level,
where it seemed most threatened.[6]

In Red Lodge, the initial efforts toward this new preservation and presentation of the past began in 1974, the year remembered for the controversy over
the burial of Liver-Eating Johnson and for the convening of the first Montana
Historical Conference. It was also the year that townspeople formed the Red
Lodge Historical Study Group and set to work collecting and recording "material to help establish or illustrate the history of the community."[7] The growth
of the local historical group mirrored that of hundreds of other such organizations around the country. Within two months the group had obtained old
copies of the town's newspapers, gathered up historic pictures, solicited histories from local organizations, and discussed boardinghouses, bootlegging,
and labor unions at formal meetings. They also set in motion plans to gather
oral histories from old-time residents.

Within a few years the renamed Carbon County Historical Society obtained a bicentennial grant, set up a county preservation office, and began the
exhausting task of researching and documenting all of the buildings that
seemed eligible for listing on the National Register of Historic Places.
Although spearheaded by a few especially energetic individuals, this was very
much a community effort. Volunteers put in hundreds of hours working on
the applications for the National Register, gathering materials for a town history book, and raising money for a new museum. Two significant milestones
occurred in 1979 and 1983. The first was the publication of a four-hundred-
page history of Red Lodge compiled by Shirley Zupan and Harry Owens. The

second was the official listing of the Red Lodge downtown area and the Hi Bug as historic districts by the National Register.[8]

"Historic district" was a relatively new designation, created by Congress in 1966 to address national concerns about the loss of America's cultural heritage. The National Historic Preservation Act of that year created the National Register of Historic Places under the supervision of the National Trust, which allowed not only houses and individual buildings but also entire districts to be listed as historic. Residents could apply to have an area of a city — its downtown, residential neighborhoods, or industrial core — officially recognized for its historic value. Although the designation did not necessarily protect buildings from destruction, the listing provided an impetus for preservation. To make preservation preferable to demolition, Congress added tax incentives in 1976 that provided credits to owners for undertaking "appropriate" improvements on designated structures such as using "historic" paint colors. To aid the national effort, states created their own historic preservation offices to work more closely with groups trying to encourage owners to maintain the historical integrity of their buildings and thus their communities.[9]

The National Register gained great popularity in the 1970s as building and business owners realized the economic rewards of preservation. Quite simply, saving old structures made sound economic sense. First of all, renovating older buildings was cheaper than building new ones, especially with the government providing tax incentives for preservation on designated historical properties. In the recession years of the 1970s, developers actually sought to get historic site status for the financial perks; by 1983, over $2 billion worth of historical projects received preservation tax credits. Second, revitalization of older, decaying neighborhoods increased property values and could even turn historic places into popular tourist attractions. Once cleaned up and made pretty, historic sites like the French Quarter in New Orleans pulled in thousands of tourists who flocked into bars, nightclubs, restaurants, and cafes in the charming old neighborhood. *Fortune* magazine summed it up: "Anachronism can be made to pay off in urban civilization."[10]

In Red Lodge, economic motivation had everything to do with the effort to preserve the downtown district as historic. In the early 1980s, when Red Lodge was only slowly recovering from its decades-long economic decline, leaders of the Carbon County Historical Society took an interest in a federal program developed by the National Trust called the Main Street Project. Using nationally televised conferences to encourage local business communities, the National Trust promoted the concept that preserving historic downtown areas could "revitalize" older commercial districts.[11] That is, while saving and enhancing what remained of the community's structural heritage, Red Lodge residents could not only help themselves financially but also preserve important connections to the town's past. In 1983, the board of the Carbon County Historical Society convinced many of the town's business operators to watch one of these conferences, and shortly thereafter the city council accepted the organization's plan to boost the downtown area by encouraging residents to rehabilitate it according to specific guidelines from the National Trust.

The revitalization master plan was a success. Encouraged by tax incentives and provided with a clear guide for rehabilitation, downtown building owners took the advice of preservationists and began to strip away the layers of history to reveal the "honest" faces of their properties. One by one, owners erected the desired awnings, installed leaded windows, and fixed up old brickwork. Others removed rustic sidings meant to make structures look more western for the rodeo crowds. Slowly, building by building, the downtown district took on the air of the prosperous, industrial hub it used to be. The restored Pollard Hotel epitomized the historic reinvention of many downtown buildings.

Constructed in 1893 by the Rocky Fork Town and Electric Company to pull Red Lodge's downtown area onto land owned by the company, the Pollard (originally named the Spofford) stood out as the grandest structure in town. With its elegant dining room, beautiful lobby, and a bar room featuring an ornately carved mahogany bar, the Pollard was a center of social life in early Red Lodge. But like so much of Red Lodge, the Pollard fell on hard times in the mid–twentieth century when mine closures stopped the flow of coal money into town. Like many of the other downtown buildings, it took on a shabby, unkempt appearance. Then in 1991, new owners took over with a vision to restore the hotel's former elegance, carefully painting and preserving the brick exterior and remodeling the interior to re-create the glory of the late Victorian era. Beautifully restored as a high-end hostelry (room rates are much higher than any other hotel in town), the Pollard lent an air of grandeur to the revitalizing downtown district, which gradually assumed the historic look envisioned in the Historical Society's master plan. To be sure, some owners didn't comply with the guidelines, and others completely disregarded them (like the old Montana Power Company building that took on a pink adobe facade in the mid-1990s). But overall, the repainted bricks and picturesque awnings helped the downtown assume a brighter, more cohesive appearance.

Together the revitalized downtown and Hi Bug areas worked to pull Red Lodge's mining past into the town's public identity. The buildings did not shout "industrial mining" like the rodeo and Festival of Nations so clearly trumpeted "Wild West" and "ethnic diversity." The message was more sub-dued but much more *present* because the structures constituted the actual and visual heart of Red Lodge. Big, solid, permanent — these buildings, especially those along Broadway Avenue, contained the stores, government agencies, and business offices that kept Red Lodge going. Everyone driving through town passed by these buildings. Residents dressed them up with flags for the Festi-val of Nations and Wild West banners for the Fourth of July rodeo. Few peo-ple probably looked carefully at the structures and contemplated the work and capital that made them possible, but many at least paused to peruse the plaques describing the historical significance of each building. The overall appearance of the downtown and Hi Bug imbued Red Lodge with a sense of history and that history had everything to do with a West of trains, corporate capital, brick, and coal. With its newly designated historic districts, Red Lodge had acquired a new, very visible sense of itself and its history.

Historic districts such as Red Lodge's downtown and Hi Bug area are inter-esting creations. Meant to preserve the past, they generate new interpretations of that past at the same time that they produce new realities for the present. At first glance, the work done on preserving and revitalizing Red Lodge's downtown adhered to a strictly accurate interpretation of local history. Iden-tifying, rehabilitating, and celebrating appropriately historic buildings re-volved around the concept that preservationists were somehow saving and publicly displaying an accurate version of the local past. Preservationists sharply criticized previous efforts to falsify Red Lodge's history through the addition of rugged, western materials to the original brick facades. These attempts to make Red Lodge buildings more appealing by making them more western had produced, according to Historical Society members, a "bizarre, and comical" look in the downtown area.

The town's revitalization master plan asked readers to "imagine how the Italianate style stone mason would cringe if he were to return from the past to discover his beautiful masonry hidden beneath a barnboard or wild west facade." Rather, the preservationists argued, local building owners should strive for "recapturing the original character" of Red Lodge by appreciating and revealing the "honesty generated by the building itself." With grant money obtained through the State Historic Preservation Office, these historical boosters created a master plan that detailed block by block how building owners should "revive" their properties from the roofs and exterior walls to the windows and gutters. With the appropriate attention to detail, Red Lodge could "revive its rich turn-of-the-century character and demonstrate its community pride in tradition and quality."[12]

Not everyone, however, saw such efforts as true — or appropriate — historical preservation. Historic preservation and revitalization like that pursued in Red Lodge was going on around the nation by the 1980s, often to the dismay of urban designers who saw something fake in this movement to create cleaned-up historic districts. In places like the South Street Seaport in New York City, for example, academics have criticized, perhaps justly, the city's move to create a "historic tableau" out of a run-down center of fishing commerce by rehabilitating nineteenth-century merchant houses, reconstructing old warehouses, and opening up a new boardwalk complete with renovated ships. Camouflaged behind attractive historic facades lie Banana Republic and The Nature Store outlets side by side with pizzerias and burger shops. Reconstructed as an outdoor museum dedicated to presenting aspects of New York's seafaring past, South Street Seaport did not even feature a working fish market because tourists didn't like the smell of real fish. Developers cleaned up the once dirty, sometimes dangerous wharf district that stunk of fish and created an appealing reconstruction of what a seaport *should* have looked (and smelled) like. In addition to altering the physical appearance of a place, preservation, critics argued, often led to gentrification, which could quickly mark the end of the original community of people in historically saved areas. Once districts like the French Quarter and South Street Seaport became attractive to higher income dwellers, property values would drive out the older residents in favor of wealthier, upwardly mobile types who could afford to pay for the ambiance created by preservation.[13]

One of the favorite terms used by scholars like M. Christine Boyer in the examination of such "historic" districts is "Disneyfication." Communities and developers have drawn from the artificial (and very successful) world of Walt

Disney's theme parks to create districts and neighborhoods that are attractively nostalgic simulations of the past. As Boyer puts it, such "city tableaux" become simply "recycled and revalued territories . . . that have been turned into gentrified, historicized, commodified, and privatized places."[14] Such historic revitalization, according to the title of Michael Sorkin's anthology on urban development, amounts to not much more than "Variations on a Theme Park." Historic districts become like theme parks in part because, like Disney's Frontier Land and Main Street, U.S.A., they are historicized. Historical geographer David Hamer argues that members of local historical groups have tended to make over historical districts "in the image of a particular interpretation of their past that it suits contemporary needs to establish."[15] Such districts freeze time; they attempt to preserve an idealized moment from the community's past and disregard all that happened between the chosen moment and the time of preservation.

In Red Lodge, for example, preservationists decided that the downtown area should reflect the period between 1894 and 1920, when most of the downtown structures were built. Much of what was added after 1920 was denounced as fraud. In the Carbon County Historical Society's plan for downtown revitalization, designers derided the "barnboard or wild west facade" that hid the "honest" faces of the town's masonry buildings.[16] Never mind that those rustic facades represented an important historical development — the town's concerted effort in the 1930s to attract tourists through the creation of a Wild West imagery — they were dishonest to the original construction and had to go. Preservationists turned back local history to uncover the moment that defined the apex of the community's development; they found a kind of usable history that would reflect what these town leaders wanted their community to be. Here was mining without pollution, immigrant workers with no class or ethnic tensions, and an authentic historic downtown with paved streets that stunk of horse manure only after the annual Fourth of July parade.

Red Lodge preservationists, in their efforts to revive a historic district, actually made their own history. Like the self-consciously optimistic Festival of Nations, Red Lodge's public presentation of its mining heritage glossed over significant differences and disputes that had defined the town's industrial past, particularly those involving class divisions. For those who really looked, the brick buildings of downtown and the freshly renovated houses of the Hi Bug clearly marked the very real class differences that had divided the community in its early years, yet public displays of mining and miners in Red Lodge rarely even hinted at such divisions. Interpretations of the town's mining past such as those presented in the mine exhibit at the Labor Temple museum or the plaque at Coal Miners' Park emphasized the courage, sacrifice, and hardiness of miners, not the grudges they bore against mine operators or Northern Pacific Railroad efforts to control local unions in the World War I years. Dioramas of immigrant women focused on ethnic clothing and cooking utensils, not on the resentment young Italian-American girls felt about cleaning the houses of the Hi Bug matrons. As with the annual rodeo and Festival of Nations, residents shaped a very public interpretation of what Red Lodge *should* have been; they created a present-day historical Red Lodge that was really an idealized, cleaned-up version of the original coal town.

The most dramatic marker of the eradication of the dirty side of the town's industrial past had to be the physical removal of the enormous slack piles that for so long had punctuated the Red Lodge townscape. Motivated out of concerns for public health and safety, federal and state government agencies in the 1980s and 1990s had initiated massive efforts to reclaim abandoned coal mines around the nation, which meant the removal not only of mine waste but also of many unused mine structures. Under the provisions of the National Historic Preservation Act (the same act used by Red Lodge residents to preserve and protect the downtown area), historically significant mining structures could be saved and preserved as part of the region's industrial heritage. Although some preservationists petitioned the state to consider the former Red Lodge mines for the National Register, evaluators found nothing in the Northwestern Improvement Company site to warrant such a listing. Researchers singled out a few structures in the Bearcreek and Washoe fields for consideration, but they concluded that the former NWIC holdings in Red Lodge "lack integrity." Except for the slack piles, all other evidence of the town's rich mining past had long since been removed or destroyed. And since investigators determined that there was "no evidence of cultural materials" in the waste dumps, these too should be removed.[17] Reclamation of the slack piles would eliminate the health and safety hazards posed by the industrial remnants of decades of coal mining and return the area to its "pre-mining condition." Accordingly, government contractors bulldozed away both slack piles, trucking away some of the decades-old waste and spreading out the rest and covering it over with layers of dirt and grass until the legacy of the town's coal mining years remained only in the facades of the downtown buildings and the memories of old-time residents.

Significantly, in removing tons of coal waste, peeling away layers of Wild West shingles, and repainting brickwork, residents did not so much uncover their past as create a new and very public version of the town's working-class heritage. They took away the eyesores and replaced them with pretty exteriors and soothing stories of heroic miners and steadfast immigrant workers. Such historical "fudging" was not unique to Red Lodge. Heritage creation — pulling together pieces of the past for public purposes — after all, is not so much about truth as about appearances. Heritage, as David Lowenthal points out, is something that people create out of their pasts to make their present selves look or feel good. This seems especially true when it comes to questions of social inequalities. Reviving working-class history could make people feel good; reflecting on class distinctions that still lingered in local societies could make them feel uneasy or defensive. If the huge piles of grimy coal slack needed to be removed to make the community safe, then reminders of past social inequalities also needed to be smoothed over. In Red Lodge, the public interpretation of the town's industrial past told a story of triumph and opportunity, not one of class divisions and control by outside capitalists.

Historian Linda Shopes encountered a similar kind of heritage construction in Baltimore when she initiated a community history project there. To Shopes's dismay, instead of confronting class differences in the community, participants in her neighborhood history project created an interpretation of neighborhood history that "validate[d] aspects of working-class culture, but . . . [made] no effort to examine that culture critically." In oral histories, printed books, and community plays, residents emphasized "the theme of personal survival" while obscuring the larger story of "power relationships between, for example, neighborhood and city, or employee and employer."[18] Local inhabitants told stories that put themselves at the center but that did not confront social distinctions which still divided the city and made people uncomfortable.

Historian Mary H. Blewett, in her investigation of dozens of industrial museums in New England, observed similar trends in other towns' presentations of their working-class pasts. Industrial exhibits and museums, Blewett found, tended to ignore the "economic and social implications of industrial capitalism as a system." While depicting laborers' hard working and living conditions, public displays glossed over "serious problems of power and control inherent in capitalist development and relevant to contemporary concerns."[19] Residents and tourists were happy to celebrate workers but shied away from questioning the deeper problems inherent in the capitalist system. Professional historians may thrive on digging out complicated interpretations of class struggle, but most Americans were more comfortable smoothing over the past to make it less confrontational and less dangerous to treasured ideals of democracy and equality.

Safe, nonconfrontational history appealed not only to residents wanting to celebrate their own local development but also to tourists who by the end of the century had become increasingly fascinated with attractions that seemed "historical" in any way.[20] Americans flocked to historical museums and patronized areas that successfully billed themselves as historic. Boston, for example, sold itself to potential visitors as "On the Freedom Trail," and Springfield, Illinois, boasted of being the "Land of Lincoln." Even tiny, remote towns in eastern Montana tapped into the lure of history. From "Historic Wibaux" with its centennial train coach to Richey's history museum full of "pioneer" objects, communities used public presentations of history as a selling point.[21] Local boosters understood that Americans wanted to interact with the past in some way as they traveled. As one scholar of American culture pointed out in the early 1970s, Americans seemed to be "treating history as though it were geography, themselves as though they could step out of the present into the past of their choice."[22]

This kind of tourism had much to do with Americans' continuing movement to preserve and display history of all kinds. As with the South Street Seaport and downtown Red Lodge, much of the impetus behind historical "Disneyfication" was the growing dependence on a tourist economy. Through historic preservation, communities have converted themselves into stages upon which tourists can stroll, gaze, and, of course, purchase commodities. Tourists willingly buy into these staged reconstructions, or theme parks, because they yearn to capture something of the past that seems missing in modern society. Communities and tourists thus build off each other; locals create appealing versions of a treasured past, and visitors pay for the opportunity to escape back into these nostalgic creations.

Red Lodge promoters and preservationists readily articulated this connection between history and money. Local historian Harry Owens had even made historical tourism a centerpoint in his battle to convince residents to fight for Liver-Eating Johnson's body; if Red Lodge wanted tourists, he had pointed out in 1974, residents had to understand that "the tourist is interested in history, but the Red Lodge history is pretty well hidden. If Liver Eating Johnson was brought home and interred in a suitable location with a fine monument, many people would be interested and stop."[23] The same argument made for the body of a dead trapper could also be put forward for brick buildings. In 1984, arguing for the downtown revitalization program, Dan Coats of the Red Lodge Chamber of Commerce focused local business owners' attention on "the value of the county's historic resources and the importance of preservation as it relates to the economic stability of the area."[24] Historic districts attracted tourists and new residents alike; the city could only benefit — as had other towns — from cleaning up its downtown area and making it look better, more "historic." Red Lodge historic preservation officer Edrie Vinson even tried to attract national money into the quest to revitalize the historic downtown area. In a letter to Ford Motor Company in 1986, Vinson touted the economic benefits possible to the car manufacturer. If Ford would ante up $14,000 to paint the Red Lodge Ford dealership in "historic" colors, then it could shoot a commercial in Red Lodge, moving from "the historic Ford dealership, through the historic city and up the Beartooth Highway to the south, which Charles Kuralt claims is the most beautiful highway in America."[25]

As with local marketing of the town's connection to cowboys and wilderness — notice how easily Vinson connected historic Red Lodge to the Beartooth Highway — history and preservation acquired a definite economic language among promoters. For boosters seeking tourist dollars, Red Lodge's new "historical" public identity fit nicely with the already established imagery of cowboys, immigrants, and nature. The Chamber of Commerce demonstrated this easy overlapping when it approved the "A Sip of Europe, A Slug of the Old West" promotional campaign in the 1980s. The brochure touting this theme featured a woman dressed in an elegant Edwardian dress and elaborate hat (think of the Ascot race scene in My Fair Lady) clinking glasses with a rough-and-ready cowhand against the backdrop of the Beartooth Mountains.[26] History, immigration, the Wild West, and nature mixed readily in the town's efforts to sell itself to tourists.

Not that Red Lodge's new emphasis on history and preservation was just about money. Red Lodge residents, like other Americans, proudly put their history on display for a variety of personal reasons, not just to earn a buck. Although the revitalization movement had to use economic arguments to convince building owners to spend their own money on renovations, preservation proponents also drew upon deeper feelings and ideas that local people had about their past. Those who donated scrapbooks, photos, and memoirs to the Carbon County Historical Society acted out of a sense of contributing to the community, preserving part of the past. Presenting the local past through revitalized buildings and new museums was not only about marketing history but also about proudly showing off the interesting and important people and events that had created this particular community. The local archives and museum became a repository of valued items and memories, which, concomitantly, proved that the town had a deep history and a population that cared about preserving the past. Americans liked history and liked visiting places that provided a readily accessible sense of the past; residents liked sharing their own sense of local heritage with visitors. The serendipitous joining of these twinned desires in a productive little tourist enterprise satisfied everyone.

If any serious problem existed with Red Lodge's newly renovated downtown and rehabilitated mining identity, it was that the entire project had become too successful. Cleaned up, nicely "historic," and tucked up against such stunning natural beauty, Red Lodge couldn't help but attract attention from people wanting to escape the urban and suburban grind for the simple joys of small-town living in the rural West. By the end of the twentieth century, more and more Americans were seeking out not only beautiful scenery and access to public lands but also the sense of community associated with small towns rooted in history and tradition.[27] With its historic main street district, Red Lodge was not only a small town in size but also the ideal small town in appearance. As such, it became a magnet for Americans relocating in search of a better life in a better place.

Americans, as geographer D. W. Meinig points out, have long revered the "symbolic landscape" of the small town. A symbolic landscape, according to Meinig, is a set of images, "part of a shared set of ideas and memories and feelings which bind a people together."[28] Like the New England village and the California suburbs, Main Street (the small town) conveys certain meanings to Americans: free enterprise, social morality, small-town virtues, the "real" America.[29] As the United States became urbanized, the small town represented the ideal middle ground between the remoteness of rural life and the complexity of the city. Nothing captured American nostalgia for the turn-of-the-century small town like the appeal of Walt Disney's Main Street, U.S.A. As historians have pointed out, Disney did a brilliant job of envisioning and creating the small-town business district in his three-quarter-scale Main Street display at Disneyland, which was actually modeled after a nostalgic vision of his own hometown of Marceline, Missouri. Historian Richard V. Francavigilia explains that Disney "effectively instigated a deep collective longing for pre-urban Anglo America that was and indeed still is widely embraced by Americans of all backgrounds."[30] Red Lodge's new old downtown — its historic buildings accentuated with attractive new paint and leaded windows — had certainly begun to acquire some of the aura of Disney's Main Street.[31] Red Lodge's downtown buildings lent a sense of permanence and community to the town, in part because the district epitomized what Americans had learned a small town should look like.

Indeed, by the late twentieth century, "small-town America" became one of Red Lodge's most important public identities. The community that boosters had so desperately tried to develop in the 1890s now drew new residents because it had *not* become the "metropolis" of these nineteenth-century fantasies. Newcomers to Red Lodge readily admitted that part of the community's attraction was its small-town "feel": the security, friendliness, and sense of community that Americans expected from a tightly knit community. Karen Kinser, who moved from Washington, D.C., to Red Lodge in 1992, positively gushed about how it lived up to the best stereotypes about small towns. Red Lodge, Kinser raved soon after her arrival, "is homey and comfortable, and most of all, friendly. . . . People here seemed happy, unharried, trusting and honest. . . . People take time to stop and talk and just, well, just be HUMAN."[32] Residents who had spent a bit more time in the community agreed with Kinser's initial perceptions of the town. At the 1992 kickoff meeting for a new community action group, the Beartooth Front Community Forum, participants listed things they did not want changed about Red Lodge. Their responses included many attributes associated with the idealized small town: "small-town flavor and attitudes," "sense of community," "friendliness," "security for kids," "don't have to lock houses at night."[33]

This newer vision of small-town life was part of what America was becoming by the end of the twentieth century. With the money and time to move beyond the necessities of survival, Americans wanted not only beautiful parks and forests but also reminders of older forms of community and industry. If Yellowstone National Park represented a chance to experience an older, pristine, more natural America, then history museums, preserved downtowns, and small-town ambiance provided a sense of connecting with an older, more interesting, communal America. Quality of lifestyle grew in significance to Americans as the modern world with its impersonal suburbs and dirty inner cities seemed to threaten older values of community, outdoor living, and neighborliness. Some willingly gave up high-paying careers to settle in towns like Red Lodge, where they tried to start up small businesses catering to tourists or earn a living as writers.[34] Anxious to protect the qualities that had drawn them to Red Lodge, residents worked to preserve the area's historical and environmental resources; they also banded together to save what turned out to be one of the town's greatest assets — its identity as a small, cohesive community.

Of course, the fact that so many Americans now wanted, and could afford, this kind of lifestyle threatened the very small-town qualities that residents treasured about Red Lodge. Inhabitants had only to look around the West to see how other small communities — Aspen, Sun Valley, Telluride, Jackson Hole — had been "loved to death" by newcomers looking for a piece of the good life. The consequences of growth frightened many Red Lodge locals, who pointed out that for "more renowned neighbors such as Jackson Hole, Wyoming, such growth resulted in unaffordable housing for longtime residents, and a loss of community as they once knew it." One Red Lodge resident warned his neighbors about the catastrophic growth of Telluride, where the average price for a house had shot up to $1.2 million and the town had to designate a certain road as a parking site for the VW buses and vans that served as "housing" for the town's nonmillionaire workers.[35] Although not quite a Telluride or Jackson Hole, Red Lodge *was* changing. By the early 1990s, Carbon County had experienced a 44 percent increase in subdivision activity as newcomers flocked to the Beartooth front to enjoy spectacular views and clean air. The population inside the city limits grew 15.1 percent in the 1990s. Increasing pressures on land values raised real estate and rental rates in Red Lodge by 30 to 100 percent.[36] One realtor in 1994 noted that he had forty-eight people on a waiting list for rental units; there simply were none available.[37] The little town seemed well on its way to being "Aspenized" — being co-opted

Here is the West being loved to death in the shadow of the Beartooth Mountains. Suburban
subdivisions now threaten the very amenities that many residents came to Red Lodge to
enjoy. (Author's photo)

by wealthy newcomers who would drive out not only the old old-timers but
also the less wealthy, "newer" old-timers.

Red Lodge residents were far from alone in their concerns about saving
community values. The phenomenon of Aspenization around the West had
already led to the creation of the Sonoran Institute in Tucson, Arizona, in 1990.
Dedicated to "promoting community-based strategies that preserve the ecological integrity of protected lands, and at the same time meeting the economic
aspirations of adjoining land owners and communities," the Sonoran Institute
reached out to towns like Red Lodge whose residents were trying to take control of local growth.[38] With the help of the institute, Red Lodge residents
formed the Beartooth Front Community Forum (BFCF), which launched a
series of town meetings from 1992 to 1995 with the ultimate goal of developing a comprehensive plan for city growth that would maintain Red Lodge's
small-town ambiance. Dozens of local residents attended each meeting of the
town planning forum, contributing thoughts and concerns that helped to generate a Red Lodge Master Plan for community development. Local residents
also regularly sat in on town council meetings and voiced opposition to many
planned developments that would increase the community's size or threaten

the local environment. Townspeople, for example, refused to permit a proposed housing development on land reclaimed from the East Side Mine. While the land owner, who had spent $700,000 on the parcel, fumed about impediments to free-market capitalism, residents held the line against expansion and growth.[39]

Perhaps the most telling event in the quest to preserve Red Lodge as a small-town community was a victory over the U.S. Postal Service in the mid-1990s. In 1994—as the BFCF was midway through its town planning meetings— postal service officials announced plans to build a new facility on the edge of town where open spaces invited expansion. Residents immediately balked at the development scheme, insisting that such a move would hurt the downtown area and erode some of Red Lodge's small-town cohesion, especially since the town did not have residential mail delivery. The local post office represented a key facet of the community's small-town identity—the hub that centered residents as they made their daily trips to pick up mail, visit neighbors, and catch up on town gossip. "It's like church on Sunday," explained local writer John Clayton, "except everyone belongs to the same denomination, and it takes place six days a week."[40]

The U.S. Postal Service, however, cared little for community cohesion and plans continued for a large new building with lots of space for parking and truck deliveries. "They were accustomed to building in a suburb, with cars," argued city councilwoman Renee Tafoya. "They have no idea how it is to live in a small community where the post office is not just a warehouse for mail but a meeting place for the community. We weren't going to let some bureaucrat from some big city come and tell us where the heart of our town would be located, and how our town would work."[41] The bureaucracy remained intransigent. Local residents, in turn, grew even more militant, rallying congressmen and senators to back up local demands to preserve the heart of the small town. In the end, the residents won; the post office remained in the middle of the town, a victory celebrated not only in the local newspaper but also in regional forums like the *High Country News* and a book on community action published by the Sonoran Institute and the Conservation Fund. A small town had taken on the federal government and preserved its local cohesion and integrity. Red Lodge, the small town, had become not only a very personal commitment for many residents but also a vibrant public identity.

So, ironically, even as they reshaped their town into the image of the bustling prosperity of Red Lodge's boom days of coal mining, residents were already seeking to prevent the kind of mineral extraction, development, and expansion that characterized the very era they had tried to recapture. By the late 1990s, most locals wanted no part of the grand booster dreams of the 1890s; the "coal metropolis" no longer appealed to people who had sought out Red Lodge because of its proximity to nature and its small-town appeal. The celebration of the coal mining past so evident in the revitalized downtown and the new museum did not mean a return to the prodevelopment beliefs of the town's early promoters. If boosters in past decades had sought to "grow" Red Lodge, modern-day activists in their rehabilitated downtown were determined to control and moderate growth to maintain the amenities associated with life in a small community. In circling back to once again promote a local coal mining identity, town leaders sought to capture only certain, desired aspects of the town's industrial past.

On 10 June 1991, Richard and Alice Mallin sat down with oral historian Anna Zellick to discuss their eight decades of living in Red Lodge. After posing a series of questions about immigrant lifestyles, Zellick asked Richard to talk about coal mining. Trying to describe the centrality of coal in the town's early identity, Richard commented wistfully that Zellick was too late in coming to Red Lodge. "You should have been here two years or so ago," he told her, "and you'd have seen the hills of slack that were brought out of the coal mines. It's unbelievable that so much could come out and still not be coal." Richard suggested that perhaps the piles might have been left as a reminder of the town's coal mining past. Zellick, in turn, challenged Richard's reasoning. "I respect your views," she told Richard, "because you've spent your life here but if you're going to have tourism, that would help the local economy. Is there any harm in doing away with the slack piles?" Richard's reply was telling. "Let's look at your own program here," he pointed out. "You're coming around wanting old history, right? All right, those slack piles were our old history. It's the same thing. Do you see what I mean: We have nothing to talk about now because our proof of it is gone and there's nothing we can do. We can't convince you of what something is when you can't see it. . . . We can't talk about to [sic] that slack pile because it isn't there." "They leveled it all off now," added Alice, "so we don't even have the memory of those slack piles anymore."[42]

The Mallins's lamentation for the slack piles points out the complex interaction of public identity and heritage with other remembrances of the past.

By the end of the twentieth century, the industrial mining that Richard Mallin's immigrant father had made his living at again held a place in the town's public identity and heritage, but its features had changed significantly since the actual boom days of coal. Red Lodge had turned its downtown, museum, and a park into monuments to this particular heritage. The Mallins, however, remembered not only the brick buildings and homes that the mines built but also the work and workers that created the heaps of coal slack on either side of town. To them the waste piles were significant markers of the town and their family's part in building that town. The mounds of waste had been a meaningful legacy for Richard Mallin, whose father worked and died in the area's coal mines and for Alice Mallin, whose mother eked out a living for her children in the 1910s by scavenging bits of coal from the slack piles. They did not see the slack piles as dangerous or dirty, but rather as part of the story of their lives and the life of Red Lodge. They weren't alone. Other residents, too, felt a loss of personal history as the waste heaps vanished from the townscape. Soon after the state government removed the West Side slack heap, for example, Loretta Jarussi noted that one of her former students came to visit and immediately asked about the reclaimed slack pile. When returning to Red Lodge, he explained, "The first thing I looked for was that dump." Jarussi's sister added, "Some of the people think that dump should have been left there as a monument."[43]

Of course, it's not surprising that most residents did not want to have a "monument" to industrial pollution wafting across their community each time the wind blew over the tops of the two slack heaps. Pollution, like radicalism, did not fit in with the public identities that residents had established for Red Lodge by the end of the century. Only a *cleaned-up* historic mining town could mesh with its contemporary identities as nature's town, Wild West community, and festival center. With the slack piles removed and the creek running clear, no public reminder remained of the hazards, pollution, and destruction of that industry. By the 1980s, mining was far enough removed from the present to seem romantic; miners simply became figures from a far-removed past that no longer infringed on modern sentiments about nature or threatened consensus narratives about the local past. Pulled out of context, removed from the slack piles and run-down buildings, the miner made less sense historically but became a more attractive and usable symbol of Red Lodge's current identity. Like the cowboys who no longer lived in town, the immigrants who now seemed so American, and the natural world that had been conquered with a highway, industrial mining by the 1980s and 1990s could finally be idealized and celebrated and incorporated back into the town's public persona as something attractive, appealing, and useful in the construction and maintenance of the community's identity.

Besides, as Zellick pointed out, removal of the slack piles had to help Red Lodge's so-important tourist trade. Tourism was central to the creation of all of the public identities so prominent in Red Lodge by the end of the century. Residents could have completely disregarded this outside influence on their identity creation, but then the town probably would never have survived past World War II. Tourism never dominated local identity creation, but residents certainly understood the demands of tourism and made decisions about Red Lodge's public imagery based on what they thought tourists might like. As Americans themselves, though, townspeople also imbibed the same national culture as their visitors did. Dressing up as cowboys and immigrants appealed to Red Lodge residents for the same reasons that tourists liked to see the public performances of costumed locals. Like most Americans, Red Lodge residents had come to value cowboys and multiculturalism by the middle of the twentieth century. Public performances of the Wild West and immigrant diversity reinforced local pride in cherished interpretations of the past even as such pageants and displays attracted paying visitors. Neither ever really stood outside of the other.

Richard Mallin's poignant argument about *his* slack pile and *his* history reminds us, though, that what town leaders and tourists perceived as appropriate heritage and public identity was not always what each individual resident wanted to remember about his or her own life in and around Red Lodge. To some residents — and most tourists — whose memories did not stretch back to the boom days of coal, the newly developed public heritage of coal mining could mesh easily with their perceptions of what Red Lodge was and had been. For them the coal miner fit as readily into the town's western heritage and public identity as did the cowboy, the Indian, and the dancing immigrant. Residents and visitors alike could convince themselves of the legitimacy of these local icons because these figures and images, unlike the slack piles, remained to be seen and admired as integral parts of Red Lodge's public identity. It was easy to remember Red Lodge's Wild West past because cowboys and Indian tepees were displayed everywhere around town. Without public reminders, other identities just did not get reinforced. Personal memories remained, of course, but without public reinforcement — the daily reminder of the slack piles — even those memories could fade, especially as the older generation inevitably aged and passed away. Alice Mallin realized that actuality when she connected the loss of those slack piles to the loss of memories. Within a decade or so, the Mallins and Jarussis would no longer be around to recall the dirt and smoke of coal mining, but the downtown historic district would still be standing — the public symbol of the public memory of the town's mining heritage. Meanwhile, at least to these local residents, the sanitized celebration of coal mining seemed as awkward and uncomfortable as spurs and boots had to some townspeople in the 1930s rodeo festivities.

Although Mallin and Jarussi and every other resident of Red Lodge individually remembered personal and intimate details about the town's past, the more general public memory of the town became a process of picking and choosing which parts of the past and the surrounding environment to value and valorize not only for residents but also for a touring public. It is easy to simply point out the inaccuracies and ironies of these multitudinous and often conflicting public presentations; lots of historians and other academics have done so. However, it is more interesting and productive to consider carefully the motivations, interests, and controversies that surround the process of identity selection. In Red Lodge, public identity has been malleable, changing and adapting with the times. Tracing this shifting, multifaceted public identity, one can follow the development and survival of a town whose residents drew strength and inspiration from their past even while adapting that past as needed to meet the exigencies of the present. Residents did not fabricate the town's histories; instead, like all other human beings, they took what they needed from the past to survive in the present. And Red Lodge, with all its personalities and varied heritages, did survive.

INTRODUCTION

1. Philip Gleason, "Identifying Identity: A Semantic History," *Journal of American History* 69 (March 1983): 910, 924–925; Craig Calhoun, "Social Theory and the Politics of Identity," in *Social Theory and the Politics of Identity*, ed. Craig Calhoun (Oxford: Blackwell, 1994), 11–14.

2. D. W. Meinig, "Symbolic Landscapes," in *The Interpretation of Ordinary Landscapes: Geographical Essays*, ed. D. W. Meinig (New York: Oxford University Press, 1979), 164.

3. Dora Shu-fang Dien, "The Evolving Nature of Self-Identity across Four Levels of History," *Human Development* 43 (January–February 2000): 5.

4. For works on public memory, see Michael Kammen, *Mystic Chords of Memory: The Transformation of Tradition in American Culture* (New York: Vintage Books, 1993); David Lowenthal, *The Past Is a Foreign Country* (Cambridge: Cambridge University Press, 1985), and *The Heritage Crusade and the Spoils of History* (Cambridge: Cambridge University Press, 1998); John Bodnar, *Remaking America: Public Memory, Commemoration, and Patriotism in the Twentieth Century* (Princeton: Princeton University Press, 1992).

5. On the power of western mythology, see Robert G. Athearn, *The Mythic West in the Twentieth Century* (Lawrence: University Press of Kansas, 1986); Richard Slotkin, *The Fatal Environment: The Myth of the Frontier in the Age of Industrialization, 1800–1890* (New York: HarperPerennial, 1994), and *Gunfighter Nation: The Myth of the Frontier in Twentieth-Century America* (New York: HarperPerennial, 1992); Henry Nash Smith, *Virgin Land: The American West As Symbol and Myth* (Cambridge: Harvard University Press, 1970); Richard White, "Frederick Jackson Turner and Buffalo Bill," in *The Frontier in American Culture*, ed. James R. Grossman (Berkeley: University of California Press, 1994), 7–55; Malcolm J. Rohrbough, *Days of Gold: The California Gold Rush and the American Nation* (Berkeley: University of California Press, 1997), 118; Clyde A. Milner II, "America Only More So," in *The Oxford History of the American West*, ed. Clyde A. Milner II, Carol A. O'Connor, and Martha A. Sandweiss (New York: Oxford University Press, 1994), 1–7. On identity, see John Findlay, "A Fishy Proposition: Regional Identity in the Pacific Northwest," in *Many Wests: Place, Culture, and Regional Identity*, ed. David M. Wrobel and Michael C. Steiner (Lawrence: University Press of Kansas, 1997), 37–70; Bodnar, *Remaking America*; Lowenthal, *The Past Is a Foreign Country*; Kammen, *Mystic Chords of Memory*.

6. Ted Price, *Miracle Town: Creating America's Bavarian Village in Leavenworth, Washington* (Vancouver, Wash.: Price and Rodgers, 1997). For a good discussion of the phenomenon of "theming," see Michael Sorkin, ed., *Variations on a Theme Park: The New American City and the End of Public Space* (New York: Hill and Wang, 1992), and Mira Engler, "Drive-Thru History: Theme Towns in Iowa," *Landscape* 32 (1993): 8–18.

7. Hal K. Rothman, *Devil's Bargains: Tourism in the Twentieth-Century American West* (Lawrence: University Press of Kansas, 1998).

8. Yi-Fu Tuan, "Space and Place: Humanistic Perspective," in *Progress in Geography: International Reviews of Current Research*, vol. 6, ed. Christopher Board, Richard J. Charley, Peter Haggett, and David R. Stoddart (London: Edward Arnold, 1974), 236–245.

9. Lowenthal, *The Heritage Crusade and the Spoils of History*, xi–xv.

10. Louis S. Warren, *The Hunter's Game: Poachers and Conservationists in Twentieth-Century America* (New Haven: Yale University Press, 1997), 16.

1. RED LODGE IN THE 1890S

1. Richard White, "Outlaw Gangs of the Middle Border: American Social Bandits," *Western Historical Quarterly* 12 (October 1981): 387–408.

2. Works on the myth and imagery of the American West include Robert G. Athearn, *The Mythic West in Twentieth-Century America* (Lawrence: University Press of Kansas, 1986); Richard Slotkin, *The Fatal Environment: The Myth of the Frontier in the Age of Industrialization, 1800–1890* (New York: HarperPerennial, 1994), especially chaps. 1 and 2, and *Gunfighter Nation: The Myth of the Frontier in Twentieth-Century America* (New York: HarperPerennial, 1992), 1–26; Henry Nash Smith, *Virgin Land: The American West As Symbol and Myth* (Cambridge: Harvard University Press, 1970); Richard White, "Frederick Jackson Turner and Buffalo Bill," in *The Frontier in American Culture*, ed. James R. Grossman (Berkeley: University of California Press, 1994), 7–55; Malcolm J. Rohrbough, *Days of Gold: The California Gold Rush and the American Nation* (Berkeley: University of California Press, 1997), 118; Clyde A. Milner II, "America Only More So," in *The Oxford History of the American West*, ed. Clyde A. Milner II, Carol A. O'Connor, and Martha A. Sandweiss (New York: Oxford University Press, 1994).

3. Robert J. Dykstra explores some of these issues in *The Cattle Towns* (New York: Knopf, 1968).

4. Carroll Van West, *Capitalism on the Frontier: Billings and the Yellowstone Valley in the Nineteenth Century* (Lincoln: University of Nebraska Press, 1993), 165.

5. K. Ross Toole, *Montana: An Uncommon Land* (Norman: University of Oklahoma Press, 1984), 157; Joseph Kinsey Howard, *Montana: High, Wide, and Handsome* (New Haven: Yale University Press, 1948), 52–54; Michael P. Malone, Richard B. Roeder, and William L. Lang, *Montana: A History of Two Centuries*, rev. ed. (Seattle: University of Washington Press, 1991), 190; Van West, *Capitalism on the Frontier*, 175, 177–178.

6. Shirley Zupan and Harry J. Owens, *Red Lodge: Saga of a Western Area* (Billings, Mont.: Frontier Press, 1979), 22–23; E. V. Smalley, "Red Lodge, Montana," *Northwest Magazine* 10 (August 1892): 20.

7. At least nine of Red Lodge's streets were named after men with interests in the Northern Pacific or its subsidiary, the Rocky Fork Coal Company; Zupan and Owens, *Red Lodge*, 39.

8. *Picket*, 20 April 1895, 2.

9. Smalley, "Red Lodge," 22, 24; *Picket*, 25 March 1893, 3; 8 July 1893, 3; 8 June 1895, 3; 24 August 1895, 3; 31 August 1895, 2. On an original investment of $53,334.40, the trustees of the RFT&EC had received dividends of $145,000 by 1911, a modest profit. D. G. O'Shea to S. T. Hauser, 22 March 1912, 31/3; D. G. O'Shea to Geo. H. Hill, 14 October 1909, 29/46, Samuel T. Hauser Collection, MC 37, Montana Historical Society (MHS).

10. *Picket*, 19 December 1891, 2; Leona Lampi, "Red Lodge: From a Frenetic Past of Crows, Coal, and Boom and Bust Emerges a Unique Festival of Diverse Nationality Groups," *Montana: The Magazine of Western History* 11 (July 1961): 21–22; Beverly Rue Wellington, *Red Lodge Landmarks* (Red Lodge: Carbon County News, 1992), 22–23; Zupan and Owens, *Red Lodge*, 25–26.

11. Van West, *Capitalism on the Frontier*, 124.

12. Elliott West, *The Saloon on the Rocky Mountain Mining Frontier* (Lincoln: University of Nebraska Press, 1979), 13, 100, 105, 109, notes that liquor was "high in value in relation to its bulk," which made it a profitable item to ship; he also shows that saloon keeping was a popular mode of advancement taken by working-class men who wanted to enter the entrepreneurial class.

13. Zupan and Owens, *Red Lodge*, 23; Smalley, "Red Lodge, Montana," 25–26.

14. *Picket*, 15 August 1891, 3.

15. Slotkin, *Fatal Environment*, 39. On replicating eastern social and economic structures in the West, see Van West, *Capitalism on the Frontier*, 134–142, 148, and David Hamer, *New Towns in the New World: Images and Perceptions of the Nineteenth-Century Urban Frontier* (New York: Columbia University Press, 1990), 85, 130–138.

16. *Picket*, 17 October 1896, 3. See also David M. Emmons, *Garden in the Grasslands: Boomer Literature of the Central Great Plains* (Lincoln: University of Nebraska Press, 1971), 47–77, and Allan G. Bogue, "An Agricultural Empire," in *The Oxford History of the American West*, 285–287.

17. *Picket*, 30 January 1892, 3; 13 February 1892, 3; 4 March 1893, 3; 6 May 1893, 3; 7 October 1893, 2.

18. Burton M. Smith, "Politics and the Crow Indian Land Cessions," *Montana: The Magazine of Western History* 36 (Autumn 1986): 24–37.

19. *Stinking Water Prospector* (Red Lodge), 24 June 1891, 3.

20. *Stinking Water Prospector*, 24 June 1891, 3; *Picket*, 19 December 1891, 3. Red Lodge's 1890 population figures are included in U.S. Department of Commerce, Bureau of the Census, *Thirteenth Census of the United States, Taken in the Year 1910, Characteristics of the Population, Volume 2* (Washington, D.C.: Government Printing Office, 1913), 1138.

21. Smalley, "Red Lodge," 21.

22. *Stinking Water Prospector*, 24 June 1891.

23. Frederick Jackson Turner, "The Significance of the Frontier in American History," in *The Early Writings of Frederick Jackson Turner*, comp. Everett E. Edwards (Madison: University of Wisconsin Press, 1938), 199.

24. Athearn, *Mythic West*, 10–13; for an analysis of *Shane*, see Slotkin, *Gunfighter Nation*, 369–400.

25. Smith, *Virgin Land*, 123–124.

26. Leo Marx, *The Machine in the Garden: Technology and the Pastoral Ideal in America* (London: Oxford University Press, 1978), 226.

27. Smith, *Virgin Land*, 124; *Picket*, 5 December 1896, 2.

28. Turner, "Significance of the Frontier in American History," 186–189.

29. Emmons, *Garden in the Grasslands*, 1–4; Smith, *Virgin Land*, 124–144; Frank R. Grant, "Embattled Voice for the Montana Farmers: Robert Sutherlin's *Rocky Mountain Husbandman*," (Ph.D. diss., University of Montana, 1984), 169; Richard Brown Roeder, "Montana in the Early Years of the Progressive Period" (Ph.D. diss., University of Pennsylvania, 1971), 86.

30. *Picket*, 5 December 1896, 2.

31. *Picket*, 16 December 1893, 2.

32. *Picket*, 5 December 1896, 2; 15 April 1893, 3; Slotkin, *Fatal Environment*, 308.

33. *Picket,* 15 April 1893, 3; 5 December 1896, 2.

34. John Bodnar, *Remaking America: Public Memory, Commemoration, and Patriotism in the Twentieth Century* (Princeton: Princeton University Press, 1992), 16, 34, 49, 92–93, 249–250.

35. Walt Whitman, *Leaves of Grass* (New York: Penguin Books, 1980), 169–172.

36. In his classic study of the mythology of the yeoman farmer, *Virgin Land,* Henry Nash Smith's index reference for pioneer reads simply "*see* Farmer" (p. 303).

37. Turner quotes from *Peck's New Guide to the West* (1837) in this passage on towns, "Significance of the Frontier," 208–209.

38. James U. Sanders, ed., *Society of Montana Pioneers,* vol. 1 (Akron, Ohio: Werner Company, 1899). The Montana Society of Pioneers tried to control the term by applying it only to those who had arrived in Montana by 1864 (later extended to 1868), excluding only Indians and outlaws from the category. Conditions for society membership did not preclude other Montanans from using the term, however. Clyde A. Milner II, "The Shared Memory of Montana Pioneers," *Montana: The Magazine of Western History* 37 (Winter 1987): 13.

39. *Picket,* 15 August 1891, 3; 19 December 1891, 3.

40. *Picket,* 19 December 1891, 3.

41. *Picket,* 15 April 1893, 3.

42. Slotkin, *Fatal Environment,* 45.

43. Lampi, "Red Lodge," 20.

44. *Picket,* 5 September 1891, 3; 19 December 1891, 2; 6 February 1892, 3; 20 August 1892, 3; 15 October 1892, 3; 22 October 1892, 3; 29 October 1892, 3; 10 December 1892, 3; 11 March 1893, 3; 18 March 1893, 3; 15 April 1893, 3; 16 September 1893, 3; 10 March 1894, 2; 15 September 1894, 3; 6 October 1894, 3; 29 June 1895; 3 August 1895, 3; 8 February 1896, 2.

45. Michael Denning, *Mechanic Accents: Dime Novels and Working-Class Culture in America* (London: Verso, 1987), 157–158; Smith, *Virgin Lands,* 90–111; Jane Tompkin, *West of Everything: The Inner Life of Westerns* (New York: Oxford University Press, 1992); Heribert Frhr. v. Feilitzsch, "Karl May: The 'Wild West' as Seen in Germany," *Journal of Popular Culture* 27 (Winter 1993): 173–189. For examples of dime-novel Westerns, see Ned Buntline, *Buffalo Bill and His Adventures in the Wild West* (New York: J. S. Ogelvie, 1884), or Edward L. Wheeler, *Deadwood Dick's Big Deal, or the Gold Brick of Oregon* (New York: Beadle and Adams, 1883).

46. White, "Frederick Jackson Turner and Buffalo Bill," 27; L. G. Moses, *Wild West Shows and the Images of American Indians, 1883–1933* (Albuquerque: University of New Mexico Press, 1996), 1.

47. Michael Denning, *Mechanic Accents,* 157–160, argues that in a particular version of dime-novel Westerns, the outlaw tale, the hero briefly emerged as a social bandit who "openly defied laws, reacted violently against social restraint." Deadwood Dick and later Jesse James were the most popular of these working-class heroes. Between 1877 and 1883, as Denning puts it, "Outlaws defied the law and got away with it, escaping the moral universe of both genteel and sensational fiction." But middle-class morality quickly caught up with these wild outlaws; the postmaster general squelched distribution of such novels in 1893, and the West returned to the control of "proper" heroes who killed only Indians and rustlers.

48. Quoted in Slotkin, *Gunfighter Nation,* 48.

49. Owen Wister, *The Virginian* (New York: Popular Library, Eagle Books, 1962), 93.

50. Boosters, for example, insisted that the white settlers should, of course, supersede Indians on area lands. *Picket,* 6 October 1894, 3; 18 January 1896, 2; 8 February 1896, 2.

51. James Welch noted that in his research for a novel on Blackfeet Indians, *Fools Crow,* he had to search out the site of the Marias massacre. Unlike the Custer Battlefield, which became a national monument, the Marias site is just an unmarked field of grass. William Kittredge relates this story in *Who Owns the West* (San Francisco: Mercury House, 1996), 122; see also Richard Maxwell Brown, "Violence," in *The Oxford History of the American West,* 416.

52. White, "Frederick Jackson Turner and Buffalo Bill," 27–32; Moses, *Wild West Shows and the Images of American Indians,* 1; Slotkin, *Gunfighter Nation,* 76; Glenda Riley, *Women and Indians on the Frontier, 1825–1915* (Albuquerque: University of New Mexico Press, 1984), 250.

53. In at least three separate incidents, rural residents near Red Lodge fled their homes in fear of Indian attacks. *Picket,* 29 October 1892, 3; 11 March 1893, 3; 18 March 1893, 3. Some residents, even in the early 1890s, feared Indians just because they were Indians. For example, Mrs. Hicox, an early Red Lodge resident, wrote: "I dreaded the arrival of the Crows, for I feared them so. Every time I saw them coming, I hid and pretended I wasn't home" (Zupan and Owens, *Red Lodge,* 22).

54. Zupan and Owens, *Red Lodge,* 22, 324.

55. *Picket,* 29 October 1892, 3.

56. *Picket,* 11 March 1893, 3. The man who shot the Indian was later acquitted on the grounds of self-defense; he argued that the Crow had been reaching for his gun; *Picket,* 15 April 1893, 3.

57. *Picket,* 11 March 1893, 3

58. *Picket,* 18 March 1893, 3. White notes this tendency of eastern newspapers to seize upon rumors of Indian attacks in "Frederick Jackson Turner and Buffalo Bill," 29.

59. *Picket,* 6 October 1894, 3; 18 January 1896, 2; 8 February 1896, 2.

60. Van West, *Capitalism on the Frontier,* 8–66.

61. *Picket,* 6 October 1894, 3; Hamer, *New Towns in the New World,* 219.

62. Van West, *Capitalism on the Frontier,* 178.

63. Slotkin, *Gunfighter Nation,* 170.

64. Red Lodge, though, never erupted into the kind of violence that marked the struggle between ranchers and farmers in the so-called Johnson County War in Wyoming. Richard White, *"It's Your Misfortune and None of My Own": A History of the American West* (Norman: University of Oklahoma Press, 1991), 345–346.

65. J. R. Dilworth to Williamson, 28 February 1887, Dilworth Cattle Company Records, MF 308a, MHS.

66. J. N. Tolman to D. J. Campbell, 23 March 1893, and J. N. Tolman to John Wilson, 1 May 1893, Dilworth Cattle Company Records, MF 308a, MHS.

67. Quote from *Picket,* 15 September 1894, 3. For other references to ranchers and Indians working together to keep land from farmers, see *Picket,* 20 August 1892, 3; 22 October 1892, 3; 6 October 1894, 3; 3 August 1895, 3; 8 February 1896, 2.

68. Most Montanans of this period supported the idea that farming was a higher and better

use of resources than cattle ranching was; Roeder, "Montana in the Early Years of the Progressive Period," 86. Red Lodge boosters may have been aware that the land surrounding the town was currently hard to cultivate, but they laid their hopes on irrigation projects and the promises of dry-land farming techniques. In the early 1900s, for example, local merchant W. A. Talmadge helped to organize a series of dry-land farming conferences in the state; *Republican Picket* (Red Lodge), 26 August 1909, 1.

69. *Picket,* 11 March 1893, 3; 10 March 1894, 2; 6 October 1894, 3; 29 June 1895, 3.

70. Efforts to control the "wild" imagery of the town's industrial miners are discussed in Chapter 2.

71. J. N. Tolman to W. J. Anderson, 30 August 1891, Dilworth Cattle Company Records, MF 308a, MHS.

72. *Picket,* 19 December 1891, 2.

73. Most cowboys lost their jobs during the winter and wandered around western towns. Kristine Fredericksson, *American Rodeo: From Buffalo Bill to Big Business* (College Station: Texas A&M University Press, 1985), 13; Blake Allmendinger, *The Cowboy: Representations of Labor in an American Work Culture* (New York: Oxford University Press, 1992), 84–86.

74. *Picket,* 5 September 1891, 3.

75. *Picket,* 15 October 1892, 3.

76. See, for example, the classic Western, Wister's *The Virginian,* for this ideal of the fun-loving, noble cowhand.

77. Quoted in Slotkin, *Gunfighter Nation,* 39.

78. *Picket,* 15 October 1892, 3.

79. *Picket,* 10 December 1892, 3.

80. *Picket,* 6 February 1892, 3. "Hobo" was a reference also to the multitudes of unemployed workers wandering around the country in the late nineteenth century. It did not necessarily refer to cowboys, but the local newspaper sometimes used the two terms interchangeably; *Picket,* 6 February 1892, 6; 15 October 1892, 3. On hobos, see Eric H. Monkkonen, ed., *Walking to Work: Tramps in America, 1790–1935* (Lincoln: University of Nebraska Press, 1984).

81. Zupan and Owens, *Red Lodge,* 16.

82. By early 1893, the jail was in such bad shape that the marshal had to physically guard prisoners who could not pay their fines; *Picket,* 11 February 1893, 3.

83. *Picket,* 16 September 1893, 3.

84. *Picket,* 15 October 1892, 3

85. A movement to "reform" women's clothing gained momentum in the 1890s; advocates argued that looser and lighter clothing would make women healthier and better workers. Some reformers advocated the "Mother Hubbard" dress, which was popular in the West because it was so simple to make and comfortable to wear. Some western towns like Red Lodge prohibited the dress because it seemed indecent; others, like Pendleton, Oregon, outlawed Mother Hubbards because the loose-flowing cloth was likely to blow in the wind and frighten horses. Lee Hall, *Common Threads: A Parade of American Clothing* (Boston: Little, Brown, 1992). For examples of dress reform arguments, see almost any *Arena* magazine from the 1890s.

86. *Picket,* 26 May 1894, 3.

87. *City of Red Lodge v. Mary McDonald* (1897), appeal from Justice Court, Carbon County District Court (CCDC), Criminal Records no. 3-35; *Picket,* 25 March 1893, 3.

88. *Picket,* 24 December 1892, 3.

89. *Picket,* 21 January 1893, 3; 10 December 1892, 3. The marshal could simply shoot any unlicensed dog that appeared to be without value (a mutt) but was required to take any dog that seemed valuable to the pound, a profound class distinction for the hounds; *Picket,* 14 January 1893, 3.

90. *Picket,* 21 January 1893, 3.

91. *Picket,* 14 January 1893, 3; 21 January 1893, 3.

92. *Picket,* 11 February 1893, 3; 25 March 1893, 3; 13 May 1893, 3. Anne M. Butler noted the ambivalent attitude of the frontier press toward prostitution in *Daughters of Joy, Sisters of Misery: Prostitutes in the American West, 1865–90* (Urbana: University of Illinois Press, 1985), 29, 81. See also Paula Petrik, *No Step Backward: Women and Family on the Rocky Mountain Mining Frontier, 1865–1900* (Helena: Montana Historical Society Press, 1987).

93. Butler, *Daughters of Joy,* 153.

94. *Carbon County Gazette* (Red Lodge), 11 May 1905, 1. The town collected $225.25 in April 1905 from "red light fines, gambling and drunks" (*Picket,* 11 May 1905, 1, 2).

95. For example, Zupan and Owens, *Red Lodge,* 243–245.

96. Lampi, "Red Lodge," 24.

97. T. J. Jackson Lears, *No Place of Grace: Antimodernism and the Transformation of American Culture, 1880–1920* (New York: Pantheon Books, 1981), xii.

98. Lears, *No Place of Grace,* 4–5.

99. Slotkin, *Gunfighter Nation,* 37.

100. Earl Pomeroy, *In Search of the Golden West: The Tourist in Western America* (Lincoln: University of Nebraska Press, 1990), 74–75; Malcolm S. Mackay, *Cow Range and Hunting Trail* (New York: G. P. Putnam's Sons, 1925), 146, 156.

101. Mackay, *Cow Range and Hunting Trail,* 18–32, 146, 156, once hired VanDyke to take him bear hunting.

102. Zupan and Owens, *Red Lodge,* 8–9.

103. *Picket,* 28 May 1892, 3.

104. Pomeroy, *In Search of the Golden West,* 131–133.

105. Harry Owens, "John (Liver-Eating) Johnston," in Zupan and Owens, *Red Lodge,* 15. A local historian, Owens has made something of a crusade out of redeeming Johnson's name and character after the publication of *Crow Killer* in 1958, a book that portrayed Johnson as a bloodthirsty and insatiable Indian killer, and the movie *Jeremiah Johnson,* which he considered an inaccurate depiction of the mountain man. Owens also insists on the spelling of Johnson's name as Johnston, since that was the name he signed on the homestead patent he took out on land just south of Red Lodge in 1897. I have used Johnson throughout this work, since it is the name by which he is generally known.

106. Zupan and Owen, *Red Lodge,* 12–13; E. C. Abbott and Helena Huntington Smith, *We Pointed Them North: Recollections of a Cowpuncher* (Norman: University of Oklahoma Press, 1989, 1939), 117–118. In Raymond W. Thorp and Robert Bunker, *Crow Killer: The Saga of Liver-Eating Johnson* (Bloomington: Indiana University Press, 1958), a sensationalistic, bloody version of Johnson's life, the authors claim Johnson killed hundreds of Indians, many of them with his bare hands.

107. Abbott, *We Pointed Them North*, 117–118. The *Helena Independent* published a letter on Johnson in 1893, reprinted in the *Picket*, 13 May 1893, 3; a story on Johnson from the *Billings Gazette* was reprinted in the *Picket*, 28 December 1895, 3. A reporter from *Field and Stream* met with Johnson in 1894 to get a "narrative on Indian warfare and life in the early days of Montana" (*Picket*, 28 April 1894, 3).

108. See, for example, the portrait of Yellowstone Kelly at the front of his memoirs, *"Yellowstone Kelly": The Memoirs of Luther S. Kelly*, ed. M. M. Quaife (Lincoln: University of Nebraska Press, 1926), ii.

109. *Picket*, 27 May 1893, 3.

110. *Picket*, 13 May 1893, 3; 27 May 1893, 3.

111. *Picket*, 11 June 1892, 3; 9 June 1894, 2; 23 February 1895, 3; 6 April 1895, 3; 15 May 1897, 3; 17 July 1897, 3; 6 November 1897, 3.

2. THE INDUSTRIAL WEST

1. Loretta and Lillian Jarussi, OH 1487, 1–2, Montana Historical Society Collections (MHS).

2. Erika A. Kuhlman, "From Farmland to Coalvillage: Red Lodge's Finnish Immigrants, 1890–1922" (master's thesis, University of Montana, 1987), 21–22.

3. *Picket*, 21 September 1905, 1.

4. For more on the transformation of natural resources to capital in the industrial age, see William Cronon, *Nature's Metropolis: Chicago and the Great West* (New York: W. W. Norton, 1991), and Richard White, *The Organic Machine: The Remaking of the Columbia River* (New York: Hill and Wang, 1995).

5. *Picket*, 5 January 1895, 3; 9 March 1895, 3.

6. *Republican Picket* (Red Lodge), 26 August 1909, 1.

7. For example, Patricia Nelson Limerick, *The Legacy of Conquest: The Unbroken Past of the American West* (New York: W. W. Norton, 1987); Robert G. Athearn, *The Mythic West in Twentieth-Century America* (Lawrence: University Press of Kansas, 1986); William Cronon, "Kennecott Journey: The Paths out of Town," in *Under an Open Sky: Rethinking America's Western Past*, ed. William Cronon, George Miles, and Jay Gitlin (New York: W. W. Norton, 1992), 28–51; Donald Worster, "Beyond the Agrarian Myth," in *Trails: Toward a New Western History*, ed. Patricia Nelson Limerick, Clyde A. Milner II, and Charles E. Rankin (Lawrence: University Press of Kansas, 1991), 3–25; Carlos A. Schwantes, "Wage Earners and Wealth Makers," in *The Oxford History of the American West*, ed. Clyde A. Milner II, Carol A. O'Connor, and Martha A. Sandweiss (New York: Oxford University Press, 1994), 431–467.

8. Carlos A. Schwantes, *The Pacific Northwest: An Interpretive History* (Lincoln: University of Nebraska Press, 1989), 239–243; Richard Maxwell Brown, "Violence," in *The Oxford History of the American West*, 411.

9. Price V. Fishback, "An Alternative View of Violence in Labor Disputes in the Early 1900s: The Bituminous Coal Industry, 1890–1930," *Labor History* 36 (Summer 1995): 426–456, points out that the contemporary press and general public blamed miners for this violence, while workers themselves blamed the coal operators. Violence was not actually the norm in mining camps, but what is important for this study is the common *perception* of great violence in the mines.

10. U.S. Congress, Industrial Commission, *Report of the Industrial Commission on Immi-*

gration, Vol. 25 *of the Commission's Report* (Washington, D.C.: Government Printing Office, 1901), 399–405.

11. In 1899, bituminous mines in the United States operated on average 171 to 234 days a year; *Report of the Industrial Commission on Immigration*, 398.

12. T. J. Jackson Lears, *No Place of Grace: Antimodernism and the Transformation of American Culture, 1880–1920* (New York: Pantheon Books, 1981), 29–31.

13. *Picket*, 24 October 1896, 3.

14. *Picket*, 1 June 1895, 3; 8 June 1895, 3; 24 October 1896, 2; 5 December 1896, 2; also see Meyer and Chapman Bank, "Red Lodge," n.d., CCHS.

15. *Picket*, 25 March 1893, 3; 11 August 1894, 3; Meyer and Chapman, "Red Lodge."

16. E. V. Smalley, "Red Lodge, Montana," *Northwest Magazine* 10 (August 1892): 21.

17. *Picket*, 15 June 1900, 3.

18. *Carbon County v. F. D. Beguette* (1896), Carbon County District Court (CCDC), Criminal Records no. 1-6.

19. See, for example, the *Picket*'s "Illustrated Industrial Souvenir Edition," 1907, CCHS, which, although it had a small drawing of a miner on the front cover, otherwise made little mention of miners or immigrants beyond a formal photograph of the Red Lodge Finnish Ladies' Band showing a dozen or so women in neatly pressed white shirtwaists and dark skirts. Also, a promotional story in the *Billings Gazette* on Carbon County written by the editor of the *Carbon County Journal*, circa 1905, made only passing reference to miners. Clipping in Vertical File, "Carbon County," Parmly Billings Library Collections.

20. *Republican*, 8 June 1906, 1.

21. *Gazette* (Red Lodge), 17 November 1905, 1.

22. Testimony in *State v. Gust Jarvi, Erik Kanga, and August Hokolo* (1911) CCDC, Criminal Records no. 290.

23. The *Picket*, for example, carried stories from Finland on 7 December 1905 and 8 March 1906. The *Republican Picket*'s Finnish-language page ran from May to July 1909.

24. *Picket*, 24 May 1906, 2; *Republican*, 6 July 1906, 1; 28 June 1907, 1.

25. For images of early Red Lodge, see the photograph collections at the Carbon County Historical Society. On railroads and the flow of raw materials and capital, see Cronon, *Nature's Metropolis*.

26. Richard V. Francaviglia provides a good overview of mining landscapes in *Hard Places: Reading the Landscape of America's Historic Mining Districts* (Iowa City: University of Iowa Press, 1991). On vernacular architecture in the West, see Thomas Carter, ed., *Images of an American Land: Vernacular Architecture in the Western United States* (Albuquerque: University of New Mexico Press, 1997).

27. Arthur A. Hart, "Sheet Iron Elegance: Mail Order Architecture in Montana," *Montana: The Magazine of Western History* 40 (Autumn 1990): 27–31; Kingston Heath, "False-Front Architecture on Montana's Urban Frontier," in *Images of an American Land*, 21–39.

28. Henry Van Brunt, "Architecture in the West," in *Architecture and Society: Selected Essays of Henry VanBrunt*, ed. William A. Coles (Cambridge: Belknap Press of Harvard University Press, 1969), 182; see also Pamela H. Simpson, "Cheap, Quick, and Easy, Part II: Pressed Metal Ceilings, 1880–1930," in *Gender, Class, and Shelter: Perspectives in Vernacular Architecture*, vol. 5, ed. Elizabeth Collins Cromley and Carter L. Hudgins (Knoxville: University of Tennessee Press, 1995), 158–159.

29. Hart, "Sheet Iron Elegance," 30–31; Simpson, "Cheap, Quick, and Easy," 152–156.

30. For a discussion on conformity and diversity in the modern age, see John Sinton, "When Moscow Looks Like Chicago: An Essay on Uniformity and Diversity in Land-scapes and Communities," *Environmental History Review* 17 (Fall 1993): 23–41.

31. On pattern book architecture, see Jan Jennings, "Cheap and Tasteful Dwellings in Popular Architecture," in *Gender, Class, and Shelter*, 133–151.

32. In 1900, 33 percent of heads of households in Red Lodge owned their own homes; Kuhlman, "From Farmland to Coalvillage," 22. On crowding, see the oral history of Tony Persha, who claimed that many houses held two to three families each (Tony Persha Oral History, OH 305, 1A); on families taking in boarders to get by, see Rose Jurkovich Oral History, OH 1486, 1–2; Rose Naglich MacFarland Oral History, OH 1474, 6; J. N. "Buck" Cornelio Oral History, OH 546, 1A, MHS.

33. Edward Blazina Oral History, OH 1485, 9–11, 14; John Kastelitz Oral History, OH 1478, 15–17; Persha Oral History, 1A; John Barovich Oral History, OH 1482, 5–8; Mike Barovich Oral History, OH 1480, 9; John Michunovich Oral History, OH 1491, 19–21; Jurkovich Oral History, 13; Edi G. Massa Sernel Oral History, OH 1081; Mildred Cheserek Harboldt Oral History, OH 1483, 22–25; Ollie Anderson Oral History, OH 302, 5, 24; Mac-Farland Oral History, 29–31, MHS.

34. *Picket-Journal*, 24 December 1919, 1.

35. On fetching the bucket of beer, see Tony and Shirley Zupan Oral History, OH 1479, 30, MHS, and Michunovich Oral History, 18; on boardinghouse meals around mine whistles, Leoni Lampi Oral History, OH 303, 13–15, MHS; on listening to the whistle to find out about work, Persha Oral History, 1A.

36. Vera Marincheck Naglich Oral History, OH 1490, 7; Walpas Koski Oral History, OH 359, 25–26, MHS; Blazina Oral History, 23–24.

37. Deryck W. Holdsworth, "'I'm a Lumberjack and I'm OK': The Built Environment and Varied Masculinities in the Industrial Age," in *Gender, Class, and Shelter*, 15–17; Susan L. Johnson, "Sharing Bed and Board: Cohabitation and Cultural Difference in Central Arizona Mining Towns, 1863–1873," in *The Women's West*, ed. Susan Armitage and Elizabeth Jameson (Norman: University of Oklahoma Press, 1987), 77–91.

38. U.S. Department of Commerce, Bureau of the Census, *Thirteenth Census of the United States, Taken in the Year 1910, Population, Volume 2* (Washington, D.C.: Government Printing Office, 1913), 1160.

39. Shirley Zupan and Harry J. Owens, *Red Lodge: Saga of a Western Area* (Billings, Mont.: Frontier Press, 1979), 29–31.

40. Women, first of all, were simply not allowed in many of the public places where men gathered. State laws actually forbade women from entering saloons unless the establishment had a separate "Ladies Lounge" (which most did not have), while local authorities frowned on such activities as disturbing the peace. The county sheriff readily arrested women who tried to break the barrier and enter these male bastions. Women, of course, worked in the town's many brothels, but local officials gradually moved these residences into discrete parts of the community where such women made the least possible public impact; *Picket*, 11 May 1905, 1, 2.

41. Jurkovich Oral History, 12–13; D. W., William M., William N., and Dan Dimich Oral History, OH 1478, 8; Daisy Pekich Lazetich Oral History, OH 1488, 6–7, MHS; MacFarland Oral History, 11–12; Zupan Oral History, 10.

42. Holdsworth, "'I'm a Lumberjack and I'm OK,'" 15–17.
43. Senia Kallio Oral History, OH 357, 38, MHS.
44. Indeed, some women, like John and Mike Barovich's mother, refused to learn English; John Barovich Oral History, 10, and Mike Barovich Oral History, 7.
45. Kallio Oral History, 9.
46. Alice and Richard Mallin Oral History, OH 1481, MHS, 5; Koski Oral History, 8; "Montana" Vera Buening Oral History, OH 358, 2A, MHS. See also Michunovich Oral History, 34; Jurkovich Oral History, 12–13.
47. For a good overview of coal mining in the West, see Priscilla Long, *Where the Sun Never Shines: A History of America's Bloody Coal Industry* (New York: Paragon Books, 1991), especially part 2, "Coal in the American West."
48. Local reminiscences and oral histories are filled with references to mine accidents and injuries. Richard Mallin's father's leg was amputated after a 1912 accident; he was then given the position of check weighman by the union; Mallin Oral History, 3. Edward Blazina's father carried huge scars from his varied accidents underground; Blazina Oral History, 12–13. When William Tweedie's father was injured in the mines, young William had to quit school and go into the mines himself to support his family; William Tweedie Oral History, OH 222, 1A, MHS. Rose Jurkovich's father injured his back while mining; Jurkovich Oral History, 9. William Glancy recalled that many old miners died struggling for breath; William Glancy Oral History, OH 516, 50, MHS. Rose Naglich MacFarland's father developed consumption at the age of twenty-four and had to quit mining; MacFarland Oral History, 3.
49. *James H. McAllister v. Rocky Fork Coal Co. of Montana* (1902), CCDC, Civil Records no. 272. Being Irish probably helped McAllister's local job prospects since Irish immigrants at the turn of the century held a number of important municipal posts in Red Lodge; Zupan and Owens, *Red Lodge*, 43–44.
50. Walpas Koski recalled that his father, like other miners, looked old before his time; Koski Oral History, 41. See also Alan Derickson, "The United Mine Workers of America and the Recognition of Occupational Respiratory Diseases, 1902–1968," *American Journal of Public Health* 81 (June 1991) 782–784.
51. Local oral histories bring up mine deaths quite often. For example, John Kastelitz lost his father in the mines; Kastelitz Oral History, 3. Tony Persha's brother and Ollie Anderson's two brothers were all killed in the mines; Persha Oral History, Ollie Anderson Oral History, 4.
52. On the hazards of underground mining, see Jack Reardon, "Injuries and Illnesses among Bituminous and Lignite Coal Miners," *Monthly Labor Review* 116 (October 1993): 51; Jacqueline Karnell Corn, "'Dark as a Dungeon': Environment and Coal Miners' Health and Safety in Nineteenth-Century America," *Environmental Review* 7 (Fall 1983): 257–268; Long, *Where the Sun Never Shines*, 24–51.
53. Ollie Anderson's brother died in the mines; Anderson Oral History, 6. Lillian Lampi's husband helped to care for many of the widows living in Red Lodge; Lampi Oral History, 16–17. Senia Kallio also noted the large numbers of widows in town; Kallio Oral History, 33.
54. Kuhlman, "From Farmland to Coalvillage," 79.
55. Rocky Fork Coal Company Records, 136/D/17/3B, Minnesota Historical Society.
56. Northwestern Improvement Company Records, 138/C/6/2, Box 53, Volume 119, Minnesota Historical Society.

57. *Picket* (Red Lodge), 17 October 1896, 3.

58. *Republican* (Red Lodge), 23 March 1906, 1.

59. *Picket,* 16 February 1905, 1; 22 June 1905, 1; *Republican,* 23 March 1906, 1.

60. *Thirteenth Census of the United States, Population, Volume 2,* 1160; Kuhlman, "From Farmland to Coalvillage," 25–26.

61. U.S. Department of Commerce, Bureau of the Census, *Fourteenth Census of the United States, Taken in the Year 1920, Volume 3, Population* (Washington, D.C.: Government Printing Office, 1922), 574.

62. Elizabeth Jameson, *All That Glitters: Class, Conflict, and Community in Cripple Creek* (Urbana: University of Illinois Press, 1998), 140–160; Richard White, *"It's Your Misfortune and None of My Own": A History of the American West* (Norman: University of Oklahoma Press, 1991), 194, 289.

63. A good account of this kind of migration pattern is in John Gjerde, *From Peasants to Farmers: The Migration from Balestrand, Norway, to the Upper Middle West* (New York: Cambridge University Press, 1985).

64. Mikko Marttunen typified this pattern of migration; he left Finland in 1910 and worked in the mines at Bessemer, Michigan, for a few months before heading off for Red Lodge, where he had heard there were good jobs in the coal mines; Kuhlman, "From Farmland to Coalvillage," 111–114. See also Reino Kero, "Migration Traditions from Finland to North America," in *A Century of European Migrations, 1830–1930,* ed. Rudolph J. Vecoli and Suzanne M. Sinke (Urbana: University of Illinois Press, 1991): 111–120; Al Gedicks, "Ethnicity, Class Solidarity, and Labor Radicalism among Finnish Immigrants in Michigan's Copper Country," *Politics and Society* 7 (1977): 127–128, 136, 154; Eugene Van Cleef, "The Finn in America," *Geographical Review* 6 (September 1918): 185–189.

65. Timothy J. Sarbaugh, "The Irish in the West: An Ethnic Tradition of Enterprise and Innovation, 1848–1991," *Journal of the West* (April 1992): 5, argues that because the western frontier lacked the entrenched bigotries of the East, it "proved to be frightfully liberating for Irish immigrants." On Irish success in the West, see also David M. Emmons, *The Butte Irish: Class and Ethnicity in an American Mining Town, 1875–1925* (Urbana: University of Illinois Press, 1990); James P. Walsh, "The Irish in the New America: 'Way Out West,'" in *America and Ireland, 1776–1976: The American Identity and the Irish Connection,* ed. David Noel Doyle and Owen Dudley Edwards (Westport, Conn.: Greenwood Press, 1980), 165–176; Thomas J. Noel, "The Immigrant Saloon in Denver," in *Immigrant Institutions: The Organization of Immigrant Life,* ed. George E. Pozzetta (New York: Garland Publishing, 1991): 209–212; Marlene S. McCleary Bosanko, "Among Colored Hats and Other Gewgaws: The Early Irish in Washington State," *Journal of the West* (April 1992): 33–40; Timothy J. Sarbaugh, "Celts with the Midas Touch: The Farmers, Entrepreneurs, and Millionaires of Spokane's City and County Pioneer Community," *Journal of the West* 31 (April 1992): 41–51.

66. *An Illustrated History of the Yellowstone Valley Embracing the Counties of Park, Sweet Grass, Carbon, Yellowstone, Rosebud, Custer and Dawson, State of Montana* (Spokane, Wash.: Western Historical Publishing, 1907), 634; Beverly Rue Wellington, *Red Lodge Landmarks* (Red Lodge: Carbon County News, 1992), 63–64.

67. Wellington, *Red Lodge Landmarks,* 53–54.

68. *Picket,* 8 June 1905, 1.

69. On grapes, see Naglich Oral History, 27; Leslie Lyons Oral History, OH 301, 2B, MHS; Faye Anderson Oral History, 1A, Mike Barovich Oral History, 10; Dimich Oral History, 8; Patten Oral History, 1B; Harboldt Oral History, 27; Daniel M. McDonald Oral History, OH 356, 1A, MHS. For picnics, see Naglich Oral History, 22; Lazelich Oral History, 12, Blazina Oral History, 18–19; Zupan Oral History, 26–27; Jarussi Oral History, 16. On ethnic celebrations, see Lazelich Oral History, 7; *Picket*, 29 December 1894, 3; 7 June 1896, 3; 13 June 1896, 3; 5 March 1898, 3. On saunas in Red Lodge, see Kallio Oral History. For saunas in Finnish-American culture, see Cotton Mather and Matti Kaups, "The Finnish Sauna: A Cultural Index to Settlement," *Annals of the Association of American Geographics* 53 (December 1963): 494–499.

70. "White" in the late nineteenth century did not have the same meaning that the term carries today. Americans made a variety of distinctions between different European groups, choosing to define only "Anglo" or "Nordic" types as "white." For contemporary examples of these distinctions, see, for example, Edward A. Ross, *The Old World in the New: The Significance of Past and Present Immigration to the American People* (New York: Century, 1914), and Jacob Riis, *How the Other Half Lives: Studies among the Tenements of New York* (Boston: St. Martin's Press, 1996). For good historical discussions of the construction of "whiteness," see Noel Ignatiev, *How the Irish Became White* (New York: Routledge, 1995); David R. Roediger, *The Wages of Whiteness: Race and the Making of the American Working Class* (London: Verso, 1991); and George Lipsitz, "The Possessive Investment in Whiteness: Racialized Social Democracy and the 'White' Problem in American Studies," *American Quarterly* 47 (September 1995): 369–387.

71. "Non-white" residents appear only spottily in the public record of Red Lodge, including the local newspapers. In 1892, Chinese laundryman Ben Kee left Red Lodge to visit China (*Picket*, 30 July 1892, 3); a story in 1893 refers to prostitutes "Miss Lulu and Miss Belle, both of African descent," being arrested in Red Lodge (*Picket*, 11 February 1893, 3); Lulu died two years later (*Picket*, 30 November 1895, 3); a "colored woman of unsavory reputation known as 'Old Mary' was arrested for drunkenness in 1893 before leaving town," (*Picket*, 13 May 1893, 3); Pleasant Draper, a "colored boy who was employed as a second cook at the Spofford" left Red Lodge in 1895 (*Picket* 1 June 1895, 3); a "colored prospector" packed out of Red Lodge in 1896 (*Picket*, 20 June 1896, 3).

72. *Republican*, 27 April 1906, 1.

73. *Thirteenth Census of the United States, Volume 2, Population*, 1160.

74. *Fourteenth Census of the United States, Volume 3, Population*, 585.

75. In several oral histories, residents made note of the absence of nonwhites in Red Lodge. Tony Persha, a miner, recalled that there were no Chinese or colored people working at the mines; he knew that a few Mexicans worked in the Red Lodge mines at one time, but they did not stay long; Persha Oral History 1A. John Barovich noted that a few Chinamen lived in Bearcreek for a while; Barovich Oral History, 21.

76. *Picket*, 5 May 1894, 3; 8 September 1894, 3.

77. Red Lodge newspapers in the 1900s were filled with stories about local unions and union activities. See, for example, *Republican*, 8 June 1906, 1; 6 July 1906, 1; 15 March 1907, 4; 23 August 1907, 1; *Gazette*, 28 September 1905, 1; 8 December 1905, 1; *Picket*, 14 March 1907, 1; 17 May 1907, 1; 23 August 1907, 1.

78. *Gazette*, 28 September 1905, 1.

79. The Labor Temple cost $36,000 to build; in late August 1909, District 22 of the UMWA agreed to loan the Red Lodge unions the $10,000 needed to complete the project. *Republican Picket*, 23 September 1909, 7; 26 August 1909, 1.

80. Finnish laborers built Workers' Hall in 1912. The Kaleva Cooperative operated from the early 1900s until 1923 when it was reorganized into the Blum and Company story; Zupan and Owens, *Red Lodge*, 183–184. There were a variety of cooperative industries in Carbon County in the early twentieth century, but most had gone out of business by the early 1920s, as evidenced by the number of bankruptcy proceedings in these years, for example, *In the Matter of Voluntary Dissolution of the Slavonic Co-Operative Mercantile Association, A Corporation* (1919), and *In the Matter of the Assignment of Farmers Co-Operative Elevator Company of Joliet, for the Benefit of Creditors* (1921), CCDC, Civil Records no. 2363 and no. 2615.

81. Workers' Hall housed community activities ranging from high school graduations and dances to funerals and gymnastics exhibitions; in 1916, Clarence Darrow spoke against prohibition in this venue; Zupan and Owens, *Red Lodge*, 183–184. In the late 1910s and 1920s, Lillian Lampi and her husband produced plays that were held in the hall; they put on a "big play" once a month and a "small play" every second week; Lampi Oral History, 18–19.

82. For example, see *Picket*, 18 June 1898, 3; 6 August 1898, 2; 7 September 1900, 1, 2; 6 September 1907, 1; *Republican*, 6 September 1907, 1. In 1898, the local chapter of the WFM also held a grand ball attended by over two hundred residents; *Picket*, 26 February 1898, 3.

83. *Picket*, 7 September 1900, 1, 2.

84. *Republican*, 28 June 1907, 1; *Picket*, 28 June 1907, 1.

85. *Picket*, 17 May 1907, 1.

86. *The Montana and Wyoming Telephone Co. v. The Miners' Union of Red Lodge, et al.* (1906), CCDC, Civil Records no. 591. The Red Lodge unions' declaration came upon the request of Billings's workers who were fighting a local businessmen's organization led by the phone company manager that was trying to limit union wages in that city. *Republican*, 5 October 1906, 1; 23 November 1906, 1; *Picket*, 4 October 1906, 1; 1 November 1906, 1.

87. *Republican Picket*, 7 July 1910, 1. Labor reform was part of a much wider progressive movement in the United States and Montana in these years. Between the turn of the century and 1917, the Montana legislature, for example, passed a series of laws meant to benefit industrial workers: maximum working hours, safety and health regulations, workers' compensation acts, and laws defining liability for industrial accidents. Specifically regarding miners, the state first guaranteed the eight-hour day only to those who worked in underground mines, gradually extending that provision by 1907 to "all labor connected with mining, washing, reducing and treating of coal at coal mines from the mining of coal until it is ready for market." The UMWA and Montana coal operators, meanwhile, agreed to an eight-hour day for miners in 1903 in their first annual convention. In 1907, the legislature also mandated that every coal mine provide a washhouse for miners; children would no longer enjoy the eerie sight of steaming miners striding up the streets as the bitter winter cold froze the day's sweat to their bodies. Richard B. Roeder, "Montana Progressivism, Sound and Fury — And One Small Tax Reform," in *Montana's Past: Selected Essays*, ed. Michael P. Malone and Richard B. Roeder

(Missoula: University of Montana Publications in History, 1973), 394; Kuhlman, "From Farmland to Coalvillage," 69; *Picket*, 14 March 1907; 10 May 1907, 1. For general works on progressivism, see Peter Levine, *A. G. Spaulding and the Rise of Baseball: The Promise of American Sport* (New York: Oxford University Press, 1986), and Aileen Kraditor, *The Ideas of the Woman Suffrage Movement, 1890–1920* (New York: Norton, 1981).

88. *Picket*, 16 August 1906, 1. Support of labor, however, often took a patronizing form among progressive reformers. In Red Lodge, Senator Meyer, who so vocally supported the eight-hour day and improved wages, could not resist the chance at a Labor Day oration in 1909 to stress that workers should spend their additional leisure time in constructive ways. He warned his listeners not to waste that time in dissolution, but to work on improving themselves and bettering the lives of their children; *Republican Picket*, 9 September 1909, 3. Like so much of progressivism, the movement and its supporters took the moral high ground, presuming to know what workers should do. See, for example, Paul S. Boyer, *The Urban Masses and Moral Order in America, 1820–1920* (Cambridge: Harvard University Press, 1978).

89. A good account of conditions in southern Colorado mines leading up to the Ludlow massacre is in Long, *Where the Sun Never Shines*, 172–304.

90. Jameson, *All That Glitters*, 199–225.

91. Managers complained about the "difficulty of procuring mining labor" as early as 1889; Report to Board of Directors, 16 December 1889, Northern Pacific Railroad Company Records, Secretary's Files, Rocky Fork Railroad and Coal Mines, 1889–1990, File 64, 137/I/19/6F, Minnesota Historical Society. For later managers' complaints about workers and responses from company officials, see Minutes of the Rocky Fork Coal Company for 1898, Rocky Fork Coal Company Records, 136/D/17/3B, Box 1, Volume 1, Minnesota Historical Society. Also see Edward Johnson to Edwin W. Winter, 5 February 1897; F. G. Prest to J. W. Kendrick, 23 February 1898; second vice president to C. S. Mellen, 30 March 1900; C. R. Claghorn to Howard Elliott, 8 January 1907; B. F. Bush to Elliot, 27 February 1907; C. C. Anderson to C. R. Claghorn, 21 October 1907, 25 October 1907; Elliot to Claghorn, 18 November 1907; Claghorn to Elliot, 28 December 1908; Claghorn to Elliott, 23 February 1912; Charles Donnelly to J. M. Hannaford, 25 September 1920, Great Northern Railroad Records, 137/B/16/1B, Minnesota Historical Society.

92. Samuel Hauser's correspondence with the Rocky Fork Town and Electric Company made clear his interest in the dividends from sales of Red Lodge properties. See, for example, D. G. O'Shea to S. T. Hauser, 13 August 1913, Samuel T. Hauser Papers, MC 37, 9/10 MHS.

93. Indeed, around 1908, several dozen Red Lodge citizens, including the mayor and most of the town's prominent businessmen, petitioned the NPRR protesting a rumored company store. The residents argued that it would be "manifestly unfair and contrary to public opinion and to the spirit of the times in which we live" for the company to "engage in petty retail business" in the community; Great Northern Railroad Records, 137/B/16B, Minnesota Historical Society.

94. Translated and quoted in Kuhlman, "From Farmland to Coalvillage," 116.

95. Kuhlman, "From Farmland to Coalvillage," 71.

96. *Picket*, 7 September 1900, 1.

97. In its 1901 report on coal mining, the U.S. Industrial Commission found that most UMWA delegates to state and interstate conferences as well as the leading officers in

the union were Irish or Irish American; *Report of the Industrial Commission on Immigration*, 407. See also John H. M. Laslett, "British Immigrant Colliers and the Origins and Early Development of the UMWA, 1870–1912," in *The United Mine Workers of America: A Model of Industrial Solidarity?* ed. John H. M. Laslett (University Park: Pennsylvania State University Press, 1996), 29–50. Local sources support this observation of English-speaking leadership in the mines and in the unions. For example, Richard Mallin's father was an experienced Scottish miner when he went to work in the Red Lodge mines in 1911; he worked the mines in Red Lodge and Bearcreek until killed in the Smith Mine explosion of 1942; Mallin Oral History, 11–12, 23. William A. Romek, a mine supervisor, noted that Slavs simply were not very good mechanics, while the Welsh made the best miners; Anthony Romek Oral History, OH 1477, 9, 15, MHS. John Barovich, son of a Yugoslavian immigrant, recalled that the Scots felt superior to other immigrants, held the better mine jobs, and mostly lived in the upper-crust neighborhood of Hi Bug; John Barovich Oral History, 23–24. Mildred Chesarek Harboldt, whose family came from Yugoslavia, also recalled that the Scots held the higher positions at the mines; Harboldt Oral History, 12. Ollie Anderson noted that Scots tended to be union members; Anderson Oral History, 3.

98. Kuhlman, "From Farmland to Coalvillage," 71. On Irish as labor leaders, see Robert D. Cross, "The Irish," in *Ethnic Leadership in America*, ed. John Higham (Baltimore: Johns Hopkins University Press, 1978), 186–188.

99. Carlos A. Schwantes, "The Concept of the Wageworkers' Frontier: A Framework for Future Research," *Western Historical Quarterly* 18 (January 1987): 44–45, refers to these more invested workers as the "home guards" as opposed to the transient "bindlestiffs." In her study of miners in Cripple Creek, Colorado, Susan Jameson, *All That Glitters*, 78–84, found that union leaders tended to be "older and more experienced workers who could marry and establish homes and families" and thus less able than younger, rootless workers to pick up and move elsewhere.

100. Kuhlman, "From Farmland to Coalvillage," 69–71.

101. Michael Nash, *Conflict and Accommodation: Coal Miners, Steel Workers, and Socialism, 1890–1920* (Westport, Conn.: Greenwood Press, 1982), 92.

102. Quoted in Kuhlman, "From Farmland to Coalvillage," 72.

103. "Radical" is, of course, a relative term. I use it here to differentiate between the members of the UMWA locals in Red Lodge and the area miners who pushed beyond that union's moderate attempts to work with management to create gradual change in the industry. In Red Lodge, the two main groups of "radicals" were socialists and IWW members. For a discussion of radicalism in the western labor force, see Jameson, *All That Glitters*, 161–196; Melvyn Dubofsky, *We Shall Be All: A History of the Industrial Workers of the World*, 2d ed. (Urbana: University of Illinois Press, 1988); Phil Mellinger, "How the IWW Lost its Western Heartland: Western Labor History Revisited," *Western Historical Quarterly* 27 (Autumn 1996): 303–324.

104. Al Gedicks, "The Social Origins of Radicalism among Finnish Immigrants in Midwest Mining Communities," *Review of Radical Political Economics* 8 (Fall 1976): 1–31.

105. Mellinger, "How the IWW Lost Its Western Heartland," 303. For other works on the IWW, see Salvatore Salerno, *Red November, Black November: Culture and Community in the Industrial Workers of the World* (Albany: State University of New York Press,

1989); Dubofsky, *We Shall Be All;* Archie Green, *Wobblies, Pile Butts, and Other Heroes: Laborlore Explorations* (Urbana: University of Illinois Press, 1993); Philip S. Foner, ed., *Fellow Workers and Friends: I.W.W. Free-Speech Fights as Told by Participants* (Westport, Conn.: Greenwood Press, 1981); Ann Schofield, "Rebel Girls and Union Maids: The Woman Question in the Journals of the AFL and IWW, 1905–1920," *Feminist Studies* 9 (Summer 1983): 335–358.

106. The quotation is from the preamble of the IWW constitution, quoted in Philip S. Foner, "Introduction," in *"Fellow Workers and Friends,* 4.

107. The origin of this nickname is unclear, but it first appeared in 1914. Archie Green devotes a chapter to the name "Wobbly" in *Wobblies, Pile Butts, and other Heroes,* 97–138.

108. That violence included the notorious Everett Massacre of 1916 in which up to twelve people were killed, most of them Wobblies. Foner, "Introduction," 3–22; Schwantes, "Wage Earners and Wealth Makers," 444–445.

109. Finnish immigrants, in fact, had a widespread reputation as radical agitators. In 1911, for example, an employer from the Lake Superior mining district testified before Congress that Finns were "good laborers but trouble breeders . . . and agitators of the worst type" (Gedicks, "Ethnicity, Class Solidarity, and Labor Radicalism among Finnish Immigrants," 136). On Finnish radicalism, see also Peter Kivisto, "Finnish Americans and the Homeland, 1918–1958," *Journal of American Ethnic History* 7 (Fall 1987): 7–27, and Gedicks, "The Social Origins of Radicalism among Finnish Immigrants in Midwest Mining Communities," 1–4.

110. On the socialists' gambling crusade, see *State of Montana v. Jalmer Kumpula* (1913) no. 341, *State of Montana v. Steve Hanni* (1913) no. 339, and *State of Montana v. Henry Niemi and Ed Vingren* (1913) no. 345, CCDC, Criminal Records. In 1906, townspeople elected a slate of socialists to city positions, but internal squabbling destroyed any power the party had and the members were not reelected. *Republican,* 6 April 1906, 1; 21 December 1906, 4; 11 January 1907, 1; 5 April 1907, 1.

111. The number of Wobblies in Red Lodge at any one time is difficult to determine. Coal operators and their supporters inflated the numbers to the point that at one time they estimated the number of local Wobblies at about three-quarters of the mines' workforce. In 1918, the U.S. attorney general estimated that of fifteen thousand miners in Butte — a much larger industrial city — less than five hundred were Wobblies. Judging from the size of the Red Lodge workforce (less than twelve hundred) and evidence from a court case against an alleged Wobbly during World War I, I estimate the number of Wobblies in Red Lodge in 1917 and 1918 to be less than fifty. Kuhlman, "From Farmland to Coalvillage," 91; K. Ross Toole, *Twentieth-Century Montana: A State of Extremes* (Norman: University of Oklahoma Press, 1972), 142; *State of Montana v. Nels Lahti* (1918), CCDC, Criminal Records no. 463.

112. Quoted in Kuhlman, "From Farmland to Coalvillage," 72.

3. THE END OF AN ERA

1. "Parades," Photograph Collection, Carbon County Historical Society Collections (CCHS); *Picket-Journal* (Red Lodge), 17 December 1919, 4.

2. *Picket-Journal,* 17 December 1919, 4.

3. For general works on wartime hysteria directed toward immigrants and radicals, see John Higham, *Strangers in the Land: Patterns of American Nativism, 1860–1925* (New Brunswick, N.J.: Rutgers University Press, 1955); Ronald Schaffer, *America in the Great War: The Rise of the War Welfare State* (New York: Oxford University Press, 1991), 13–30. For a discussion of World War I in Montana, one of the best sources is K. Ross Toole, *Twentieth-Century Montana: A State of Extremes* (Norman: University of Oklahoma Press, 1972), 139–193.

4. *Picket,* 24 March 1894, 2; see also 9 April 1892, 3. The hostility toward immigrants who returned to Europe after earning money in the United States was widespread; see Neil Larry Shumsky, "'Let No Man Stop to Plunder!' American Hostility to Return Migration, 1890–1924," *Journal of American Ethnic History* 11 (Winter 1992): 56–75.

5. *Picket,* 10 March 1894, 2.

6. On unions using patriotic symbolism in parades, see *Picket,* 7 September 1900, 1, 2; *Republican,* 6 September 1907, 1. For Irish and Italian marching in Fourth of July parades, see *Picket,* 11 July 1896, 3; *Republican,* 5 July 1907, 1. On Budas, see *Republican,* 26 October 1906, 4.

7. This kind of "frivolous" celebration of the Fourth of July was quite popular in the early twentieth century. See Raymond W. Smilor, "Creating a National Festival: The Campaign for a Safe and Sane Fourth, 1903–1916," *Journal of American Culture* 2 (Winter 1980): 611–622. Also see Michael Kammen, *Mystic Chords of Memory: The Transformation of Tradition in American Culture* (New York: Vintage Books, 1993), 105, 256; and John Bodnar, *Remaking America: Public Memory, Commemoration, and Patriotism in the Twentieth Century* (Princeton: Princeton University Press, 1992), 83–86.

8. See, for example, *Picket,* 23 May 1896, 3; 3 July 1897, 3; *Gazette,* 8 June 1905, 1; *Republican,* 10 May 1907, 1.

9. *Picket-Journal,* 23 April 1919, 6.

10. The Montana Sedition Act of 1918 actually made it a crime to speak against the war or conscription; Congress modeled its own federal sedition law on this Montana legislation. Toole, *Twentieth-Century Montana,* 139–156. In Red Lodge there were at least three court cases involving charges of sedition or "criminal syndicalism" against men who had allegedly spoken against the war. Ben Kahn, a salesman from Billings, was sentenced to up to twenty years in jail for stating that "this is a rich man's war and we have no business in it." Kahn also claimed that the United States was warned about the *Lusitania* carrying munitions. *State of Montana v. Ben Kahn* (1918), Carbon County District Court (CCDC), Criminal Records no. 457; also see *State of Montana v. Nels Lahti* (1918) no. 463 and *State of Montana v. Frank B. Rakstis* (1918) no. 475, CCDC, Criminal Records. On conformity to "100% Americanism," see Hans Vought, "Division and Reunion: Woodrow Wilson, Immigration, and the Myth of American Unity," *Journal of American Ethnic History* 13 (Spring 1994): 24–26, and Lawrence H. Fuchs, *American Kaleidoscope: Race, Ethnicity, and the Civic Culture* (Middletown, Conn.: Wesleyan University Press, 1990), 57–61.

11. Higham, *Strangers in the Land,* 215.

12. *Picket,* 11 April 1918, 1. A list of the Liberty Committee members is in the papers of H. A. Simmons, former district attorney for Red Lodge. This list includes Finnish names like Emil Hekkola, M. T. Koski, and Nestor Makela. H. A. Simmons Collection, MC 204, 5/15 Montana Historical Society Collection (MHS).

13. For the Serbians: *Picket*, 13 April 1917, 1; 20 April 1917, 1; 27 April 1917, 1; 8 June 1917, 1; 6 July 1917, 1. On the Italians: *Picket*, 16 November 1917, 1, and *Steve Roman v. Societa Italiana E Fratellanzadi Mutuo Soccorso, a Corporation* (1918), CCDC, Civil Records no. 2118.

14. With the outbreak of the Bolshevik revolution in November 1917, Finnish-American loyalties were even more torn when a civil war broke out in Finland between the Reds and Whites; P. George Hummasti, "World War I and the Finns of Astoria, Oregon: The Effects of the War on an Immigrant Community," *International Migration Review* 11 (Fall 1977): 340–341. For the Serbians, see *Picket*, 13 April 1917, 1; 20 April 1917, 1; 27 April 1917, 1. Local Italian Americans made a point of emphasizing the masculinity of their soldiers; for a good example of this pride in combat, see the testimony in *Steve Roman v. Societa Italiana*.

15. According to K. Ross Toole, *Twentieth-Century Montana*, 140, almost every small town in the state had Liberty Committees, which became "the local arbiters of patriotism." Other states also organized local and statewide patriotic committees to ferret out opponents of war. Schaffer, *America in the Great War*, 17–23.

16. Toole, *Twentieth-Century Montana*, 140–143, 148–154; Arnon Gutfield, "The Murder of Frank Little: Radical Labor Agitation in Butte, Montana, 1917," in *Montana's Past: Selected Essays*, ed. Michael P. Malone and Richard B. Roeder (Missoula: University of Montana Publications in History, 1973), 370–390.

17. Higham, *Strangers in the Land*, 215–218.

18. *Picket*, 23 November 1917, 1.

19. When Nels Tahti, one of the town's sidewalk orators, was arrested for criminal syndicalism in 1918, he had a list of those pledging financial support for Wobblies imprisoned during the war; the list and all the names on it were Finnish. In his trial and in Liberty Committee proclamations, Finns and Wobblies became publicly and prominently intertwined; *State of Montana v. Nels Tahti*.

20. In an investigation of the Liberty Committee's accusations against the county draft board, the County Council of Defense concluded that the Liberty Committee "is an organization which was originally conceived through patriotic motives, but which has evidently deteriorated into a one or two man affair [led by Alderson and Potter] which is detrimental to the best interests of the Government and the community and should no longer exist" ("Report of Proceeding Had at Meeting of Council of Defense, Carbon County, State of Montana, 1918," Council of Defense Records RS 19, 6/1 MHS). On the numbers of Wobblies in Red Lodge, miner Ollie Anderson insisted that there was "very little" IWW activity in the town, although "there was a lot of them that got blamed for that, you know, during the war years" (Anderson Oral History, 2).

21. *Picket*, 14 December 1917, 1.

22. Koski's killing of Jackson was ruled accidental; *Picket*, 21 December 1917, 1, 8.

23. Senia Kallio Oral History, OH 357, 18–20, MHS.

24. Edward Blazina Oral History, OH 1485, 28, MHS.

25. *Picket*, 21 December 1917, 1.

26. *Solomen Homi, et al. v. Workers Building Association et al.* (1918), CCDC, Civil Records no. 2163.

27. Gary Gerstle, *Working-Class Americanism: The Politics of Labor in a Textile City* (Cambridge: Cambridge University Press, 1989), 8.

28. Gary Gerstle, *Working-Class Americanism*, 1–4, found that in Woonsocket, R.I., too, the

cultural diversity of immigrant residents and their children had begun to narrow by the 1920s, in part because of the sweeping anti-socialism/Americanism movements that started during World War I.

29. In the 1 May 1917 organizational meeting for the Carbon County Red Cross, there was only one name listed that seemed Finnish, a "Miss Haaland." Mrs. Heikkala had joined the group by 8 October 1917, and she assumed the liaison position between the new Finnish auxiliary and the original Red Cross group. The older group assigned Mrs. Joe Romersa, Mrs. Julio, and Mrs. Curto "to see to the Italian ladies" and gave them charge of the Thursday evening workroom meeting; Red Lodge Red Cross, "Minutes," 1 May 1917, 8 October 1917, 3 January 1918, CCHS. The women of the Finnish association Kalevan Naiset Mielikintupa No. 1 took the initiative in forming the leadership for the new Finnish Ladies' Auxiliary to the Carbon County chapter of the American Red Cross; *Picket*, 28 December 1917, 1. The Finnish and Italian auxiliaries marched in uniform in the 1918 Fourth of July parade; *Picket*, 4 July 1918, 1.

30. This was part of a larger, national effort to control miners' wages. See Joseph A. McCartin, *Labor's Great War: The Struggle for Industrial Democracy and the Origins of Modern American Labor Relations, 1912–1921* (Chapel Hill: University of North Carolina Press, 1997), 125; Erika A. Kuhlman, "From Farmland to Coalvillage: Red Lodge's Finnish Immigrants, 1890–1922" (Master's thesis, University of Montana, 1987), 73. Union leaders, of course, countered with the assertion that the patriotically celebrated "American standard of living" meant that workers needed to be paid well enough to enjoy that ideal. James R. Barrett, "Americanization from the Bottom Up: Immigration and the Remaking of the Working Class in the United States, 1880–1930," *Journal of American History* 79 (December 1992): 1009.

31. *Picket*, 19 September 1918, 1, 4. The local district attorney immediately began to close down alleged houses of prostitution; for example, *State of Montana et al. v. Lola Hannula, alias Blanch Webber* (1918) no. 2235, and *State of Montana et al. v. Pearl Petrea, alias Pearl Davis* (1918) CCDC, Civil Cases no. 2231.

32. *Picket*, 19 September 1918, 1.

33. William Glancy Oral History, OH 516, 53–54, MHS; Anderson Oral History, 18.

34. Kuhlman, "From Farmland to Coalvillage," 95–97; *Picket*, 14 December 1917, 1.

35. After the Koski shooting and the Finnish town meeting, the Liberty Committee degenerated into a one- or two-man operation led by retired newspaper publisher Alderson and former sheriff Potter. These men largely discredited themselves in 1918 when they called upon state authorities to investigate the local draft board on charges of bribery and corruption. Attacking prominent local authorities — Sheriff George Headington, County Clerk H. P. Sandels, and physician E. M. Adams — was not so easy as intimidating Finnish Wobblies. Investigation of Carbon County Draftboard, State Council of Defense Records, RS 19, 1/9 MHS; Kuhlman, "From Farmland to Coalvillage," 99–100.

36. Daniel S. McCorkle to Frank P. Walsh, 11 January 1918, Daniel S. McCorkle Papers, MC 59, 2/10 MHS; also Anderson Oral History, OH 302, 18–20, MHS; and Glancy Oral History, 53–54.

37. Glancy Oral History, 53.

38. On John L. Lewis, see Alan J. Singer, " 'Something of a Man': John L. Lewis, the UMWA, and the CIP, 1919–1943," in *The United Mine Workers of America: A Model of Industrial*

Solidarity? ed. John H. Laslett (University Park: Pennsylvania State University Press, 1996), 104–150; Priscilla Long, *Where the Sun Never Shines: A History of America's Bloody Coal Industry* (New York: Paragon Books, 1991), 323–331.

39. In their oral histories, former Red Lodge miners remembered John L. Lewis as a hero of the workers' cause. Ollie Anderson, for example, credited Lewis with improving conditions in the nation's coal mines. Anderson, who had a photograph of Lewis displayed in his home, told an interviewer that "you can thank ol' John L. Lewis, the miners can, for everything that he done for 'em." Anderson combined his admiration for Lewis with contempt for coal operators: "Well, you're always supposed to work to produce as much as you can. The more you produce, that means the more money for the big boys to put in the pocketbook" (Anderson Oral History, 18, 21). Tony Persha, likewise, admired Lewis greatly, informing his interviewer that "he was something!" Persha not only had a picture of himself with Lewis, but he also owned a copy of Lewis's biography; Persha Oral History, 1B. Mine manager William A. Romek recalled Lewis less fondly, maintaining that Lewis maintained a tight grip over the national and state union organizations. "John L. Lewis," he stated, "was the czar over the coal industry in the entire nation" (Anthony Romek Oral History, OH 1477, 17, MHS).

40. *Picket-Journal*, 30 August 1922, 1; 27 September 1922, 1; Kuhlman, "From Farmland to Coalvillage," 75–76.

41. Ollie Anderson Oral History, 21.

42. Letters translated and quoted in Kuhlman, "From Farmland to Coalvillage," 75–76.

43. William B. Evans and Robert L. Peterson, "Decision at Colstrip: The Northern Pacific Railway's Open-Pit Mining Operation," in *Montana's Past*, 445–460.

4. THE "WILD WEST" IN THE TWENTIETH CENTURY

1. Oral History of John Barovich, OH 1482, Montana Historical Society Collections (MHS).

2. For discussions of the "mythic West," see Richard Slotkin, *Gunfighter Nation: The Myth of the Frontier in Twentieth-Century America* (New York: HarperPerennial, 1992); Richard G. Athearn, *The Mythic West in Twentieth-Century America* (Lawrence: University Press of Kansas, 1986); Earl Pomeroy, *In Search of the Golden West: The Tourist in Western America* (Lincoln: University of Nebraska Press, 1957); Anne M. Butler, "Selling the Popular Myth," in *The Oxford History of the American West*, ed. Clyde A. Milner II, Carol A. O'Connor, and Martha A. Sandweiss (New York: Oxford University Press, 1994), 771–801; Hal K. Rothman, *Devil's Bargains: Tourism in the Twentieth-Century West* (Lawrence: University Press of Kansas, 1998). For general discussions of how people use history in public performances, see Michael Kammen, *Mystic Chords of Memory: The Transformation of Tradition in American Culture* (New York: Random House, 1991); David Lowenthal, *The Past Is a Foreign Country* (Cambridge: Cambridge University Press, 1985), and *The Heritage Crusade and the Spoils of History* (Cambridge: Cambridge University Press, 1998); John Bodnar, *Remaking America: Public Memory, Commemoration, and Patriotism in the Twentieth Century* (Princeton: Princeton University Press, 1992).

3. Meredith Nelson Wiltsie, "Land Use and Landscape Evolution in the West: A Case Study of Red Lodge, Montana, 1884–1995" (Master's thesis, Montana State University, 1998), 89–90, 98, 108; *Picket-Journal*, 18 July 1934, 1, 4.

4. Slotkin, *Gunfighter Nation*, 61–62.

5. *Picket-Journal* (Red Lodge), 26 May 1920, 4.

6. In addition to the actual "See America First" movement, railroads also actively promoted western tourism in these years. Anne Farrar Hyde, *An American Vision: Far Western Landscape and National Culture, 1820–1920* (New York: New York University Press, 1990), 244–245; Pomeroy, *In Search of the Golden West*, 135–136, 153–165; Marguerite S. Shaffer, " 'See America First': Re-envisioning Nation and Region through Western Tourism," *Pacific Historical Review* 65 (November 1996): 559–582.

7. For stories on local interest in tourism, see *Picket-Journal*, 17 March 1920, 6; 18 August 1920, 1, 4; 28 June 1923, 4; 3 July 1924, 1.

8. Jesse Lynch Williams, "Joy-Ranching and Dude-Wrangling," *Colliers* 51 (9 August 1913): 22; Athearn, *The Mythic West*, 137; Pomeroy, *In Search of the Golden West*, 167–172; William Cronon, "Landscapes of Abundance and Scarcity," in *The Oxford History of the American West*, 630; Butler, "Selling the Popular Myth," 787–789.

9. Michael P. Malone, Richard B. Roeder, and William L. Lang, *Montana: A History of Two Centuries*, rev. ed. (Seattle: University of Washington Press, 1991), 340.

10. In the early twentieth century, "dude" had not yet acquired the negative connotations that would later induce dude ranchers to rename their businesses "guest ranches." In the 1920s and 1930s, "dude" simply referred to someone who paid to stay at a western ranch. Variations included "dudine" or less commonly "dudette" for a female guest. Lawrence R. Borne explains these distinctions in his celebratory history of the industry, *Dude Ranching: A Complete History* (Albuquerque: University of New Mexico Press, 1983), 8, 38.

11. *Picket-Journal*, 8 July 1926, 6.

12. M. M. Goodsill, "What Dudes Tell the Railroads: Remarks on Their Vacations," *Minutes of the Fourth Annual Dude Ranchers' Meeting Held at Billings, Montana, November 18, 19, 20, 1929* (Casper: S. E. Boyer, 1930), 61–75. The Dude Ranchers' Association represented dude ranchers from around Wyoming and Montana. Red Lodge rancher Al Croonquist was a founding member of the organization in 1927 and its first vice president; he also served as executive secretary for many years. Shirley Zupan and Harry J. Owens, *Red Lodge: Saga of a Western Area* (Billings, Mont.: Frontier Press, 1979), 280.

13. *Picket-Journal*, 3 June 1926, 1.

14. *Picket-Journal*, 8 July 1926, 1.

15. *Picket-Journal*, 28 June 1923, 4.

16. Kristine Fredericksson, *Rodeo: From Buffalo Bill to Big Business* (College Station: Texas A&M University Press, 1985), 140–141. Michael Allen, *Rodeo Cowboys in the North American Imagination* (Reno and Las Vegas: University of Nevada Press, 1998), 17, argues that although Cody took credit for the first rodeo, so did several other communities.

17. Fredericksson, *Rodeo*, 13.

18. Women in early-twentieth-century rodeos frequently came to the sport either from Wild West shows or from work on family ranches. Most contracted for their appearances but also competed against other women in events such as saddle bronc riding and wild heifer riding. Mary Lou LeCompte argues that actor/rodeo promoter Gene Autry played a key role in shifting women's rodeo performances away from bronco events when he took over the major eastern rodeos in the 1940s. Although women continued to ride broncs in all-girls rodeos from the 1940s on, in mainstream rodeos they served

primarily as "sponsor girls" who carried corporate flags. Mary Lou LeCompte, *Cowgirls of the Rodeo: Pioneer Professional Athletes* (Urbana: University of Illinois Press, 1993), 137, 114–116, 142–143. On woman rodeo riders, see also Teresa Jordan, *Cowgirls: Women of the American West* (Lincoln: University of Nebraska Press, 1982), 187–275; Liz Stiffler and Tona Blake, "Fannie Sperry-Steele: Montana's Champion Bronc Rider," *Montana: The Magazine of Western History* 32 (Spring 1982): 44–57; and Doris Loeser, director, *"I'll Ride That Horse!": Montana Women Bronc Riders* (Rattatosk Films, n.d.).

19. Fredericksson, *Rodeo,* 36.

20. Jacob M. Schwoob, "Relation of the Retailer to the Dude Rancher," *Minutes of the Fourth Annual Dude Ranchers' Meeting,* 53–59.

21. *Picket-Journal,* 7 July 1927, 1.

22. *Picket-Journal,* 4 July 1929, 1.

23. *Picket-Journal,* 26 June 1930, 4.

24. *Picket-Journal,* 2 July 1931, 1.

25. *Picket-Journal,* 22 June 1933, 1.

26. *Picket-Journal,* 17 July 1930, 1.

27. *Picket-Journal,* 10 July 1930, 1; 21 June 1934, 4; 12 July 1934, 1; 11 July 1936, 1.

28. *Picket-Journal,* 9 July 1931, 1.

29. *Picket-Journal,* 6 July 1937, 1; 4 July 1939, 1.

30. *Picket-Journal,* 20 February 1936, 1; 6 July 1937, 1.

31. *Picket-Journal,* 12 July 1934, 1.

32. *Picket-Journal,* 29 June 1933, 1.

33. Beverly Rue Wellington, *Red Lodge Landmarks* (Red Lodge: Carbon County News, 1992), 95–97; newspaper clipping, "Camp Senia" Collection, n.d., Carbon County Historical Society Collections (CCHS).

34. Michels Raffety Architects and Carbon County Historical Preservation Office, *Red Lodge Commercial Historic District Revitalization Master Plan* (Livingston, Mont.: Michels Raffety Architects, 1986), 47–48.

35. See, for example, Malcolm S. Mackay's memoir, *Cow Range and Hunting Trail* (New York: G. P. Putnam's Sons, 1925), the correspondence of Ben Greenough in the Greenough Collection, CCHS, and the "Montana" Vera Buening Oral History, OH 358, MHS.

36. Photograph Collections, CCHS.

37. Constance J. Poten, "Robert Yellowtail: The New Warrior," *Montana: The Magazine of Western History* 39 (Summer 1989): 36–37; Peter Iverson, *When Indians Became Cowboys: Native People and Cattle Ranching in the American West* (Norman: University of Oklahoma Press, 1994), 63.

38. Iverson, *When Indians Became Cowboys,* 190–191. Famous Indian rodeo cowboys like Jackson Sundown wore much the same attire as non-Indian cowboys did, right down to the woolly chaps and ostentatious belt buckle; unlike most cowboys, however, Sundown wore long braids tied under his chin. Rowena L. Alcorn and Gordon D. Alcorn, "Jackson Sundown: Nez Perce Horseman," *Montana: The Magazine of Western History* 33 (Autumn 1983): 46–48.

39. *Picket-Journal,* 3 July 1930, 1.

40. The *Picket-Journal* listed the top placers (up to four or five) in all of the rodeo events. After 1931, Indian names did not appear in the lists for the "non-Indian" events,

although some may have participated in these categories. Rodeo promoters, though, created specific "Indian races" and other events exclusively for the visiting Crow, in part to assure the Indians that they would be guaranteed a certain amount of the event's prize money; *Picket-Journal*, 1 June 1937, 1.

41. *Picket-Journal*, 22 June 1933, 8; 11 July 1935, 1; 5 July 1938, 1; 27 June 1939, 1.

42. Philip Deloria, *Playing Indian* (New Haven: Yale University Press, 1998), 123.

43. L. G. Moses, *Wild West Shows and the Images of American Indians, 1883–1933* (Albuquerque: University of New Mexico Press, 1996), 1–8, 205–206. Red Lodge residents had invited show Indians into town for celebrations long before the 1930 rodeo, but on a very irregular basis. In 1909, for example, the town council paid Crow Indians six steers, fifty pounds of coffee, one thousand pounds of sugar, and some other items in return for the presence of Chief Plenty Coups and two hundred other Indians at the annual Carbon County Fair. These Crow not only competed in special Indian relay races but also demonstrated sham war dances and camped in "full regalia" to entertain curious visitors; Zupan and Owens, *Red Lodge*, 5–6.

44. Moses, *Wild West Shows*, 8. As Moses points out, even in the Wild West shows, where they portrayed a "defeated but colorful people," Indians were never simply victims. "Instead they were portrayed as worthy adversaries, for how else could the showmen-entrepreneurs like Cody validate their prowess in battle?" Disturbed by this glamorization of the "old-time habits and pagan ways," reformers and concerned Indian agents fought against the practice of "show Indians" (*Wild West Shows*, 131–142, 253–257). See also Jeffrey Steele, "Reduced to Images: American Indians in Nineteenth-Century Advertising," in *Dressing in Feathers: The Construction of the Indian in American Popular Culture*, ed. S. Elizabeth Bird (Boulder, Colo.: Westview Press, 1996), 46.

45. See, for example, Zupan and Owens, *Red Lodge*, 6.

46. *Picket-Journal*, 9 May 1935, 1, 8; *Carbon County News*, 1 May 1947, 1; 24 June 1948, 4; 24 May 1949, 1.

47. *Carbon County News*, 11 April 1950, 1.

48. Marcella Littlefield to Mrs. Herbert Richel, 22 March 1931, Richel Lodge Collection, CCHS.

49. A 1929 Beartooth promotional pamphlet had a cover design with "a view of an Indian buck and squaw beside a 'Red Lodge' tepee pitched on the shore of a mountain lake" (*Picket-Journal*, 4 July 1929, 1). The unoccupied tepee showed up on the cover of other brochures, such as a "Beartooth Forest" pamphlet, circa 1930, the "Welcome to Red Lodge" brochure for the 1949 Fraternal Order of Eagles Convention, and "Howdy Folks," a Red Lodge Cafe pamphlet, 1949, CCHS.

50. *Carbon County News*, 10 May 1959, 8.

51. "Beartooth Forest." See also "Welcome to Red Lodge," "Howdy Folks," and "Have Fun . . . Relax in Red Lodge, Montana," 1953 brochure, CCHS.

52. Athearn, *The Mythic West*, 265–266.

53. From *Rider of the Purple Sage* (1919) to Tex Ritter's *Hitting the Trail* (1937) and Gene Autry's *Gold Mine in the Sky* (1946), cowboy movies made regular appearances at local movie houses. Local newspapers like the *Picket-Journal* also ran serialized versions of works by Zane Grey and other Western writers, catering to the demand from readers for these tales of the Wild West. *Picket-Journal*, 12 March 1919, 10; 20 September 1934, 4; 3 August 1937, 5; *Carbon County News*, 29 March 1946.

54. Carey McWilliams, "Myths of the West," *North American Review* 232 (November 1931): 428. See also "The Real, Not the Reel, Cowboy," *Literary Digest* 22 (20 May 1922): 56. Cowboys, as Richard Slatta, *Cowboys of the Americas* (New Haven: Yale University Press, 1990), 121–122, points out, were voracious readers. In one small Texas town, ranchmen and cowboys snapped up every Western novel that bookstore owner Eulalia Turner ordered in the early 1930s. When the Western books arrived, Turner reported, "I dropped my cowboys and ranchmen postal cards. In they came, hard, bronzed faces eager, great sombreros held shyly in hand as they fumbled through the books. Their great, coppery hands snatched them up and away they went back to their ranches." Favorites included the rough-riding stories of Zane Grey, Friend, Mann, Hoffman, Gregory, and Celtzer. Ernie Phillips, "Cowboys Like to Read Westerns," *Publishers' Weekly* 122 (13 August 1932): 509.

55. Jo Rainbolt, *The Last Cowboy: Twilight Era of the Horseback Cowhand, 1900–1940* (Helena, Mont.: American and World Geographic Publications, 1992), 25; see also Mackay, *Cow Range and Hunting Trail*, 9–10. The romantic appeal of cowboying actually hurt those cowpunchers who tried to make a profession of riding the range. According to David E. Lopez, "Cowboy Strikes and Unions," *Labor History* 18 (Summer 1977): 327–329, "Cowboys were perhaps the first occupational group to suffer directly from mass media romanticization." Ranchers took advantage of the popularity of cowboying to stifle attempts by ranch hands to strike for higher wages; for every cowboy who went out on strike, three or four eager greenhorns stood ready to take his place as mounted "nobility."

56. *Majestic Montana: Land of Mountains, Lakes and Streams — Yellowstone and Glacier National Park* (Billings, Mont.: Reporter Printing and Supply, circa 1940), CCHS.

57. *State of Montana v. Herbert Moon* (1937), Carbon County District Court Records (CCDC), Criminal Records no. 1014.

58. Borne, *Dude Ranching*, 110–111.

59. LeCompte, *Cowgirls of the Rodeo*, 33–36; *Picket-Journal*, 14 December 1937, 3. For photographs of the dashing outfits of women performers in Wild West shows in the early twentieth century, see "Daring Beautiful Western Girls: Sweethearts of the Wild West Shows," *American West* 22 (July/August 1985): 44–48.

60. Jordan, *Cowgirls*, 214–215.

61. Michael Amundsen, director, *Take Willy With 'Ya: The Ridin' Greenoughs and the Golden Age of Rodeo* (Snowflake, Ariz.: Rodeo Video, 1989); Zupan and Owens, *Red Lodge*, 211–212; David L. Cohn, *A History of American Morals and Manners as Seen through the Sears, Roebuck Catalogs, 1905 to the Present* (New York: Simon and Schuster, 1940), 398–399. Several of these scrapbooks are housed at the Carbon County Historical Society.

62. Michael Allen, *Rodeo Cowboys in the North American Imagination*, 12–13, argues that by the late twentieth century the rodeo cowboy, carrying on the "cowboy code," remained the best representative of the cowboy in North America.

63. Athearn, *The Mythic West*, 269.

64. Frederick Errington, "The Rock Creek Rodeo: Excess and Constraint in Men's Lives," *American Ethnologist* 17 (September 1990): 629.

65. Mackay, *Cow Range and Hunting Trail*, vii.

66. Mackay, *Cow Range and Hunting Trail*, vii.

67. Amundsen, *Take Willy With 'Ya*; Zupan and Owens, *Red Lodge*, 208–209.

68. C. E. Thompson, the interviewer and compiler of a WPA project on the regional cattle industry, included several of Greenough's stories in his collection. On the first story, Thompson made the notation "an excellent source, should get more if possible" (WPA Writers' Program Records, Reel 15, "Western Range Cattle Industry Study," MF 250, MHS). Also, *Picket-Journal*, 28 November 1939, 1; Zupan and Owens, *Red Lodge*, 208–209.

69. *Carbon County News*, 13 July 1948, 1.

70. *Picket-Journal*, 7 November 1939, 8.

71. Greenough's enjoyment in playing this role of Wild West cowboy is clear in his letters from New York to his wife, Myrtle, who remained at the family ranch just outside of Red Lodge. See, for example, Ben Greenough to Myrtle Greenough, 5 October 1939, 9 October 1939, 19 October 1939, Greenough Collection, CCHS.

72. Mackay, *Cow Range and Hunting Trail*, vi.

73. E. C. Abbott and Helena Huntington Smith, *We Pointed Them North: Recollections of a Cowpuncher* (Norman: University of Oklahoma Press, 1989), 191.

74. Mackay, *Cow Range and Hunting Trail*, 28.

75. Mackay, *Cow Range and Hunting Trail*, 10.

76. Mackay, *Cow Range and Hunting Trail*, vii..

77. Frederic G. Renner, ed., *Paper Talk: Illustrated Letters of Charles M. Russell* (Fort Worth, Tex.: Amon Carter Museum of Western Art), 115.

78. Almost every summer, rodeo promoters started pleading with residents to "dress western" to make Red Lodge look more appropriately western for the tourists. See, for example, *Picket-Journal*, 9 July 1931, 1; 28 March 1935, 1, 8; 16 April 1936, 1; *Carbon County News*, 6 June 1941, 1; 20 June 1946, 1; 10 June 1948, 1; 1 July 1948, 8.

79. Laurel Wilson, "The American Cowboy: Development of the Mythic Image," in *Dress in American Culture*, ed. Patricia A. Cunningham and Susan Voso Lab (Bowling Green, Ohio: Bowling Green State University Popular Press, 1993), 80–93.

80. Richard W. Etulain, "Changing Images: The Cowboy in Western Films," *Colorado Heritage* 1 (1981): 40.

81. *Carbon County News*, 6 June 1941, 1.

82. At Camp Sawtooth, F. I. Johnson (a Red Lodge pharmacist who presumably understood the dangers of hypothermia) warned dudes to bring plenty of wool clothing so they could enjoy trail rides, fishing, and hiking in comfort. "Remember," he told guests, "we are one and five-eighths miles above sea-level. There are no formalities at camp and outing togs are the rule." To easterners, western clothes were democratic and liberating, and ranchers emphasized this connection. As Al Croonquist assured his guests at Camp Senia: "There are no formalities or conventionalities. You don your boots, breeches and a flannel shirt, fill your lungs with pure mountain air; and all out doors is yours" (*Picket-Journal*, 17 June 1926, 2–3).

83. "Dressing the Dude," *Vogue* 87 (1 May 1936): 140–141.

84. Helena Warila, "A Dude's Idea of the West," *Carbon Review* 5 (May 1934): 15, CCHS.

85. See, for example, Jacob M. Schwoob's 1929 address, "Relation of the Retailer to the Dude Rancher." Westerners, Schwoob contended, needed to cater to dudes. Schwoob praised Cody, Wyoming, merchants who let themselves be "guided by the dude rancher in the selection of his stocks" so they would appeal to eastern visitors. Nothing, he concluded,

was more "pitiful than to see the old western storekeeper, who won't change his methods" (*Minutes of the Fourth Annual Dude Ranchers' Meeting*, 55, 59).

86. *Picket-Journal*, 9 July 1931, 1. Rodeo promoters in other areas have also regularly urged spectators to "get into the spirit" of the festivities by wearing western-style clothing. In the 1970s, for example, Calgary Stampede officials gave prizes to visitors for "dressing Western." Elizabeth Atwood Lawrence, *Rodeo: An Anthropologist Looks at the Wild and the Tame* (Chicago: University of Chicago Press, 1982), 93.

87. *Picket-Journal*, 28 March 1935, 1, 8; 16 April 1936, 1; *Carbon County News*, 10 June 1948, 1. Bernard DeVoto lamented this kind of civic pressure to make westerners look the way that the Chamber of Commerce wanted them to look. The beard grower, he groused, "is just a coerced advertiser" ("The Anxious West," *Harper's Magazine* 193 [December 1946]: 485).

88. Oral History of Tony and Shirley Zupan, 35, OH 1479, MHS.

89. *Carbon County News*, 6 June 1941, 1.

90. *Carbon County News*, 1 July 1948, 8.

91. *Carbon County News*, 20 June 1946, 1.

92. *Carbon County News*, 10 June 1948, 1.

93. Advertisement for RCA Radiola in *Literary Digest* 89 (29 May 1926): 1.

94. Warila, "A Dude's Idea of the West," 15.

95. *Picket-Journal*, 27 June 1935, 1; 16 June 1936, 1.

96. *Picket-Journal*, 12 June 1930, 8.

97. *Picket-Journal*, 10 July 1930, 1.

98. See, for example, Gerald P. Nye, "Speaking of Backward States," *North American Review* 229 (April 1930): 406–413.

99. Warila, "A Dude's Idea of the West," 15.

100. *Picket-Journal*, 9 July 1931, 4.

101. *Picket-Journal*, 11 July 1935, 1.

102. *Picket-Journal*, 3 July 1930, 1.

103. "Dismal Moments in the American West," *Forbes* 156 (23 October 1995): FYI 128; Zupan and Owens, *Red Lodge*, 204.

104. DeVoto, "The Anxious West," 481–482.

105. "Howdy Folks," 1949, CCHS.

106. Fraternal Order of Eagles, "Welcome to the Land of the Shining Mountains," 1949, CCHS.

107. *Carbon County News*, 17 March 1948, 4.

5. PUBLIC ETHNICITY IN THE WEST

1. *Carbon County News* (Red Lodge), 23 August 1951, 1; 30 August 1951, 1.

2. *Carbon County News*, 13 August 1953, 1. Although a few Jewish families lived in Red Lodge over the years, the Festival of Nations and Red Lodge's local histories make little if any reference to Jews in the town. One reference to local Jews is in the "Family Sketches" section of the town's 1979 published history, which has a few paragraphs on I. Joe and Henrietta Hasterlick, "First Jewish Family of Red Lodge." The Hasterlicks moved to Red Lodge in 1906. Shirley Zupan and Harry J. Owens, *Red Lodge: Saga of a Western Area* (Billings: Frontier Press), 321.

3. *Carbon County News* (Red Lodge), 20 December 1940, 1.

4. U.S. Department of Commerce, Bureau of the Census, *A Report of the Seventeenth Decennial Census of the United States, Census of Population: 1950, Volume 2, Part 26, Montana* (Washington, D.C.: Government Printing Office, 1952), 44.

5. John Bodnar discusses "narrative structures" in "Power and Memory in Oral History: Workers and Managers at Studebaker," *Journal of American History* 75 (March 1989): 1201–1202.

6. For work on memory and history, see Michael Kammen, *Mystic Chords of Memory: The Transformation of Tradition in American Culture* (New York: Vintage Books, 1993); John Bodnar, *Remaking America: Public Memory, Commemoration, and Patriotism in the Twentieth Century* (Princeton: Princeton University Press, 1992). For historical festivals, see David Glassberg, *American Historical Pageantry: The Uses of Tradition in the Early Twentieth Century* (Chapel Hill: University of North Carolina Press, 1990); for ethnic festivals, see Victor Turner, ed., *Celebration: Studies in Festivity and Ritual* (Washington, D.C.: Smithsonian Institution Press, 1982); Ray B. Browne and Michael T. Marsden, eds., *The Cultures of Celebrations* (Bowling Green, Ohio: Bowling Green State University Popular Press, 1994); Ramon A. Guitierrez and Genevieve Fabre, eds., *Feasts and Celebrations in North American Ethnic Communities* (Albuquerque: University of New Mexico Press, 1995); Stephen Stern and John Allan Cicala, eds., *Creative Ethnicity: Symbols and Strategies of Contemporary Ethnic Life* (Logan: Utah State University Press, 1991); Michael D'Innocenzo and Josef P. Sirefman, eds., *Immigration and Ethnicity: American Society— "Melting Pot" or "Salad Bowl"?* (Westport, Conn.: Greenwood Press, 1992).

7. See, for example, Zupan and Owens, *Red Lodge,* 169–198; Leona Lampi, "Red Lodge: From a Frenetic Past of Crows, Coal, and Boom and Bust Emerges a Unique Festival of Diverse Nationality Groups," *Montana: The Magazine of Western History* 11 (July 1961): 20–31; any of the historical "blurbs" in the Red Lodge Chamber of Commerce Visitor's Guide from the 1950s to the present, including the 1996–1997 edition, p. 16, Carbon County Historical Society Collections (CCHS); and the *Carbon County News* from 1950 to the present, CCHS.

8. Bob Moran, comments at the Festival of Nations All-Nations Day program, Red Lodge, Montana, 11 August 1996.

9. Richard Weiss, "Ethnicity and Reform: Minorities and the Ambiance of the Depression Years," *Journal of American History* 66 (December 1979): 569–571, 582.

10. U.S. Department of Commerce, Bureau of the Census, *Fourteenth Census of the United States, Taken in the Year 1920, Population, Volume 3* (Washington, D.C.: Government Printing Office, 1922), 585, and *Fifteenth Census of the United States, Taken in the Year 1930, Population, Volume 3, Part 2* (Washington, D.C.: Government Printing Office, 1932), 31.

11. Weiss, "Ethnicity and Reform," 568–570.

12. Bodnar, *Remaking America,* 70; Glassberg, *American Historical Pageantry,* 232–234.

13. A group of young Italian-American women formed the Italian Girls Victory Club during World War I to support the war effort at the local level. After the war, the club continued as a community service organization and still exists.

14. *Picket-Journal* (Red Lodge), 7 April 1932, 1.

15. *Picket-Journal,* 7 April 1932, 1; 14 April 1932, 1, 8; 28 April 1932, 1, 4.

16. *Picket-Journal,* 16 May 1939, 1.
17. On displaying "safe" aspects of immigrant culture, see Bodnar, *Remaking America,* 70–77.
18. *Picket-Journal,* 23 May 1939, 1; emphasis added.
19. Bodnar, *Remaking America,* 70–77.
20. Community reform groups like the YWCA and the Playground Association of America began promoting international folk dancing at the turn of the century as a moral and healthy exercise for young people. Victor Greene, "Old-time Folk Dancing and Music among the Second Generation, 1920–50," in *American Immigrants and Their Generations: Studies and Commentaries on the Hansen Thesis after Fifty Years,* ed. Peter Kivisto and Dag Blanck (Urbana: University of Illinois Press, 1990), 144–148. For an example of the popularity of folk dancing, see the books from the 1940s series, *Handbooks of European National Dances,* such as Louise Witzig, *Dances of Switzerland* (London: Max Parrish, 1949).
21. Greene, "Old-time Folk Dancing and Music," 147–148.
22. *Picket-Journal,* 14 April 1932, 1, 8.
23. Linda Degh, "Grape-Harvest Festival of Strawberry Farmers: Folklore or Fake?" *Ethnologia Europaea* 10 (1977/1978): 114–131; Phyllis G. Tortora and Keith Eubank, *Survey of Historic Costume: A History of Western Dress,* 2d ed. (New York: Fairchild Publications, 1994), 6.
24. Patricia Williams, "From Folk to Fashion: Dress Adaptations of Norwegian Immigrant Women in the Midwest," in *Dress in American Culture,* ed. Patricia A. Cunningham and Susan Voso Lab (Bowling Green, Ohio: Bowling Green State University Popular Press, 1993), 95–108.
25. Dean MacCannell, *The Tourist: A New Theory of the Leisure Class* (New York: Schoken Books, 1976), 168.
26. *Picket-Journal,* 16 May 1939, 1.
27. Richard Polenberg, *One Nation Divisible: Class, Race, and Ethnicity in the United States since 1938* (New York: Penguin Books, 1980).
28. *Carbon County News,* 16 October 1950, 1.
29. *Carbon County News,* 1 May 1942, 1. Larger ethnic celebrations were popular in other parts of the country where people feared a replay of the xenophobic actions that had occurred during World War I; Polenberg, *One Nation Divisible,* 54.
30. Ronald Takaki, *A Different Mirror: A History of Multicultural America* (Boston: Little, Brown, 1993), 399.
31. Quoted in Polenberg, *One Nation Divisible,* 51.
32. Richard Slotkin, *Gunfighter Nation: The Myth of the Frontier in Twentieth-Century America* (New York: HarperPerennial, 1992), 322, 326.
33. Zupan and Owens, *Red Lodge,* 84–88.
34. *Carbon County News,* 22 March 1945, 1; 21 June 1945, 1.
35. U.S. Department of Commerce, Bureau of the Census, *A Report of the Seventeenth Decennial Census of the United States, Census of the Population: 1950, Volume 2, Characteristics of the Population, Part 26, Montana* (Washington, D.C.: Government Printing Office, 1952), 44, 46.
36. *Carbon County News,* 2 February 1948, 2.

37. Allan M. Winkler, *Home Front U.S.A.: America during World War II* (Arlington Heights, Ill.: Harlan Davidson, 1986), 43; Polenberg, *One Nation Divisible*, 17; Gerald D. Nash, *The American West in the Twentieth Century: A Short History of an Urban Oasis* (Albuquerque: University of New Mexico Press, 1985), 213–214.

38. *Carbon County News*, 11 April 1950, 1. On "saving" Red Lodge, also see the series of newspaper ads run in the *Carbon County News* in 1950 by Charles W. Stevens of the Red Lodge Cafe touting civic improvements and enthusiasm.

39. *Carbon County News*, 12 March 1948, 1; 30 May 1950, 1; 28 September 1950, 1.

40. *Carbon County News*, 22 December 1949, 1; 2 March 1950, 1.

41. *Carbon County News*, 17 May 1949; 5 July 1949, 4. The quotation is from the Northern Pacific Railroad brochure "The Spectacular Red Lodge Highway over the Rockies," Northern Pacific, Yellowstone Park Line, n.d., CCHS.

42. The town received a federal subsidy for rural hospitals. At the launching of the hospital construction campaign, Governor Sam Ford noted that "a modern hospital keeps money at home." Without a hospital, he observed, Red Lodge would become a "dying community" (*Carbon County News*, 17 May 1948, 1).

43. *Carbon County News*, 27 April 1950, 1; 19 October 1950, 6.

44. *Carbon County News*, 6 September 1949, 4.

45. *Carbon County News*, 26 October 1950, 1.

46. According to the *Carbon County News*, the original steering committee for the festival was made up of Mrs. Joe Bailey, Mrs. J. H. MacDonough, Mrs. J. H. Patten, and Miss Lucile Ralston. Since all the women assumed their husbands' names, ethnic affiliations are difficult to ascertain, but all appear to be native-born women of Anglo-American descent. A second steering committee, composed of Laura Weaver, Roger Davis, and John Lampi, included members of two older Anglo families and Lampi, a Finnish immigrant who moved to Red Lodge from British Columbia in 1917. Zupan and Owens, *Red Lodge*, 307–308, 336–338; Lillian Lampi Oral History, OH 303, 18–23, Montana Historical Society Collections (MHS).

47. *Billings Gazette*, 5 August 1996, clipping in "Red Lodge" vertical file, Parmly Billings Library.

48. *Carbon County News*, 19 April 1951, 1; 21 June 1951, 1.

49. *Carbon County News*, 11 April 1950, 1.

50. *Carbon County News*, 2 August 1951, 4.

51. *Carbon County News*, 11 April 1950, 1; 5 July 1951, 1.

52. *Carbon County News*, 8 September 1955, 1, 8.

53. *Carbon County News*, 26 August 1954, 1; 18 July 1957, 1.

54. MacCannell, *The Tourist*.

55. Although the Festival of Nations never presented an "authentic" presentation of Old World culture, many visitors eagerly accepted this re-creation as the real thing. Most tourists, Erik Cohen argues, do not demand "total authenticity" and are content if "they perceive part of the whole as authentic" ("Authenticity and Commoditization in Tourism," *Annals of Tourism Research* 15 [1988]: 377–378).

56. Cohen, "Authenticity and Commoditization in Tourism," 383.

57. *Carbon County News*, 30 August 1951, 1; 25 August 1955, 1.

58. *Carbon County News*, 17 January 1952, 1; 27 August 1953, 1.

59. *Carbon County News*, 1 August 1974, 4.

60. Bodnar, *Remaking America*, 138–139.

61. Gary W. Glantz to Mrs. Berver, 28 December 1962, Red Lodge Festival of Nations Collection, CCHS.

62. References to the United Nations flag, so prominent in the first few festivals, became increasingly rare in newspaper stories about the Festival of Nations in the late 1950s. By the mid-1990s, the U.N. flag was simply one of the hundreds of flags displayed in the Civic Center and not included at all among the flags displayed along Broadway Avenue.

63. Werner Sollors, ed., *The Invention of Ethnicity* (New York: Oxford University Press, 1989), xiv.

64. *Carbon County News*, 30 August 1951, 1; 25 August 1955, 4; 19 July 1956, 1; 29 August 1957, 1.

65. *Carbon County News*, 11 June 1959, 1; 23 July 1959, 1; 6 August 1959, 1; "Minutes," 1 August 1960, 17 November 1982, Red Lodge Festival of Nations Collection, CCHS.

66. See, for example, Kathleen Neils Conzen, David A. Gerber, Ewa Morawska, George E. Pozzetta, and Rudolph J. Vecoli, "The Invention of Ethnicity: A Perspective from the USA," *Altreitalie* 2 (April 1990): 37–62; Russell A. Kazal, "Revisiting Assimilation: The Rise, Fall, and Reappraisal of a Concept in American Ethnic History," *American Historical Review* 100 (April 1995): 437–471; and Oliver Zunz, "American History and the Changing Meaning of Assimilation," *Journal of American Ethnic History* 4 (Spring 1985): 53–72.

67. J. N. "Buck" Cornelio, a second-generation Italian, reported that Red Lodge had different Italian "factions." Most, he said, were from northern Italy, some from Rome, but there were no Sicilians in Red Lodge. Oral History of J. N. "Buck" Cornelio, OH 546, MHS. See also Conzen et al., "The Invention of Ethnicity," 48–49, and Zupan and Owens, *Red Lodge*, 177–179.

68. Conzen et al., "The Invention of Ethnicity," 42–43.

69. For example, Italians testified about the profound distinctions between Tyrolian Italians and other Italians in *Steve Roman v. Societa Italiana E Fratellanzadi Mutuo Soccorso, a corporation* (1918), Carbon County District Court (CCDC), Civil Records no. 2118.

70. *Carbon County News*, 23 August 1951, 1.

71. Zupan and Owens, *Red Lodge*, 171–173.

72. Zupan and Owens, *Red Lodge*, 172–173.

73. "21st Annual Festival of Nations, Special Souvenir Edition," 1971, 12, CCHS.

74. Slavic Day program, Festival of Nations, 9 August 1997, Red Lodge, Montana.

75. George Lipsitz, "The Possessive Investment in Whiteness: Racialized Social Democracy and the 'White' Problem in American Studies," *American Quarterly* 47 (September 1995): 379.

76. Edward A. Ross, *The Old World in the New: The Significance of Past and Present Immigration to the American People* (New York: Century, 1914), 117–118.

77. Jacob Riis, *How the Other Half Lives: Studies among the Tenements of New York* (Boston: St. Martin's Press, 1996), 94–95.

78. Quoted in Slotkin, *Gunfighter Nation*, 97.

79. D. G. O'Shea to S. T. Hauser, 13 August 1913, Box 9, Folder 10, Samuel T. Hauser Papers, MC 37, MHS; Zupan and Owen, *Red Lodge*, 368.

80. Noel Ignatiev, *How the Irish Became White* (New York: Routledge, 1995), 96; David R. Roediger, *The Wages of Whiteness: Race and the Making of the American Working Class*

(London: Verso, 1993), 179–180. See also Lipsitz, "The Possessive Investment in White-ness," 370.

81. Old-time miner Tony Persha recalled that "we didn't have any Chinese, or, we never had any colored people there, working in the mines or even living there. I understand at one time here in Red Lodge they did have one negro living here for quite a number of years" (this was Jack White who had a little shoe shine parlor on Billings Avenue). Persha added that at one point there were a few Mexicans in the Red Lodge mines, but they didn't stay long. Tony Persha Oral History, OH 305, 1A, MHS; see also Edward Blazina Oral History, OH 1485, 8, MHS.

82. Lampi, "Red Lodge," 24.

83. *Carbon County News*, 21 August 1958, 3.

84. Patricia Nelson Limerick, *The Legacy of Conquest: The Unbroken Past of the American West* (New York: W. W. Norton, 1987).

85. *Carbon County News*, 26 October 1950, 7.

86. Polenberg, *One Nation Divisible*, 101–104. For 1930s studies on class, see, for example, Earl H. Bell, "Social Stratification in a Small Community," *Scientific Monthly* 38 (Feb-ruary 1934): 157–164.

87. "The People of the U.S.A. — A Self-Portrait," *Fortune* 21 (February 1940): 14.

88. "A Sociologist Looks at an American Community," *Life* 27 (12 September 1949): 110.

89. Festival of Nations brochures have routinely described these European immigrants as "pioneers" of Red Lodge. See also Zupan and Owens, *Red Lodge*. The town's 100th anniversary edition of the local newspaper ran a section on long-lived residents, "Profiles of Red Lodge Area Pioneers," that included several second-generation immi-grants as well as the 101-year-old Blaz Sneider who had been born in Fuzina, Croatia. "Red Lodge: Tales of the First 100 Years," 44–48, CCHS.

90. Lampi, "Red Lodge," 22.

91. Lampi, "Red Lodge," 25.

92. Lampi, "Red Lodge," 31.

93. Zupan and Owen, *Red Lodge*, 36–37.

94. Zupan and Owen, *Red Lodge*, 30.

95. This tendency to insist on class rather than ethnicity was evident both in a 1980s oral history project by Laurie Mercier, "Montanans at Work," and one done in the early 1990s by Anna Zellick, which focused primarily on South Slavic immigrants and their children. All interviews are at the Montana Historical Society.

96. Walpas Koski Oral History, OH 359, 5, MHS.

97. Persha Oral History, 1B.

98. John Kastelitz Oral History, OH 1478, 19, MHS.

99. Daniel M. McDonald Oral History, OH 356, 1A, MHS.

100. Tony and Shirley Zupan Oral History, OH 1479, 42, MHS. See also Alice and Richard Mallin Oral History, OH 1481, 30–31, MHS.

101. Zupan Oral History, 41.

102. Senia Kallio Oral History, OH 357, 20; Rose Jurkovitch Oral History, OH 1486, 9, 16; Zupan Oral History, 37, MHS.

103. Jurkovitch Oral History, 16.

104. V. A. Burr to Joseph H. Roe, 11 June 1947, director of the Division of Public Assistance's

Responses to State Field Supervisors' Field Reports, Central Counties, 1/3, Montana Department of Public Welfare Records, RS 236, MHS.

105. *Carbon County News,* 6 November 1975, 1.

106. *Carbon County News,* 6 November 1975, 1.

107. For more on consensus history, see Peter Novick, *That Noble Dream: The "Objectivity Question" and the American Historical Profession* (Cambridge: Cambridge University Press, 1988), 333.

108. Frederick Errington, "Reflexivity Deflected: The Festival of Nations as an American Cultural Performance," *American Ethnologist* 14 (November 1987): 662.

109. *Carbon County News,* 5 June 1952, 1; 26 May 1955, 1; 27 July 1967, 1; "Minutes," 19 July 1960, Red Lodge Festival of Nations Collection, CCHS.

110. Bureau of the Census, *Census of Population: 1950, Volume 2, Part 26,* 44.

111. See, for example, Zupan Oral History, Mallin Oral History, Blazina Oral History, Persha Oral History.

112. Herbert J. Gans, "Symbolic Ethnicity: The Future of Ethnic Groups and Cultures in America," *Ethnic and Racial Studies* 2 (January 1979): 1–19.

113. Mary C. Waters, "The Construction of a Symbolic Ethnicity: Suburban White Ethnics in the 1980s," in *Immigration and Ethnicity,* 88; see also Waters, *Ethnic Options: Choosing Identities in America* (Berkeley: University of California Press, 1990).

114. Werner Sollors, *Beyond Ethnicity: Consent and Descent in American Culture* (New York: Oxford University Press, 1986), 14.

115. Gans, "Symbolic Ethnicity."

116. Degh, "Grape-Harvest Festival of Strawberry Farmers," 129, observed this process with Hungarian-American folk dancers performing at the Smithsonian Folk Festival.

117. "Festival of Nations," 1974 program, 12, CCHS.

118. "Minutes," 19 September 1984, 26 November 1984, 16 October 1985, Red Lodge Festival of Nations Collection, CCHS.

119. *Billings Gazette,* 5 August 1996, "Carbon County" vertical file, Parmly Billings Library.

120. Quoted in Zunz, "American History and the Changing Meaning of Assimilation," 55.

6. NATURE'S WEST

1. For historical studies on the interactions between communities and the environment, see William Cronon, "Kennecott Journey: The Paths out of Town," in *Under an Open Sky: Rethinking America's Western Past,* ed. William Cronon, George Miles, and Jay Gitlin (New York: W. W. Norton, 1992), 28–51, and "The Trouble with Wilderness; or, Getting Back to the Wrong Nature," in *Uncommon Ground: Rethinking the Human Place in Nature,* ed. William Cronon (New York: W. W. Norton, 1996), 69–90; Anne F. Hyde, "Round Pegs in Square Holes: The Rocky Mountains and Extractive Industry," in *Many Wests: Place, Culture, and Regional Identity,* ed. David M. Wrobel and Michael C. Steiner (Lawrence: University Press of Kansas, 1997), 93–113; John M. Findlay, "A Fishy Proposition: Regional Identity in the Pacific Northwest," in *Many Wests,* 37–70; Richard White, *Land Use, Environment, and Social Change: The Shaping of Island County, Washington* (Seattle: University of Washington Press, 1980).

2. Cronon, "The Trouble with Wilderness," 20.

3. On knowing nature through work, see Richard White, *The Organic Machine: The*

Remaking of the Columbia River (New York: Hill and Wang, 1995), 30–58, and " 'Are You an Environmentalist or Do You Work for a Living?': Work and Nature," in *Uncommon Ground*, 171–185; also see William Dietrich, *The Final Forest: The Battle for the Last Great Trees of the Pacific Northwest* (New York: Penguin Books, 1992), 26–46.

4. Erika A. Kuhlman, "From Farmland to Coalvillage: Red Lodge's Finnish Immigrants, 1890–1922" (Master's thesis, University of Montana, 1987), 22.

5. Ollie Anderson Oral History, OH 302, 19, Montana Historical Society Collections (MHS).

6. Leo Michelcic Oral History, OH 304, 1B, MHS.

7. Tony Persha Oral History, OH 305, 2B, MHS.

8. Daniel McDonald Oral History, OH 356, 1A, MHS.

9. Daniel McDonald Oral History, 2A.

10. Earl Pomeroy, *In Search of the Golden West: The Tourist in Western America* (Lincoln: University of Nebraska Press, 1990), 142–143; Roderick Nash, *Wilderness and the American Mind*, rev. ed. (New Haven: Yale University Press, 1973), 147.

11. John F. Sears, *Sacred Places: American Tourist Attractions in the Nineteenth Century* (New York: Oxford University Press, 1989); Anne Farrar Hyde, *An American Vision: Far Western Landscape and National Culture, 1820–1920* (New York: New York University Press, 1990); Richard West Sellars, *Preserving Nature in the National Parks: A History* (New Haven: Yale University Press, 1997); Alfred Runte, *National Parks: The American Experience* (Lincoln: University of Nebraska Press, 1979); John F. Reiger, "Wildlife, Conservation, and the First Forest Reserve," in *Origins of the National Forests: A Centennial Symposium*, ed. Harold K. Steen (Durham, N.C.: Forest History Society, 1992), 79–92.

12. Nash, *Wilderness and the American Mind*, 147.

13. Helen Hunt Jackson, "Puget Sound," *Atlantic Monthly* 51 (February 1983): 220.

14. Isabella L. Bird, *A Lady's Life in the Rocky Mountains* (Norman: University of Oklahoma Press, 1960), 194.

15. Pomeroy, *In Search of the Golden West*, 201.

16. E. V. Smalley, "Red Lodge, Montana," *The Northwest Magazine* 10 (August 1892): 21–22.

17. *Picket* (Red Lodge), 6 May 1893, 3.

18. *Picket*, 1907 Special Edition, 1.

19. Hyde, *An American Vision*, 245–254.

20. Nash, *Wilderness and the American Mind*, 150–151.

21. Hyde, *An American Vision*, 247.

22. "Junior Wa-Wa: Annual of the Carbon County High School, 1909," Carbon County Historical Society Collections (CCHS). Admittedly, this annual went out to only the more affluent members of the community; although the sophomore class in 1909 started out with twenty-four students in the eighth grade, it had only eleven students by the tenth grade.

23. *Picket*, 10 September 1892, 3; 24 September 1892, 3; 10 August 1895, 3; 7 August 1897, 3.

24. Several of these scrapbooks, with pictures from the 1900s through the 1940s, are on display at the Carbon County Historical Society archives.

25. Red Lodge oral histories are full of stories about picnics at these various campgrounds. See, for example, Walpas Koski Oral History, OH 359, 12; Lillian Lampi Oral History, OH 303, 23; Edward Blazina Oral History, OH 1485, 18, MHS. The local newspaper also

made note of large picnic gatherings outside town; for example, *Picket*, 10 August 1895, 3, and 25 June 1898, 3. The "funny stories" is from *State v. Gust Jarvi, Erik Kangas, and August Hokolo* (1911), Carbon County District Court (CCDC), Criminal Records no. 290.

26. Pomeroy, *In Search of the Golden West*, 141–143.

27. Shirley Zupan and Harry J. Owens, *Red Lodge: Saga of a Western Area* (Billings: Frontier Press, 1979), 7–9; Malcolm S. Mackay, *Cow Range and Hunting Trail* (New York: G. P. Putnam's Sons, 1925), 118.

28. Edward Nordstrom, "The Art of Dude Ranching," *The Review* (Carbon County High School) 3 (May 1932): 24.

29. Marcella Littlefield to Vera, 23 January 1932, Richel Lodge Collection, CCHS.

30. Zupan and Owens, *Red Lodge*, 329.

31. For example, Nordstrom's article "The Art of Dude Ranching" was published in the high school literary magazine, *The Review*, in 1932. In 1934, Helena Warila wrote both "Entertaining Dudes" and "A Dude's Idea of the West" for the high school publication; *Carbon Review* 5 (May 1934): 2, 15, CCHS. When Marcella Littlefield left for college in Bozeman, she maintained a steady correspondence with local residents in which she frequently mentioned her dude ranching experiences. Littlefield's correspondence is in the Richel Lodge Collection, CCHS.

32. I have borrowed from Leo Marx, *The Machine in the Garden: Technology and the Pastoral Ideal in America* (London: Oxford University Press, 1978), for the metaphor of the machine in the garden.

33. For a good overview of American auto tourism, see Warren James Belasco, *Americans on the Road: From Autocamp to Motel, 1910–1945* (Baltimore: Johns Hopkins University Press, 1979).

34. Belasco, *Americans on the Road*; Robert G. Athearn, *The Mythic West in Twentieth-Century America* (Lawrence: University Press of Kansas, 1986).

35. U.S. Congress, Senate, *Use of Automobiles in National Parks, Letter from the Acting Secretary of the Interior*, 1912, Senate Document 433 (62-2) SS 6181, 2.

36. U.S. Congress, House, *Roads: Hearings before the Committee on Roads, Part 1* (Washington, D.C.: Government Printing Office, 1928), 424.

37. House, *Roads: Hearings*, 540–541; Athearn, *The Mythic West*, 150.

38. Carl Abbott, "The Federal Presence," in *The Oxford History of the American West*, ed. Clyde A. Milner II, Carol A. O'Connor, and Martha A. Sandweiss (New York: Oxford University Press, 1994), 475–476; William Cronon, "Landscapes of Abundance and Scarcity," in *The Oxford History of the American West*, 629; Gerald D. Nash, *The American West in the Twentieth Century: A Short History of an Urban Oasis* (Albuquerque: University of New Mexico Press, 1985), 88.

39. *Picket-Journal* (Red Lodge), 29 January 1931, 1, 8.

40. Richard White, *The Organic Machine*, 57, and *"It's Your Misfortune and None of My Own": A History of the American West* (Norman: University of Oklahoma Press, 1991), 475.

41. Edgar W. Allen, the Red Lodge Commercial Club, to Senator Burton K. Wheeler, 26 April 1938, U.S. Forest Service Records, Msla-CCC, RG 95, Box 37/5, National Archives, Pacific Northwest Region, Seattle.

42. Memorandum, 12 May 1938, U.S. Forest Service Records, Msla-CCC, RG 95, Box 37/5.

43. Quoted in White, *The Organic Machine*, 57. See also Wesley Arden Dick, "When Dams

Weren't Damned: The Public Power Crusade and Visions of the Good Life in the Pacific Northwest in the 1930s," *Environmental Review* 13 (Fall/Winter 1989): 121, 135.

44. For local bounty hunters, see *Picket,* 10 February 1894, 3, and *Republican Picket* (Red Lodge), 13 May 1909, 1. For government agencies sponsoring elimination of "undesirable" animals, see Thomas Dunlap, *Saving America's Wildlife* (Princeton: Princeton University Press, 1988), and Bonnie Christensen, "From Divine Nature to Umbrella Species: The Development of Wildlife Science in the United States," in *Forest and Wildlife Science in America: A History,* ed. Harold K. Steen (Durham, N.C.: Forest History Society, 1999), 212–213.

45. Sports fishers were planting fish in the area as early as 1898; see *Picket,* 26 February 1898, 3.

46. *Picket-Journal,* 12 April 1922, 1; 30 August 1922, 1; 31 March 1932, 1, 8.

47. The newspaper reported that in three trips from Billings the airplane carrying the young fish had dropped over fifteen thousand fish into three isolated, unnamed lakes. Workers dropped the fish from a height of 150 feet. Planted species included California golden trout, albino eastern trout, and rainbow trout. The golden trout, though scarce in California, were still thriving in Beartooth lakes into the 1970s. *Picket-Journal,* 17 October 1939, 1; *Villager* (Red Lodge), 12 June 1975, 6.

48. *Billings Gazette,* "Land of Shining Mountains, Scenic Grandeur Supplement," 1936, CCHS.

49. *Picket,* 6 May 1893, 3; 22 July 1893, 3.

50. House, *Roads: Hearings,* 548.

51. D. W. Columbus, Red Lodge mayor, Resolution no. 849, 14 March 1967, Lee Metcalf Papers, MC 172, 112/14, MHS; William H. Browning to local chambers, 31 March 1958, and E. T. S., National Park Service, to Mike Mansfield, 1 April 1958, Montana Chamber of Commerce Records, MC 199, 1/11, MHS.

52. The Northern Pacific Railroad, for example, published a nationally distributed brochure entitled "The Spectacular Red Lodge Highway over the Rockies, Newest Gateway to Yellowstone Park"; a copy is in the collections of the Carbon County Historical Society. The Billings *Gazette* routinely extolled the "scenic grandeur" of the Beartooth Highway; see, for example, "The Land of Shining Mountains" supplements from the *Gazette,* CCHS.

53. Edward Weydt, "The New Road," *Carbon Review* 4 (1934): 2, CCHS.

54. *Carbon County News* (Red Lodge), 21 November 1934, 4.

55. *Carbon County News,* 21 August 1952, 8; "Montana" Vera Buening Oral History, OH 358, 1A, MHS.

56, *Have Fun . . . Relax in Red Lodge, Montana* (Red Lodge: Carbon County News, 1953), CCHS.

57. See, for example, the picture in the *Carbon County News,* 14 August 1952, 5.

58. *Carbon Review* 5 (1934), CCHS.

59. *Picket-Journal,* 26 June 1930.

60. *Picket-Journal,* 29 June 1933, 1.

61. Auto touring in this period, as Warren James Belasco points out, "remained predominately middle class" (*Americans on the Road,* 115).

62. U.S. Congress, Senate, *Hearings on the Highway from Red Lodge, Mont., to Cooke City, Mont., 20 April 1928,* SS 8831, 1.

63. U.S. Congress, Senate, *Hearings before a Subcommittee of the Committee on Public Lands and Surveys, Part 16, 29 August 1925* (Washington, D.C.: Government Printing Office, 1926), 4558–4559.

64. Zupan and Owens, *Red Lodge,* 19.

65. Senia Kallio Oral History, OH 357, 31, MHS. See also Michelcic Oral History, 1B, and Koski Oral History, 23.

66. Zupan and Owens, *Red Lodge*, 35.

67. *Picket-Journal*, 19 October 1937, 1.

68. J. N. "Buck" Cornelio Oral History, OH 546, 2B, MHS. Other Red Lodge area miners who worked in the park included Frank DeVille (bus driver), Ollie Anderson, and Leo Michelcic ("sanitation engineer"). DeVille Oral History, 2B; Anderson Oral History, 9; Michelcic Oral History, 1A.

69. *Carbon County News*, 9 October 1946, 1.

70. Meredith Nelson Wiltsie, "Land Use and Landscape Evolution in the West: A Case Study of Red Lodge, Montana, 1884–1995" (Master's thesis, Montana State University, 1998), 98.

71. *Picket-Journal*, 29 September 1932, 1, 8; 15 June 1937, 4.

72. *Picket-Journal*, 27 October 1932, 1.

73. The local newspaper printed the three prize-winning essays; *Picket-Journal*, 18 May 1933, 1, 5.

74. Federal Writers' Project, *Montana: A State Guide Book* (New York: Hastings House, 1939), 342; Leslie Lyons Oral History, OH 301, MHS; *Picket-Journal*, 18 May 1933, 1, 8; Leslie Lyons Collection, MHS; Photograph Collection, CCHS; Zupan and Owens, *Red Lodge*, 62–63. For more on the commodification of "nature," see Jennifer Price, *Flight Maps: Adventures with Nature in Modern America* (New York: Basic Books, 1999), and Susan G. Davis, *Spectacular Nature: Corporate Culture and the Sea World Experience* (Berkeley: University of California Press, 1997).

75. Lyons Oral History, 1B, MHS.

76. *Picket-Journal*, 18 May 1933, 1, 8.

77. *Picket-Journal*, 9 June 1936, 1, 4. Of course, many Montanans actually don't mind "seein' 'em dead" either, as evidenced by the preponderance of mounted stuffed animals in many of the state's public establishments; the Great Falls and Missoula airports, for example, display dozens of these "trophy" animals (perhaps to show incoming tourists what they can expect to see in their national park visits).

78. Quoted in Louis S. Warren, *The Hunter's Game: Poachers and Conservationists in Twentieth-Century America* (New Haven: Yale University Press, 1997), 112.

79. Nash, *Wilderness and the American Mind*, 207.

80. Quoted in Craig W. Allin, *The Politics of Wilderness Preservation* (Westport, Conn.: Greenwood Press, 1982), 74.

81. The Cody Commercial Club representative summarized these points on behalf of dude ranchers at the 1928 Senate hearings on the Beartooth Highway, *Highway from Red Lodge, Mont. to Cooke City, Mont.*, 407. For a general discussion of dude ranchers as stewards of wild lands, see Lawrence R. Borne, *Dude Ranching: A Complete History* (Albuquerque: University of New Mexico Press, 1983), esp. 143–158.

82. Area dude ranchers continued to lobby for wilderness areas. In 1958, for example, the Dude Ranchers' Association sent a resolution to the Montana Chamber of Commerce opposing "multiple use" interpretations for wilderness areas that would permit the construction of access roads around and leading to these areas. The ranchers did not want more cars driving up to and around the wilderness areas. "Resolution: Wilderness Areas, Trails, and Access Roads," 1958, Montana Chamber of Commerce Records, MHS.

83. Samuel P. Hays, *Beauty, Health, and Permanence: Environmental Politics in the United States, 1955–1985* (Cambridge: Cambridge University Press, 1989), 22.

84. For a comprehensive discussion of how the Echo Park controversy influenced American conservationists, see Mark W. T. Harvey, *A Symbol of Wilderness: Echo Park and the American Conservation Movement* (Albuquerque: University of New Mexico Press, 1994).

85. Quoted in Nash, *Wilderness and the American Mind,* 213–214.

86. Harvey, *A Symbol of Wilderness.*

87. By 1970, the median age of residents in Red Lodge was 51.5 years, the highest for a town its size in Montana; 27 percent of the town's population was over 65, the second highest average among towns with a population between 1,000 and 2,500. U.S. Department of Commerce, Bureau of the Census, *1970 Census of Population, Characteristics of the Population, Volume 1, Part 28, Montana* (Washington, D.C.: Government Printing Office, 1973), 28–60, and *The Eighteenth Decennial Census of the United States, Census of Population: 1960, Volume 1, Characteristics of the Population, Part 28, Montana* (Washington, D.C.: Government Printing Office, 1961), 28–29.

88. U.S. Department of Commerce, Bureau of the Census, "Red Lodge City: 1990 Census of Population and Housing — Summary Tape File 3A," *http://ceic.commerce.state.mt.us/demog/1990dec.*

89. Hal K. Rothman, *Devil's Bargains: Tourism in the Twentieth-Century American West* (Lawrence: University Press of Kansas, 1998), 26. On population statistics, see Carbon County Planning Board, "Carbon County Comprehensive Plan" (c. 1972), 33–34, 45–50, CCHS. This transition in the population and concern about the environment can be seen anecdotally in the publications of the Brokedown Palace Project (CCHS) and in a series of town meetings held in 1994 and 1995 by the Beartooth Front Community Forum. In these meetings, residents defined perceived problems with the community and laid out goals to address these concerns. One of the concerns voiced at the 3 August 1994 meeting was the high number of seasonal homes in and around Red Lodge; there were 170 seasonal homes in Red Lodge according to the 1990 census and 700 such homes in the immediate vicinity of Red Lodge. Videotapes of these meetings are available through the Beartooth Front Community Forum in Red Lodge.

90. Brokedown Palace Project, "Annual Report, Program Year 1974–1975," 14, and "Sunbind" (1976), 33, CCHS.

91. For an overview of the wilderness plan, see U.S. Department of Agriculture, Forest Service, "A Proposal: Beartooth Wilderness," 1974, CCHS. For Red Lodge's response, I used the local newspaper, the *Carbon County News,* looking at both articles and letters to the editor, all of which favored unified wilderness. Microfilmed copies of the wilderness hearing process include much testimony from Big Timber residents opposed to the unified wilderness, but few Red Lodge voices. For Mackay's quote, see U.S. Congress, House and Senate, *Joint Hearings on the Absaroka-Beartooth Wilderness, State of Montana,* held in Billings, Montana, 1977, 78 S311-12, 79. Red Lodge resident Kenneth Shesne testified in 1984 that the wilderness bill favored by the Forest Service (with the corridors) was "unbelievably bad" and "skewed strongly toward the competing exploitative and mechanized recreationist factions" (U.S. Congress, Senate, *Montana Wilderness Act of 1984, Hearings before the Subcommittee on Public Lands and Reserved Water of the Committee on Energy and Natural Resources on S. 2850,* Washington, D.C., 1984, 85 S311-28, 643).

92. Few of the public hearings on record contain input from people identified as Red Lodge residents. See, for example, *Joint Hearings on the Absaroka-Beartooth Wilderness*, and U.S. Congress, Senate, *Hearings on San Antonio Missions National Historic Park, Texas; Absaroka-Beartooth Wilderness, Montana; and Chattahoochee River National Recreation Area, Georgia, Washington D.C.*, 1977, 78 S311-15. See also letters to U.S. Senator Lee Metcalf regarding the Absaroka-Beartooth Wilderness, Lee Metcalf Collection, 30/4, 25/1, 24/5, MHS.

93. Big Timber business interests lobbied forcefully for the creation of their own gateway highway to Yellowstone National Park, and the National Forest Service vigorously supported the town's efforts to bisect the proposed wilderness area with a road. Arne M. Petaja to Senator Lee Metcalf, 10 May 1965, Lee Metcalf Collection, 112/14, MHS; testimony of Conrad B. Fredericks and the Big Timber City Council, *Joint Hearings on the Absaroka-Beartooth Wilderness*, 47–50.

94. *Carbon County News*, 7 March 1974, 2. For an example of more stridently environmentalist arguments about the wilderness, see the Montana Wilderness Association, "Wilderness Hearing Alert: Absaroka-Beartooth Primitive Areas," Lee Metcalf Collection, 25/1, MHS.

95. Bob Anderson, *Beartooth Country: Montana's Absaroka and Beartooth Mountains* (Helena, Mont.: American and World Geographic Publishing, 1994), 57.

96. Anderson, *Beartooth Country*, 90; *Carbon County News*, 24 November 1977.

97. For example, see Lloyd Schweizer's letter to the editor, *Montana Free Press* (Red Lodge), October 1991, 5–7.

98. "Minutes," 31 October 1986, Red Lodge Chamber of Commerce, Red Lodge Visitors' Center Collections.

99. "Carbon County Comprehensive Plan," 33–34, 45–50.

100. U.S. Department of Commerce, "Red Lodge City: 1990 Census of Population and Housing."

101. Television journalist Charles Kuralt, for example, listed the Beartooth Highway at the top of his list of the most beautiful highways in the United States. See Harry J. Owens to Charles Kuralt, 27 February 1980, "Kuralt and Other Celebrities" file, CCHS; see also almost any Red Lodge booster publication from 1980 to the present; the Kuralt listing is a topic constantly brought up whenever there is mention of the Beartooth Highway. Red Lodge Mountain, as far as I know, has not topped any comparable lists of beautiful ski areas.

102. See, for example, Dick Overturf to Linda Ward Williams, district ranger, n.d., Carbon County Clerk's Office File; U.S. Department of Agriculture, Forest Service, Northern Region, "Record of Decision for the Expansion of Red Lodge Mountain Ski Area Master Development Plan," January 1996, "Chapter 5: Response to Public Comment." Mark Harvey, *A Symbol of Wilderness*, makes clear in his study of the Echo Park fight that these legal weapons — environmental impact statements, endangered species listings — have changed the shape of conservation battles since the late 1960s.

103. On the growth of skiing in the West in the postwar years, see Rothman, *Devil's Bargains*, 168–286.

104. See "Ski Red Lodge Mountain" brochures, CCHS; also vertical file, "Red Lodge, Montana — Amusements," MHS.

105. "Red Lodge Visitors Guide 1986," 46–47, CCHS.

106. "Red Lodge Visitors Guide 1990–91," 6–7W, CCHS.

107. *Montana Free Press,* June 1992, 16–17.

108. *Montana Free Press,* September 1991, 3.

109. *Montana Free Press,* September 1991, 6.

110. The 1971 proposal fell through because of lack of funding; Red Lodge Grizzly Peak, "Ski Red Lodge: A Master Plan," 21 April 1971, CCHS; Forest Service, Northern Region, "Record of Decision for the Expansion of Red Lodge Mountain." Although the 1996 RLM report did not list the place of residency of respondents to the Draft Environmental Impact Statement, I cross-checked these names with the Red Lodge phone book to determine local residency. On business owners' objections to RLM, see Minutes, 14 January 1986, Red Lodge Chamber of Commerce.

111. Linda Ward-Williams, Beartooth district ranger of the Custer National Forest, wrote a letter to the editor of the *Montana Free Press* in 1993 (August, 3) urging public participation in the National Environmental Protection Act process for the expansion of RLM. She argued that the proposed action would turn RLM into a "regional, ski area resort" that would improve the mountain's declining market shares.

112. Forest Service, Northern Region, "Record of Decision for the Expansion of Red Lodge Mountain," Jan Roat, V-11.

113. Forest Service, Northern Region, "Record of Decision for the Expansion of Red Lodge Mountain," Ron Gerondale, V-12.

114. Forest Service, Northern Region, "Record of Decision for the Expansion of Red Lodge Mountain," Ron Gerondale, V-71.

115. Hyde, "Round Pegs in Square Holes," 96.

7. PRESERVING A PAST

1. *Carbon County News,* 9 May 1974, 1.

2. *National Tombstone Epitaph,* 16, clipping in "Liver-Eating Johnson" vertical file, Montana Historical Society Collections (MHS).

3. Michael Kammen, *Mystic Chords of Memory: The Transformation of Tradition in American Culture* (New York: Vintage Books, 1993), 641–643.

4. T. Allan Comp, "The Best Arena: Industrial History at the Local Level," *History News* 37 (May 1982): 8–11; Marsha Mullin and Geoffrey Huys, "Industrial History: How to Research, Collect, and Display Industrial Artifacts," *History News* 37 (May 1982): 12–16.

5. Michael Wallace, "Visiting the Past: History Museums in the United States," in *Presenting the Past: Essays on History and the Public,* ed. Susan Porter Benson, Stephen Brier, and Roy Rosenzweig (Philadelphia: Temple University Press, 1986), 155; David Lowenthal, "Pioneer Museums," in *History Museums in the United States: A Critical Assessment,* ed. Warren Leon and Roy Rosenzweig (Urbana: University of Illinois Press, 1989), 119–124; Linda Shopes, "Oral History and Community Involvement: The Baltimore Neighborhood Heritage Project," in *Presenting the Past,* 249–263; Mary H. Blewett, "Machines, Workers, and Capitalists: The Interpretation of Textile Industrialization in New England Museums," in *History Museums in the United States,* 262–293.

6. Michael Wallace, "Reflections on the History of Historic Preservation," in *Presenting the Past,* 175.

7. "Minutes," Historical Society, 23 September 1974, Carbon County Historical Society Collections (CCHS), Red Lodge, Montana.

8. Carbon County Historical Society File, CCHS.

9. David Hamer, *History in Urban Places: The Historic Districts of the United States* (Columbus: Ohio State University Press, 1998), 18–20. See also National Trust for Historic Preservation, *Preservation: Toward an Ethic in the 1980s* (Washington, D.C.: Preservation Press, 1980); William J. Murtagh, *Keeping Time: The History and Theory of Preservation in America*, rev. ed. (New York: Preservation Press, 1997); Arthur P. Ziegler Jr. and Walter C. Kidney, *Historic Preservation in Small Towns: A Manual of Practice* (Nashville, Tenn.: American Association for State and Local History, 1980); National Trust for Historic Preservation, *Economic Benefits of Preserving Old Buildings* (Washington, D.C.: Preservation Press, 1976); Robert E. Stipe and Antoinette J. Lee, eds., *The American Mosaic: Preserving a Nation's Heritage* (Washington, D.C.: U.S. Committee of the International Council on Monuments and Sites, 1987).

10. Quote is in Wallace, "Reflections on the History of Historic Preservation," 176; David Lowenthal, *The Past Is a Foreign Country* (Cambridge: Cambridge University Press, 1985), 387.

11. J. Myrick Howard, "Where the Action Is: Preservation and Local Governments," in *The American Mosaic*, 126–127.

12. Michels Raffety Architects and Carbon County Historical Preservation Office, *Red Lodge Commercial Historic District Revitalization Master Plan* (Livingston, Mont.: Michels Rafferty Architects, 1986), 8–9, 15, 47.

13. M. Christine Boyer, "Cities for Sale: Merchandising History at South Street Seaport," in *Variations on a Theme Park: The New American City and the End of Public Space*, ed. Michael Sorkin (New York: Hill and Wang, 1992), 181–204; Wallace, "Reflections on the History of Historic Preservation," 180–181.

14. Boyer, "Cities for Sale," 204.

15. Hamer, *History in Urban Places*, ix.

16. Michels Raffety Architects, *Red Lodge Revitalization*, 15.

17. Paul Anderson, "Cultural Resource Inventory and Evaluation, Red Lodge East Bench — Washoe-Highway-Burns-Smith Mines," 12–20, CCHS; William A. Babcock and Alan S. Newell, *Cultural Resource Management Report: Beartooth (Brophy) Mine Site, Carbon County, Montana* (Missoula: Historical Research Associates, 1980), 5–8; GCM Services, "Definition and Evaluation of the Bear Creek Mining District, Carbon County, Montana," November 1993, 75–88, CCHS; Marcella Sherfy to Ben Mundie, 1 June 1983, CCHS.

18. Shopes, "Oral History and Community Involvement," 258–260.

19. Blewett, "Machines, Workers, and Capitalists," 262, 273.

20. John A. Jakle, *The Tourist: Travel in Twentieth-Century North America* (Lincoln: University of Nebraska Press, 1985), 293.

21. Custer Country Tourism Region of Montana, *Montana's Custer Country Regional Tour Guide* (Hardin, Mont.: Custer Country Montana, 1989).

22. Stephen Spender, quoted in Kammen, *Mystic Chords of Memory*, 673.

23. *Carbon County News*, 23 May 1974, 2.

24. Dan Coats to Shirley Zupan, 20 April 1984, Historical Preservation Grant file, CCHS.

25. Edrie Vinson to Wally W. Edmands Jr., 9 April 1986, Downtown Revitalization file, CCHS.

26. "A Sip of Europe, A Slug of the Old West," brochure, CCHS.

27. Lowenthal, "The Past Is a Foreign Country," 399.

28. D. W. Meinig, "Symbolic Landscapes," in *The Interpretation of Ordinary Landscapes: Geographical Essays,* ed. D. W. Meinig (New York: Oxford University Press, 1979), 164.

29. Meinig, "Symbolic Landscapes," 167; also see John A. Jakle, *The American Small Town: Twentieth-Century Place Images* (Hamden, Conn.: Archon Books, 1982), 5–7.

30. Richard V. Francaviglia, "Main Street U.S.A.: A Comparison/Contrast of Streetscapes in Disneyland and Walt Disney World," *Journal of Popular Culture* 15 (Summer 1981): 143.

31. Meinig, "Symbolic Landscapes," 179. Even some local residents noted the town's increasing tendency toward "Disneyfication." One of the respondents in the Beartooth Front Community Forum (BFCF) meetings, for example, asserted that the group should work to preserve the community's historic identity, but not so that the downtown looked like a "theme park" (BFCF video, "Land Use Planning Meetings," 17 September 1994).

32. *Montana Free Press* (Red Lodge), June 1992, 16–17.

33. BFCF, "Land Use Planning Meetings," 17 September 1994.

34. *Montana Free Press,* June 1992, 16–17.

35. BFCF, "Land Use Planning Meetings," 1 December 1994.

36. Montana Consensus Council, *Solving Community Problems by Consensus: A Celebration of Success Stories* (Bozeman, Mont.: Robert J. Buzzas CIVIC Consulting, 1995), 8.

37. BFCF, "Land Use Planning Meetings," 1 December 1994.

38. Jim Howe, Ed McMahon, and Luther Propst, *Balancing Nature and Commerce in Gateway Communities* (Washington, D.C.: Island Press, 1997).

39. *Billings Gazette,* 14 August 1997, 1–5C.

40. John Clayton, "Keeping the Heart in the Center of Town," *High Country News* 28 (23 December 1996); *www.hcn.org/1996/dec23/dir/Profile_Keeping_th.html.*

41. Clayton, "Keeping the Heart in the Center of Town."

42. Alice and Richard Mallin Oral History, OH 1481, 12–13, 25–26, MHS.

43. Loretta and Lillian Jarussi Oral History, OH 1487, 21, MHS.

BIBLIOGRAPHY

ARCHIVAL MATERIAL

Carbon County District Court, Red Lodge, Montana
   Carbon County District Court, Criminal and Civil Records
   County Clerk's Office File
Carbon County Historical Society, Red Lodge, Montana
   Edwards Collection
   Festival of Nations Collection
   Greenough Collection
   Leslie Lyons Collection
   Photograph Collection
   Reading Room Collection
   Red Lodge Red Cross Minutes
   Red Lodge Woman's Club Minutes
   Richel Lodge Collection
Minnesota Historical Society, St. Paul
   Great Northern Railroad Records, 137/B/16/1B
   Northern Pacific Railroad Company Records, Secretary's Files, 137/I/19/6F
   Northwestern Improvement Company Records, 138/C/6/2
   Rocky Fork Coal Company Records, 136/D/17/3B
Montana Historical Society, Helena
   Anaconda Copper Mining Company Records, MC 169
   Council of Defense Records, RS 19
   Dilworth Cattle Company Records, MF 308a
   Samuel T. Hauser Collection, MC 37
   Daniel S. McCorkle Papers, MC 59
   Lee Metcalf Papers, MC 172
   Montana Chamber of Commerce Records, MC 199
   Montana Department of Public Welfare Records, RS 236
   Montana Forestry Records, RS 283
   Montana State Planning Records, RG 80
   Oral Histories Collection
   William Anthony Romek Reminiscence, SC 1453
   H. A. Simmons Collection, MC 204
   WPA Writers' Program Records
National Archives, Pacific Northwest Region, Seattle, Washington
   United States Forest Service Records, Msla-CCC, RG 95
Parmly Billings Library, Billings, Montana
   Vertical Files, "Carbon County"
Red Lodge Visitors' Center
   Red Lodge Chamber of Commerce Minutes

GOVERNMENT DOCUMENTS

U.S. Congress. House. *Roads: Hearings before the Committee on Roads, Part 1.* Washington, D.C.: U.S. Government Printing Office, 1928.

U.S. Congress. House and Senate. *Joint Hearings on the Absaroka-Beartooth Wilderness, State of Montana.* Billings, Montana, 1977. 78 S311-12.

U.S. Congress. Industrial Commission. *Report of the Industrial Commission on Immigration, Volume 25.* Washington, D.C.: Government Printing Office, 1901.

U.S. Congress. Senate. *Hearings before a Subcommittee of the Committee on Public Lands and Surveys, Part 16, 29 August 1925.* Washington, D.C.: Government Printing Office, 1926.

———. *Hearings on the Highway from Red Lodge, Mont. to Cooke City, Mont., 20 April 1928.* SS 8831.

———. *Hearings on San Antonio Missions National Historic Park, Texas; Absaroka-Beartooth Wilderness, Montana; and Chattahoochee River National Recreation Area, Georgia.* 1977. 78 S311-15.

———. *Montana Wilderness Act of 1984: Hearings before the Subcommittee on Public Lands and Reserved Water of the Committee on Energy and Natural Resources on S. 2850.* 1984. 85 S311-28.

———. *Use of Automobiles in National Parks, Letter from the Acting Secretary of the Interior.* 1912. Senate Document 433 (62-2) SS 6181.

U.S. Department of Agriculture. Forest Service, Northern Region. "Record of Decision for the Expansion of Red Lodge Mountain Ski Area Master Development Plan." January 1996.

U.S. Department of Commerce. Bureau of the Census. *Twelfth Census of the United States, Taken in the Year 1900, Population, Volume 2, Part 2.* Washington, D.C.: U.S. Census Office, 1902.

———. *Thirteenth Census of the United States, Taken in the Year 1910, Population, Volume 2.* Washington, D.C.: Government Printing Office, 1913.

———. *Fourteenth Census of the United States, Taken in the Year 1920, Population, Volume 1.* Washington, D.C.: Government Printing Office, 1921.

———. *Fourteenth Census of the United States, Taken in the Year 1920, Population, Volume 3.* Washington, D.C.: Government Printing Office, 1922.

———. *Fifteenth Census of the United States, Taken in the Year 1930, Population, Volume 3, Part 2.* Washington, D.C.: Government Printing Office, 1932.

———. *A Report of the Seventeenth Decennial Census of the United States, Census of Population: 1950, Volume 2, Characteristics of the Population, Part 26, Montana.* Washington, D.C.: U.S. Government Printing Office, 1952.

———. *The Eighteenth Decennial Census of the United States, Census of Population: 1960, Volume 1, Characteristics of the Population, Part 28, Montana.* Washington, D.C.: Government Printing Office, 1961.

———. *1970 Census of Population, Characteristics of the Population, Volume 1, Part 28, Montana.* Washington, D.C.: Government Printing Office, 1973.

———. "Red Lodge City: 1990 Census of Population and Housing — Summary Tape File 3A." http://ceic.commerce.state.mt.us/demog/1990dec.

———. "Profile of General Demographic Characteristics: 2000. Geographic Area: Red Lodge City, Montana."

NEWSPAPERS

Billings Gazette (Billings, Montana)
Carbon County Gazette (Red Lodge)
Carbon County News (Red Lodge)
Montana Free Press (Red Lodge)
Picket (Red Lodge)
Picket-Journal (Red Lodge)
Republican (Red Lodge)
Republican-Picket (Red Lodge)
Stinking Water Prospector (Red Lodge)

BOOKS

Abbott, E. C., and Helena Huntington Smith. *We Pointed Them North: Recollections of a Cowpuncher.* Norman: University of Oklahoma Press, 1989.

Allen, Michael. *Rodeo Cowboys in the North American Imagination.* Reno and Las Vegas: University of Nevada Press, 1998.

Allin, Craig W. *The Politics of Wilderness Preservation.* Westport, Conn.: Greenwood Press, 1982.

Allmendinger, Blake. *The Cowboy: Representations of Labor in an American Work Culture.* New York: Oxford University Press, 1992.

Anderson, Bob. *Beartooth Country: Montana's Absaroka and Beartooth Mountains.* Helena, Mont.: American and World Geographic Publishing, 1994.

Armitage, Susan, and Elizabeth Jameson, eds. *The Women's West.* Norman: University of Oklahoma Press, 1987.

Athearn, Robert G. *The Mythic West in Twentieth-Century America.* Lawrence: University Press of Kansas, 1986.

Belasco, Warren James. *Americans on the Road: From Autocamp to Motel, 1910–1945.* Baltimore: Johns Hopkins University Press, 1979.

Benson, Susan Porter, Stephen Brier, and Roy Rosenzweig, eds. *Presenting the Past: Essays on History and the Public.* Philadelphia: Temple University Press, 1986.

Bird, Isabella L. *A Lady's Life in the Rocky Mountains.* Norman: University of Oklahoma Press, 1960.

Bird, S. Elizabeth, ed. *Dressing in Feathers: The Construction of the Indian in American Popular Culture.* Boulder, Colo.: Westview Press, 1996.

Bodnar, John. *Remaking America: Public Memory, Commemoration, and Patriotism in the Twentieth Century.* Princeton: Princeton University Press, 1992.

Borne, Lawrence R. *Dude Ranching: A Complete History.* Albuquerque: University of New Mexico Press, 1983.

Boyer, Paul S. *The Urban Masses and Moral Order in America, 1820–1920.* Cambridge: Harvard University Press, 1978.

Browne, Ray B., and Michael T. Marsden, eds. *The Cultures of Celebration.* Bowling Green, Ohio: Bowling Green State University Popular Press, 1994.

Buntline, Ned. *Buffalo Bill and His Adventures in the Wild West.* New York: J. S. Ogelvie, 1884.

Butler, Anne M. *Daughters of Joy, Sisters of Misery: Prostitutes in the American West, 1865–90.* Urbana: University of Illinois Press, 1985.

Carter, Thomas, ed. *Images of an American Land: Vernacular Architecture in the Western United States*. Albuquerque: University of New Mexico Press, 1997.

Cohn, David L. *A History of American Morals and Manners as Seen through the Sears, Roebuck Catalogs, 1905 to the Present*. New York: Simon and Schuster, 1940.

Cromley, Elizabeth Collins, and Carter L. Hudgins, eds. *Gender, Class, and Shelter: Perspectives in Vernacular Architecture*. Vol. 5. Knoxville: University of Tennessee Press, 1995.

Cronon, William. *Nature's Metropolis: Chicago and the Great West*. New York: W. W. Norton, 1991.

Cronon, William, ed. *Uncommon Ground: Rethinking the Human Place in Nature*. New York: W. W. Norton, 1996.

Cronon, William, George Miles, and Jay Gitlin, eds. *Under an Open Sky: Rethinking America's Western Past*. New York: W. W. Norton, 1992.

Cunningham, Patricia A., and Susan Voso Lab, eds. *Dress in American Culture*. Bowling Green, Ohio: Bowling Green State University Popular Press, 1993.

Davis, Susan G. *Spectacular Nature: Corporate Culture and the Sea World Experience*. Berkeley: University of California Press, 1997.

Deloria, Philip. *Playing Indian*. New Haven: Yale University Press, 1998.

Denning, Michael. *Mechanic Accents: Dime Novels and Working-Class Culture in America*. London: Verso, 1987.

Dietrich, William. *The Final Forest: The Battle for the Last Great Trees of the Pacific Northwest*. New York: Penguin Books, 1992.

D'Innocenzo, Michael, and Josef P. Sirefman, eds. *Immigration and Ethnicity: American Society "Melting Pot" or "Salad Bowl"?* Westport, Conn.: Greenwood Press, 1992.

Doyle, David Noel, and Owen Dudley Edwards, eds. *America and Ireland, 1776–1976: The American Identity and the Irish Connection*. Westport, Conn.: Greenwood Press, 1980.

Dubofsky, Melvyn. *We Shall Be All: A History of the Industrial Workers of the World*. 2d ed. Urbana: University of Illinois Press, 1988.

Dunlap, Thomas. *Saving America's Wildlife*. Princeton: Princeton University Press, 1988.

Dykstra, Robert R. *The Cattle Towns*. New York: Knopf, 1968.

Emmons, David M. *The Butte Irish: Class and Ethnicity in an American Mining Town, 1875–1925*. Urbana: University of Illinois Press, 1990.

———. *Garden in the Grasslands: Boomer Literature of the Central Great Plains*. Lincoln: University of Nebraska Press, 1971.

Fazio, Michael W., and Peggy Whitman Prenshaw, eds. *Order and Image in the American Small Town*. Jackson: University Press of Mississippi, 1981.

Federal Writers' Project. *Montana: A State Guide Book*. New York: Hastings House, 1939.

Foner, Philip S., ed. *Fellow Workers and Friends: I.W.W. Free-Speech Fights As Told by Participants*. Westport, Conn.: Greenwood Press, 1981.

Francaviglia, Richard V. *Hard Places: Reading the Landscape of America's Historic Mining Districts*. Iowa City: University of Iowa Press, 1991.

Fredricksson, Kristine. *American Rodeo: From Buffalo Bill to Big Business*. College Station: Texas A&M University Press, 1985.

Fuchs, Lawrence H. *American Kaleidoscope: Race, Ethnicity, and the Civic Culture*. Middletown, Conn.: Wesleyan University Press, 1990.

Gerstle, Gary. *Working-Class Americanism: The Politics of Labor in a Textile City*. Cambridge: Cambridge University Press, 1989.

Gjerde, John. *From Peasants to Farmers: The Migration from Balestrand, Norway, to the Upper Middle West*. New York: Cambridge University Press, 1985.

Glassberg, David. *American Historical Pageantry: The Uses of Tradition in the Early Twentieth Century*. Chapel Hill: University of North Carolina Press, 1990.

Green, Archie. *Wobblies, Pile Butts, and Other Heroes: Laborlore Explorations*. Urbana: University of Illinois Press, 1993.

Grossman, James R., ed. *The Frontier in American Culture*. Berkeley: University of California Press, 1994.

Guitierrez, Ramon A., and Genevieve Fabre, eds. *Feasts and Celebrations in North American Ethnic Communities*. Albuquerque: University of New Mexico Press, 1995.

Hall, Lee. *Common Threads: A Parade of American Clothing*. Boston: Little, Brown, 1992.

Hamer, David. *History in Urban Places: The Historic Districts of the United States*. Columbus: Ohio State University Press, 1998.

———. *New Towns in the New World: Images and Perceptions of the Nineteenth-Century Urban Frontier*. New York: Columbia University Press, 1990.

Harvey, Mark W. T. *A Symbol of Wilderness: Echo Park and the American Conservation Movement*. Albuquerque: University of New Mexico Press, 1994.

Hays, Samuel P. *Beauty, Health, and Permanence: Environmental Politics in the United States, 1955–1985*. Cambridge: Cambridge University Press, 1989.

Higham, John. *Strangers in the Land: Patterns of American Nativism, 1860–1925*. New Brunswick, N.J.: Rutgers University Press, 1955.

Higham, John, ed. *Ethnic Leadership in America*. Baltimore: Johns Hopkins University Press, 1978.

Howard, Joseph Kinsey. *Montana: High, Wide, and Handsome*. New Haven: Yale University Press, 1948.

Howe, Jim, Ed McMahon, and Luther Propst. *Balancing Nature and Commerce in Gateway Communities*. Washington, D.C.: Island Press, 1997.

Hyde, Anne Farrar. *An American Vision: Far Western Landscape and National Culture, 1820–1920*. New York: New York University Press, 1990.

Ignatiev, Noel. *How the Irish Became White*. New York: Routledge, 1995.

An Illustrated History of the Yellowstone Valley Embracing the Counties of Park, Sweet Grass, Carbon, Yellowstone, Rosebud, Custer and Dawson, State of Montana. Spokane: Western Historical Publishing, 1907.

Iverson, Peter. *When Indians Became Cowboys: Native Peoples and Cattle Ranching in the American West*. Norman: University of Oklahoma Press, 1994.

Jakle, John A. *The American Small Town: Twentieth-Century Place Images*. Hamden, Conn.: Archon Books, 1982.

———. *The Tourist: Travel in Twentieth-Century North America*. Lincoln: University of Nebraska Press, 1985.

Jameson, Elizabeth. *All That Glitters: Class, Conflict, and Community in Cripple Creek*. Urbana: University of Illinois Press, 1998.

Jordan, Teresa. *Cowgirls: Women of the American West*. Lincoln: University of Nebraska Press, 1982.

Kammen, Michael. *Mystic Chords of Memory: The Transformation of Tradition in American Culture*. New York: Vintage Books, 1993.

Kittredge, William. *Who Owns the West*. San Francisco: Mercury House, 1996.

Kivisto, Peter, and Dag Blanck, eds. *American Immigrants and Their Generations: Studies and Commentaries on the Hansen Thesis after Fifty Years.* Urbana: University of Illinois Press, 1990.

Kraditor, Aileen. *The Ideas of the Woman Suffrage Movement, 1890–1920.* New York: Norton, 1981.

Laslett, John H. M., ed. *The United Mine Workers of America: A Model of Industrial Solidarity?* University Park: Pennsylvania State University Press, 1996.

Lawrence, Elizabeth Atwood. *Rodeo: An Anthropologist Looks at the Wild and the Tame.* Chicago: University of Chicago Press, 1982.

Lears, T. J. Jackson. *No Place of Grace: Antimodernism and the Transformation of American Culture, 1880–1920.* New York: Pantheon Books, 1981.

LeCompte, Mary Lou. *Cowgirls of the Rodeo: Pioneer Professional Athletes.* Urbana: University of Illinois Press, 1993.

Leon, Warren, and Roy Rosenzweig, eds. *History Museums in the United States: A Critical Assessment.* Urbana: University of Illinois Press, 1989.

Levine, Peter. *A. G. Spaulding and the Rise of Baseball: The Promise of American Sport.* New York: Oxford University Press, 1986.

Limerick, Patricia Nelson. *The Legacy of Conquest: The Unbroken Past of the American West.* New York: W. W. Norton, 1987.

Limerick, Patricia Nelson, Clyde A. Milner II, and Charles E. Rankin, eds. *Trails: Toward a New Western History.* Lawrence: University Press of Kansas, 1991.

Long, Priscilla. *Where the Sun Never Shines: A History of America's Bloody Coal Industry.* New York: Paragon Books, 1991.

Lowenthal, David. *The Heritage Crusade and the Spoils of History.* Cambridge: Cambridge University Press, 1998.

———. *The Past Is a Foreign Country.* Cambridge: Cambridge University Press, 1985.

MacCannell, Dean. *The Tourist: A New Theory of the Leisure Class.* New York: Schoken Books, 1976.

Mackay, Malcolm S. *Cow Range and Hunting Trail.* New York: G. P. Putnam's Sons, 1925.

Malone, Michael P., and Richard B. Roeder, eds. *Montana's Past: Selected Essays.* Missoula: University of Montana Publications in History, 1973.

Malone, Michael P., Richard B. Roeder, and William Lang. *Montana: A History of Two Centuries.* Rev. ed. Seattle: University of Washington Press, 1991.

Marx, Leo. *The Machine in the Garden: Technology and the Pastoral Ideal in America.* London: Oxford University Press, 1978.

McCartin, Joseph A. *Labor's Great War: The Struggle for Industrial Democracy and the Origins of Modern American Labor Relations, 1912–1921.* Chapel Hill: University of North Carolina Press, 1997.

Michels Raffety Architects and Carbon County Historical Preservation Office. *Red Lodge Commercial Historic District Revitalization Master Plan.* Livingston, Mont.: Michels Raffety Architects, 1986.

Milner, Clyde A., II, Carol A. O'Connor, and Martha A. Sandweiss, eds. *The Oxford History of the American West.* New York: Oxford University Press, 1994.

Monkkonen, Eric H., ed. *Walking to Work: Tramps in America, 1790–1935.* Lincoln: University of Nebraska Press, 1984.

Montana Consensus Council. *Solving Community Problems by Consensus: A Celebration of Success Stories.* Bozeman, Mont.: Robert J. Buzzas CIVIC Consulting, 1995.

Moses, L. G. *Wild West Shows and the Images of American Indians, 1883–1933.* Albuquerque: University of New Mexico Press, 1996.

Murtagh, William J. *Keeping Time: The History and Theory of Preservation in America.* Rev. ed. New York: Preservation Press, 1997.

Nash, Gerald D. *The American West in the Twentieth Century: A Short History of an Urban Oasis.* Albuquerque: University of New Mexico Press, 1985.

Nash, Michael. *Conflict and Accommodation: Coal Miners, Steel Workers, and Socialism, 1890–1920.* Westport, Conn.: Greenwood Press, 1982.

Nash, Roderick. *Wilderness and the American Mind.* Rev. ed. New Haven: Yale University Press, 1973.

National Trust for Historic Preservation. *Economic Benefits of Preserving Old Buildings.* Washington, D.C.: Preservation Press, 1976.

———. *Preservation: Toward an Ethic in the 1980s.* Washington, D.C.: Preservation Press, 1980.

Novick, Peter. *That Noble Dream: The "Objectivity Question" and the American Historical Profession.* Cambridge: Cambridge University Press, 1988.

Petrik, Paula. *No Step Backward: Women and Family on the Rocky Mountain Mining Frontier, 1865–1900.* Helena: Montana Historical Society Press, 1987.

Polenberg, Richard. *One Nation Divisible: Class, Race, and Ethnicity in the United States Since 1938.* New York: Penguin Books, 1980.

Pomeroy, Earl. *In Search of the Golden West: The Tourist in Western America.* Lincoln: University of Nebraska Press, 1957.

Pozzetta, George E., ed. *Immigrant Institutions: The Organization of Immigrant Life.* New York: Garland Publishing, 1991.

Price, Jennifer. *Flight Maps: Adventures with Nature in Modern America.* New York: Basic Books, 1999.

Price, Ted. *Miracle Town: Creating America's Bavarian Village in Leavenworth, Washington.* Vancouver, Wash.: Price and Rodgers, 1997.

Quaife, M. M., ed. *"Yellowstone Kelly": The Memoirs of Luther S. Kelley.* Lincoln: University of Nebraska Press, 1926.

Rainbolt, Jo. *The Last Cowboy: Twilight Era of the Horseback Cowhand, 1900–1940.* Helena, Mont.: American and World Geographic Publications, 1992.

Renner, Frederic G., ed. *Paper Talk: Illustrated Letters of Charles M. Russell.* Fort Worth, Tex.: Amon Carter Museum of Western Art, 1962.

Riis, Jacob. *How the Other Half Lives: Studies among the Tenements of New York.* Boston: St. Martin's Press, 1996.

Riley, Glenda. *Women and Indians on the Frontier, 1825–1915.* Albuquerque: University of New Mexico Press, 1984.

Roediger, David R. *The Wages of Whiteness: Race and the Making of the American Working Class.* London: Verso, 1991.

Rohrbough, Malcolm J. *Days of Gold: The California Gold Rush and the American Nation.* Berkeley: University of California Press, 1997.

Ross, Edward A. *The Old World in the New: The Significance of Past and Present Immigration to the American People.* New York: Century, 1914.

Rothman, Hal K. *Devil's Bargains: Tourism in the Twentieth-Century American West.* Lawrence: University Press of Kansas, 1998.

Runte, Alfred. *National Parks: The American Experience.* Lincoln: University of Nebraska Press, 1979.

Salerno, Salvatore. *Red November, Black November: Culture and Community in the Industrial Workers of the World.* Albany: State University of New York Press, 1989.

Sanders, James U., ed. *Society of Montana Pioneers.* Vol. 1. Akron, Ohio: Werner, 1899.

Schaffer, Ronald. *America in the Great War: The Rise of the War Welfare State.* New York: Oxford University Press, 1991.

Schwantes, Carlos A. *The Pacific Northwest: An Interpretive History.* Lincoln: University of Nebraska Press, 1989.

Sears, John F. *Sacred Places: American Tourist Attractions in the Nineteenth Century.* New York: Oxford University Press, 1989.

Sellars, Richard West. *Preserving Nature in the National Parks: A History.* New Haven: Yale University Press, 1997.

Slatta, Richard. *Cowboys of the Americas.* New Haven: Yale University Press, 1990.

Slotkin, Richard. *The Fatal Environment: The Myth of the Frontier in the Age of Industrialization, 1800–1890.* New York: HarperPerennial, 1994.

———. *Gunfighter Nation: The Myth of the Frontier in Twentieth-Century America.* New York: HarperPerennial, 1992.

Smith, Henry Nash. *Virgin Land: The American West as Symbol and Myth.* Cambridge: Harvard University Press, 1970.

Sollors, Werner. *Beyond Ethnicity: Consent and Descent in American Culture.* New York: Oxford University Press, 1986.

Sollors, Werner, ed. *The Invention of Ethnicity.* New York: Oxford University Press, 1989.

Sorkin, Michael, ed. *Variations on a Theme Park: The New American City and the End of Public Space.* New York: Hill and Wang, 1992.

Steen, Harold K., ed. *Forest and Wildlife Science in America: A History.* Durham, N.C.: Forest History Society, 1999.

———. *Origins of the National Forests: A Centennial Symposium.* Durham, N.C.: Forest History Society, 1992.

Stern, Stephen, and John Allan Cicala, eds. *Creative Ethnicity: Symbols and Strategies of Contemporary Ethnic Life.* Logan: Utah State University Press, 1991.

Stipe, Robert E., and Antoinette J. Lee, eds. *The American Mosaic: Preserving a Nation's Heritage.* Washington, D.C.: U.S. Committee of the International Council on Monuments and Sites, 1987.

Stout, Tom, ed. *Montana: Its Story and Biography.* Chicago: American Historical Society, 1912.

Takaki, Ronald. *A Different Mirror: A History of Multicultural America.* Boston: Little, Brown, 1993.

Thorp, Raymond W., and Robert Bunker. *Crow Killer: The Saga of Liver-Eating Johnson.* Bloomington: Indiana University Press, 1958.

Tompkin, Jane. *West of Everything: The Inner Life of Westerns.* New York: Oxford University Press, 1992.

Toole, K. Ross. *Montana: An Uncommon Land.* Norman: University of Oklahoma Press, 1984.

———. *Twentieth-Century Montana: A State of Extremes.* Norman: University of Oklahoma Press, 1972.

Tortora, Phyllis G., and Keith Eubank. *Survey of Historic Costume: A History of Western Dress.* 2d ed. New York: Fairchild Publications, 1994.

Turner, Victor, ed. *Celebration: Studies in Festivity and Ritual.* Washington, D.C.: Smithsonian Institution Press, 1982.

Van West, Carroll. *Capitalism on the Frontier: Billings and the Yellowstone Valley in the Nineteenth Century.* Lincoln: University of Nebraska Press, 1993.

Vecoli, Rudolph J., and Suzanne M. Sinke, eds. *A Century of European Migrations, 1830–1930.* Urbana: University of Illinois Press, 1991.

Wallace, Mike. *Mickey Mouse History and Other Essays on American Memory.* Philadelphia: Temple University Press, 1996.

Warren, Louis S. *The Hunter's Game: Poachers and Conservationists in Twentieth-Century America.* New Haven: Yale University Press, 1997.

Waters, Mary C. *Ethnic Options: Choosing Identities in America.* Berkeley: University of California Press, 1990.

Wellington, Beverly Rue. *Red Lodge Landmarks.* Red Lodge, Mont.: Carbon County News, 1992.

West, Elliott. *The Saloon on the Rocky Mountain Mining Frontier.* Lincoln: University of Nebraska Press, 1979.

Wheeler, Edward L. *Deadwood Dick's Big Deal, or the Gold Brick of Oregon.* New York: Beadle and Adams, 1883.

White, Richard. *"It's Your Misfortune and None of My Own": A History of the American West.* Norman: University of Oklahoma Press, 1991.

———. *Land Use, Environment, and Social Change: The Shaping of Island County, Washington.* Seattle: University of Washington Press, 1980.

———. *The Organic Machine: The Remaking of the Columbia River.* New York: Hill and Wang, 1995.

Whitman, Walt. *Leaves of Grass.* New York: Penguin Books, 1980.

Winkler, Allan M. *Home Front U.S.A.: America during World War II.* Arlington Heights, Ill.: Harlan Davidson, 1986.

Wister, Owen. *The Virginian.* New York: Popular Library, Eagle Books, 1962.

Witzig, Louise. *Dances of Switzerland.* London: Max Parrish, 1949.

Wrobel, David M., and Michael C. Steinger, eds. *Many Wests: Place, Culture, and Regional Identity.* Lawrence: University Press of Kansas, 1997.

Ziegler, Arthur P., Jr., and Walter C. Kidney. *Historic Preservation in Small Towns: A Manual of Practice.* Nashville, Tenn.: American Association for State and Local History, 1980.

Zupan, Shirley, and Harry J. Owens. *Red Lodge: Saga of a Western Area.* Billings, Mont.: Frontier Press, 1979.

ARTICLES AND CHAPTERS IN BOOKS

Abbott, Carl. "The Federal Presence." In *The Oxford History of the American West,* ed. Clyde A. Milner II, Carol A. O'Connor, and Martha A. Sandweiss, 475–476. New York: Oxford University Press, 1994.

Alcorn, Rowena L., and Gordon D. Alcorn. "Jackson Sundown, Nez Perce Horseman." *Montana: The Magazine of Western History* 33 (Autumn 1983): 46–51.

Barrett, James R. "Americanization from the Bottom Up: Immigration and the Remaking of the Working Class in the United States, 1880–1930." *Journal of American History* 79 (December 1992): 996–1020.

Bell, Earl H. "Social Stratification in a Small Community." *Scientific Monthly* 38 (February 1934): 157–164.

Bodnar, John. "Power and Memory in Oral History: Workers and Managers at Studebaker." *Journal of American History* 75 (March 1989): 1201–1221.

Bogue, Allan G. "An Agricultural Empire." In *The Oxford History of the American West,* edited by Clyde A. Milner II, Carol A. O'Connor, and Martha A. Sandweiss, 275–313. New York: Oxford University Press, 1994.

Bosanko, Marlene S. McCleary. "Among Colored Hats and Other Gewgaws: The Early Irish in Washington State." *Journal of the West* 31 (April 1992): 33–40.

Boyer, M. Christine. "Cities for Sale: Merchandising History at South Street Seaport." In *Variations on a Theme Park: The New American City and the End of Public Space,* edited by Michael Sorkin, 181–204. New York: Hill and Wang, 1992.

Brown, Richard Maxwell. "Violence." In *The Oxford History of the American West,* edited by Clyde Milner II, Carol A. O'Connor, and Martha A. Sandweiss, 393–425. New York: Oxford University Press, 1994.

Butler, Anne. M. "Selling the Popular Myth." In *The Oxford History of the American West,* edited by Clyde A. Milner II, Carol A. O'Connor, and Martha A. Sandweiss, 771–801. New York: Oxford University Press, 1994.

Calhoun, Craig. "Social Theory and the Politics of Identity." In *Social Theory and the Politics of Identity,* edited by Craig Calhoun, 9–36. Oxford: Blackwell, 1994.

Christensen, Bonnie. "From Divine Nature to Umbrella Species: The Development of Wildlife Science in the United States." In *Forest and Wildlife Science in American: A History,* edited by Harold K. Steen, 209–229. Durham, N.C.: Forest History Society, 1999.

Clayton, John. "Keeping the Heart in the Center of Town." *High Country News* 28 (23 December 1996), www.hcn.org/1996/dec23/dir/Profile_Keeping_th.html.

Cohen, Erik. "Authenticity and Commoditization in Tourism." *Annals of Tourism Research* 15 (1988): 371–386.

Comp, T. Allan. "The Best Arena: Industrial History at the Local Level." *History News* 37 (May 1982): 8–11.

Conzen, Kathleen Neils, David A. Gerber, Ewa Morawska, George E. Pozzetta, and Rudolph J. Vecoli. "The Invention of Ethnicity: A Perspective from the USA." *Altreitalie* 2 (April 1990): 37–62.

Corn, Jacqueline Karnell. " 'Dark as a Dungeon': Environment and Coal Miners' Health and Safety in Nineteenth Century America." *Environmental Review* 7 (Fall 1983): 257–268.

Cronon, William. "Forward to the Paperback Edition." In *Uncommon Ground: Rethinking the Human Place in Nature,* edited by William Cronon, 19–22. New York: W. W. Norton, 1996.

———. "Kennecott Journey: The Paths out of Town." In *Under an Open Sky: Rethinking America's Western Past,* edited by William Cronon, George Miles, and Jay Gitlin, 28–51. New York: W. W. Norton, 1992.

———. "Landscapes of Abundance and Scarcity." In *The Oxford History of the American West,* edited by Clyde A. Milner II, Carol A. O'Connor, and Martha A. Sandweiss, 603–637. New York: Oxford University Press, 1994.

———. "The Trouble with Wilderness; or, Getting Back to the Wrong Nature." In *Uncommon Ground: Rethinking the Human Place in Nature,* edited by William Cronon, 69–90. New York: W. W. Norton, 1996.

Cross, Robert D. "The Irish." In *Ethnic Leadership in America*, edited by John Higham, 176–197. Baltimore: Johns Hopkins University Press, 1978.

"Daring Beautiful Western Girls: Sweethearts of the Wild West Shows." *American West* 22 (July/August 1985): 44–48.

Degh, Linda. "Grape-Harvest Festival of Strawberry Farmers: Folklore or Fake?" *Ethnologia Europaea* 10 (1977/1978): 114–131.

Derickson, Alan. "The United Mine Workers of America and the Recognition of Occupational Respiratory Diseases, 1902–1968." *American Journal of Public Health* 81 (June 1991): 782–790.

DeVoto, Bernard. "The Anxious West." *Harper's Magazine* 193 (December 1946): 481–491.

———. "Footnote on the West." *Harper's Monthly Magazine* 155 (November 1927): 713–722.

Dick, Wesley Arden. "When Dams Weren't Damned: The Public Power Crusade and Visions of the Good Life in the Pacific Northwest in the 1930s." *Environmental Review* 13 (Fall/Winter 1989): 113–151.

Dien, Dora Shu-fang. "The Evolving Nature of Self-Identity across Four Levels of History." *Human Development* 43 (January–February 2000): 1–18.

"Dismal Moments in the American West." *Forbes* 156 (23 October 1995): FYI 128.

"Dressing the Dude." *Vogue* 87 (1 May 1936): 140–141.

Engler, Mira. "Drive-Thru History: Theme Towns in Iowa." *Landscape* 32 (1993): 8–18.

Errington, Frederick. "Reflexivity Deflected: The Festival of Nations As an American Cultural Performance." *American Ethnologist* 14 (November 1987): 654–667.

———. "The Rock Creek Rodeo: Excess and Constraint in Men's Lives." *American Ethnologist* 17 (September 1990): 638–645.

Etulain, Richard W. "Changing Images: The Cowboy in Western Films." *Colorado Heritage* 1 (1981): 36–55.

Evans, William B., and Robert L. Peterson. "Decision at Colstrip: The Northern Pacific Railway's Open-Pit Mining Operation." In *Montana's Past: Selected Essays*, edited by Michael P. Malone and Richard B. Roeder, 445–460. Missoula: University of Montana Publications in History, 1973.

Feilitzsch, Heribert Frhr. v. "Karl May: The 'Wild West' As Seen in Germany." *Journal of Popular Culture* 27 (Winter 1993): 173–189.

Findlay, John M. "A Fishy Proposition: Regional Identity in the Pacific Northwest." In *Many Wests: Place, Culture, and Regional Identity*, edited by David M. Wrobel and Michael C. Steiner, 37–70. Lawrence: University Press of Kansas, 1997.

Fishback, Price V. "An Alternative View of Violence in Labor Disputes in the Early 1900s: The Bituminous Coal Industry, 1890–1930." *Labor History* 36 (Summer 1995): 426–456.

Gans, Herbert J. "Symbolic Ethnicity: The Future of Ethnic Groups and Cultures in America." *Ethnic and Racial Studies* 2 (January 1979): 1–19.

Gedicks, Al. "Ethnicity, Class Solidarity, and Labor Radicalism among Finnish Immigrants in Michigan's Copper Country." *Politics and Society* 7 (1977): 127–156.

———. "The Social Origins of Radicalism among Finnish Immigrants in Midwest Mining Communities." *Review of Radical Political Economics* 8 (Fall 1976): 1–31.

Gleason, Philip. "Identifying Identity: A Semantic History." *Journal of American History* 69 (March 1983): 910–931.

Goodsill, M. M. "What Dudes Tell the Railroads; Remarks on their Vacations." *Minutes of the Fourth Annual Dude Ranchers' Meeting Held at Billings, Montana, November 18, 19, 20, 1929.* Pp. 61–75. Casper, Wyo.: S. E. Boyer, 1930.

Greene, Victor. "Old-time Folk Dancing and Music Among the Second Generation, 1920–50." In *American Immigrants and Their Generations: Studies and Commentaries on the Hansen Thesis after Fifty Years,* edited by Peter Kivisto and Dag Blanck, 142–163. Urbana: University of Illinois Press, 1990.

Gutfeld, Arnon. "The Murder of Frank Little: Radical Labor Agitation in Butte, Montana, 1917." In *Montana's Past: Selected Essays,* edited by Michael P. Malone and Richard B. Roeder, 370–390. Missoula: University of Montana Publications in History, 1973.

Hart, Arthur A. "Sheet Iron Elegance: Mail Order Architecture in Montana." *Montana: The Magazine of Western History* 40 (Autumn 1990): 27–31.

Heath, Kingston. "False-Front Architecture on Montana's Urban Frontier." In *Images of an American Land: Vernacular Architecture in the Western United States,* edited by Thomas Carter, 21–39. Albuquerque: University of New Mexico Press, 1997.

Holdsworth, " 'I'm a Lumberjack and I'm OK': The Built Environment and Varied Masculinites in the Industrial Age." In *Gender, Class, and Shelter: Perspectives in Vernacular Architecture,* vol. 5., edited by Elizabeth Collins Cromley and Carter L. Hudgins, 11–25. Knoxville: University of Tennessee Press, 1995.

Howard, J. Myrick. "Where the Action Is: Preservation and Local Governments." In *The American Mosaic: Preserving a Nation's Heritage,* edited by Robert E. Stipe and Antoinette J. Lee, 113–144. Washington, D.C.: U.S. Committee of the International Council on Monuments and Sites, 1987.

Hummasti, P. George. "World War I and the Finns of Astoria, Oregon: The Effects of the War on an Immigrant Community." *International Migration Review* 11 (Fall 1977): 340–341.

Hyde, Anne F. "Round Pegs in Square Holes: The Rocky Mountains and Extractive Industry." In *Many Wests: Place, Culture, and Regional Identity,* edited by David M. Wrobel and Michael C. Steiner, 93–113. Lawrence: University Press of Kansas, 1997.

Jackson, Helen Hunt. "Puget Sound." *Atlantic Monthly* 51 (February 1983): 218–231.

Jennings, Jan. "Cheap and Tasteful Dwellings in Popular Architecture." In *Gender, Class, and Shelter: Perspectives in Vernacular Architecture,* vol. 5, edited by Elizabeth Collins Cromley and Carter L. Hudgins, 133–151. Knoxville: University of Tennessee Press, 1995.

Johnson, Susan L. "Sharing Bed and Board: Cohabitation and Cultural Difference in Central Arizona Mining Towns, 1863–1873." In *The Women's West,* edited by Susan Armitage and Elizabeth Jameson, 77–91. Norman: University of Oklahoma Press, 1987.

Kazal, Russell A. "Revisiting Assimilation: The Rise, Fall, and Reappraisal of a Concept in American Ethnic History." *American Historical Review* 100 (April 1995): 437–471.

Kero, Reino. "Migration Traditions from Finland to North America." In *A Century of European Migrations, 1830–1930,* edited by Rudolph J. Vecoli and Suzanne M. Sinke, 111–133. Urbana: University of Illinois Press, 1991.

Kivisto, Peter. "Finnish Americans and the Homeland, 1918–1958." *Journal of American Ethnic History* 7 (Fall 1987): 7–27.

Lampi, Leona. "Red Lodge: From a Frenetic Past of Crows, Coal, and Boom and Bust Emerges a Unique Festival of Diverse Nationality Groups." *Montana: The Magazine of Western History* 11 (July 1961): 20–31.

Laslett, John H. M. "British Immigrant Colliers and the Origins and Early Development of the UMWA, 1870–1912." In *The United Mine Workers of America: A Model of Industrial Solidarity?* edited by John H. M. Laslett, 29–50. University Park: Pennsylvania State University Press, 1996.

Lipsitz, George. "The Possessive Investment in Whiteness: Racialized Social Democracy and the 'White' Problem in American Studies." *American Quarterly* 47 (September 1995): 369–387.

Lopez, David E. "Cowboy Strikes and Unions." *Labor History* 18 (Summer 1977): 325–340.

Lowenthal, David. "Pioneer Museums." In *History Museums in the United States: A Critical Assessment,* edited by Warren Leon and Roy Rosenzweig, 115–127. Urbana: University of Illinois Press, 1989.

Mather, Cotton, and Matti Kaups. "The Finnish Sauna: A Cultural Index to Settlement." *Annals of the Association of American Geographics* 53 (December 1963): 494–504.

McWilliams, Carey. "Myths of the West." *North American Review* 232 (November 1931): 424–432.

Meinig, D. W. "Symbolic Landscapes." In *The Interpretation of Ordinary Landscapes: Geographical Essays,* edited by D. W. Meinig, 164–192. New York: Oxford University Press, 1979.

Mellinger, Phil. "How the IWW Lost Its Western Heartland: Western Labor History Revisited." *Western Historical Quarterly* 27 (Autumn 1996): 303–324.

Milner, Clyde A., II. "America Only More So." In *The Oxford History of the American West,* edited by Clyde A. Milner II, Carol A. O'Connor, and Martha A. Sandweiss, 1–7. New York: Oxford University Press, 1994.

———. "The Shared Memory of Montana Pioneers." *Montana: The Magazine of Western History* 37 (Winter 1987): 2–13.

Mullin, Marsha, and Geoffrey Huys. "Industrial History: How to Research, Collect, and Display Industrial Artifacts." *History News* 37 (May 1982): 12–16.

Noel, Thomas J. "The Immigrant Saloon in Denver." In *Immigrant Institutions: The Organization of Immigrant Life,* edited by George E. Pozzetta, 205–223. New York: Garland Publishing, 1991.

Nordstrom, Edward. "The Art of Dude Ranching." *The Review* 3 (May 1932): 24.

Nye, Gerald P. "Speaking of Backward States." *North American Review* 229 (April 1930): 406–413.

"The People of the U.S.A. — A Self-Portrait." *Fortune* 21 (February 1940): 14, 20, 28, 133–134, 136.

Philips, Ernie. "Cowboys Like to Read Westerns." *Publishers' Weekly* 122 (13 August 1932): 509.

Poten, Constance J. "Robert Yellowtail, the New Warrior." *Montana: The Magazine of Western History* 39 (Summer 1989): 36–41.

"The Real, Not the Reel, Cowboy." *Literary Digest* 22 (20 May 1922): 56–58.

Reardon, Jack. "Injuries and Illnesses among Bituminous and Lignite Coal Miners." *Monthly Labor Review* 116 (October 1993): 49–55.

Reiger, John F. "Wildlife, Conservation, and the First Forest Reserve." In *Origins of the National Forests: A Centennial Symposium,* edited by Harold K. Steen, 106–121. Durham, N.C.: Forest History Society, 1992.

Roeder, Richard B. "Montana Progressivism, Sound and Fury — And One Small Tax Reform." In *Montana's Past: Selected Essays,* edited by Michael P. Malone and Richard Roeder, 391–404. Missoula: University of Montana Publications in History, 1973.

Sarbaugh, Timothy J. "Celts with the Midas Touch: The Farmers, Entrepreneurs, and Millionaires of Spokane's City and County Pioneer Community." *Journal of the West* 31 (April 1992): 41–51.

———. "The Irish in the West: An Ethnic Tradition of Enterprise and Innovation, 1848–1991." *Journal of the West* 31 (April 1992): 5–8.

Schofield, Ann. "Rebel Girls and Union Maids: The Woman Question in the Journals of the AFL and IWW, 1905–1920." *Feminist Studies* 9 (Summer 1983): 335–358.

Schwantes, Carlos A. "The Concept of the Wageworkers' Frontier: A Framework for Future Research." *Western Historical Quarterly* 18 (January 1987): 39–55.

———. "Wage Earners and Wealth Makers." In *The Oxford History of the American West*, edited by Clyde A. Milner II, Carol A. O'Connor, and Martha A. Sandweiss, 431–467. New York: Oxford University Press, 1994.

Schwoob, Jacob M. "Relation of the Retailer to the Dude Rancher." *Minutes of the Fourth Annual Dude Ranchers' Meeting Held at Billings, Montana, November 18, 19, 20, 1929*. Pp. 53–59. Casper, Wyo.: S. E. Boyer, 1930

Shaffer, Marguerite S. " 'See America First': Re-envisioning Nation and Region through Western Tourism." *Pacific Historical Review* 65 (November 1996): 559–582.

Shumsky, Neil Larry. " 'Let No Man Stop to Plunder!': American Hostility to Return Migration, 1890–1924." *Journal of American Ethnic History* 11 (Winter 1992): 56–75.

Simpson, Pamela H. "Cheap, Quick, and Easy, Part II: Pressed Metal Ceilings, 1880–1930." In *Gender, Class, and Shelter: Perspectives in Vernacular Architecture*, vol. 5, edited by Elizabeth Collins Cromley and Carter L. Hudgins, 152–163. Knoxville: University of Tennessee Press, 1995.

Singer, Alan J. " 'Something of a Man': John L. Lewis, the UMWA, and the CIP, 1919–1943." In *The United Mine Workers of America: A Model of Industrial Solidarity?* edited by John H. Laslett, 104–150. University Park: Pennsylvania State University Press, 1996.

Sinton, John. "When Moscow Looks Like Chicago: An Essay on Uniformity and Diversity in Landscapes and Communities." *Environmental History Review* 17 (Fall 1993): 23–41.

Smalley, E.V. "Red Lodge, Montana." *Northwest Magazine* 10 (August 1892): 20–27.

Smilor, Raymond W. "Creating a National Festival: The Campaign for a Safe and Sane Fourth, 1903–1916." *Journal of American Culture* 2 (Winter 1980): 611–622.

Smith, Burton M. "Politics and the Crow Indian Land Cessions." *Montana: The Magazine of Western History* 36 (Autumn 1986): 24–37.

"A Sociologist Looks at an American Community." *Life* 27 (12 September 1949): 108–119.

Steele, Jeffrey. "Reduced to Images: American Indians in Nineteenth-Century Advertising." In *Dressing in Feathers: The Construction of the Indian in American Popular Culture*, edited by Elizabeth S. Bird, 45–64. Boulder, Colo.: Westview Press, 1996.

Stiffler, Liz, and Tona Blake. "Fanny Sperry-Steele: Montana's Champion Bronc Rider." *Montana: The Magazine of Western History* 32 (Spring 1982): 44–57.

Tuan, Yi-Fu. "Space and Place: Humanistic Perspective." In *Progress in Geography: International Reviews of Current Research*, vol. 6, edited by Christopher Board, Richard J. Charley, Peter Haggett, and David R. Stoddart, 211–252. London: Edward Arnold, 1974.

Turner, Frederick Jackson. "The Significance of the Frontier in American History." In *The Early Writings of Frederick Jackson Turner*, compiled by Everett E. Edwards, 185–229. Madison: University of Wisconsin Press, 1938.

Van Brunt, Henry. "Architecture in the West." In *Architecture and Society: Selected Essays of Henry Van Brunt*, edited by William A. Coles, 180–194. Cambridge: Belknap Press of Harvard University Press, 1969.

Van Cleef, Eugene. "The Finn in America." *Geographical Review* 6 (September 1918): 185–214.

Vought, Hans. "Division and Reunion: Woodrow Wilson, Immigration, and the Myth of American Unity." *Journal of American Ethnic History* 13 (Spring 1994): 24–50.

Wallace, Michael. "Reflections on the History of Historic Preservation." In *Presenting the Past: Essays on History and the Public*, edited by Susan Porter Benson, Stephen Brier, and Roy Rosenzweig, 165–199. Philadelphia: Temple University Press, 1986.

———. "Visiting the Past: History Museums in the United States." In *Presenting the Past: Essays on History and the Public*, edited by Susan Porter Benson, Stephen Brier, and Roy Rosenzweig, 137–161. Philadelphia: Temple University Press, 1986.

Walsh, James P. "The Irish in the New America: 'Way Out West.'" In *America and Ireland, 1776–1976: The American Identity and the Irish Connection*, edited by David Noel Doyle and Owen Dudley Edwards, 165–176. Westport, Conn.: Greenwood Press, 1980.

Warila, Helena. "A Dude's Idea of the West." *Carbon Review* 5 (May 1934): 15.

———. "Entertaining Dudes." *Carbon Review* 5 (May 1934): 2.

Waters, Mary C. "The Construction of a Symbolic Ethnicity: Suburban White Ethnics in the 1980s." In *Immigration and Ethnicity: American Society — "Melting Pot" or "Salad Bowl"?* edited by Michael D'Innocenzo and Josef P. Sirefman. Westport, Conn.: Greenwood Press, 1992.

Weiss, Richard. "Ethnicity and Reform: Minorities and the Ambience of the Depression Years." *Journal of American History* 66 (December 1979): 566–585.

Weydt, Edward. "The New Road." *Carbon Review* 4 (1934): 2.

White, Richard. "'Are You an Environmentalist or Do You Work for a Living?': Work and Nature." In *Uncommon Ground: Rethinking the Human Place in Nature*, edited by William Cronon, 171–185. New York: W. W. Norton, 1996.

———. "Frederick Jackson Turner and Buffalo Bill." In *The Frontier in American Culture*, edited by James R. Grossman, 7–65. Berkeley: University of California Press, 1994.

———. "Outlaw Gangs of the Middle Border: American Social Bandits." *Western Historical Quarterly* 12 (October 1981): 387–408.

Williams, Jesse Lynch. "Joy-Ranching and Dude-Wrangling." *Colliers* 51 (9 August 1913): 22–23.

Williams, Patricia. "From Folk to Fashion: Dress Adaptations of Norwegian Immigrant Women in the Midwest." In *Dress in American Culture*, edited by Patricia A. Cunningham and Susan Voso Lab, 95–108. Bowling Green, Ohio: Bowling Green State University Popular Press, 1993.

Wilson, Laurel. "The American Cowboy: Development of the Mythic Image." In *Dress in American Culture*, edited by Patricia A. Cunningham and Susan Voso Lab, 80–93. Bowling Green, Ohio: Bowling Green State University Popular Press, 1993.

Worster, Donald. "Beyond the Agrarian Myth." In *Trails: Toward a New Western History*, edited by Patricia Nelson Limerick, Clyde A. Milner II, and Charles E. Rankin, 3–25. Lawrence: University Press of Kansas, 1991.

Zunz, Oliver. "American History and the Changing Meaning of Assimilation." *Journal of American Ethnic History* 4 (Spring 1985): 53–72.

THESES AND DISSERTATIONS

Grant, Frank R. "Embattled Voice for the Montana Farmers: Robert Sutherlin's *Rocky Mountain Husbandman*." Ph.D. dissertation, University of Montana, 1984.

Kuhlman, Erika A. "From Farmland to Coalvillage: Red Lodge's Finnish Immigrants, 1890–1922." Master's thesis, University of Montana, 1987.

Roeder, Richard Brown. "Montana in the Early Years of the Progressive Period." Ph.D. dissertation, University of Pennsylvania, 1971.

Wiltsie, Meredith Nelson. "Land Use and Landscape Evolution in the West: A Case Study of Red Lodge, Montana, 1884–1995." Master's thesis, Montana State University, 1998.

VIDEOS

Amundsen, Michael. *Take Willy With 'Ya: The Ridin' Greenoughs and the Golden Age of Rodeo.* Snowflake, Ariz.: Rodeo Video, 1989.

Loeser, Doris. *"I'll Ride that Horse!": Montana Women Bronc Riders.* Rattatosk Films, n.d.

INDEX

Abbott, Teddy Blue, 36, 115
Absaroka-Beartooth Wilderness Area,
    203–206
Adirondack Mountains, 173
African Americans, 63, 154, 251n71, 270n81
Agrarian west, 4, 5, 12–14, 16, 17, 42. *See also*
    Farmers
Alaska-Pacific-Yukon Exhibition, 104
Albright, H. M., 182
Alcohol consumption, 30–31, 84. *See also*
    Saloons
Alderson, Walter, 79, 85, 258n35
American Federation of Labor, 64, 71
American identity, xiv, 162, 164
Americanism
    anti-immigrant sentiment, 75–76, 81, 130
    conformity, 77
    criticism of war opponents, 78–79
    ethnic pluralism within, 132–133, 137–138,
        146–147, 167
    in Festival of Nations, 146–147
    of immigrants, 76, 77–78, 81–83
    interest in history, 218–220
    Liberty Committees, 77, 78–81, 85, 256n12,
        257n20, 258n35
    in 1950s, 139
    promotion during World War I, 74–75,
        76–78
    public attitudes toward, 75
    public rhetoric, 82
    in Red Lodge, 76, 132, 139
    small towns as embodiment of, 230–231
    tourism promotion, 93
    violence, 78–79, 80–81
    See also Patriotism
Anderson, C. C., 70
Anderson, Ollie, 86, 171, 253n97, 259n39
Animals
    dogs, 31, 245n89
    raised by miners' families, 53
    in Red Lodge area, 185–186, 197
    zoo, 196–197
    See also Hunting
Architecture. *See* Buildings, in Red Lodge
Aspen (Colorado), xix
Athearn, Robert G., 107, 112
Austrian immigrants, 149
Authenticity, 101, 145, 148–149, 223
Automobiles, 182, 184. *See also* Highways

Automobile tourism, 181–182, 184, 192, 200
Autry, Gene, 260n18, 262n53

Balkans. *See* Slavic immigrants; Yugoslavian
    immigrants
Baltimore (Maryland), 219, 227
Barovich, John, 88, 126, 253n97
Baseball games, 103
Bearcreek (Montana)
    disappearance of town, 128, 139
    mines, 87, 88, 92, 138, 226
Beartooth Forest Preserve, 176
Beartooth Front Community Forum (BFCF),
    231, 233, 234
Beartooth Highway
    associated with Red Lodge events, 189–191
    beauty of, 229, 277n101
    construction, 184, 189–190, 191, 192–193
    effects on Red Lodge identity, 169, 183, 189
    jobs created, 191, 192–193
    Opening Day Ceremony, 132–133, 135–136,
        191
    opponents, 200, 205
    photographs and paintings of, 189
    pride in, 188–189, 205, 215
    promotion of, 139, 188, 192, 200
    proposal, 186–187, 200
    route, 187
    season, 187–188
    snowfall on route, 186–187
    as tourist attraction, 183
    visitors, 193, 194
    zoo near, 196–197
Beartooth Primitive Area, 199
Beartooth Range
    Absaroka-Beartooth Wilderness Area,
        203–206
    beauty of landscape, 168, 175
    camping in, 176–177
    coal mines, 169
    fishing in, 186
    as obstacle to transportation, 11
    photographs of, 176, 190–191
    as tourist attraction, 99, 172–173, 174
Bell for Adano, A (Hersey), 137
Bell Telephone, 63, 66
Bicentennial, U.S., 218–219
Big Nose, Max, 104
Big Timber (Montana), 204, 205, 277n93

Billings, Frederick, 6–7, 68
Billings (Montana)
    cowboy statue, 108
    law enforcement, 29
    proximity to Red Lodge, 168
    rodeo, 114
Billings Mutual Telephone Company, 66–67
Biological racism, 152–154
Bird, Isabella L., 174
Bird Hat, Sampson, 103
Bird-in-Ground, Sam, 102
Blackfeet Indians, 22
Blazina, Edward, 249n48
Blazina, Steve, 81
Blewett, Mary H., 227–228
Boone, Daniel, 34
Boone and Crockett Club, 34
Boosters. *See* Entrepreneurs
Borne, Lawrence R., 109
Boston, 228
Bowlen, Charles, 9
Boyer, M. Christine, 224–225
Boy Scouts, 173
Bracey, J. E., 48
British ethnicity, 150–151, 253n97
Brokedown Palace Project (BPP), 202–203,
    276n89
Brothels, 9, 28, 31–32, 55, 84. *See also*
    Prostitutes
Budas, Albert, 76, 77
Buening, Vera, 165
Buffalo Bill's Wild West shows, 20
    audience, 20, 21
    cowboys, 13, 95, 117
    cowgirls, 110
    imagery, 33, 91
    images of Indians, 22, 23, 104
    influence on rodeo, 95
    See also Cody, William "Buffalo Bill"
Buildings, in Red Lodge
    downtown district, 7–8
    effects of tourist economy, 194–196
    historic designation, 215, 220–221
    industrial materials, 50–51
    restoration, 215, 222–224, 225
    styles of early, 50–51, 52, 215, 222, 223, 225
    western architecture, 100, 123
    Wild West facades, xviii, 99–100, 215, 222,
        223, 225
Businesses
    in 1890s Red Lodge, 9
    of immigrants, 56, 60
    tourist economy, 90, 172–173, 181, 193–194
    See also Corporations; Entrepreneurs

Busy Bee Café, 194
Butler, Anne M., 32
Butte (Montana)
    attacks on Wobblies, 78–79, 80
    ethnic groups, 145

Calamity Jane, 90, 110, 113, 114
California, immigrant population, 59
Camp Beartooth, 180
Campfire Club, 173
Camping, 173, 176–177, 178. *See also* Nature
    tourism
Camp Sawtooth, 94, 180, 264n82
Camp Senia, 94, 100, 180, 264n82
Capital, 6–7, 8, 9–10, 14–15, 41
Carbon County (Montana)
    farming in, 16, 19, 243n68
    government stationery, 47
    landscape, 175
    name, 41
    pioneer society, 114
    ranches, 115–116
    Red Lodge as county seat, 29
Carbon County High School, 176, 189
Carbon County Historical Society
    formation, 218, 220
    historic preservation programs, 221–222
    items donated to, 230
    museum, 213, 214–215, 220, 226, 230
    revitalization plan, 221–222, 225
Carbon County News, 138, 155–156, 205
Carbon County Red Cross auxiliaries, 83,
    258n29
Carbon County Republican, 63, 106
Carpenters and Joiners Union, 66
Cattle companies. *See* Ranchers
Cattleman's Association, 203
Chain migration, 59–60
Chapman, John, 52
Chapman-Meyer Bank, 67
Cheyenne (Wyoming), 24
Chicago
    Columbian Exposition, 104
    Haymarket Riot, 16, 44
Chicago Advertising Club, 125
Children in immigrant families, 56
Chinese immigrants, 63, 153, 251n71
Choirs. *See* Musical groups
Civilian Conservation Corps (CCC), 184–185
Class
    American attitudes toward, 157–158
    fears based on, 16
    ignored in local history, 157, 158–159, 162,
        225–226, 227–228

in Red Lodge, 8, 63, 158–162, 225–226
tourism and, 191–192
upward mobility, 157–158
in Wild West mythology, 21
See also Entrepreneurs; Middle class;
    Neighborhoods; Workers
Clayton, John, 209, 234
Clothing
cowboy, xvii, 88–89, 91, 117
cowgirl, 109–110
of dude ranch guests, 94, 118, 264n82
ethnic costumes, 134–136, 143, 163, 164
fashion, 118, 134
of immigrants, 134, 161
Indian costumes for tourist
    performances, 103, 154
middle-class standards, 30
modern, 119–120
"Mother Hubbard" dresses, 30, 244n85
sold to tourists, 118, 210–211
western worn by residents, 89, 97,
    116–120, 122, 135, 155
women's, 30, 244n85
Coal Metropolis, 12, 42, 170
Coal Miners' Park, 215, 226
Coal mines in Red Lodge
accidents, 48, 55, 57–58, 67, 69, 171, 249n48
closings, 84, 86–87, 89–90, 92–93
creation by railroad, 6, 7
dominance of local economy, 14–15
East Side Mine, 49–50, 60, 86, 131
economic impact, 28, 39, 41
importance in daily life, 40, 43
locations, 49–50
managers, 7, 8, 61, 68, 85, 153, 160
monument to, 73
output, 41, 45
as part of natural world, 170–171
physical reminders of, 87, 195, 226–227
pollution caused by, 41, 195, 196, 236
sounds of operation, 53–55
strikes, 73, 84, 85–86, 171
unionized workers, 63–64, 68
West Side Mine, 40, 49–50, 60, 86, 92–93
See also Miners; Northwestern
    Improvement Company; Rocky Fork
    Coal Company
Coal mining
in Beartooth Range, 169
competition from other energy sources,
    73
eight-hour day, 252n87
immigrant workers, 59
labor tensions, 44, 67

machinery, 44, 172
in national forests, 205
operators, 44
preservation of buildings, 226
safety, 44, 57–58, 67, 69, 171
strip mines, 86, 172
unions, 44, 63–64, 65, 67, 69–70, 153, 160
Coal mining, in Red Lodge public identity,
    40–41, 43
as Coal Metropolis, 12, 42, 170
diminished importance, 84, 86–87
images of miners, 45–48, 215–217
media depictions, 45–48
memories of residents, 91–92, 235–236,
    237
physical appearance of town, 49–53
physical reminders of past, 92
in prosperous times, 72, 74
rejection of, 90
renewed interest, 215, 217, 223, 225–226,
    236–237
restored buildings, 223
Coal slack piles
creation of, 41
after mine closings, 87, 195
removal of, 226–227, 235, 238
symbolism, 235–236
Coats, Dan, 229
Cody, William "Buffalo Bill," 36–37, 96. See
    also Buffalo Bill's Wild West shows
Cody (Wyoming), 96, 100, 212–214, 264n85
Coeur d'Alene (Idaho), strikes, 44, 48
Cohen, Erik, 145
Cold war, 139, 146, 157
Collective identity, xiv, xv–xvi
Colorado, mining in, 44, 59, 67, 254n99
Colstrip (Montana), 86, 172
Columbian Exposition, 104
Columbus, D. W., 196, 197
Committee for Reburial of Liver-Eating
    Johnston, 212
Communism, 139, 146, 157
Community Fine Arts Festival, 132, 133–134
Congress, U.S.
hearings on wilderness area, 203
historic preservation laws, 221, 226
Wilderness Act, 201
Conservation Fund, 234
Conzen, Kathleen Neils, 149–150
Cornelio, J. N. "Buck," 194
Corporations
control of resort towns, xix
power, 14–15, 42
Costumes. See Clothing

Coulsten. *See* Billings (Montana)
Cowboys
    association with rodeo, 32, 106–109, 116
    attraction of life, 108
    clothing, 88–89, 91, 117
    drawl, 123–125
    easterners, 24, 114–115
    as heroes of Wild West, 13, 29, 32, 38–39
    idealized, 91, 101–102, 106–109
    Indian, 102
    in movies and novels, 107, 109, 110, 117, 125
    negative views in Red Lodge, 5, 19–20, 27
    novels read by, 107–108, 263n54
    ranchers seen as, 112–114
    real, 28–29, 32, 107, 108
    representations in rodeo, 101–102
    social control of, 27, 29–30, 32
    statues, 108
    strikes, 263n55
    symbolism, 3, 4, 91, 107
    wildness, 5, 27, 28–29, 108
Cowgirls, 109–110
Crawford, Jack, 37
Crime, 28, 29, 30
Cripple Creek (Colorado), 59, 67, 254n99
Croatian immigrants, 62, 151–152. *See also*
    Slavic immigrants
Crockett, Davy, 34
Cronon, William, 169
Croonquist, Al, 94, 100, 123, 260n12, 264n82
Crow Indian Reservation
    boundary changes, 6–7, 11, 19, 25–26, 155
    cattle and horses on, 102
    federal control, 11
Crow Indians
    alliance with United States, 23
    barter with white settlers, 23
    costumes, 103
    cowboys, 102
    disappearance from Red Lodge, 106, 155
    fear and hostility toward, 22–24, 26
    lands of, 11, 16–17, 19, 22, 23, 25
    performances in Red Lodge, 92, 97, 103,
        105, 154, 262n43
    racism toward, 155–157
    in Red Lodge, 24, 63
    relations with ranchers, 25–26
    rodeo participants, 97, 102–103, 105,
        261n40
    tensions with settlers, 23
Custer Battlefield, 22
Custer National Forest
    forestry management plans, 206
    oil drilling in, 209

    roadless areas, 176
    ski area in, 206–210
    visitors, 193

Dakotas, 24, 59
Dams, 185, 186, 201
Dancing. *See* Folk dancing
Davis, Roger S., 141, 142, 155–156
Dawes Allotment Act, 19, 25
Dawson, Jim, 109
Deloria, Philip, 103–104
Democracy, 3, 24
Depression, 184
Desert Land Act, 25
DeVoto, Bernard, 123–125, 201
Dilworth, J. R., 25
Dilworth Cattle Company, 25, 102
Dinosaur National Monument, 201
Disney, Walt, 231
Disneyfication, 224–225, 228
Disneyland, 224–225, 231
Dogs, regulation of, 31, 245n89
Downtown Red Lodge
    creation of district, 7–8
    as historic district, 215, 221–223, 229
    layout, 50
    revitalization, 215, 217, 222–224, 225, 229,
        231
    See also Buildings, in Red Lodge
Dude Ranchers' Association, 96, 260n12
Dude ranches
    association with Wild West mythology, 91
    buildings, 94, 105–106
    clothing for, 94, 118, 264n82
    economic impact, 94
    growth in 1920s, 93–95
    guests, 94, 180
    idealized version of West, 93–94, 109
    Indian associations, 105–106
    popularity, 93
    near Red Lodge, 94, 100, 180, 200, 264n82
    in Red Lodge identity, 179–181
    use of wilderness areas, 200, 275n82
    workers, 109, 121, 179–180
Dude wranglers, 109, 121, 179–180
Dutch Tulip Festival (Holland, Michigan),
    142

East Side Mine, 49–50, 60, 86, 131
Echo Park, 201
Economy, of Red Lodge
    crises in 1940s, 138
    development plans, 87
    effects of mine closings, 90, 138, 191

efforts to survive, 131, 138, 139–140, 191
historic preservation and, 221–222
impact of rodeo, 96–99
prosperity of early twentieth century, 39, 72
role of farmers, 15
role of mines, 14–15, 28, 39, 41
tourist economy, 89–90, 172–173, 181, 191, 193–194, 204–205, 210–211
See also Businesses
Edgar, Bob, 212, 213
Emerson, Ralph Waldo, 185
English immigrants, 150–151
Entrepreneurs
civic roles, 10
middle class morality, 28, 29, 30–31
negative views of Wild West, 21–22
promotion of growth, 8–10, 27, 43
relations with large companies, 14–15
self-image as pioneers, 17–19
small, 68
successful, 39
Environmentalists, 203, 206
Ethnic festivals, 140–141
in 1930s, 83, 132–136, 191
symbolic ethnicity in, 164
See also Festival of Nations
Ethnicity
attitudes in United States, 136, 137
evolution of categories, 150–151
meaning of, 147–149
melting pot image, 166
pluralism, 130–131, 132–133, 137–138, 146–147, 166, 167
relationship to race, 152–154
static, 147–149, 162, 166
symbolic, 164–166
See also Public ethnicity
Europe
interest in Wild West, 20
national identities, 149
See also Immigrants
Evans, Dale, 110

Fairgrieve, Alex, 65–66
Farmers
conflicts with ranchers, 13, 22, 25
as democratic symbols, 3
dry-land farming techniques, 42, 243n68
economic problems, 4
irrigation, 39, 186
mythology of agrarian west, 4, 5, 12–14, 16, 17, 42
pioneer image, 17

preference of Red Lodge boosters for, 13, 14–17, 45
rural history, 219
technology used, 42
Federal government
control of Indian reservations, 6–7, 11, 19
environmental regulations, 210
highway funding, 182
historic preservation programs, 219, 221
housing rehabilitation funding, 203
land opened up to farming, 16–17, 19
national forests, 11, 199, 201, 205, 209
as obstacle to transportation, 11
presence in Red Lodge area, 2, 11, 27, 42
projects funded by, 140
role in West, 42
See also Congress, U.S.
Festival of Nations
Americanism of, 146–147
authenticity, 148–149
background, 83, 137, 140
Beartooth Highway on backdrops, 189, 191
costumes, 143, 163
ethnic groups involved, 127, 128–130, 147, 150–152
first year, 127–128, 141–142, 191
flags displayed, 147
goals, 128, 136, 141–142
histories of, 158–159
interpretation of local history, 128–130, 136–137, 147, 157, 158, 162
message, 136–137, 146, 158, 163, 166–167
Montana Day, 127, 154–155, 165
organizers, 141–142, 268n46
publicity, 143–144, 145, 270n89
representations of ethnicity, 129, 166–167
resident participation, 163–164, 165–166
schedule, 143
success, 145–146, 162
as tourist attraction, 128, 142–143, 145, 162
Festivals
ethnic, 83, 132–136, 164, 191
fine arts, 132, 133–134
Fiction. *See* Novels
Fields of care, xix
Films. *See* Movies
Finland, 49, 78, 257n14
Finnish immigrants
Americanism, 77–78, 81–83
choirs, 134
clothing, 161
Festival of Nations activities, 127
miners, 59, 60, 69

Finnish immigrants, *continued*
  national identities, 149
  neighborhood, 58, 60, 65
  newspaper stories for, 49
  picnics, 177
  radicals, 71, 79–81, 85, 133, 257n19
  Red Cross auxiliary, 83, 258n29
  saunas, 56, 81
  wedding parades, 62
  Workers' Hall, 65, 80, 82, 252n80
Finnish Orchestra, 132
Fishing, 177, 186
Flags, 147
Flash's Studio, 189
Fleming, Kathryn, 61
Fleming, Roger, 61
Folk dancing, 133, 140, 163, 164, 165, 267n20
Ford, Henry, xiv, 166
Ford Motor Company, 229
Forests
  increased access to, 183
  management plans, 206
  national, 11, 199, 201, 205, 209
  primitive areas, 199, 201
  Yellowstone Forest Preserve, 175–176
  See also Custer National Forest
Forest Service. *See* National Forest Service
Fort Dodge (Iowa), xviii
Fortune, 157
Fourth of July, 73, 76, 92, 96, 103
Fox, J. M., 7, 8
Fox, Maurice, 61
Francavigilia, Richard V., 231
Fraternal Order of Eagles, 125
Frontier. *See* West
Frontier scouts. *See* Mountain men

Gallagher, Billa, 28–29, 30
Gambling, 28, 71
Gans, Herbert J., 164
Gender
  composition of Red Lodge population, 55
  male domination of public life, 55–56
  See also Masculinity; Women
Germany, interest in Wild West, 20
Gerstle, Gary, 82
Glancy, William, 85, 249n48
Golf, 123
Grand Coulee Dam, 185
Greenough, Alice, 97, 109–110, 111
Greenough, Ben, 90, 112–114, 116, 145
Greenough, Bill, 109, 123
Greenough, Marge, 109–110, 111
Greenough, Myrtle, 113

Greenough, Turk, 109, 110, 111, 121–122
Greenough family, 109–110, 111, 114, 116
Grey, Zane, 107
Grizzly Peak ski area. *See* Red Lodge
  Mountain

Haggarty, William, 85
Haley, Alex, 219
Hamer, David, 225
Hannaford, J. M., 72
Happy Brothers Camping Ground, 177
Harboldt, Mildred Chesarek, 253n97
Harley's Cottage Motel, 194
Harriman, W. Averell, xix
Hart, William S., 108
Hauser, Samuel T., 6–7, 8, 9, 68
Haymarket Riot, 16, 44
Hays, Samuel P., 201
Henry, Frank, 67
Heritage
  creation of, xx, 227
  distinction from history, xx
Hersey, John, 137, 138
Hi Bug neighborhood
  class of residents, 61, 159, 225–226
  as historic district, 215, 221, 223
  household workers, 56, 161
  houses, 51–52
  Irish residents, 61
  location, 50
Hickok, Wild Bill, 20
Higham, John, 77
Highways
  construction, 182–183, 184–185
  in West, 181–183, 184–185
  in wilderness, 200
  See also Beartooth Highway
Hill, Andrew, 58
Historic preservation movement, 217,
  224–225, 226, 228
History
  American interest in, 218–220, 228
  distinction from heritage, xx
  idealization of past, 227–228
  of rural areas, 219
  as tourist attraction, 221, 228–229
  See also Local history
Holidays
  celebrated by immigrants, 62
  Fourth of July, 73, 76, 92, 96, 103
  Labor Day, 47, 63, 65–66, 69, 76
Holland (Michigan), Dutch Tulip Festival,
  142
Homestead Acts, 16–17, 25

Homestead Strike, 16, 44
Hoopes, Gene, 109
Hospital, in Red Lodge, 140, 268n42
Housing and Urban Development,
    Department of, 203
Housing in Red Lodge
    boardinghouses, 53, 54, 55, 60
    federal funding, 203
    new construction, 232, 234
    prices, 138, 161–162, 232
    seasonal, 276n89
    of upper- and middle-class residents, 7,
        50, 51–52, 100, 225–226
    Wild West styles, 100
    of workers, 18, 50, 53, 55
Hunting
    by easterners, 33–35, 174, 178–179
    guides, 178–179
    in Red Lodge area, 178–179, 186
    Roosevelt on benefits of, 33–34
    See also Mountain men
Huovinen, Paavo, 155

Identity
    collective, xiv, xv–xvi
    individual, xiii–xiv
    multiple, xiii–xiv, 102
    national, 62
    public, xiv–xv, xix
    theories of, xiii–xiv
    See also Ethnicity; Public identity of Red
        Lodge; Western identity
Ignatiev, Noel, 153
Images
    of cowboys, 120, 125
    of miners, 45–48, 158, 215–217, 226
    of mountain men, 33–37
    in public identities, xiv–xv, xix
    in western identity, xvi–xvii, 3, 89, 125–126
Immigrant miners
    descendants, 18–19
    discrimination against, 59, 69
    ethnic origins, 153–154, 160
    families, 40, 53, 56
    motives for going west, 8
    radicals, 43–44
    recruitment of, 59, 68
    unity in union, 160
    in West, 59
    See also Miners
Immigrants
    American attitudes toward, 166
    chain migration, 59–60
    criticism of, 75–76, 130

European, 152–154, 167
    legal restrictions, 130, 153
    pluralism in United States, 130–131,
        132–133, 137–138, 166, 167
    racial classifications, 59, 63, 152–153
Immigrants in Red Lodge
    Americanism, 76, 77–78, 81–83
    Chinese, 63, 153, 251n71
    class distinctions from natives, 160, 161
    clothing, 134, 161
    criticism of, 75–76
    descendants, 18–19, 164–166
    diversity, 58–59, 130, 140, 167
    effects of World War I, 82–84
    ethnic and national identities, 62,
        149–150, 158–159
    European backgrounds, 62–63
    holidays and festivals, 62
    interpretations of history, 128–130, 140,
        226
    musical groups, 62, 132, 133–134
    neighborhoods, 58, 60, 82
    newspaper readers, 49
    proportion of population, 130, 154, 163
    in Red Lodge identity, 40–41, 58–59, 72,
        131
    unity, 129–130, 131, 136–137, 140–141, 152,
        159
    western clothing worn by, 88, 154, 155
    women, 56, 161, 226
    See also Finnish immigrants; Irish immi-
        grants; Italian immigrants; Public
        ethnicity; Slavic immigrants
Indians
    atrocities against, 22
    blamed for Red Lodge's problems in
        1890s, 19–20, 21–24
    costumes for tourist performances, 103,
        154
    cowboys, 102
    fear and hostility toward, 22–24, 26
    glamorization of, 32, 101–102
    images of, 22, 23
    multiple identities, 102
    mythology of, 103–105
    performances for tourists, 90, 103–105
    racist attitudes toward, 26, 155–157
    rodeo participants, 261n38
    white domination of, 21
    See also Crow Indians
Industrialization
    building materials, 50–51
    contrast with agrarianism, 14
    contrast with nature, 173

Industrialization, *continued*
  effects on West, 42
  interest in history of, 214–218, 219, 226,
    227–228
  in nature, 188
Industrial Workers of the World (IWW),
  70–72, 78–80, 85, 133, 255n111,
  257n19
Inland Forest Resource Council, 204
Irish immigrants
  Americanism, 76
  Festival of Nations activities, 151
  grouped into British ethnicity, 150–151
  miners, 60–62
  neighborhoods, 61
  social status, 60–62, 249n49
  union leaders, 253n97
Iron buildings, 50
Italian Girls Victory Club, xx, 83, 131, 132
Italian immigrants
  Americanism, 76, 77–78, 82
  clothing, 161
  differences among, 149
  Festival of Nations activities, 127–128
  miners, 60
  miners' families, 40
  neighborhoods, 60
  Red Cross auxiliary, 83, 258n29
  women, 56, 226

Jackson, Helen Hunt, 174
Jackson, Kaisa Kreeta, 80
Jail, Red Lodge, 30
James, Jesse, 3
Jarussi, Lillian, 40, 56
Jarussi, Loretta, 40, 236, 238
Jefferson, Thomas, 14, 16
Jeremiah Johnson, 212, 245n105
Jewish residents, 265n2
J. H. Conrad Company, 9
Johnson, Esther, 180
Johnson, F. I., 264n82
Johnson, John "Liver-Eating"
  association with Red Lodge, 35
  books on, 245n105
  cabin, 213, 215
  as constable, 29, 30
  Greenough and, 113, 114
  Indians killed by, 36, 245n106
  as mountain man, 36, 37, 178
  movie based on life, 212, 245n105
  nickname, 36
  reburial of remains, 212–214, 220, 229
  in Red Lodge, 29, 30, 37

  spelling of name, 245n105
  stories about, 90
Jurkovich, Rose, 161, 249n48

Kahn, Ben, 256n10
Kainu, Olavi, 155
Kaleva Cooperative Mercantile, 62, 65, 75,
  252n80
Kalevan Ritarit Society, 62
Kallio, Ida, 56
Kallio, Senia, 81, 193
Kastelitz, John, 160
Kelley, George W., 201
Kelly, Yellowstone, 36–37
Kinser, Karen, 209, 231
Kivistokoski, Anton, 48
Knights of Labor, 63
Koski, Emile, 80–81, 82
Kuhlman, Erika, 69
Kuralt, Charles, 229, 277n101

Labor. *See* Unions; Workers
Labor Day celebrations
  Americanism in, 76
  early, 63, 65–66, 69
  images of miners, 47
Labor Temple, 65, 69, 97, 215, 226, 252n79
Lampi, John, 141
Lampi, Leona, 158–159
Landscape. *See* Nature
Law enforcement, 28, 29, 30, 31
Leadville (Colorado), 44
Lears, T. J. Jackson, 34, 44
Leavenworth (Washington), xviii
LeCompte, Mary Lou, 109
Leopold, Aldo, 199, 201
Lewis, John L., 86, 259n39
Liberty Committees, 77, 78–81, 85, 256n12,
  257n20, 258n35
Life, 157
Limerick, Patricia Nelson, 155
Lincoln, Abraham, xiv
Lindquist, Jacob, 80
Lipsitz, George, 152
Little, Frank, 78–79, 80
Littlefield, Marcella, 105, 180
Local history
  accuracy, 223, 225
  class ignored in, 157, 158–159, 162, 225–226,
    227–228
  interest in, 214–218, 219, 220
  interpreted in Festival of Nations,
    128–130, 136–137, 147, 157, 158, 162
  of Red Lodge, 220, 229–230

Local residents, xx–xxi
Lockhart, Caroline, 109
Lowell (Massachusetts), 219
Lowenthal, David, xx, 227
Ludlow massacre, 67
Lumber companies, 59
Lyons, Les, 196, 197

MacCannell, Dean, 135
MacFarland, Rose Naglich, 249n48
Mackay, Malcolm, 35, 36, 112, 113, 114–115
Mackay, William R., Jr., 203
Madsen, Michael, 209
Magnusson, Carl, 185
Main Street, U.S.A. (Disneyland), 225, 231
Main Street Project, 222
Maki, Nestor, 58
Maki, Sue, 165
Mallin, Alice, 235–236, 238
Mallin, Richard, 235–236, 237, 249n48, 253n97
Marceline (Missouri), 231
Marias massacre, 22, 243n51
Marlboro Man, 112
Marshall, Bob, 199
Marttunen, Mikko, 68, 86, 250n64
Marx, Leo, 14
Masculinity
    of public life, 55–56
    represented by mountain men, 5, 33, 35,
        36
    of West, 34, 35, 37
    See also Gender
May, Karl, 20
McAllister, James, 57
McCarthyism, 139
McCorkle, Daniel S., 85
McDonald, Daniel, 171, 172
McWilliams, Carey, 107–108
Meinig, D. W., 230
Mellinger, Phil, 71
Memories, collective, xv–xvi
Men. See Gender; Masculinity
Mesker Brothers Iron Works, 50
Mexican immigrants, 154
Meyer, William F., 52, 67, 253n88
Michelcic, Leo, 171
Middle class
    clothing, 30
    morality, 27, 28, 29, 30–31, 46–48
    neighborhoods, 161–162
    in Red Lodge, 8–9
    in United States, 157
    See also Entrepreneurs
Miles, Frank, 36–37

Miners
    attitudes toward nature, 171–172
    class sense, 159–160
    deaths, 48, 57–58
    disembodiment, 45–46, 48
    drunkenness, 30–31
    economic status, 53
    end of work shift, 40
    English speakers, 69
    gender, 55
    housing, 53
    imagery of, 45–48, 158, 215–217, 226
    importance in Red Lodge, 43
    injuries, 57, 58, 67, 249n48
    jobs lost, 86, 138, 191, 202
    physical effects of work, 56–57
    pride, 171–172
    proportion of adult male population, 41,
        170
    recreational activities, 177
    relations with management, 160
    rules for, 30–31
    skills and knowledge, 171
    social control of, 44–45, 46–48, 55
    uncertainty of work, 53, 54–55
    wages, 41, 57, 84, 85
    as yeoman workers, 47
    See also Coal mines in Red Lodge;
        Immigrant miners; Unions
Mix, Tom, 117
Modernity
    tension with myths of Old West, 121,
        122–123
    in West, 10, 41, 42, 49, 88, 122
    See also Industrialization
Montana
    coal fields, 6
    dude ranches, 93, 94
    historic attractions, 228
    Historic Preservation Office, 224
    immigrant population, 59
    Liberty Committees, 78–79
    progressive movement, 252n87
Montana Day, Festival of Nations, 127,
    154–155, 165
Montana Historical Conference, 220
Montana Sedition Act, 256n10
Montana Society of Pioneers, 242n38
Montana-Wyoming Cowboys' Association,
    114
Montenegrin immigrants, 151–152. See also
    Slavic immigrants
Moses, L. G., 104
"Mother Hubbard" dresses, 30, 244n85

Mountain men, 5, 33–37, 38. *See also* Johnson, John "Liver-Eating"
Movies
  based on life of Liver-Eating Johnson, 212, 245n105
  cowboy heroes, 107, 109, 110, 117, 125
  ethnic pluralism in, 130
  rodeo riders in, 110
  war, 137
  Westerns, 13, 89, 262n53
Musical groups, ethnic, 62, 132, 133–134, 164, 165
Mythic spaces, 91

Nash, Michael, 70
National forests. *See* Forests
National Forest Service, 185, 187, 199, 203, 206, 209, 210
National Historic Preservation Act, 221, 226
National parks, 173, 182. *See also* Yellowstone National Park
National Park Service, 185, 187
National Register of Historic Places, 215, 220–221
National Trust, 221, 222
Native Americans. *See* Crow Indians; Indians
Natural gas, 206
Nature
  American attitudes toward, 173–174, 177–178, 183–184, 197–202
  animals in, 185–186, 197
  beauty of, 168, 174–175
  improved by humans, 184, 185, 186, 187, 208–209
  interest in living close to, 197, 202–203, 209
  machinery in, 188, 198, 199–202, 208–210
  meaning of, 169–170
  miners' views of, 171–172
  as obstacle to growth of Red Lodge, 10–11
  preservation efforts, 173–174
  recreational activities, 172–173, 176–178, 185, 199, 210–211
  Romantic view of, 173, 174
  separation from modern life, 178
  surroundings of Red Lodge, 10–11, 168, 173, 174
  See also Wilderness
Nature, in Red Lodge identity, 168–170
  dude ranching, 179–181, 200
  effects of automobile travel, 181
  hunting, 178–179, 186
  new residents attracted, 197, 202–203, 206, 209, 217

photographs of scenery, 176
physical appearance of town, 195
role of Beartooth Highway, 169, 183, 189
tourist economy, 172–173, 191, 210–211
zoo, 196–197
Nature tourism, 170, 172–173, 174–176, 181, 191–192, 210–211
Nature writing, 174
Neighborhoods
  ethnic, 58, 60, 65, 82
  middle-class, 161–162
  working-class, 53, 55
  See also Hi Bug neighborhood; Housing in Red Lodge
Neolocals, 202, 209
New Deal, 184
New England, industrial museums, 219, 227–228
Newspapers
  competition among, 48–49
  images of miners, 48
  immigrant readers, 49
  public identity communicated by, xix–xx
  support of unions, 49
  workers, 63
  See also Red Lodge *Picket;* Red Lodge *Picket-Journal*
New York City
  rodeos, 114
  South Street Seaport, 224
Nordstrom, Edward, 180
North Dakota. *See* Dakotas
Northern Pacific Railroad (NPRR)
  cleaning of Red Lodge, 210
  coal fields, 6, 68, 86, 172
  creation of Red Lodge, xvii, 6
  magazine, 46–47, 158
  Red Lodge's dependence on, 10, 11
  support of Liberty Committee, 85
  tourism promotion, 175
  unions and, 226
Northwestern Improvement Company (NWIC)
  closed mines, 86, 89–90, 92–93, 226
  East Side Mine, 49–50, 60, 86, 131
  effects of World War I, 84
  mine accidents, 58, 67
  strikes against, 86
  unionized workers, 63, 70, 84
  wages, 57
  West Side Mine, 40, 49–50, 60, 86, 92–93
  workers, 41, 60
  See also Coal mines in Red Lodge
Northwest Magazine, 46–47, 158

Novels
  cowboy heroes, 29, 107, 117, 125
  dude wrangler heroes, 109
  read by cowboys, 107–108, 263n54
  Western, 21, 89, 107–108, 242n47, 262n53

Oakley, Annie, 110
O'Connor, William, 61
Oil drilling in national forests, 205, 206, 209
Old Elk, Dan, 102
Ollila, Jack, 80
O'Shea, Daniel, 61, 153
Owens, Harry J., 213, 220, 228–229, 245n105

Paepcke, Walter, xix
Panic of 1893, 19, 75
Park City (Utah), xix
Parks, national. See National parks
Pastoralism. See Farmers
Patriotism
  of immigrants, 81
  promotion of, xv
  in Red Lodge, 76
  during World War II, 136
  See also Americanism
Persha, Tony, 160, 171, 259n39
Pete's Riverside Restaurant Club, 189
Phillips Petroleum, 206
Photography
  of Beartooth Highway, 189
  of Beartooth Range, 176, 190–191
  by tourists, 177
Picnics, 177
Pioneers, 17–19, 114, 242n38
Polish immigrants, 149
Politicians, 67, 71, 253n88
Pollard Hotel, 222. See also Spofford Hotel
Pollution from coal mining, 41, 195, 196, 236
Pomeroy, Earl, 174, 178
Population of Red Lodge
  in 1890s, 2, 7, 12
  in 1910, 50
  in 1920s, 128
  in 1950s, 128, 138
  declines, 128, 138, 202
  gender composition, 55
  median age, 202
  new residents in late twentieth century,
    197, 202–203, 206, 209, 230, 231,
    232–235
Post office, 234
Potter, Fred, 79, 85, 258n35
Progress, mythology of, 14
Progressive movement, 252n87

Prostitutes, 30, 31–32, 63, 84, 251n71. See also
  Brothels
Public ethnicity
  American context, 132–133
  cleaned up versions, 129, 133, 147, 151–152,
    162
  costumes, 134–136, 143, 163, 164
  decline in expressions of, 163–164
  effects of World War I, 82–84
  folk dancing, 133, 140, 163, 164, 165, 267n20
  performances, 135–136
  in Red Lodge identity, 129, 131, 132–133,
    136–137, 143–145, 166–167
  safe displays of, 131–132
  as tourist attraction, 131, 135, 136, 142
  See also Ethnicity; Festival of Nations
Public identities
  development of, xv, xix
  of groups, xiv
  images projected, xiv–xv, xix
Public identity of Red Lodge
  American identity, 162
  attraction of investment, 10, 12, 36
  attraction of new residents in 1890s, 12, 18
  Beartooth Highway in, 169, 183, 189
  changes in, xvii–xviii, 37–39, 84, 169,
    210–211, 213–214, 217, 238
  class differences ignored, 129, 162, 225–226
  communicated by local newspapers,
    xix–xx
  cowboy imagery, 120, 125
  development of, 37–38
  in 1890s, 4–5, 12
  ethnicity in, 128–130, 131, 132–133, 136–137,
    143–145, 166–167
  fading of ethnic differences, 162–163
  Festival of Nations in, 128–130
  idealization of past, 225–226, 227
  immigrant workers in, 40–41, 58–59, 72,
    131
  Indian symbols, 24, 101, 105–106, 155–156
  individual memories and, 235–236, 237
  as industrial town, 40–41, 43
  influence of tourism, xix, 237
  interpretations of history, xv
  mountain men in, 5, 33–37, 38
  multiple aspects, 42–43, 229, 237–238
  residents' participation in, xx
  ski area in, 207–208
  as small town, 231–235
  tension with actual physical world of
    town, 41–42, 43–45
  Wild West elements in 1890s, 33, 34–35,
    37, 38–39

Public identity of Red Lodge, *continued*
  Wild West image for tourism, 89, 90–91,
    92–93, 96, 99, 123
  workers in, 65
  See also Coal mining, in Red Lodge public
    identity; Nature, in Red Lodge identity
Puumala, Nestor, 58

Race
  attitudes toward non-whites, 26, 63
  classifications of immigrants as non-
    white, 59, 63, 152–153
  fears based on, 16
  relationship to ethnicity, 152–154
  white dominance of Red Lodge, 62–63,
    106, 153–154, 251n75, 270n81
  white domination of West, 4, 13, 21
  See also African Americans
Racism, 26, 152–154, 155–157
Radiola, 120–121
Railroads
  monopolies, 11
  to Red Lodge, 7, 11
  strikes, 44
  See also Northern Pacific Railroad
    (NPRR)
Rainier, Mount, 174
Ralston, Lucile, 141, 142
Ranchers
  alliances with Crow Indians, 25–26
  as capitalists, 112
  clothing, 88–89
  conflicts with farmers, 13, 22, 25
  connections to industrial economy, 42
  heritage of, 115–116
  land claims, 25
  mythology of, 24
  negative views in Red Lodge, 19–20,
    21–22, 24–27
  positive views of, 38–39
  power, 27
  as symbol of western identity, 88–89, 101,
    112–113, 116
  See also Dude ranches
Rand, Sally, 110
Red Cross. *See* Carbon County Red Cross
  auxiliaries
Redford, Robert, 212, 213
Red Lodge (Montana)
  bird's-eye view, 49–50
  civic center, 140, 155
  cleanup, 194–196, 210, 236–237
  climate and geography, 168
  growth in 1890s, 7–8, 28–29

incorporation, 29
lack of westernness in 1890s, 1
local government, 27, 29, 31, 32
location, 2, 10–11, 68, 175–176
master plan, 233
name of town, 24, 105, 106
origins, xvii, 6–7
street names, 7
townscape, 49–53
western characteristics, xvii, 10
See also Economy of Red Lodge;
  Population of Red Lodge; Public
  identity of Red Lodge
Red Lodge Board of Trade, 66
Red Lodge Cafe, 125, 138, 189
Red Lodge Chamber of Commerce, xx, 120,
  139, 195, 207, 208, 229
Red Lodge Coal Company (restaurant), 210
Red Lodge Historical Study Group, 220
Red Lodge Ladies' Glee Club, 132
Red Lodge Miners Union, 66
Red Lodge Mountain (RLM), 206–210
Red Lodge *Picket*, 16, 18
  on Americanism, 75–76
  descriptions of natural beauty, 175
  immigrant readers, 49
  on law enforcement, 31
  mine accident stories, 48
  on miners, 45, 47
  need for local government, 29
  views of Indians, 26
  on women's clothing, 30
Red Lodge *Picket-Journal*, 53–55, 96–97,
  121–122
Red Lodge Rod and Gun Club, 186
Red Lodge Rodeo Association, 99, 112, 115, 123
Red Lodge Woman's Club, xx, 61, 132, 133–134,
  195, 210
Remington, Frederic, 102, 115, 153, 154
Republican, 48
Republican Picket, 49
Richel Lodge, 105–106, 180
Riders of the Purple Sage (Grey), 107
Riding Greenoughs, 109–110, 111, 114, 116
Riis, Jacob, 152–153
Rinehart, Mary Roberts, 109, 174
RLM. *See* Red Lodge Mountain
Roads. *See* Highways
Rock Creek, 41, 177, 178
Rockefeller, John D., 67
Rockford (Illinois), 157–158
Rocky Fork Coal Company
  area around mine, 18
  customers, 195

economic power, 14–15
ethnicities of miners, 153
managers, 7, 8, 61, 153
rules, 30–31
unionized workers, 64
wages, 57
See also Coal mines in Red Lodge;
    Northwestern Improvement
    Company
Rocky Fork Railway, 7, 11, 14–15
Rocky Fork Town and Electric Company
    (RFT&EC), 7, 222
Rocky Mountain Bell Telephone Company,
    66
Rocky Mountains
    descriptions of, 174
    expeditions into, 179
    roads in, 181
    See also Beartooth Range
Rodeo, Red Lodge
    baseball games, 103
    Beartooth Highway associated with, 189,
        190–191
    cowboys as heroes, 32, 106–111, 116
    creation of, 96–97
    economic impact, 96–99
    Indian participants, 97, 102–103, 105,
        261n40
    locals in Western clothing, 97, 119, 122, 135
    modern elements, 122–123
    promotion of, 113, 120, 121–122, 123
    success, 97, 99
    western imagery, 99, 101–102
Rodeo riders, 109–111, 117
Rodeos
    association with Wild West mythology,
        91, 95
    development of, 95
    female participants, 95, 97, 109–110,
        260n18
    Indian participants, 261n38
Rogers, B. M., 48
Rogers, Roy, 110
Romanticism, 173, 174
Romek, William A., 253n97, 259n39
Roosevelt, Franklin D., 130, 184
Roosevelt, Theodore
    celebration of West, 33–35
    on cowboys, 29, 102
    in West, 24, 115, 174, 175
    on white domination of Indians, 21
Roots (Haley), 219
Ross, Edward A., 152
Rothman, Hal K., xix, 202

Runaways, 1
Russell, Charlie, 115
Russia, 78, 139

Saloons, 9, 28, 55, 56, 62, 84
Scandinavian immigrants, 165
Scanlin, Don, 141, 142
Scenery. *See* Nature
Schwoob, Jacob M., 96, 264n85
Scottish immigrants, 150–151
Scouts. *See* Mountain men
Seattle (Washington), Alaska-Pacific-Yukon
    Exhibition, 104
See 'Em Alive Zoo, 196–197
Serbian immigrants, 77–78, 82. *See also* Slavic
    immigrants
Serbs, xv
Seton, Ernest Thomas, 174
Shane, 13
Shelley, O. H. P., 187, 192
Shopes, Linda, 227
Shoshone Dam, 186
Show Indians, 104, 262nn43,44
Siegfriedt, J. C. F., 132, 133, 135, 142, 197
Sierra Club, 200, 201, 203
Sironen, Matt, 155
Ski area. *See* Red Lodge Mountain
Slack piles. *See* Coal slack piles
Slavic immigrants
    Americanism, 77–78, 82
    clothing, 161
    ethnic identities, 151–152
    holidays and festivals, 62
    miners, 59, 60
    neighborhoods, 60
    Western identity, 88
    See also Yugoslavian immigrants
Slotkin, Richard, xvi, 10, 18, 91
Slovenian immigrants, 62, 151–152, 177. *See*
    also Slavic immigrants
Small towns, 230–231, 233
    Red Lodge as, 217, 231–235
Social control
    of cowboys, 27, 29–30, 32
    in Red Lodge, 28, 29–32, 44–45, 55
    of women, 30, 248n40
    during World War I, 84–85
Socialists, 70, 71, 78, 133
Sollors, Werner, 148, 164
Solvang (California), xviii
Sonoran Institute, 233, 234
Sorkin, Michael, 225
Sourdough tourists, 177
South Dakota. *See* Dakotas

South Street Seaport, 224
Southward, Johnny, 1, 2, 8, 39, 89
Speech, cowboy drawl, 123–125
Spofford Hotel, 7–8, 222
Sports
    baseball, 103
    golf, 123
    high school, 161
    ski area, 206–210
Springfield (Illinois), 228
Stevens, Charles W., 138
Strikes
    ban during World War I, 84
    coal miners, 44, 66, 73, 85–86, 171
    cowboys, 263n55
    in East, 16, 44
    following World War I, 86
    in Red Lodge, 66, 69, 73, 84, 85–86, 171
    telephone operators, 66
    See also Unions
Strip mines, 86, 172
Stuart, Granville, 24
Sundown, Jackson, 102, 261n38
Sun Valley (Idaho), xix
Sygulla, Sam, 157–158
Symbolic ethnics, 164–166
Symbolic landscapes, 230–231
Symbols, public, xix

Tafoya, Renee, 234
Tahti, Nels, 257n19
Talmadge, W. A., 41–42, 243n68
Talmadge Mercantile Company, 176
Telephone companies, 63, 66–67
Tepees
    as symbol of Red Lodge, 101, 105, 106,
        155–156
    as tourist attractions, 104, 105
Theme parks, 224–225
Theme towns, xviii
Thoreau, Henry David, 174
Timber Culture Act, 25
Tolman, J. N., 25, 28
Toole, K. Ross, 78
Tourism
    by automobile, 181–182, 184, 192, 200
    campers, 176–177
    class differences, 191–192
    early, 178–179
    growth in Red Lodge, 89–90, 93
    influence on local people, 145
    influence on physical appearance of
        towns, 228

influence on Red Lodge public identity,
    xix, 237
    by local residents, 176–177
    in Red Lodge identity, 162, 191
    service businesses created, 90, 172–173,
        181, 193–194
    in West, 89, 90, 93, 168
Tourist attractions
    Beartooth Highway, 183
    Festival of Nations as, 128, 142–143, 145,
        162
    historic sites, 221, 228–229
    nature, 170, 172–173, 174–176, 181, 191–192,
        210–211
    public ethnicity as, 131, 135, 136, 142
    rodeos, 96–99
    theme towns, xviii
    western scenery, 168
    See also Dude ranches; Wilderness
Tourist camps, 100
Tourists, attracting to Red Lodge
    construction projects by CCC, 184–185
    in 1890s, 37
    historic attractions, 228–229
    natural beauty, 168, 172–173, 174–176, 191
    promotional campaigns, 229
    promotion of Beartooth Highway, 139,
        188, 192, 200
    western clothing worn by residents, 89,
        97, 116–120, 122, 135, 155
    Wild West identity of town, 89, 90, 96
Travel writing, 174
Tuan, Yi-Fu, xix
Tunnicliff, Lou, 105
Turner, Frederick Jackson, 12–13, 17, 42
Twain, Mark, 20
Tweedie, William, 249n48

Union Pacific Railroad, xix
Unions
    eight-hour day demand, 67, 70, 252n87
    fears of, 43–44
    holidays, 65–66
    leadership, 69–70, 71, 254n99
    mining, 44, 63–64, 65, 67, 69–70, 153, 160
    opponents, 59, 67, 85
    power, 66–67, 68
    radical activists, 43–44, 70–72, 77, 78–80,
        85, 133
    in Red Lodge, 63–70, 160
    relations with management, 63, 68, 69, 84,
        85, 226
    support for, 49, 67, 68

tensions in eastern United States, 16, 44
violence by members, 63
See also Labor Day celebrations; Strikes
United Mine Workers of America (UMWA),
63–64, 65, 69–70, 73, 84, 86, 252n87,
253n97
United Nations flag, 147
Unruh, Yvonne M., 209
Urbanization, 138–139
U.S. Army
coal dug by, 171
ethnicities of soldiers, 137–138
frontier scouts, 36–37
Marias massacre, 22, 243n51
soldiers from Red Lodge, 137–138
U.S. government. *See* Federal government
U.S. Postal Service, 234

VanDyke, E. E., 35–36, 37, 178, 179
Veterans' Memorial Civic Center, 140, 155
Villard, Henry, 6–7, 9, 24
Vinson, Edrie, 229
Virginian, The (Wister), 21, 29, 107, 115
Virtue, Jim, 9, 10
Vogue, 118

Wahl, Art, 108
Warila, Helena, 121, 122
Warren, Louis S., xx
Washoe (Montana), 92, 128, 139,
226
Waters, Mary C., 164
Wayne, John, 110
Webber, "Grandma," 142
Welfare system, 161
West
agrarian, 4, 5, 12–14, 16, 17, 42
competition among towns for settlers, 12,
14
effects of automobiles and roads, 181–183
idealized version at dude ranches, 93–94,
109
immigrants in, 59, 155
land available for farming, 15, 16–17
modern industrial, 10, 41, 42, 49, 88, 122
mythology of, xvi, 2, 3–4, 5–6, 8–9, 12, 89,
100–101
nature tourism, 210–211
reality of, 6
scenery, 168, 174
speech patterns, 123–125
white domination of, 4, 13, 21
See also Western identity; Wild West

Western Federation of Miners (WFM), 44,
63, 67, 69, 153
Western identity
clothing, xvii, 88–89, 91, 116–120
contradictions in, 126
development of, 88–89
eastern perceptions of, 117–118
equated to ethnic identity in Festival of
Nations, 135, 154–155, 165
heritage, 90–91, 100–101
imagery, xvi–xvii, 3, 89, 125–126
of immigrants, 88, 155
meaning of, 2–3
ranchers as symbol of, 88–89, 101, 112–113,
116
West Side Mine, 40, 49–50, 60, 86, 92–93
Wheeler, Burton K., 184
Wheeler, Edward L., 110
White, Richard, 22
Whitebear, Russell, 103
Whites
dominance in Red Lodge, 62–63, 106,
153–154, 251n75, 270n81
domination of West, 4, 13, 21
See also Race
Whitman, Walt, 17
Wilderness
American attitudes toward, 120–121, 175,
209
controversies in Red Lodge, 198, 203–206,
209–210
debates on use in United States,
198–202
meaning of, 199
roads in, 200, 201, 275n82
value, 201
See also Nature
Wilderness Act, 201
Wilderness Society, 199, 200, 201, 203
Wild West
authenticity of performances, 101
building styles, 99–100
class and race in, 21
cowboys as heroes, 13
end of wildness, 5
imagery in rodeos, 99, 101–102
modern elements, 121
mountain men, 5, 33–37, 38
mythology of, 5–6, 20–21, 91
negative views of, 5, 10, 19–20, 21–22
in Red Lodge identity, 33, 34–35, 37, 38,
96, 123
symbols of, 32

Wild West, *continued*
  violence in, 5
  See also Buffalo Bill's Wild West shows
Williamsburg (Virginia), xviii
Wilsey (Montana), 23
Wilson, Laurel, 117
Wilson, Woodrow, 74
Winturri, Jalmar, 80
Wister, Owen, 21, 24, 29, 107, 115
Wobblies. *See* Industrial Workers of the
  World
Women
  class distinctions, 161
  clothing, 30, 244n85
  cowgirls, 109–110
  immigrants, 56, 161, 226
  paid household labor, 56, 161, 226
  Red Cross work, 83, 258n29
  rodeo participants, 95, 97, 109–110, 260n18
  social control of, 30, 248n40
  social organizations, 83, 131, 132
  See also Gender
Wordsworth, William, 174
Workers
  as consumers, 46, 48, 68
  fears of radicalized, 43–44
  history, 227–228
  housing, 18, 50, 53, 55
  opportunities in Red Lodge, 8
  outdoor recreation, 177
  patronizing views of, 253n88
  in Red Lodge identity, 65
  social control of, 30–31
  See also Immigrant miners; Miners
Workers' Hall, 65, 80, 82, 252n80
World War I
  effects, 74, 82–84, 132
  opponents, 79–81, 256n10, 257n19
  propaganda, 74–75

  support of, 76–78
  travel restrictions, 93
World War II
  economic impact, 138–139
  patriotism during, 136, 137
  soldiers, 137–138
Wranglers. *See* Dude wranglers

Yellowstone Forest Preserve, 175–176
Yellowstone National Park
  automobile travel in, 182
  camping in, 176–177
  class of visitors, 192
  entrance fee, 192
  establishment, 173
  number of visitors, 175, 182
  proximity to Red Lodge, 168, 172–173,
    175–176, 195
  workers in, 194
  See also Beartooth Highway
Yellowstone Park Timberland Reserve
  Act, 11
Yellowtail, Robert, 102
YMCA, 173
Yosemite National Park, 173
Yugoslavia, xv
Yugoslavian immigrants
  Festival of Nations activities, 127, 149,
    151–152
  musical groups, 165
  See also Slavic immigrants
Yugoslavian Tamburitza Band, 165

Zaputil, Willie, 137, 138
Zellick, Anna, 235, 237
Zoo, 196–197
Zupan, Liz, 161
Zupan, Shirley, 220
Zupan, Tony, 137–138, 160–161, 193

CPSIA information can be obtained
at www.ICGtesting.com
Printed in the USA
LVOW11*0842030817

543645LV00009BA/183/P